Power & Glory

Pitch Publishing Ltd
9 Donnington Park
85 Birdham Road
Chichester
West Sussex
PO20 7AJ

Email: info@pitchpublishing.co.uk
Web: www.pitchpublishing.co.uk

First published by Pitch Publishing 2022

1

A CIP catalogue record for this book is available from the British Library.

13-digit ISBN: 9781801501590
Design and typesetting by Olner Pro Sport Media. Visit www.olnerpsm.co.uk
Printed in India by Replika Press

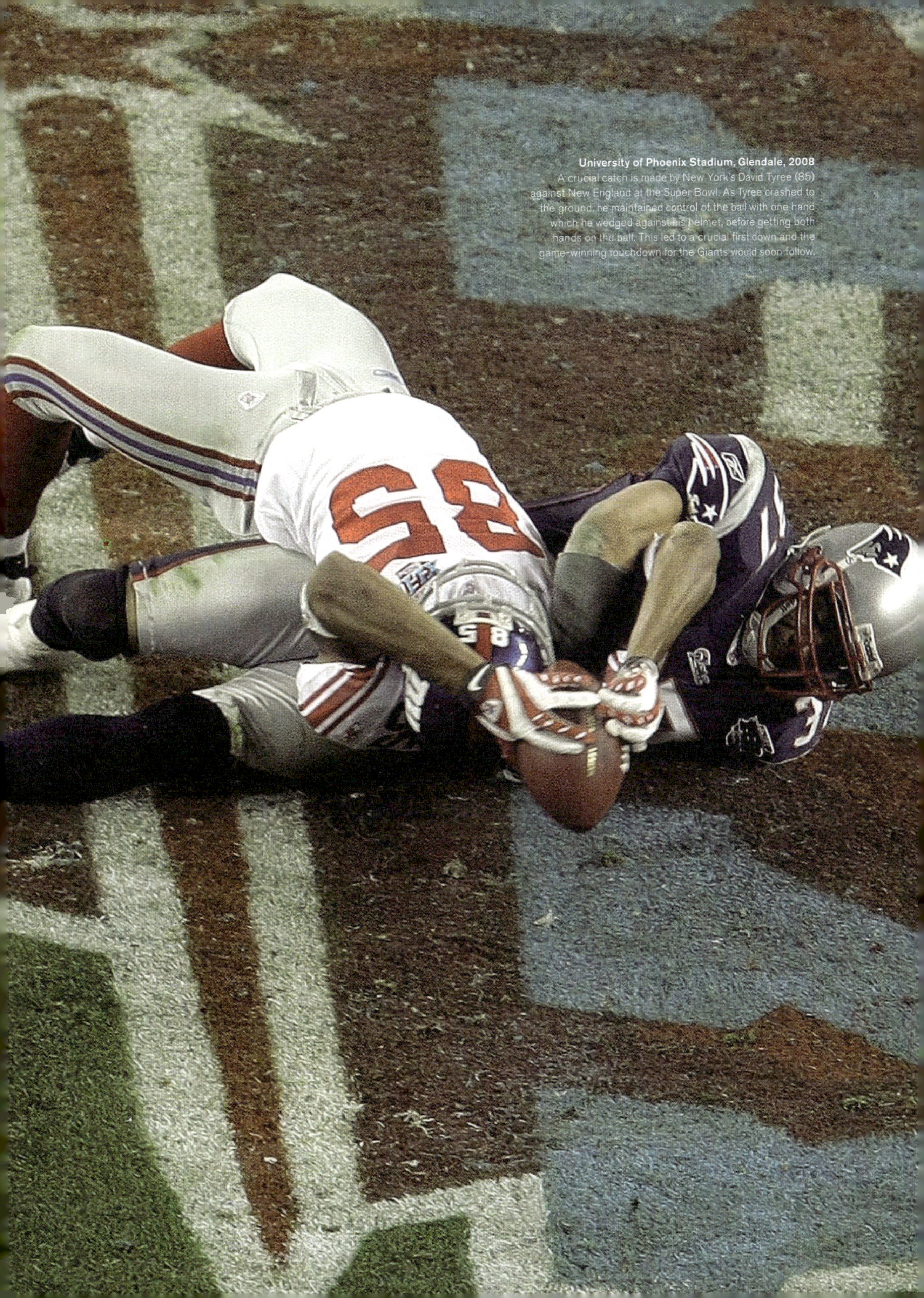

University of Phoenix Stadium, Glendale, 2008
A crucial catch is made by New York's David Tyree (85) against New England at the Super Bowl. As Tyree crashed to the ground, he maintained control of the ball with one hand which he wedged against his helmet, before getting both hands on the ball. This led to a crucial first down and the game-winning touchdown for the Giants would soon follow.

Power & Glory

A Pictorial Celebration of the NFL

Matthew Bazell

pitch

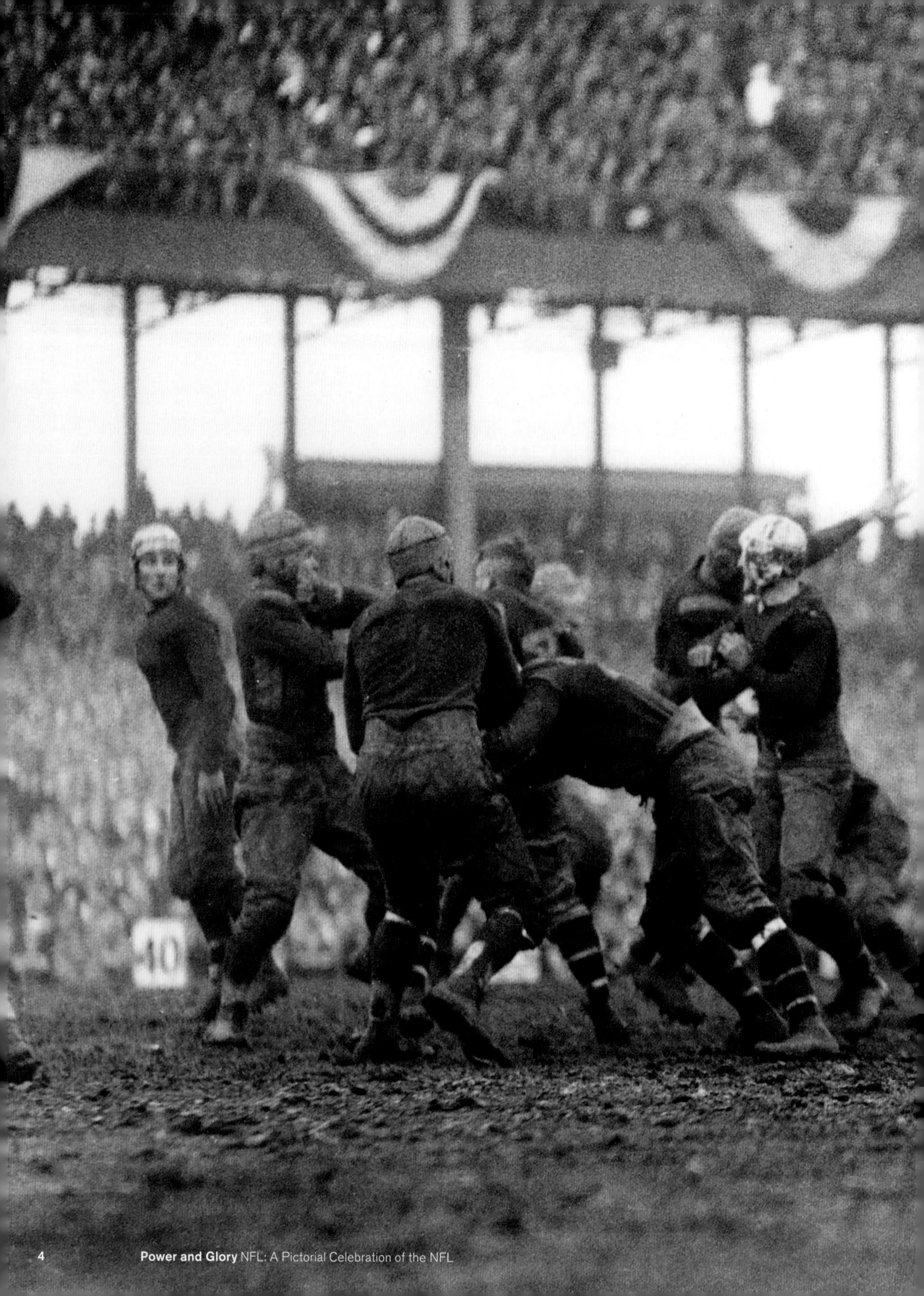

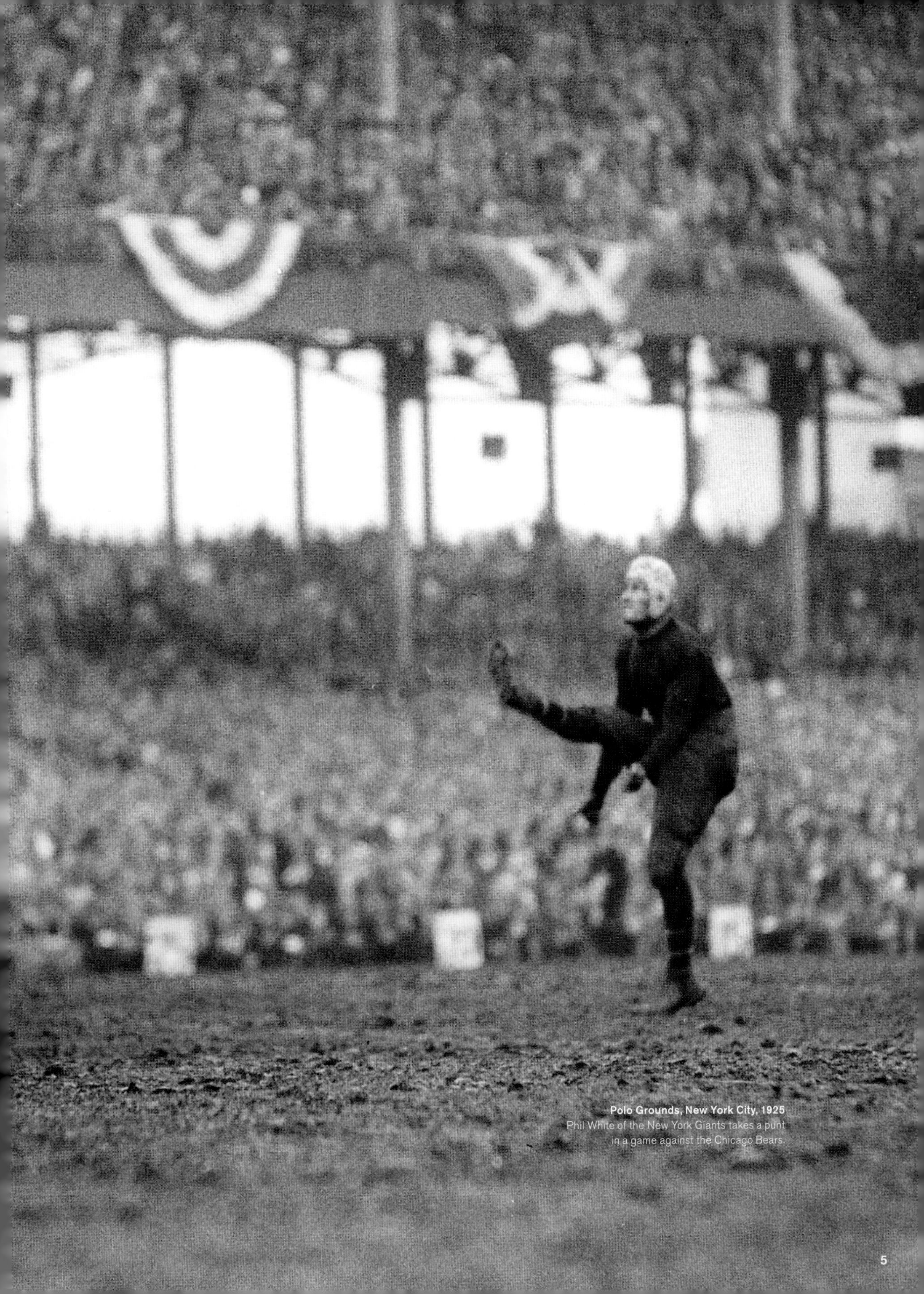

Polo Grounds, New York City, 1925
Phil White of the New York Giants takes a punt in a game against the Chicago Bears.

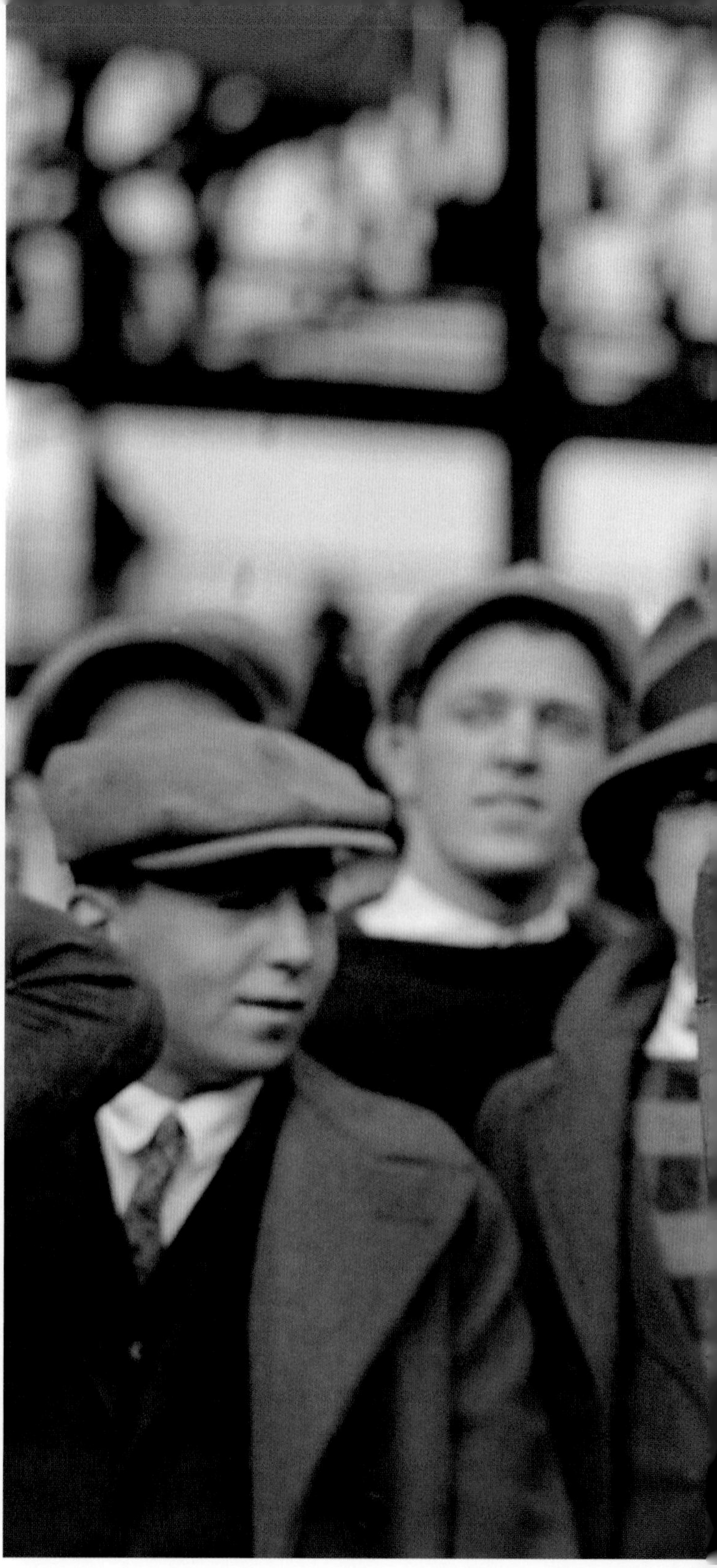

Harold 'Red' Grange of the Chicago Bears.

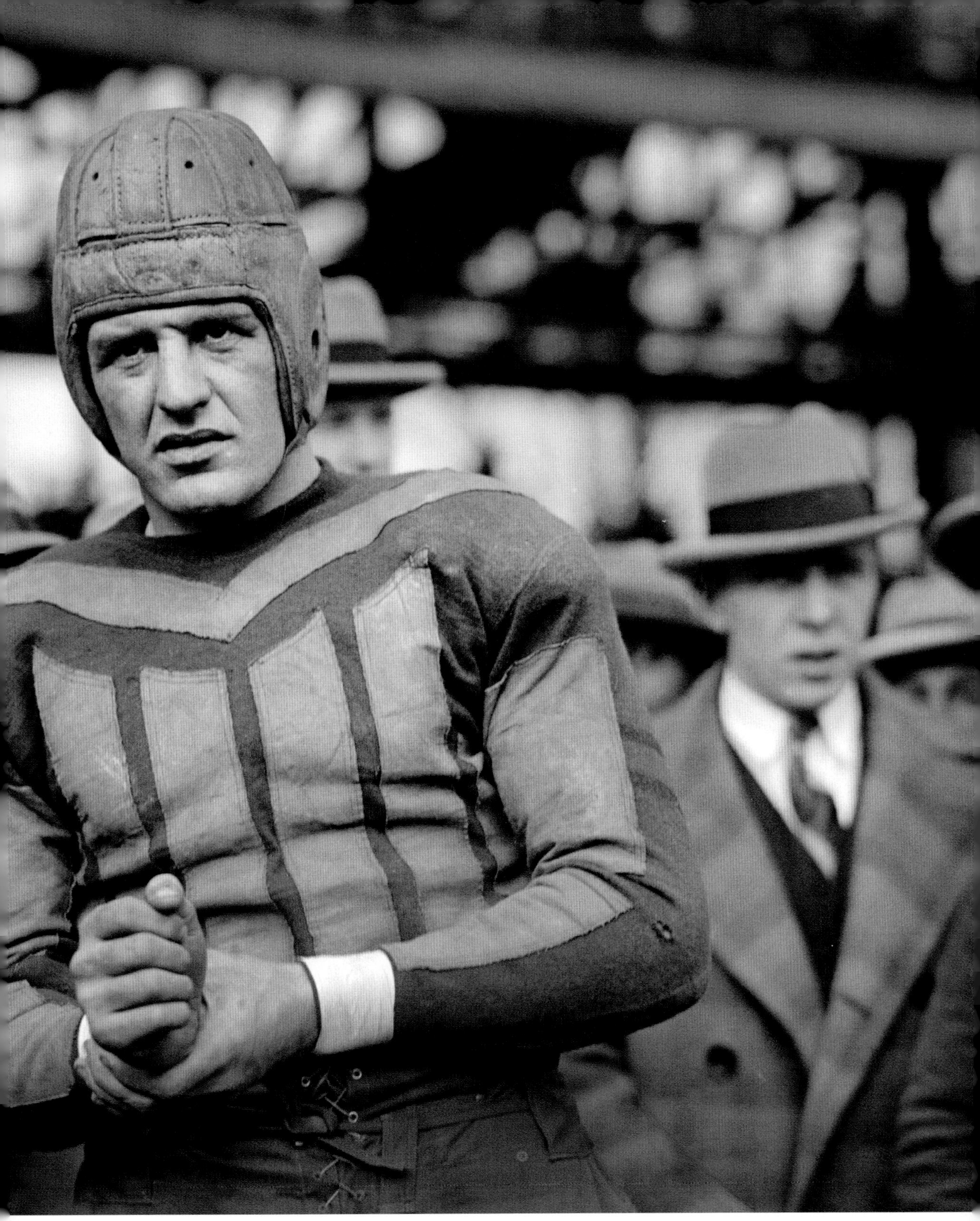

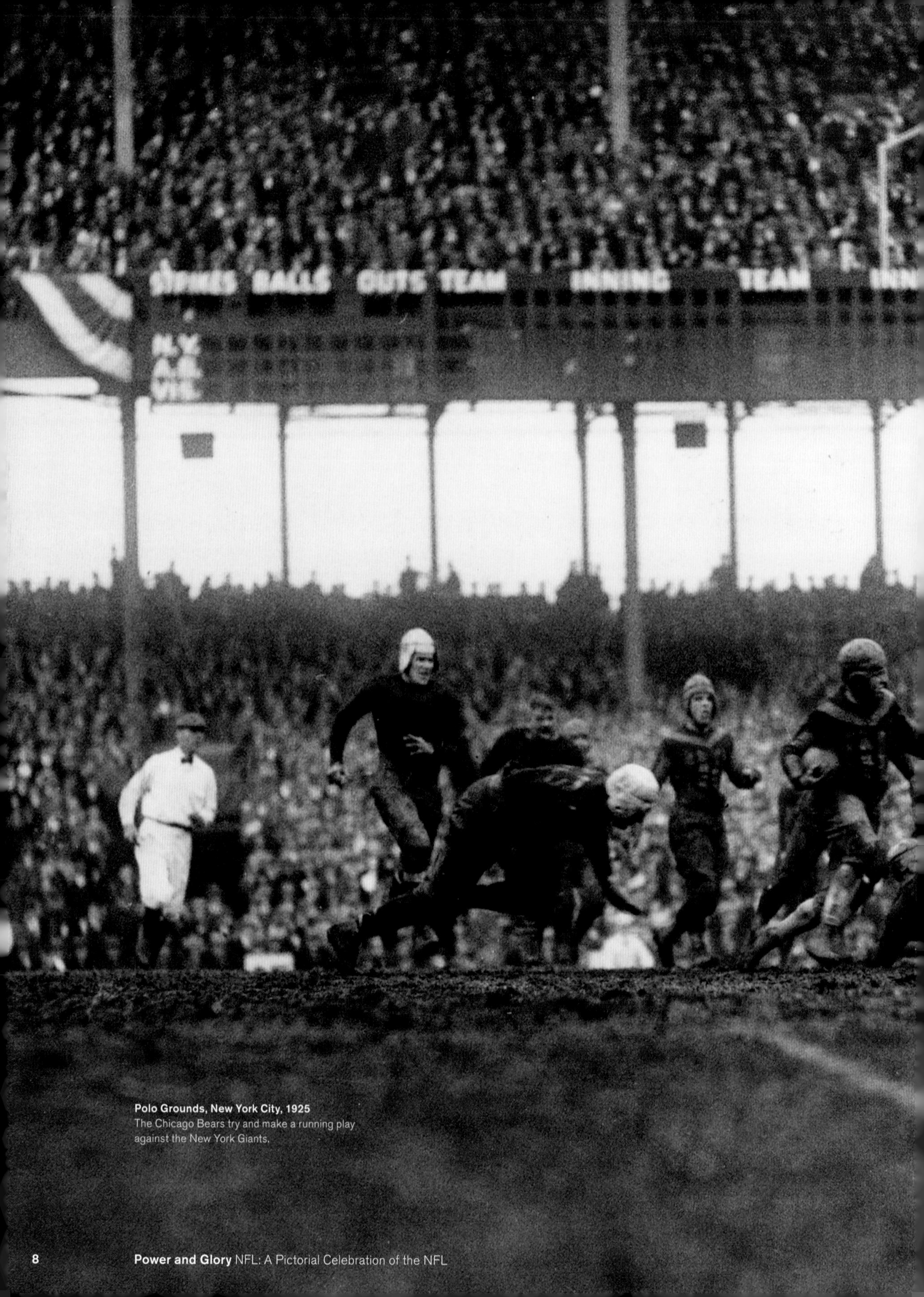

Polo Grounds, New York City, 1925
The Chicago Bears try and make a running play against the New York Giants.

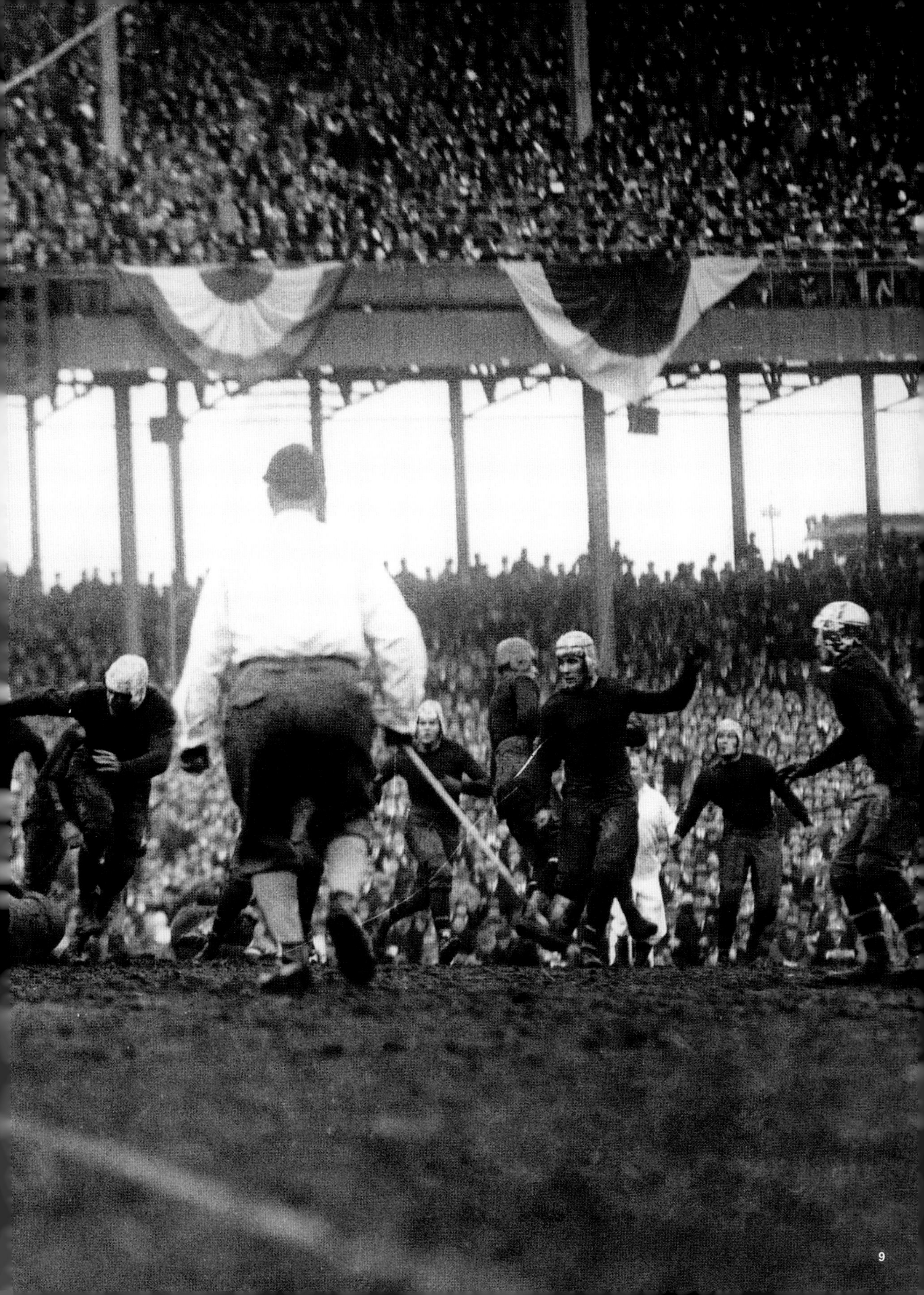

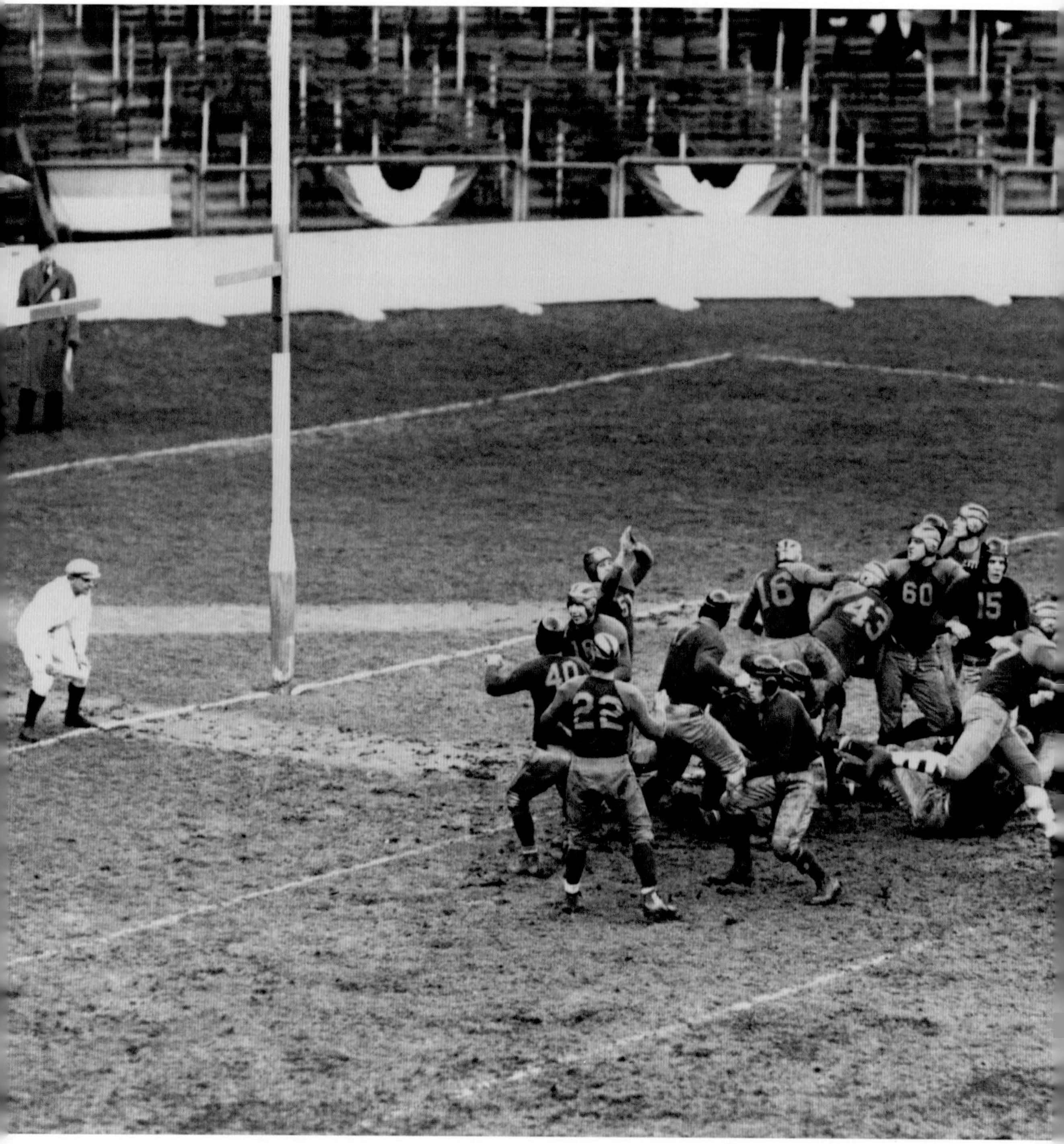

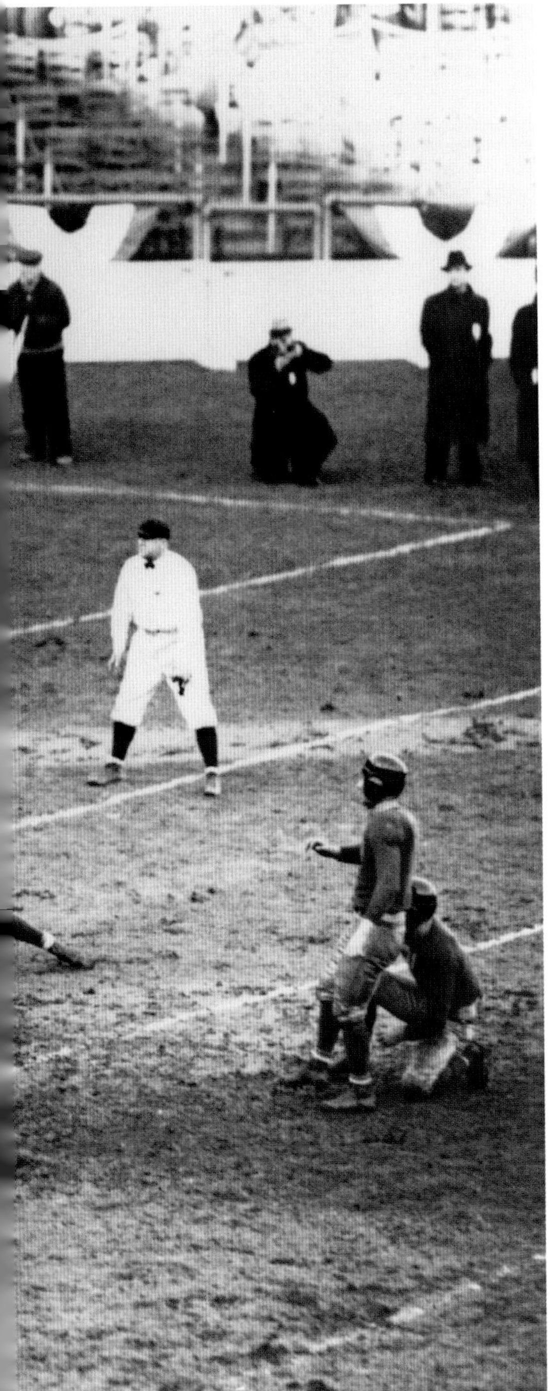

City Stadium, Green Bay, 1936
The Boston Redskins miss a field goal against the Green Bay Packers.

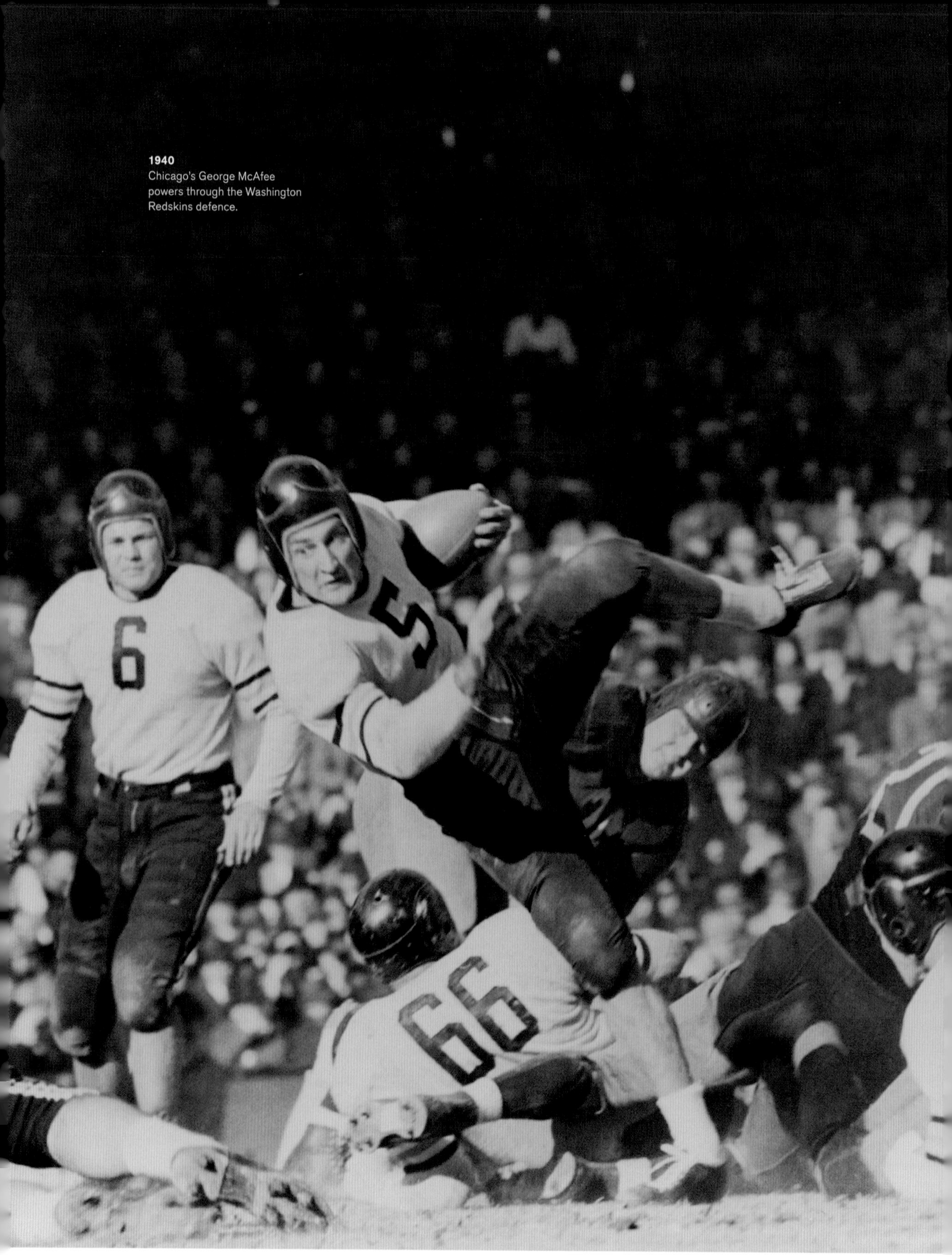

1940
Chicago's George McAfee powers through the Washington Redskins defence.

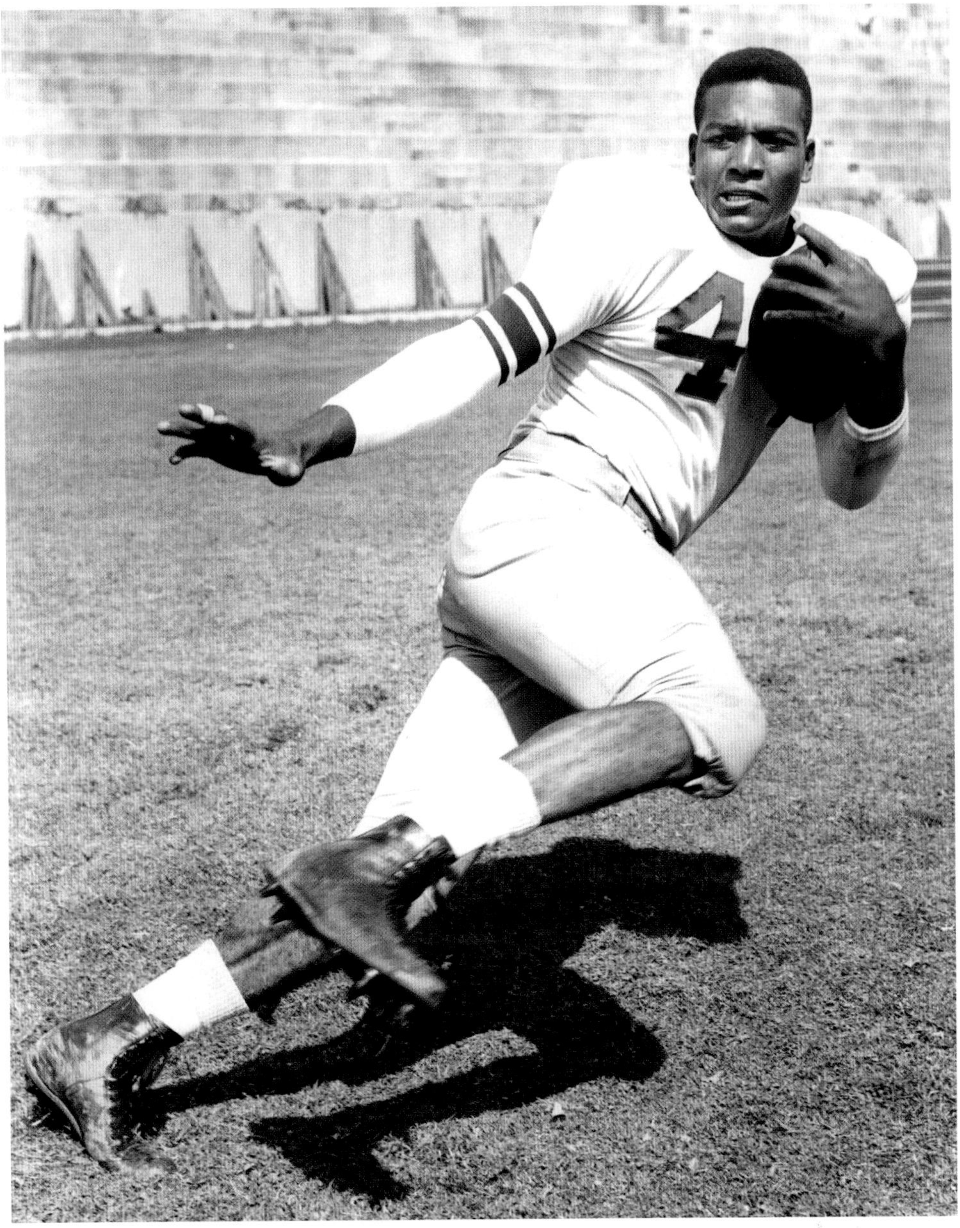

Cleveland's Jim Brown in a publicity photo, taken sometime in the mid-1950s
The running back would be one of the most dominant forces in NFL history.

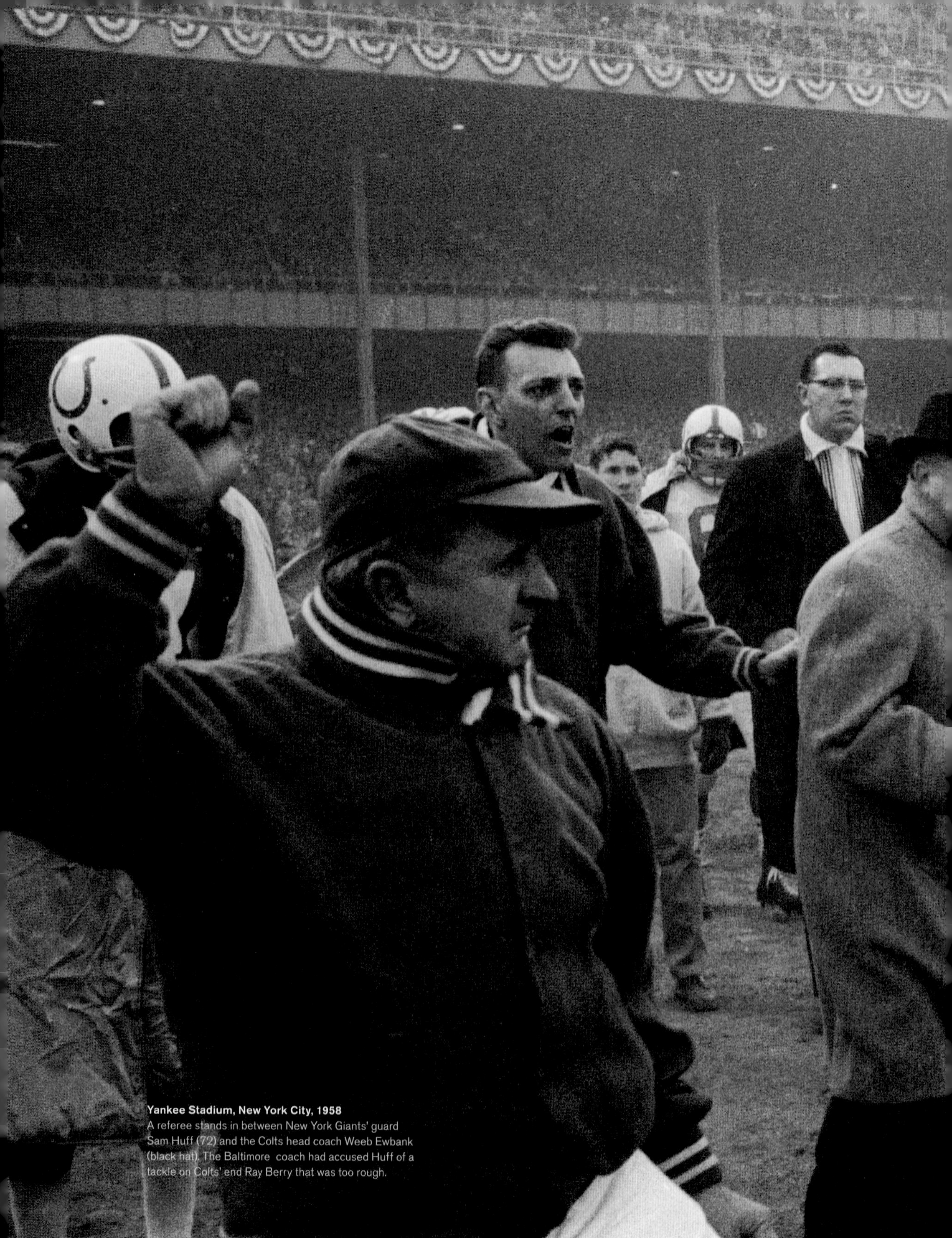

Yankee Stadium, New York City, 1958
A referee stands in between New York Giants' guard Sam Huff (72) and the Colts head coach Weeb Ewbank (black hat). The Baltimore coach had accused Huff of a tackle on Colts' end Ray Berry that was too rough.

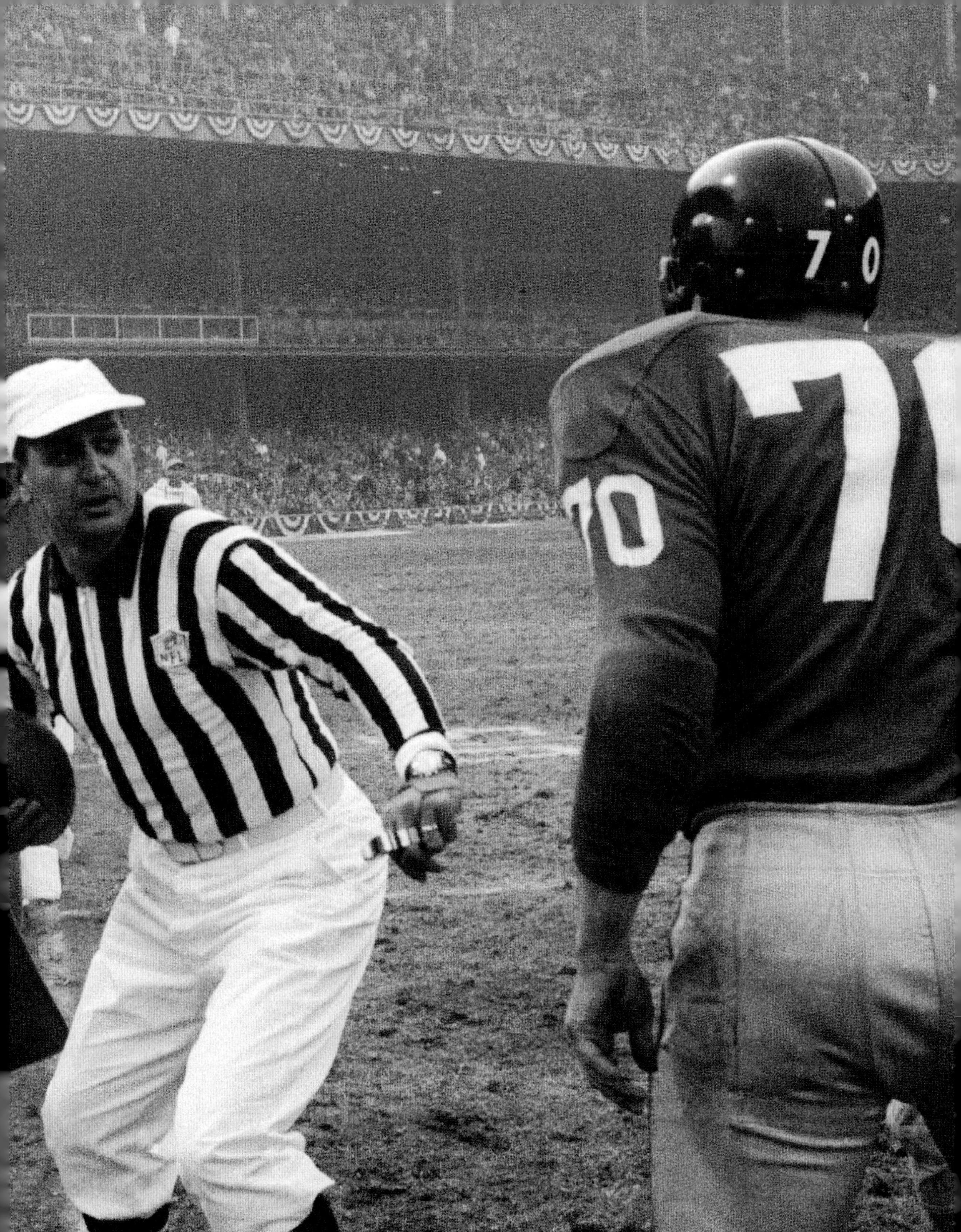
70
70
70
NFL

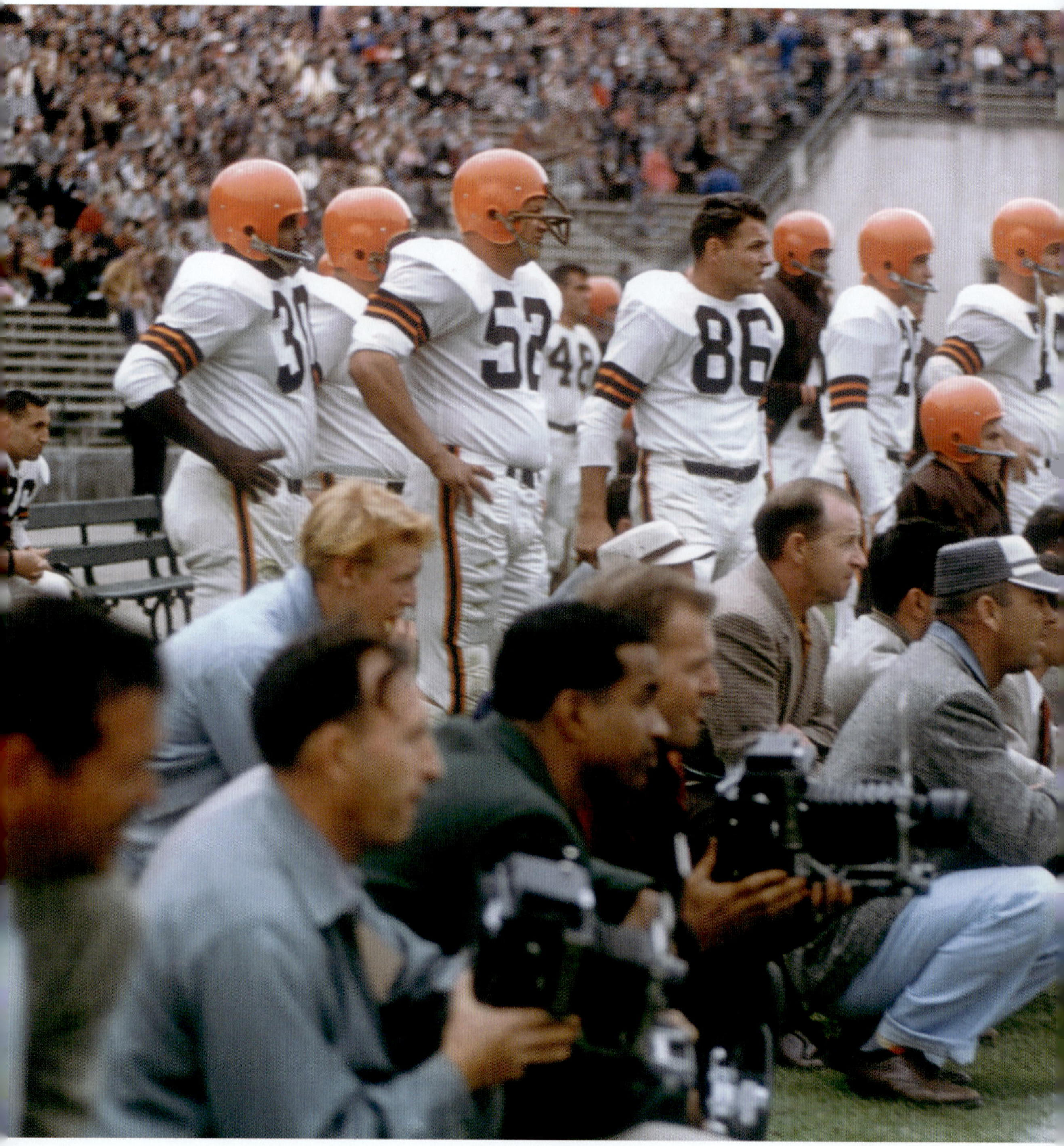

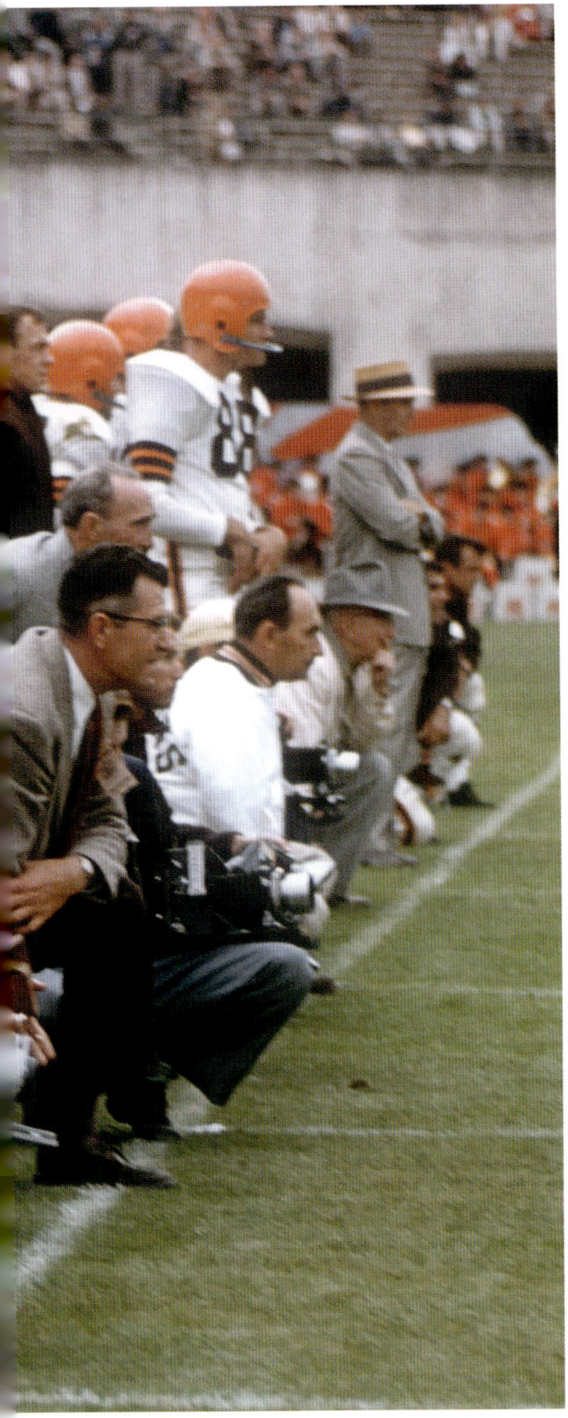

Kezar Stadium, San Francisco, 1956
Photographers line up near the Cleveland Browns sideline, in their game against the 49ers. The Browns had already won the NFL championship three times during the decade.

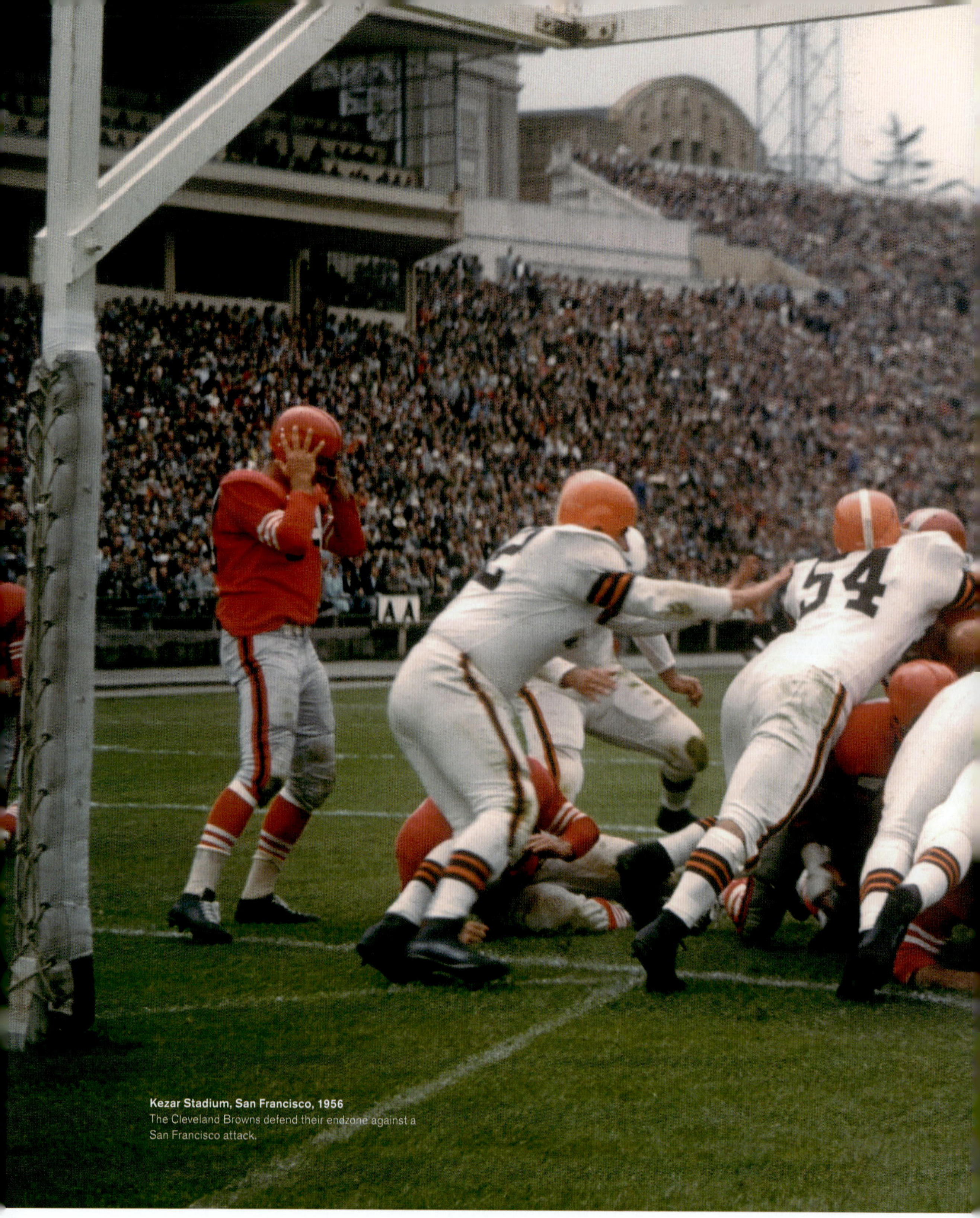
Kezar Stadium, San Francisco, 1956
The Cleveland Browns defend their endzone against a San Francisco attack.

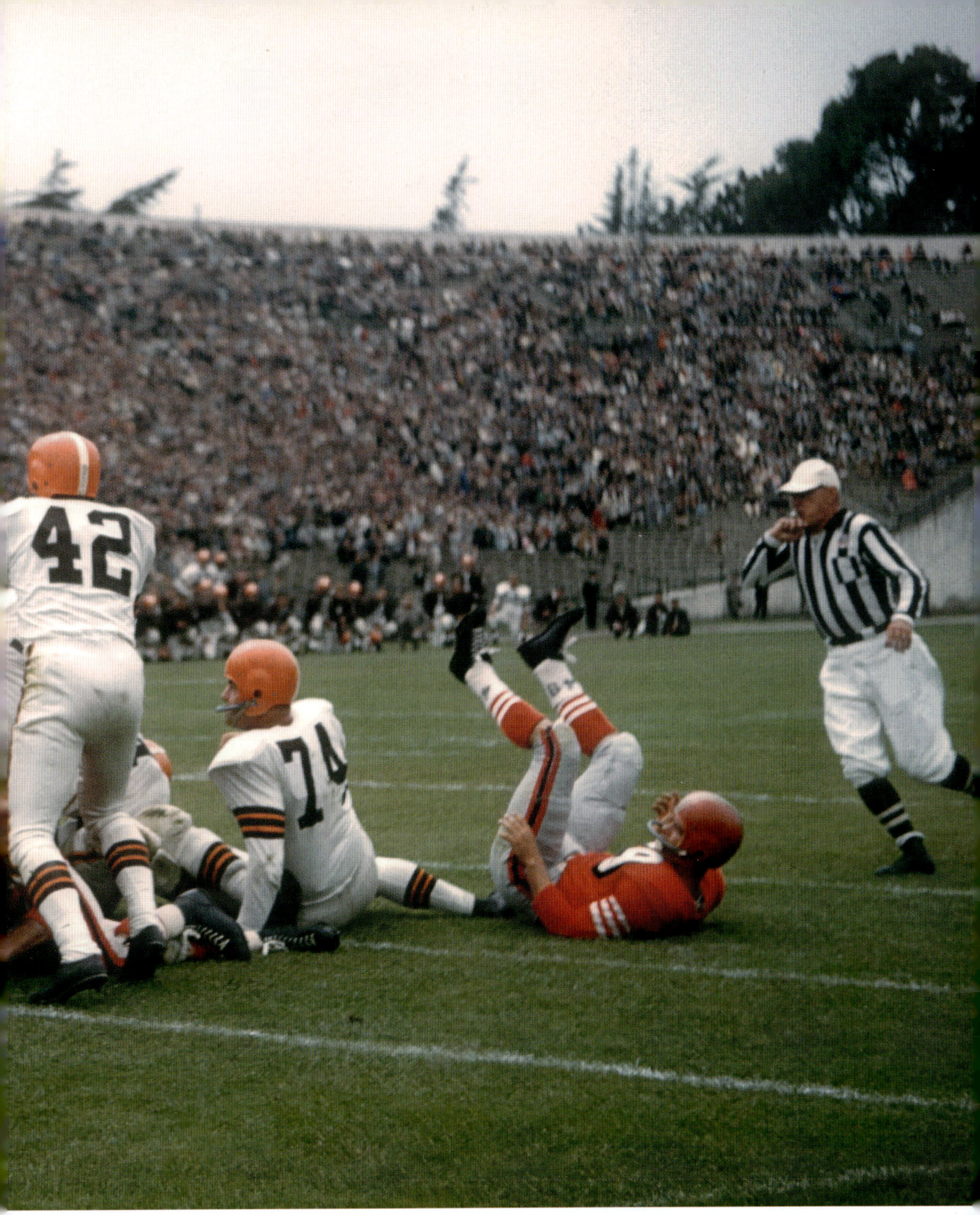

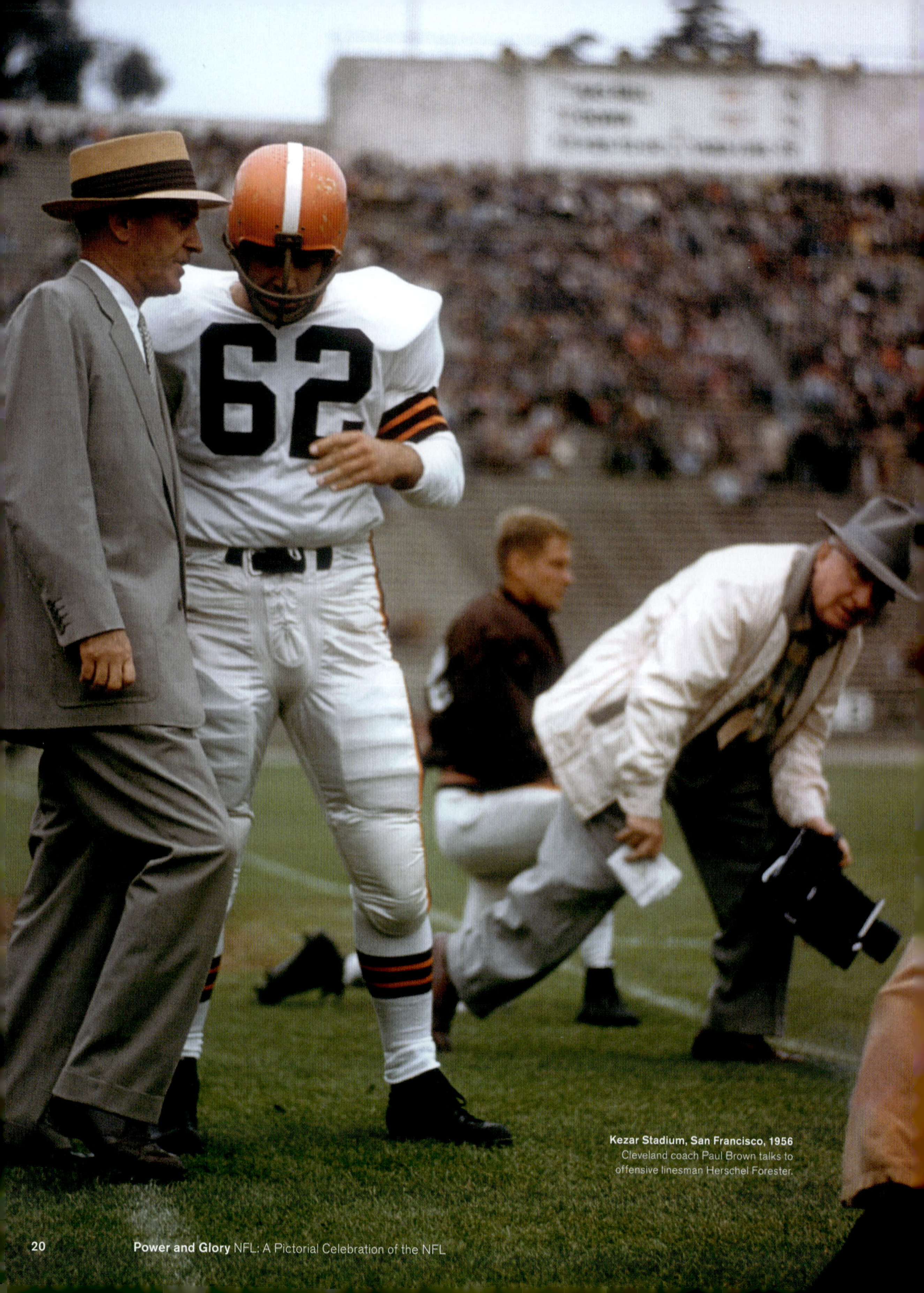

Kezar Stadium, San Francisco, 1956
Cleveland coach Paul Brown talks to offensive linesman Herschel Forester.

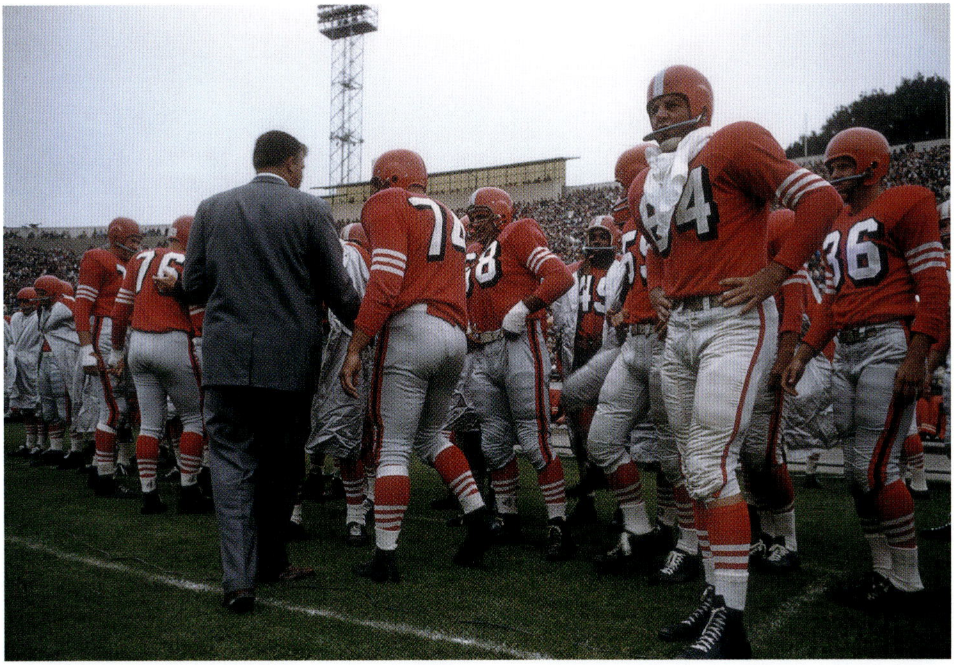

Kezar Stadium, San Francisco, 1956
The San Francisco 49ers team on the sideline during a clash with Cleveland.

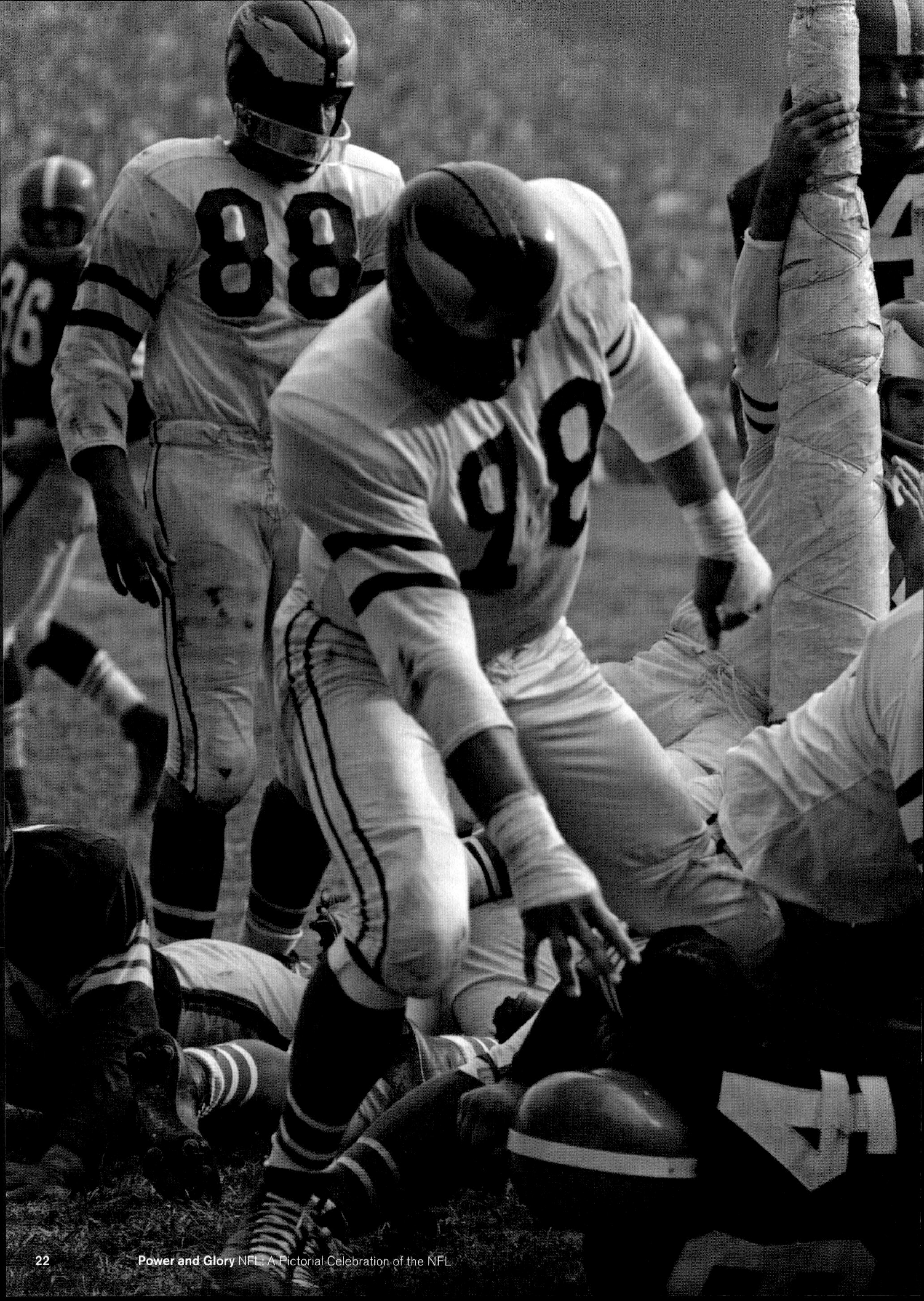

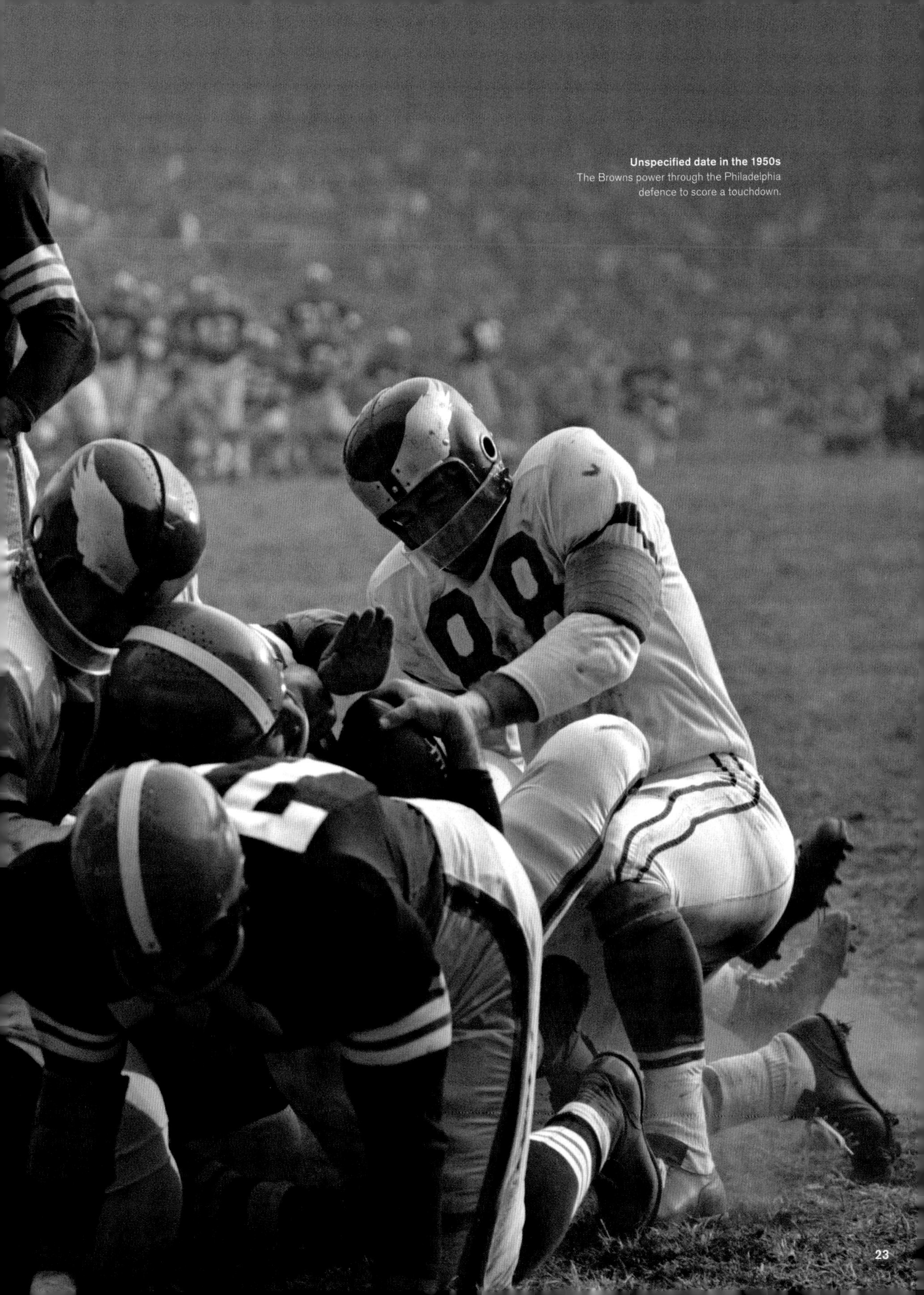

Unspecified date in the 1950s
The Browns power through the Philadelphia defence to score a touchdown.

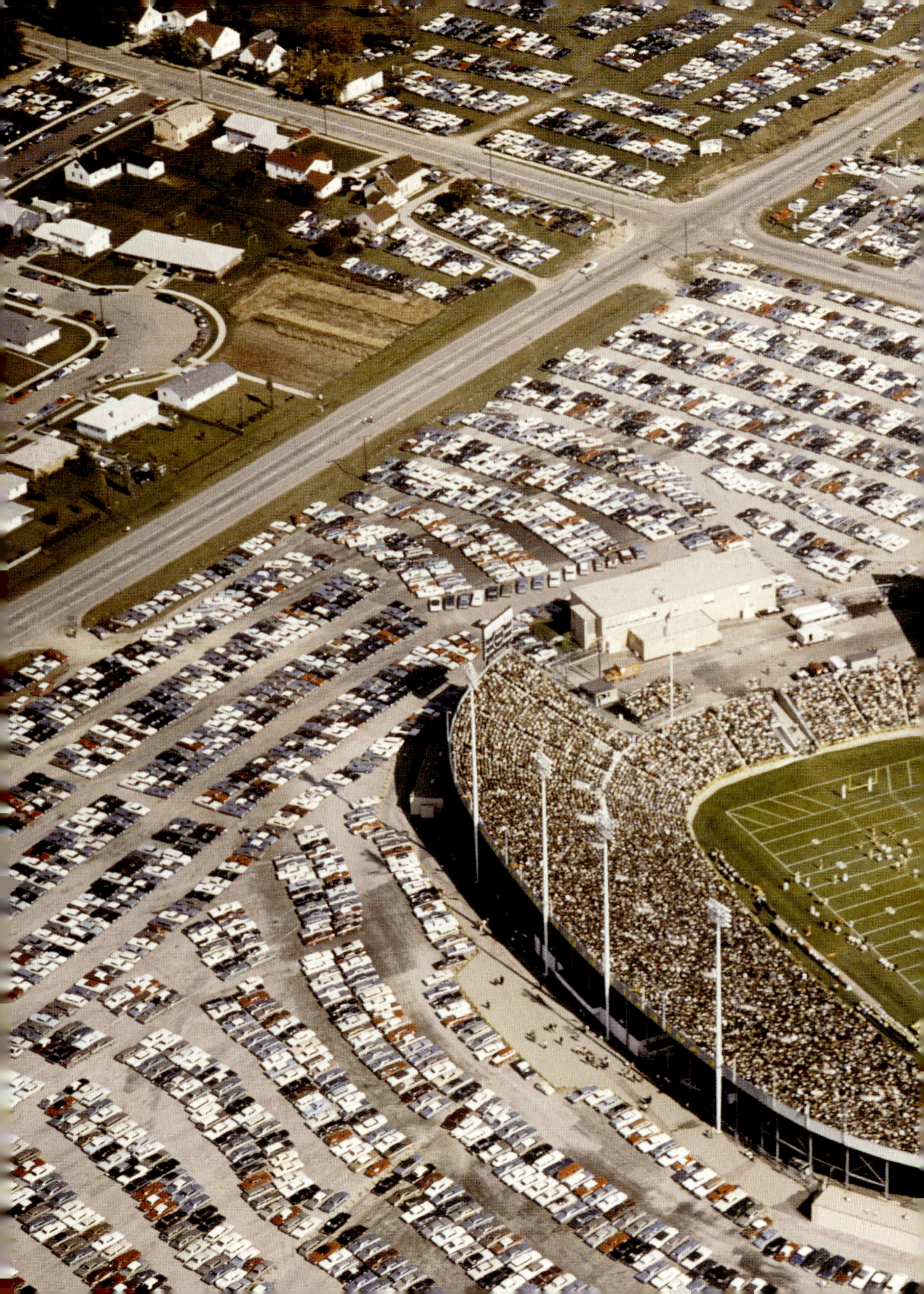

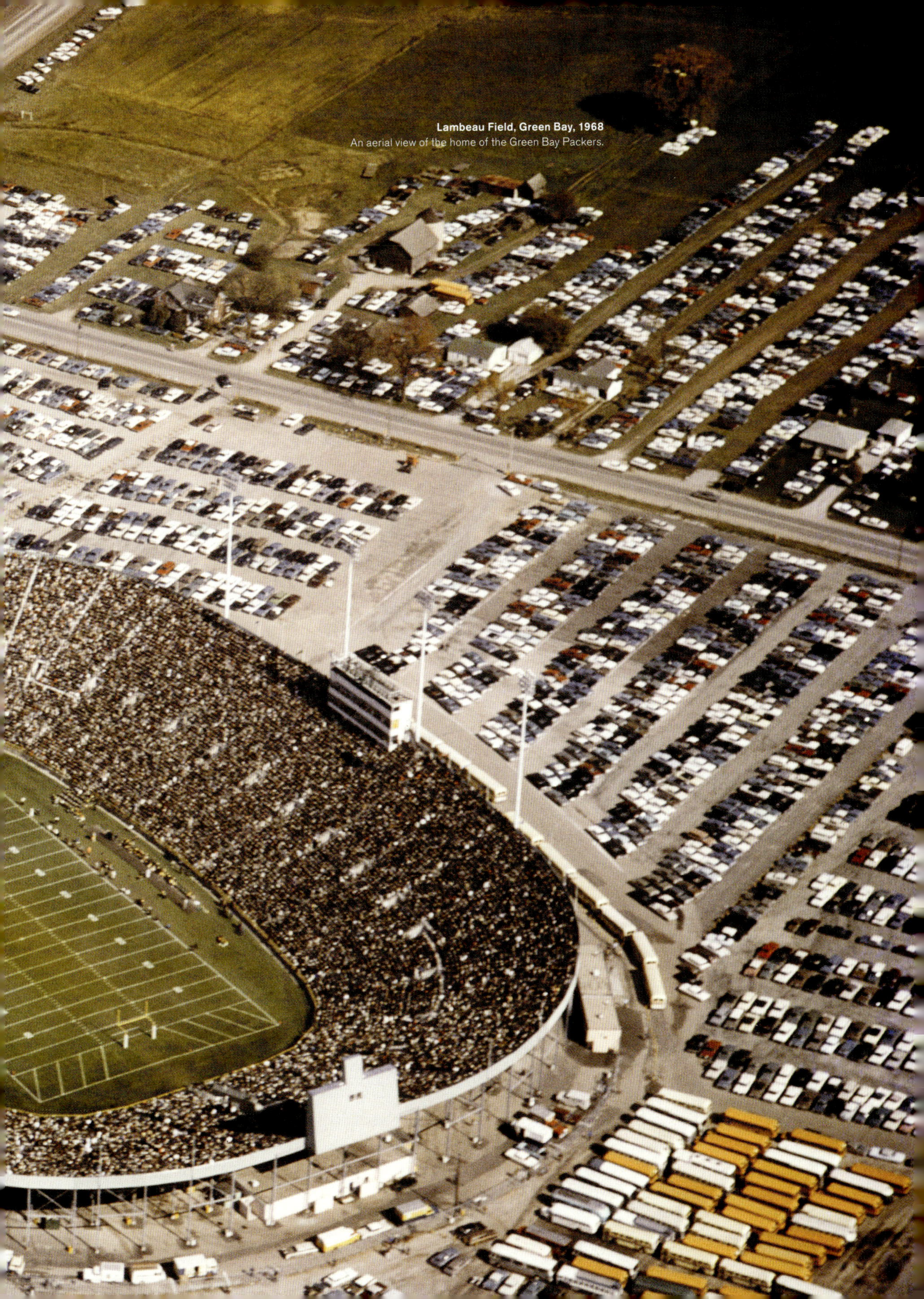

Lambeau Field, Green Bay, 1968
An aerial view of the home of the Green Bay Packers.

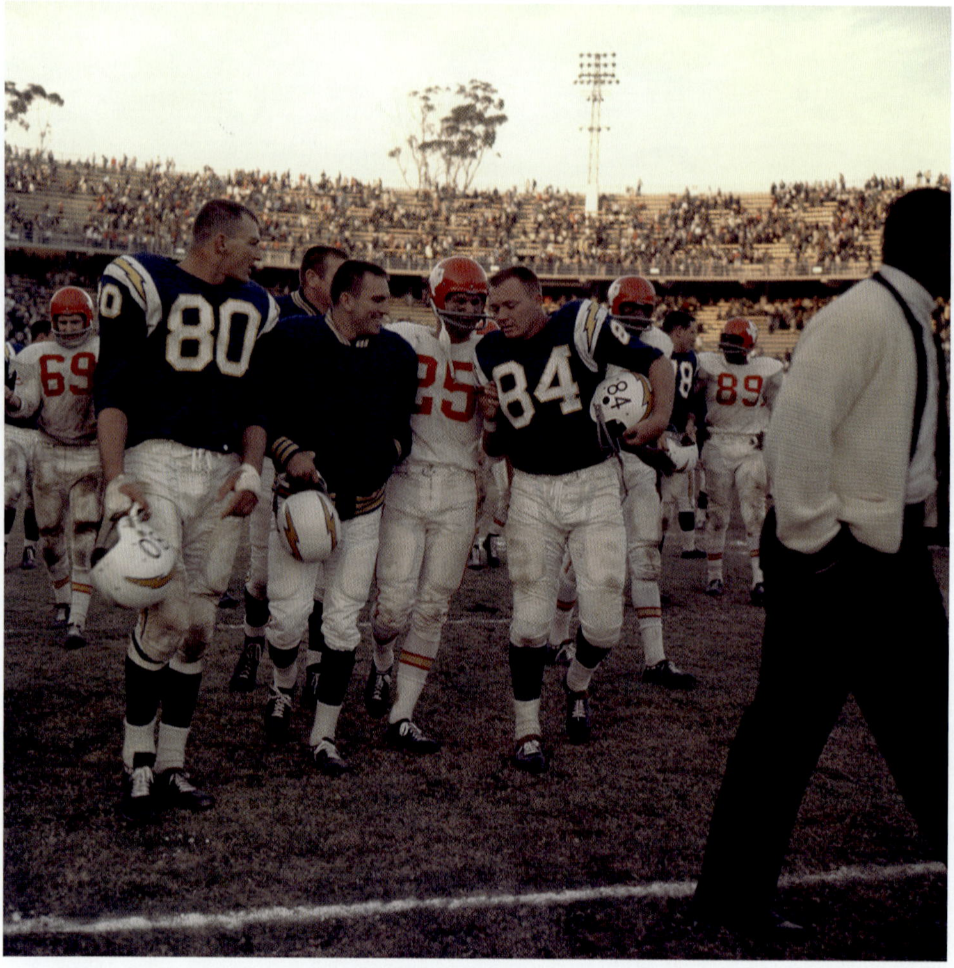

Balboa Park, San Diego, 1961
Chargers Ron Nery (80) and Paul Maguire (84) chat
with Doyle Nix (25) of the Dallas Texans.

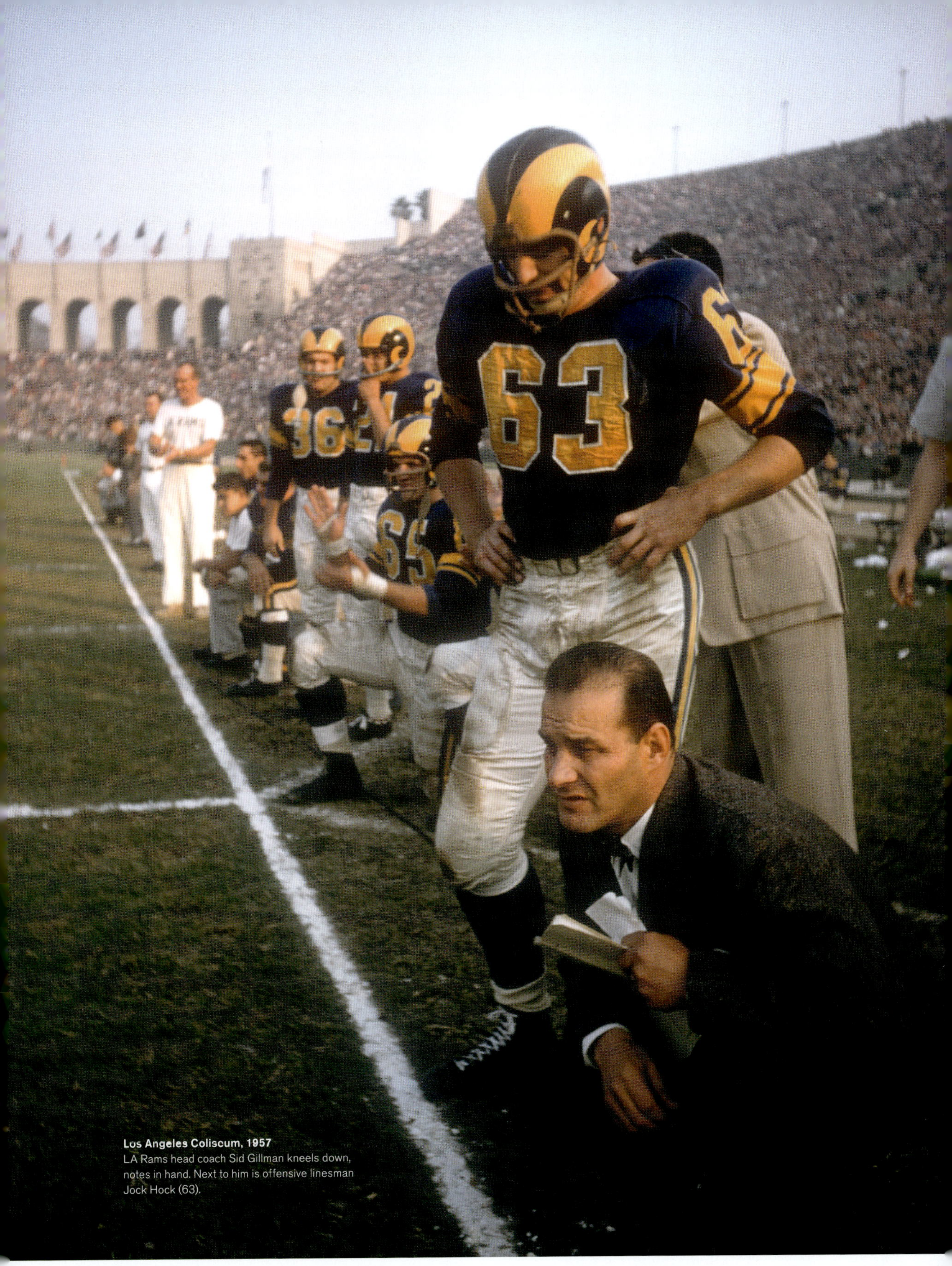

Los Angeles Coliseum, 1957
LA Rams head coach Sid Gillman kneels down, notes in hand. Next to him is offensive linesman Jock Hock (63).

Buffalo Bills: Est. 1959

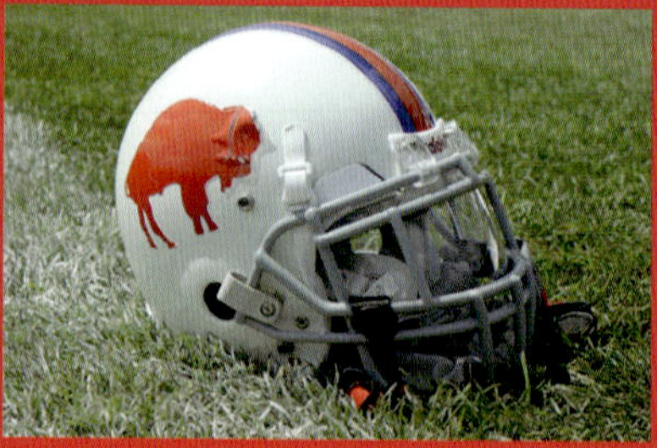

AFC East Champions: (9) 1980, 1988, 1989, 1990, 1991, 1993, 1995, 2020, 2021

AFC Conference Champions: (4) 1990, 1991, 1992, 1993

AFL Championships: (2) 1964, 1965

Super Bowl record: 0-4

When boxing legend Floyd Patterson lost his world heavyweight championship after being knocked down seven times he would go on to say, 'Yeah but I got up seven times.' The Buffalo Bills lost four Super Bowls between seasons 1990 and 1993, but many supporters would respond, 'Yeah but we got there four times in a row.'

No other team has been to four consecutive Super Bowls, and it's a record the Bills are rightly proud of, but it's mixed with a feeling of regret as their 1990s dynasty were never crowned as champs. Indeed, what compounds the sorrow of these four losses is that Buffalo has no other Super Bowl appearance to fall back on. The closest they came to winning was in their first Super Bowl appearance in the 1990 season against the New York Giants. Bill Belichick was the Giants' defensive coach and the Bills' 'no huddle' offence strategy, which had been so effective, was this time kept at bay.

With just minutes left in the final quarter the Bills were trailing 20-19, but they could still win if they got within field goal range and converted the kick. Legendary quarterback Jim Kelly, with the help of running back Thurman Thomas, got the play to the Giants' 29-yard line with eight seconds left on the clock. What followed was the classic sliding doors scenario: if kicker Scott Norwood puts the ball between the sticks from 39 yards out then he goes down in history as the man who won Buffalo the Super Bowl. He's lifted up high in the air by ecstatic team-mates and Jim Kelly, Bruce Smith and Thurman Thomas seal their legacies as greats of the era, with a Super Bowl ring on their fingers. Instead, Norwood's kick went a yard wide of the right post, in what still remains today the most heart-aching end to a Super Bowl for the losing team and 1990 remains the only Super Bowl where a kick missed in the final seconds cost a team victory.

Instead of Norwood being cast as the villain, he and his team-mates were given a heroes' reception in a parade to the town hall. The crowd chanted 'WE WANT SCOTT'. The emotional kicker thanked the fans and told them the players would do their best to get back the following season. They did just that, but got beat 37-24 by Washington, and so the narrative of the following season's Super Bowl was surely they couldn't lose three in a row. Dallas beat them 52-17, and by this point the USA had had enough of seeing the Bills at the Super Bowl. Instead of being viewed as plucky losers the message was 'anyone but the Bills'. Buffalo responded with a simple message: if you don't like it then beat us!

The Bills made it to the Super Bowls because the other 13 teams in the AFC were not as good as they were. So much for being losers, but when it came to the showpiece, it was no great surprise when Dallas won the 1993 Super Bowl in a repeat match-up, and from this point Buffalo have not been back.

A horrible barren spell followed between seasons 2000 to 2016 where the Bills never made it to one play-off game. However, in the third decade of the millennium the team looked strong again and were close to getting to Super Bowls in seasons 2020 and 2021. Quarterback Josh Allen recently joked to the owner about having an indoor stadium during a warm-up in a rain storm. It's cold in Buffalo, snow storms and bad weather days are the norm, but that's what makes it special. The town, the stadium, the weather is a wonderful antidote to the big city glamour clubs.

New England Patriots: Est. 1959

Former names: Boston Patriots (1960–1970)

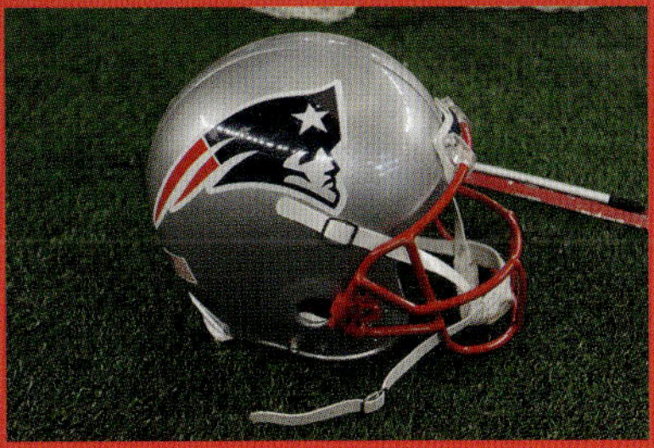

AFC East Champions: (21) 1978, 1986, 1996, 1997, 2001, 2003 , 2004, 2005, 2006, 2007, 2009, 2010, 2011, 2012, 2013, 2014, 2015, 2016, 2017, 2018, 2019

AFC Conference Champions: (11) 1985, 1996, 2001, 2003, 2004, 2007, 2011, 2014, 2016, 2017, 2018

Super Bowl titles: (6) 2001, 2003, 2004, 2014, 2016, 2018

Super Bowl record: 6-5

The Patriots used to play in the city of Boston, before relocating 30 miles to Foxboro. To represent the wider region, their name was changed to New England, made up of the states of Massachusetts, Rhode Island, New Hampshire, Maine, Vermont and Connecticut. After 30 years in Foxboro the team had made two Super Bowl appearances in seasons 1985 and 1996, but had lost them both. By the year 2000 the phrase 'The Patriots' Way' had no meaning, and when an unfancied quarterback from Michigan state called Tom Brady joined, as the 199th overall pick in that year's NFL draft, there was no great expectation that such a move would take the team remotely closer to ultimate glory.

During a game versus the New York Jets in 2001, the Patriots' starting quarterback Drew Bledsoe got injured and on came Brady as a replacement. They lost and went 0-2 on the season. At that moment in time, who could possibly have imaged that what would follow would be the most unprecedented period of success for any team of any era. By the end of the 2001 season they had made it to the Super Bowl with a sixth-round draft rookie quarterback, and were to play the highly rated St Louis Rams. The Patriots' head coach was Bill Belichick, who had tasted victory before in the 1990 season Super Bowl as defensive coach for the New York Giants. Belichick had been fired as head coach of the Cleveland Browns in 1995, after four years in charge and achieving just the one winning season. He initially joined the Patriots as assistant head coach for their 1996 season which ended in a defeat to the Green Bay Packers in Super Bowl 31. He left but would return a few years later in 2000, this time as head coach. The Brady-Belichick era was under way and defeat of the St Louis Rams in Super Bowl 36 was the catalyst to the NFL's greatest dynasty.

The last of the nine Super Bowl appearances of the Brady-Belichick era was perhaps the least eventful in terms of compelling offensive action, but its outcome carried the most significance. The Patriots defeated the LA Rams 13-3 to equal the Pittsburgh Steelers' record of six overall wins. New England's other Super Bowl conquests were not lacking in entertainment. Super Bowl 49 against the Seattle Seahawks was dramatically won by a Malcolm Butler interception on the edge of the endzone when Seattle looked certain to score and win at the very end, with no time remaining for the Patriots to come back. The 2016 season was perhaps even more dramatic and carried the biggest comeback in Super Bowl history. With the score 28-3 to the Atlanta Falcons late on in the third quarter, the 'Pats' scored 25 unanswered points to level and would win in overtime. In 2003 season they won Super Bowl 38 against the Carolina Panthers with a field goal with just seconds left on the clock. The 24-21 win against Philadelphia the following year came down to the last play of the game as the Patriots' defence held firm in the dying seconds. Their loss against Philadelphia in the 2017 season also came down to the last play, as did their two other Super Bowl defeats which were both against the New York Giants.

For all the disappointments, they were overshadowed by glory, and there may never be another dynasty quite like the one that the Patriots built up in the first two decades of the millennium.

New York Jets: Est. 1959

Former names: New York Titans (1960–1962)

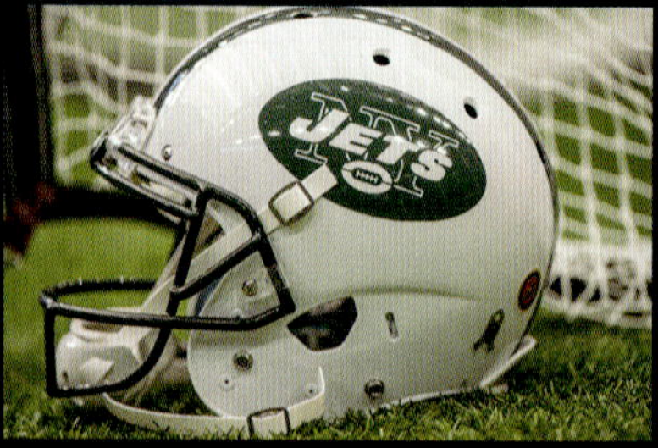

AFC East Champions: (2) 1998, 2002

AFL Championships: (1) 1968

Super Bowl titles: (1) 1968

Super Bowl record: 1-0

The New York metropolitan area was never big enough for just the one team. The long-established Giants were to be handed a noisy neighbour, and when the new team were formed at the end of 1959 they named themselves New York Titans because according to owner Harry Wismer, 'Titans are bigger and stronger than giants.' The club nearly went bankrupt and were taken over in 1962 and renamed the New York Jets for two reasons: it rhymed with the baseball team New York Mets, and because the stadium was located near to LaGuardia Airport.

The Jets image was to represent something modern, in contrast to the more traditional neighbours. The Giants had achieved success in decades past, but the Jets would be the first New York team to win the Super Bowl. When they beat Oakland in the AFL Championship game very few people gave them a chance to beat the NFL's Baltimore Colts in Super Bowl 3. In the late 1960s the build-up to the Super Bowl was a no-nonsense affair; the teams ran on, a coin was tossed, and the game started. This showdown was billed as David vs Goliath with the Colts being favoured by the bookmakers to win by a 19-point margin. Although insulted, the Jets were happy to be written off and their tackle Paul Rochester said, 'I'd rather be a 19-point underdog than 19-point favourites.' Jets quarterback Joe Namath, at a media conference, insisted, 'We're gonna win the game, I guarantee it,' which was a comment his coach Weeb Ewbank wasn't happy with.

Namath's prediction was made while drunk, but he was proven right and was named as MVP for his display of passing. The Colts' offence was shut out for most of the game as the Jets put 16 points on the board. Baltimore rallied at the very end with a touchdown followed by a recovery from an onside kick, but it was too late to overturn the deficit and the Jets became the very first team from the AFL to be declared as Super Bowl champions. It was a pivotal moment in the sport's history, and had proved the newer teams from the AFL could beat the older established teams from the NFL, a year before the two leagues merged into one. Namath, aka 'Broadway Joe', had become a true superstar, but his career peaked at Super Bowl 3, much like the Jets themselves.

The two New York teams have only played 14 competitive games against one another with the Giants 8-6 ahead overall. A New York derby in the Super Bowl is possible, which is one intriguing aspect of the Giants and the Jets being in separate conferences. With both teams sharing a stadium in New Jersey, it has led to Buffalo laying claim to being the only NFL team in the state of New York, although the Jets started off in Manhattan before moving to Shea Stadium in Queens in 1964 where they stayed until 1983.

Since Super Bowl 3 the Jets have only registered 17 winning seasons and 13 campaigns that went beyond the regular season. However, on four occasions they have been only one game away from a second Super Bowl appearance; losing against the Dolphins in 1982, the Broncos in 1998, the Colts in 2009, and the Steelers in 2010. At the end of the first decade of the millennium the Jets were serious contenders, but since that time they have not registered one play-off appearance, which at the time of writing is the longest current streak in the NFL for a team not getting to the post-season. Things can only get better and if NFL history proves one thing, it's that teams don't lose forever.

Miami Dolphins: Est. 1965

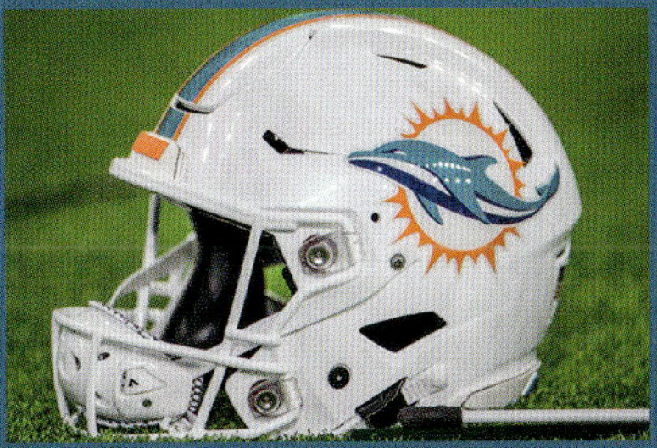

AFC East Champions: (13) 1971, 1972, 1973, 1974, 1979, 1981, 1983, 1984, 1985, 1992, 1994, 2000, 2008

AFC Conference Championships: (5) 1971, 1972, 1973, 1982, 1984

Super Bowl titles: (2) 1972, 1973

Super Bowl record: 2-3

The Dolphins went from their very foundation to being champions in just an eight-year period. They won back-to-back Super Bowls in 1972 and 1973 with the first success being one of the most celebrated seasons in NFL history. If a team is considered so strong that they could perhaps go every single game unbeaten, then part of the narrative will be, 'Can they do what the Dolphins did in the 1972 season, and go unbeaten?'

The 1972 campaign had started with the Dolphins coming off the back of a losing Super Bowl the previous season, where they had been defeated 24-3 by the Dallas Cowboys. They would go 14-0 in the regular season, before beating Cleveland in the divisional play-off and Pittsburgh in the AFC Championship match. This led to a Super Bowl showdown with Washington in LA, the outcome of which would forever make legends of the Dolphins whose season ended with a record of 17-0.

Although the games for the regular season would increase from 14 to 16 in the following years, making it harder for a team to achieve a 100 per cent winning season, the 1972 campaign remains the standard-bearer for perfection. The closest they came to losing their standalone record was in the 2007 season when their divisional rivals New England were heavy favourites to beat the Giants in Super Bowl 42 and end the season with a record of 19-0. It's said that the surviving members of the Dolphins team of 1972 always have a drink together whenever the last team in the NFL to remain undefeated loses, meaning that their status as the only perfect-record team will stay intact for yet another year. Their quarterback Bob Griese played that down slightly and said that they just have a coke, but when the Giants beat New England in the Super Bowl that coke would have tasted like vintage wine.

The Dolphins followed the perfect season by retaining their championship at Super Bowl 8 with a 24-7 win against the Minnesota Vikings, making them the first AFC team to win two Super Bowls on the trot; a feat that only six other teams in the NFL have achieved. The AFC in the 1970s would then get dominated by the Pittsburgh Steelers, but the Dolphins would reappear as a force in the 1980s with a team that won two AFC Championship games. The first in the 1982 season led them to Super Bowl 17 in which they lost 27-17 to Washington. A couple of years later, legendary quarterback Dan Marino took Miami to their second Super Bowl of the decade, where they lost 38-16 to San Francisco. Up to this point the Dolphins had been in over 25 per cent of all Super Bowls ever played, but by the time of publication they have not been back since. Overall Marino would lead the team to ten play-off campaigns in the 1980s and 1990s, but they would fall short each time and Marino would end up in the conversation for being one of the greatest quarterbacks to have never won a Super Bowl.

Miami as a team would be less of a contender as the years rolled on, winning the AFC East only four times since getting to the Super Bowl in the 1984 season. However, despite recent disappointment it remains a popular destination for players thanks to lower taxes and good weather, and due to the exploits of 1972, Miami remains the team to be able to say, 'We're the only ones to have been perfect.'

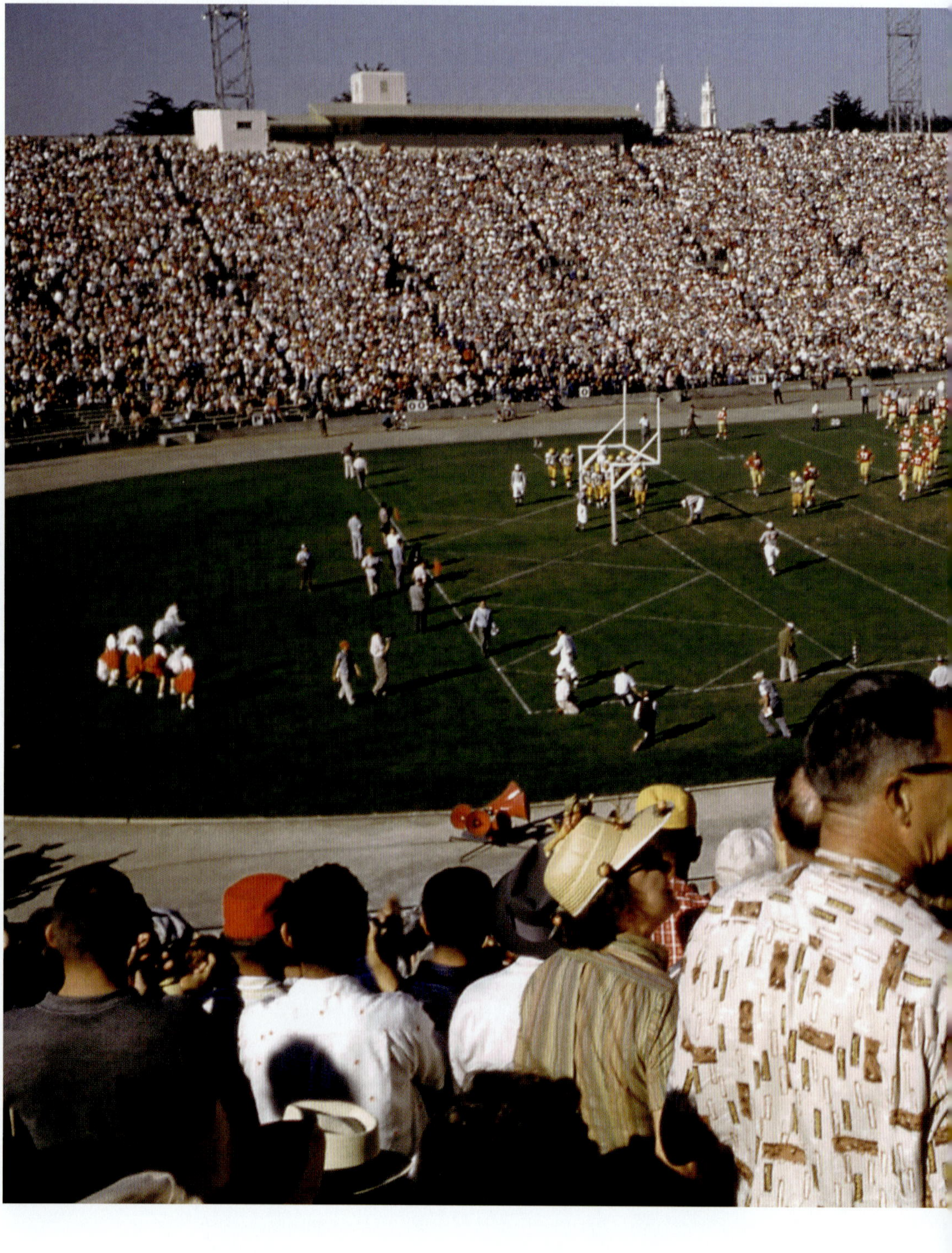

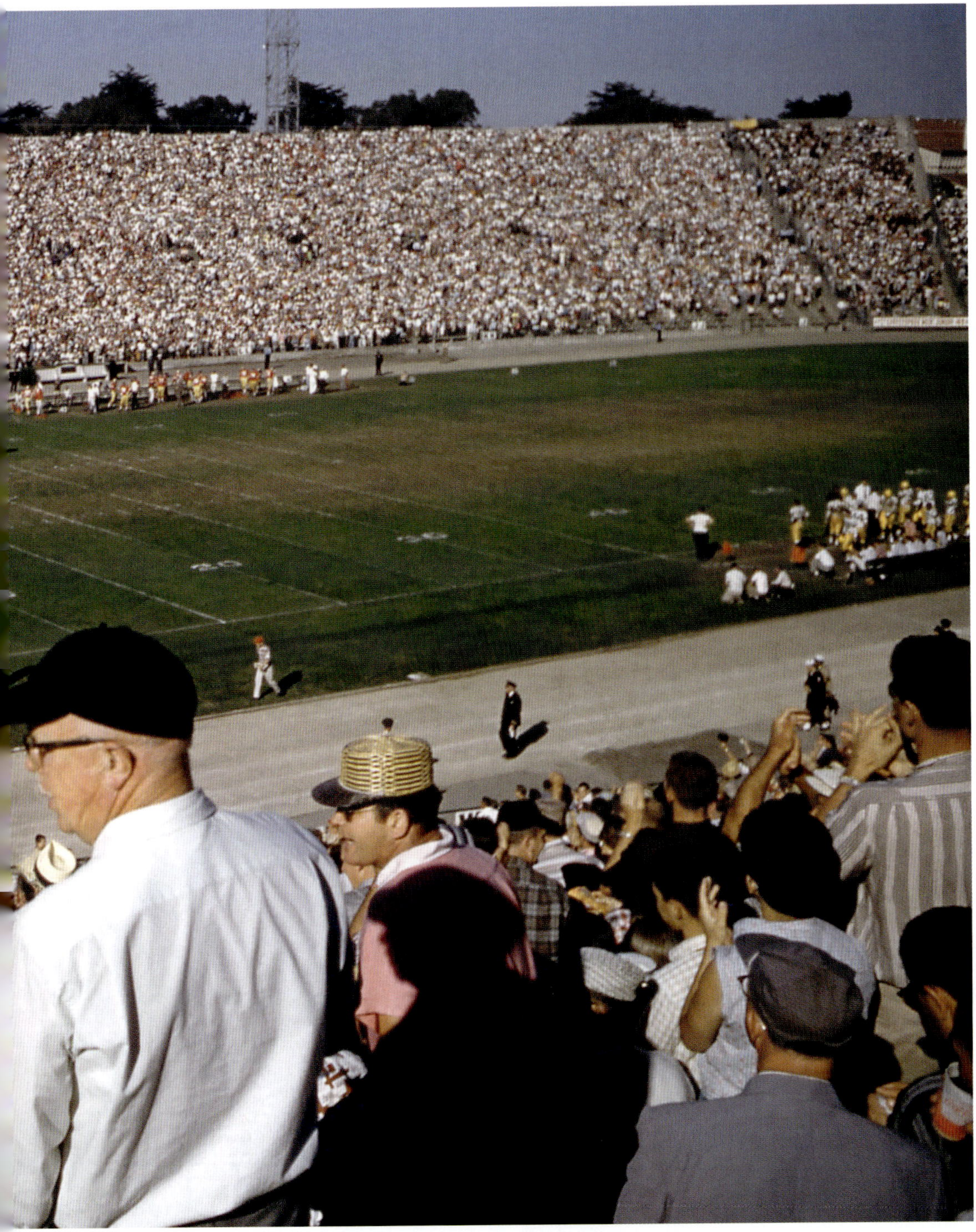

Kezar Stadium, San Francisco, 1958
The 49ers host the Pittsburgh Steelers.

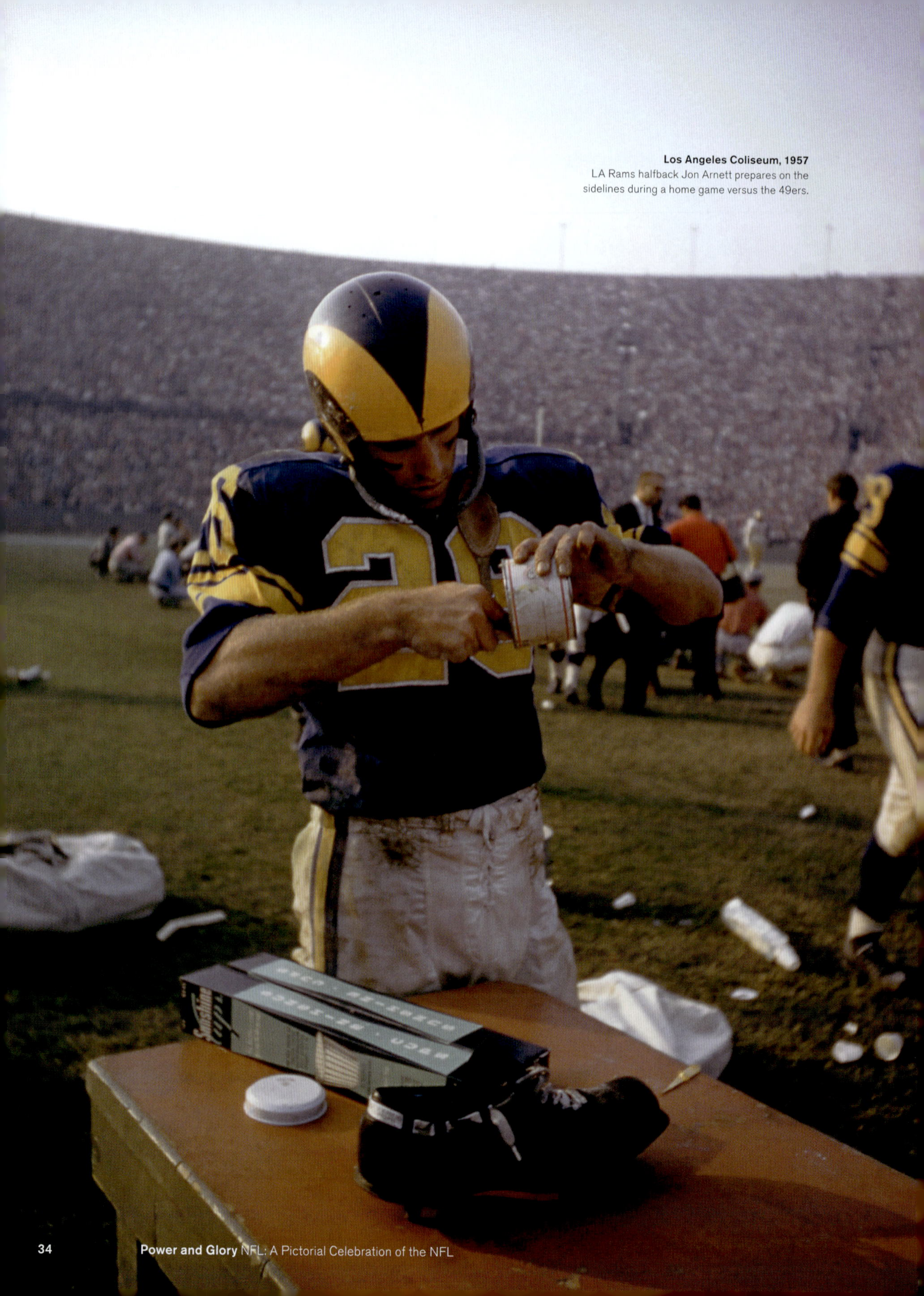

Los Angeles Coliseum, 1957
LA Rams halfback Jon Arnett prepares on the sidelines during a home game versus the 49ers.

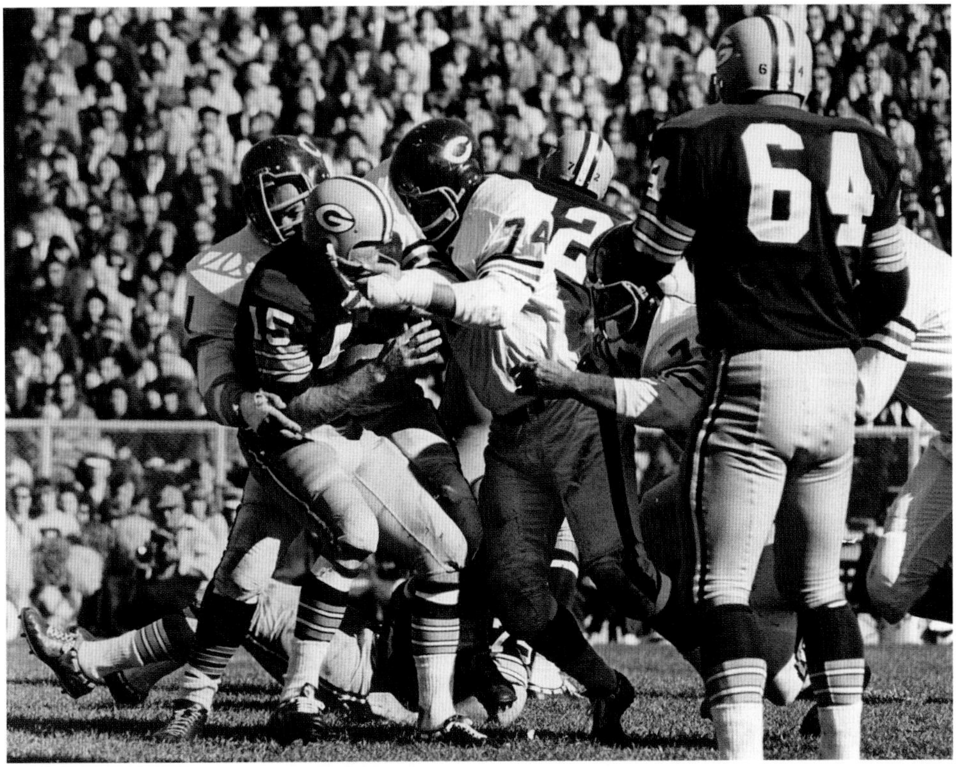

Lambeau Field, Green Bay, 1965
The Chicago Bears defence sack Green Bay quarterback Bart Starr.

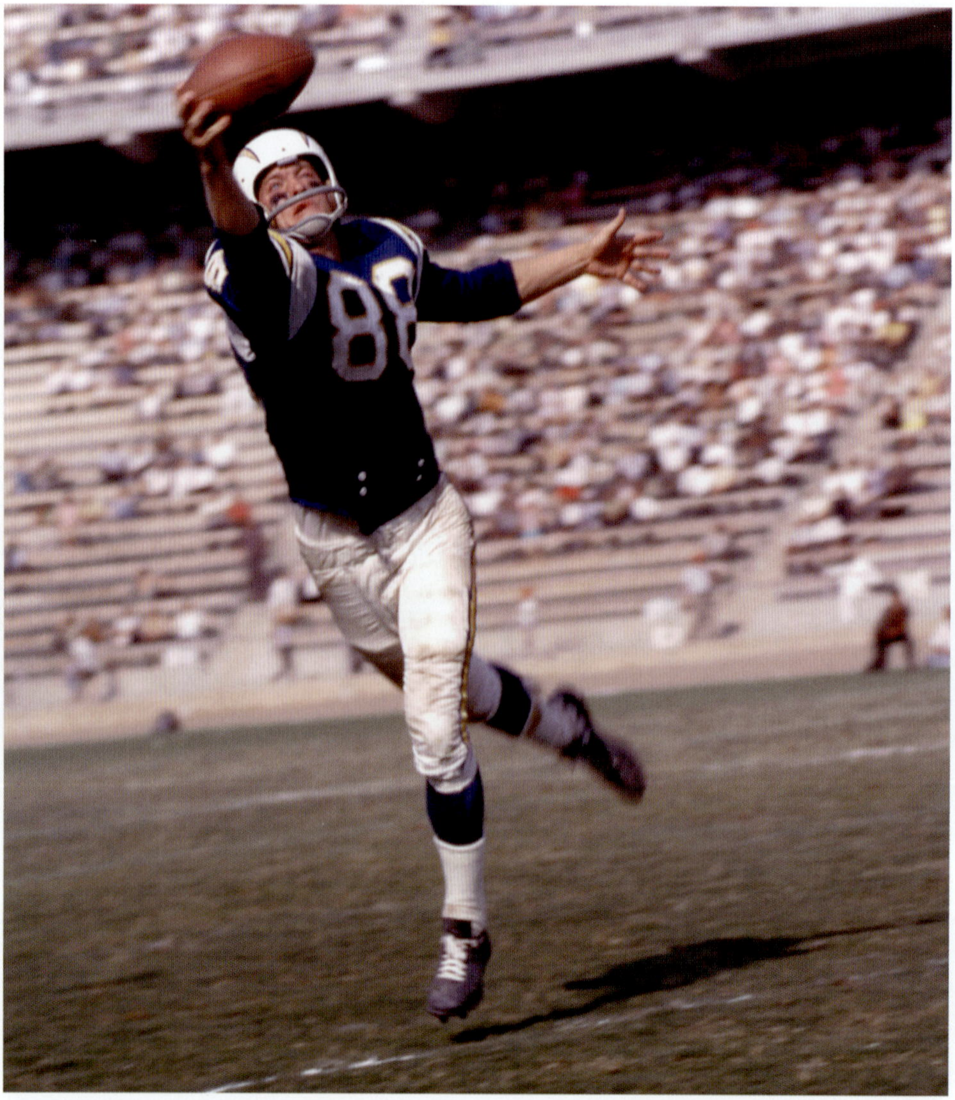

Balboa Park, San Diego, 1962
San Diego's Don Norton attempts a one-handed catch against the Houston Oilers.

Municipal Stadium, Cleveland. Unspecified date
Cleveland's Jim Brown powers though the St. Louis Cardinals defence on the one-yard line.

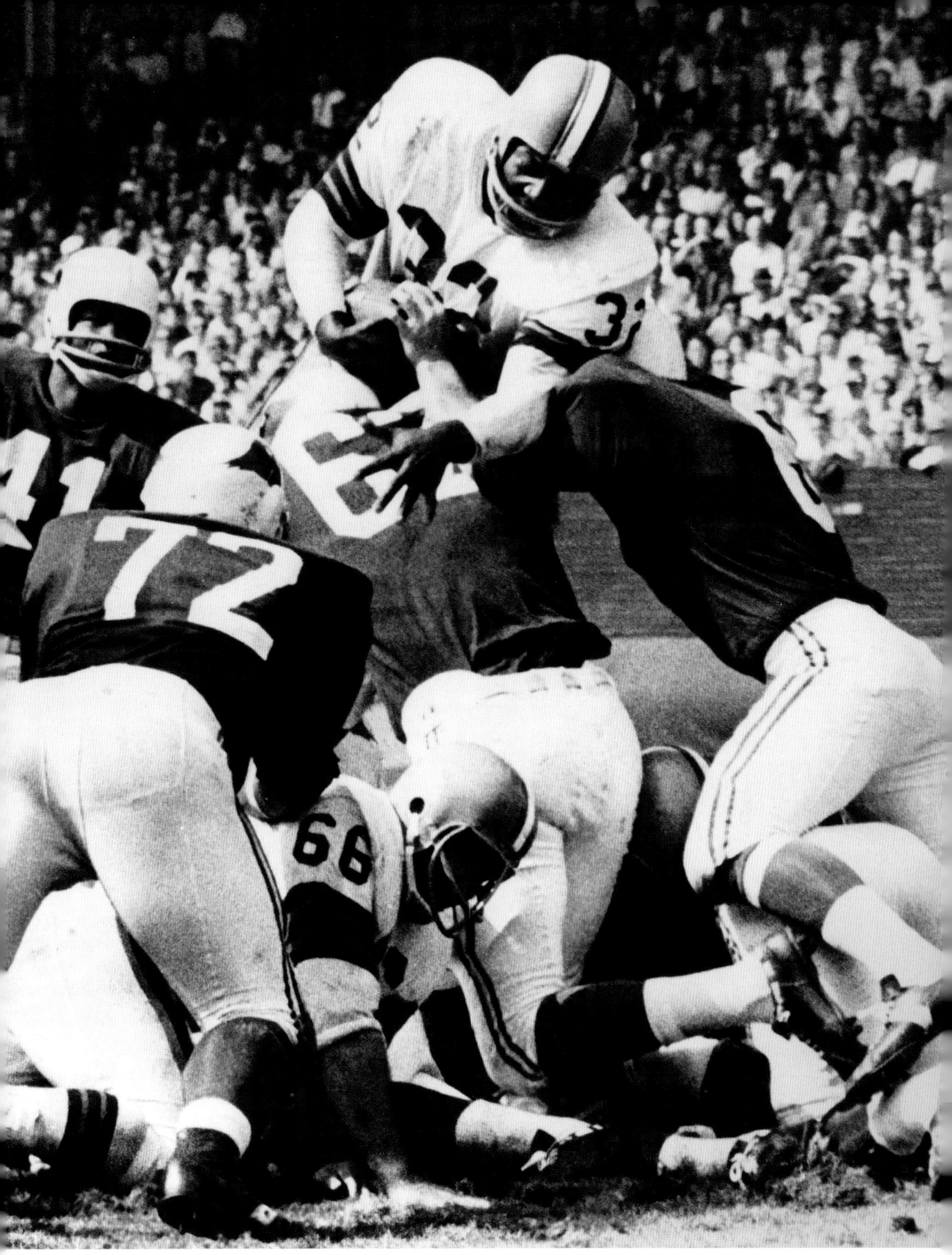
72
66

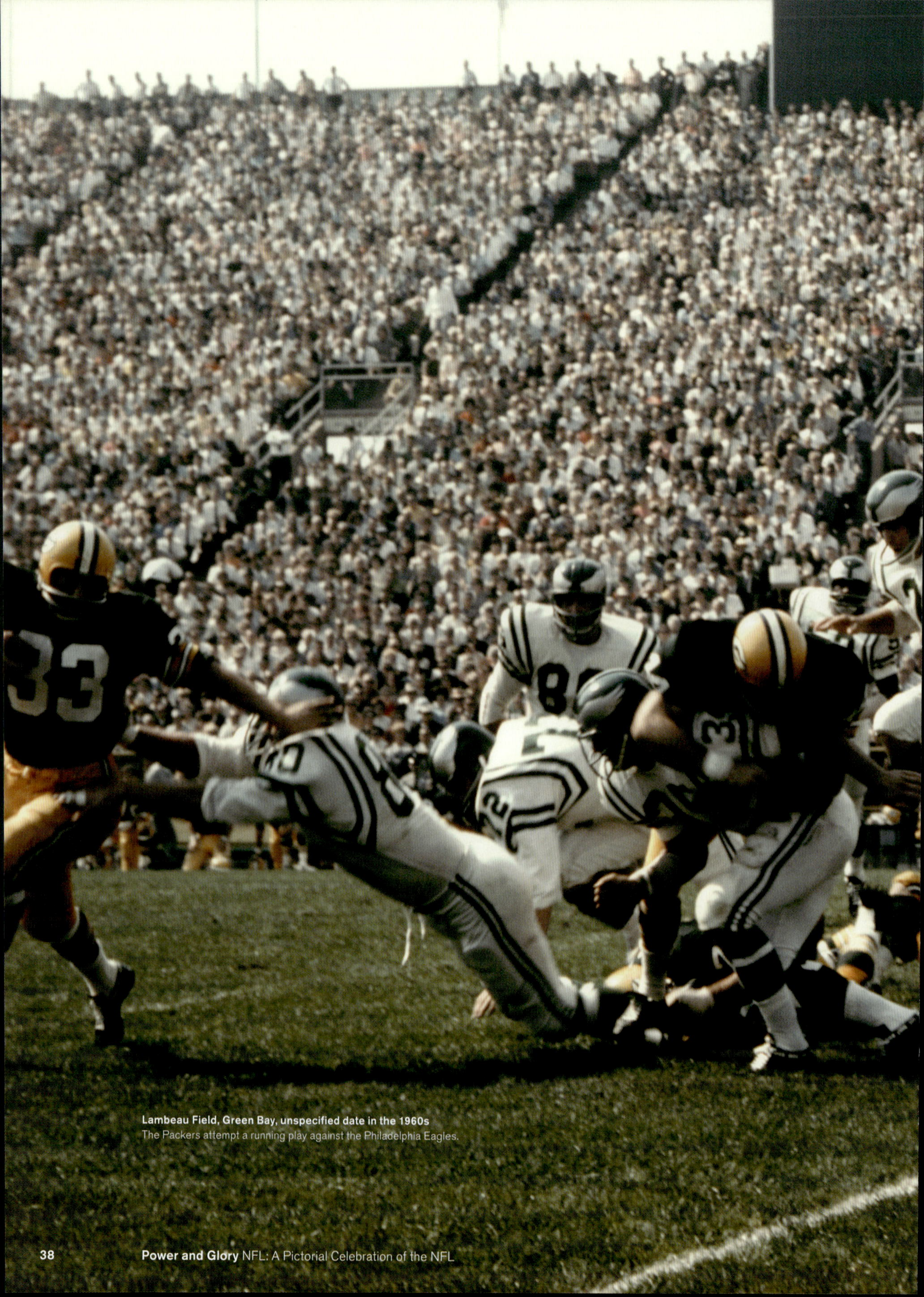

Lambeau Field, Green Bay, unspecified date in the 1960s
The Packers attempt a running play against the Philadelphia Eagles.

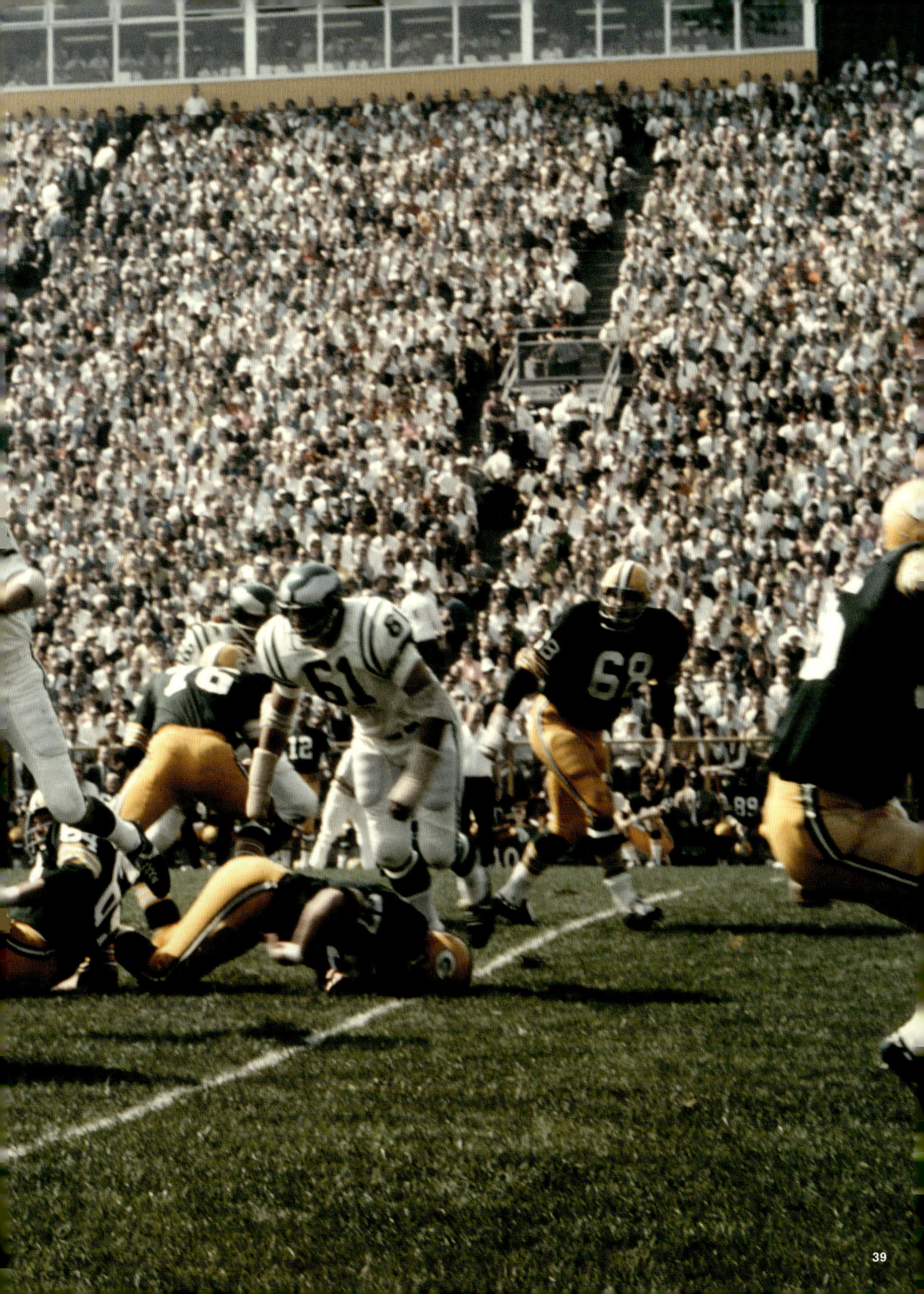
61
68
12

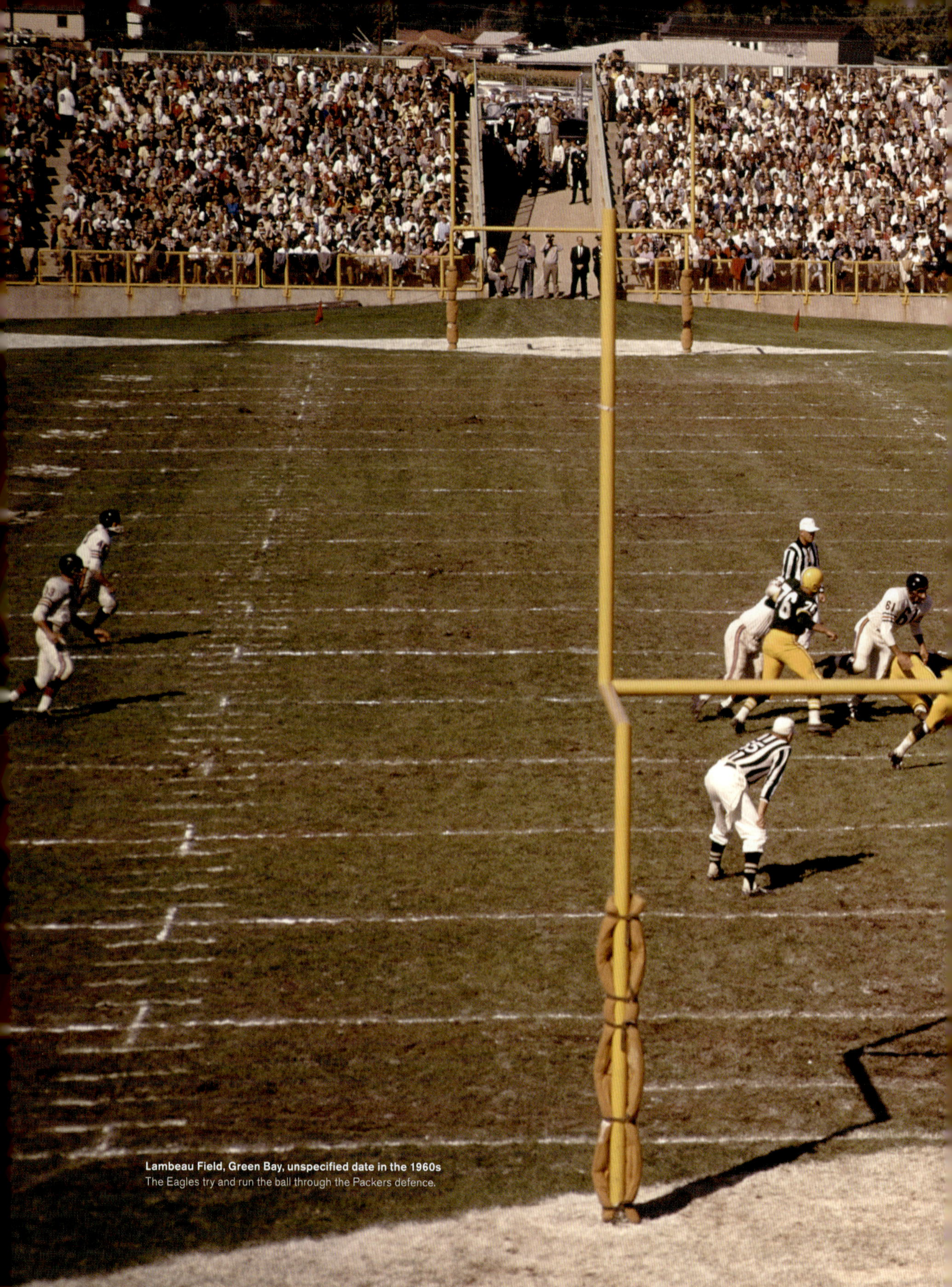

Lambeau Field, Green Bay, unspecified date in the 1960s
The Eagles try and run the ball through the Packers defence.

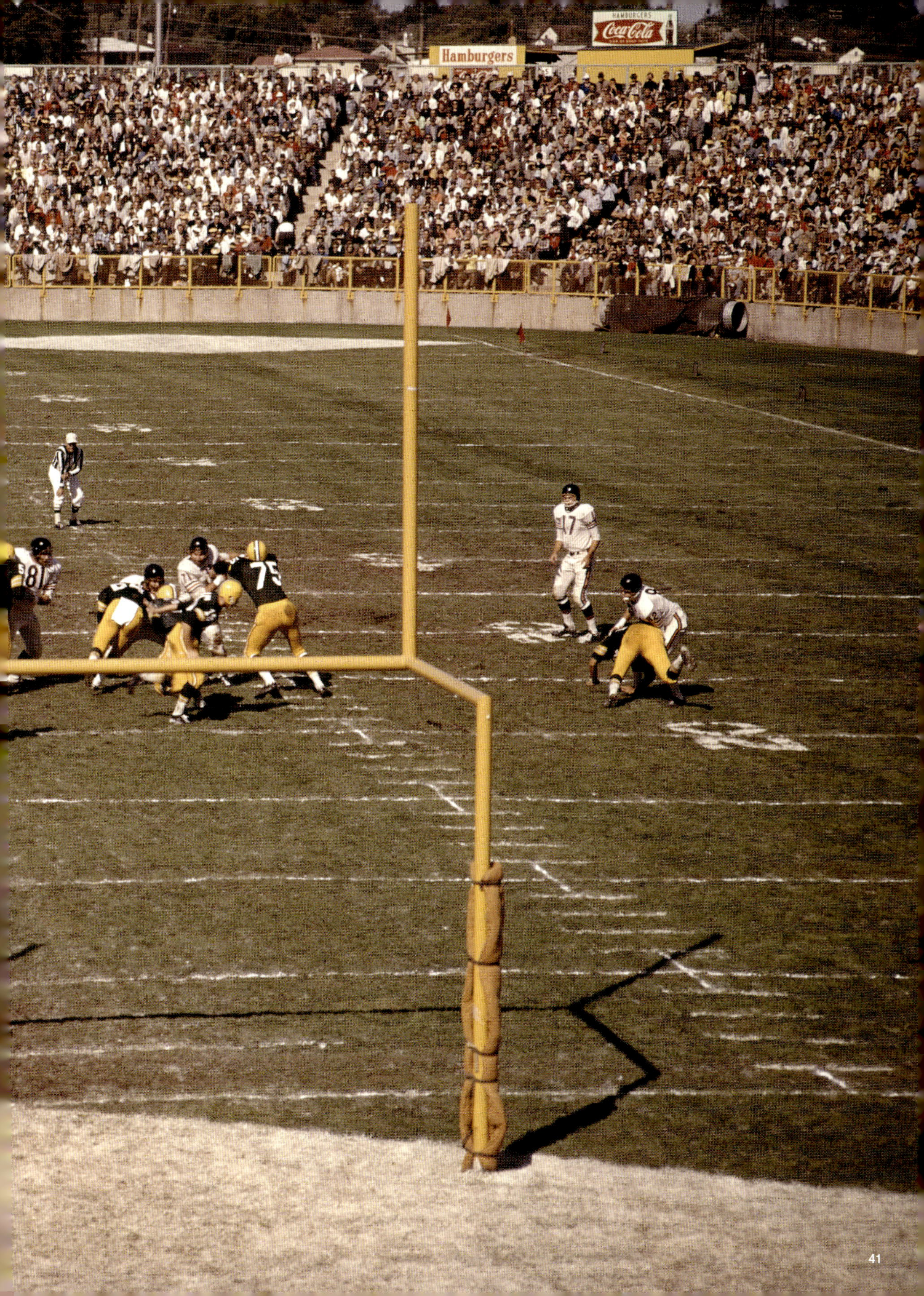
Hamburgers
HAMBURGERS
Coca-Cola

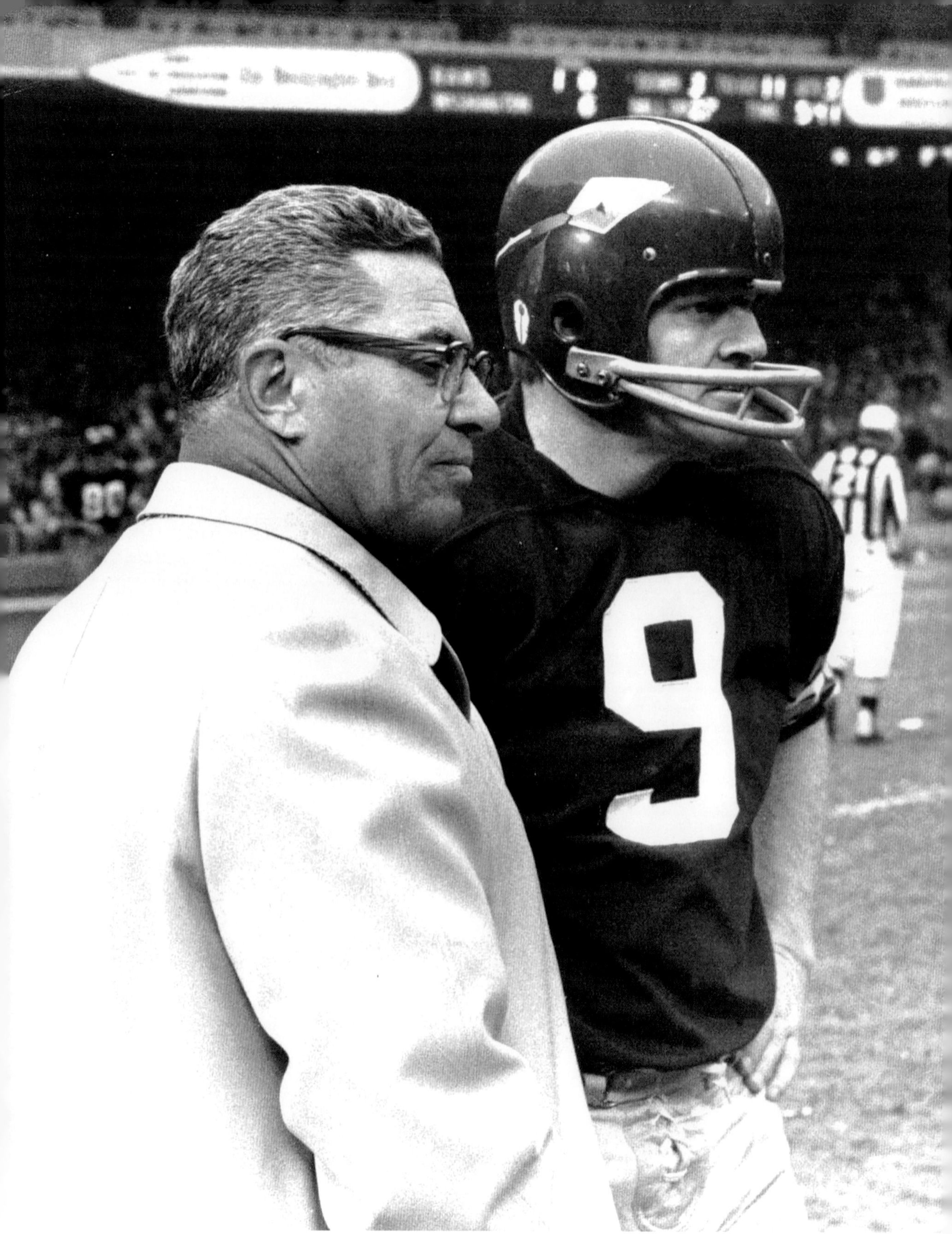

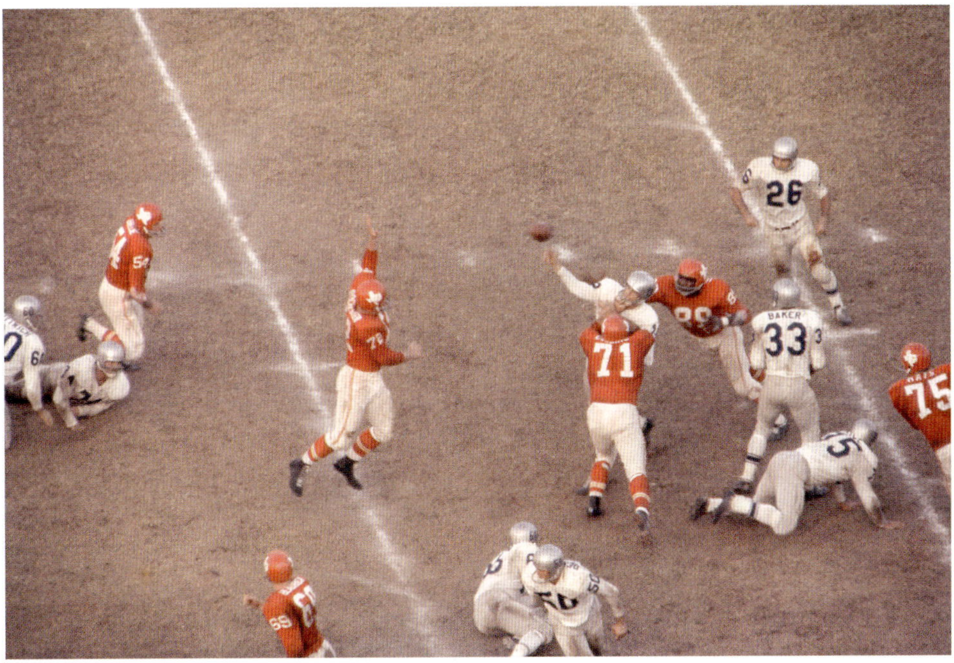

RFK Stadium, Washington, 1969
Vince Lombardi's only season as Washington's head coach. Here he is in discussion with quarterback Sonny Jurgensen. Lombardi would die a year later at the age of 57, and the Super Bowl trophy is named after him.

Cotton Bowl, Dallas, 1961
Buffalo in white take on the Dallas Texans (who would become the Kansas City Chiefs), as quarterback Johnny Green is tackled by Ray Collins (71) and Luther Jeralds (89).

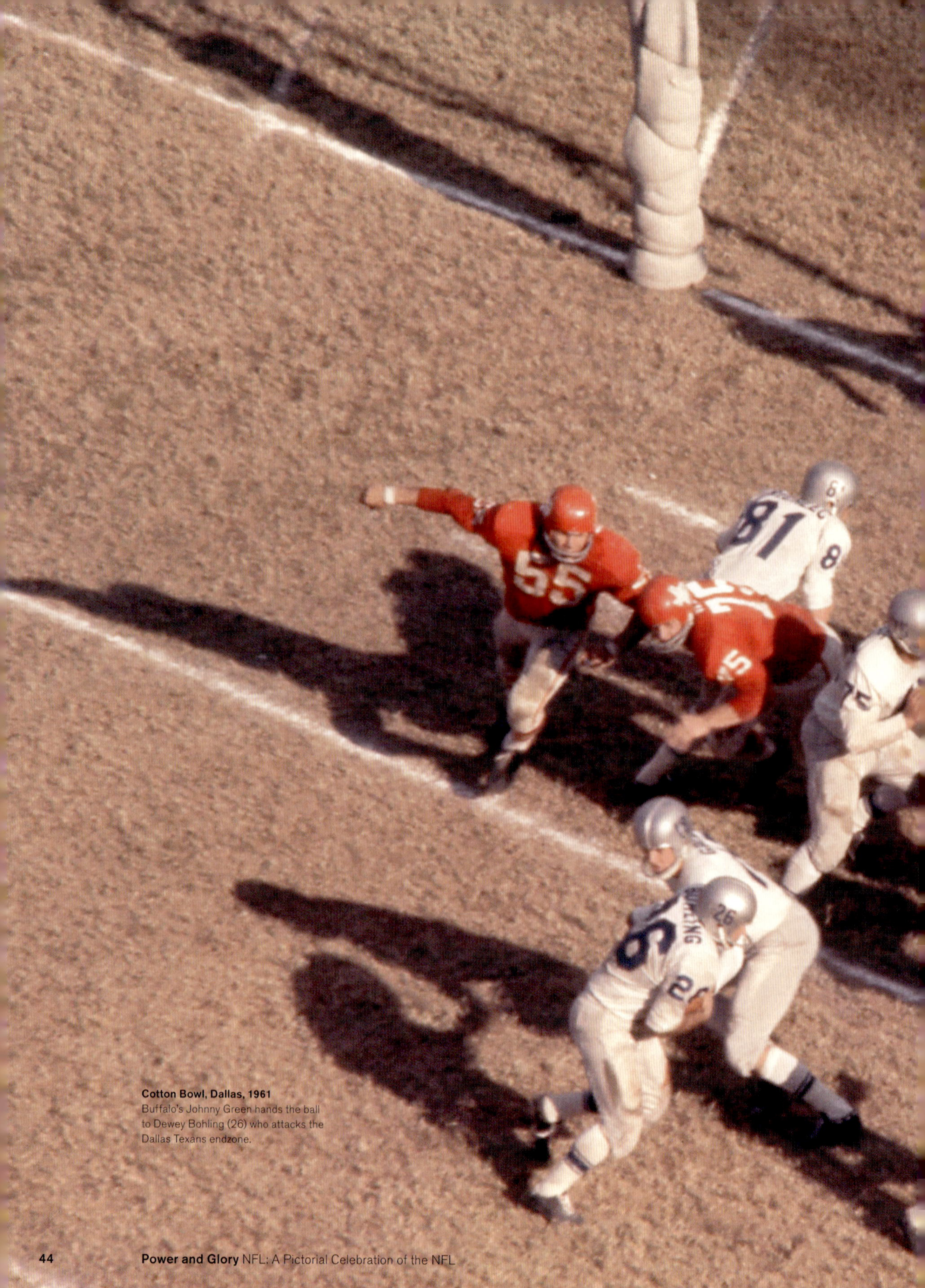

Cotton Bowl, Dallas, 1961
Buffalo's Johnny Green hands the ball to Dewey Bohling (26) who attacks the Dallas Texans endzone.

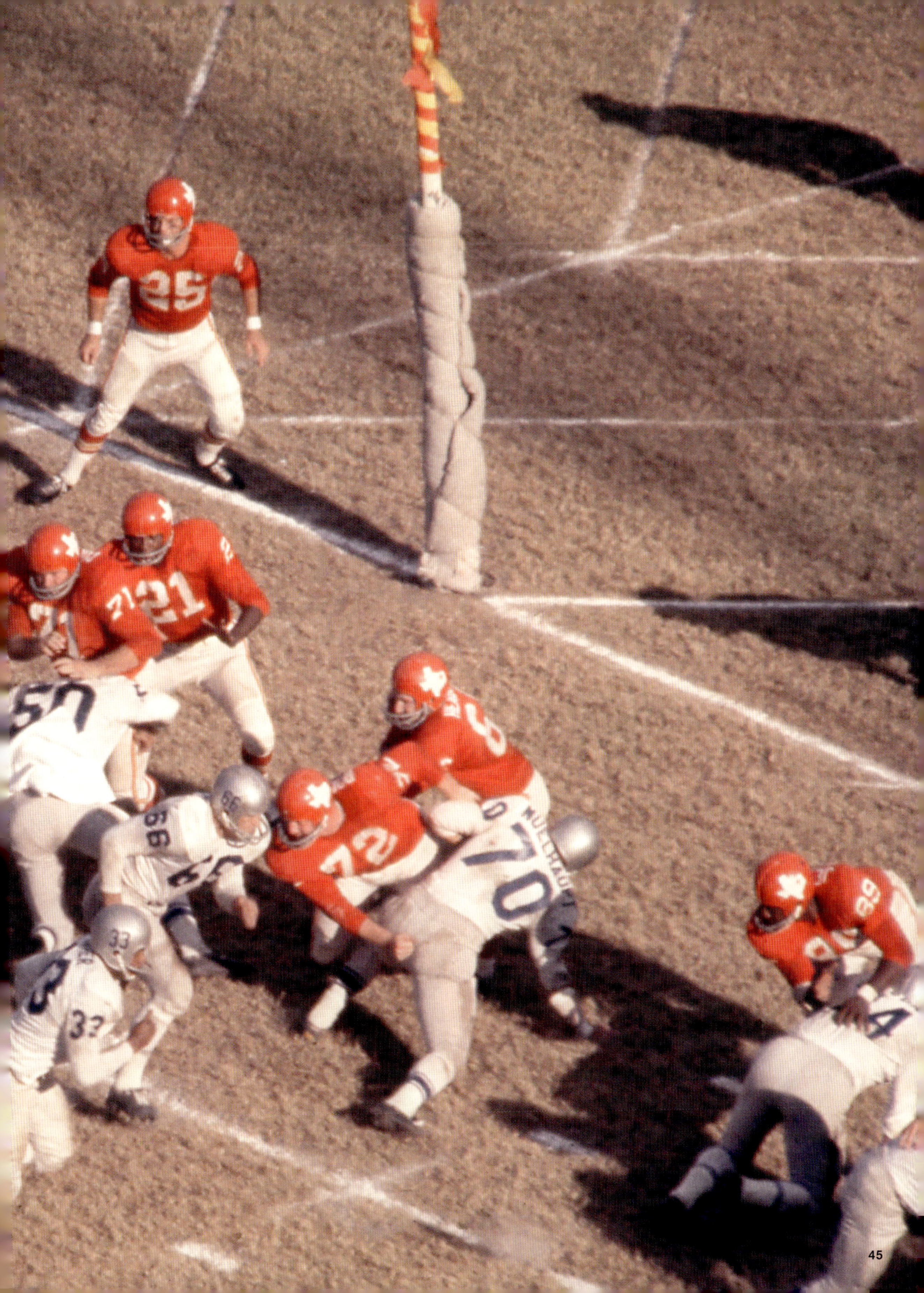

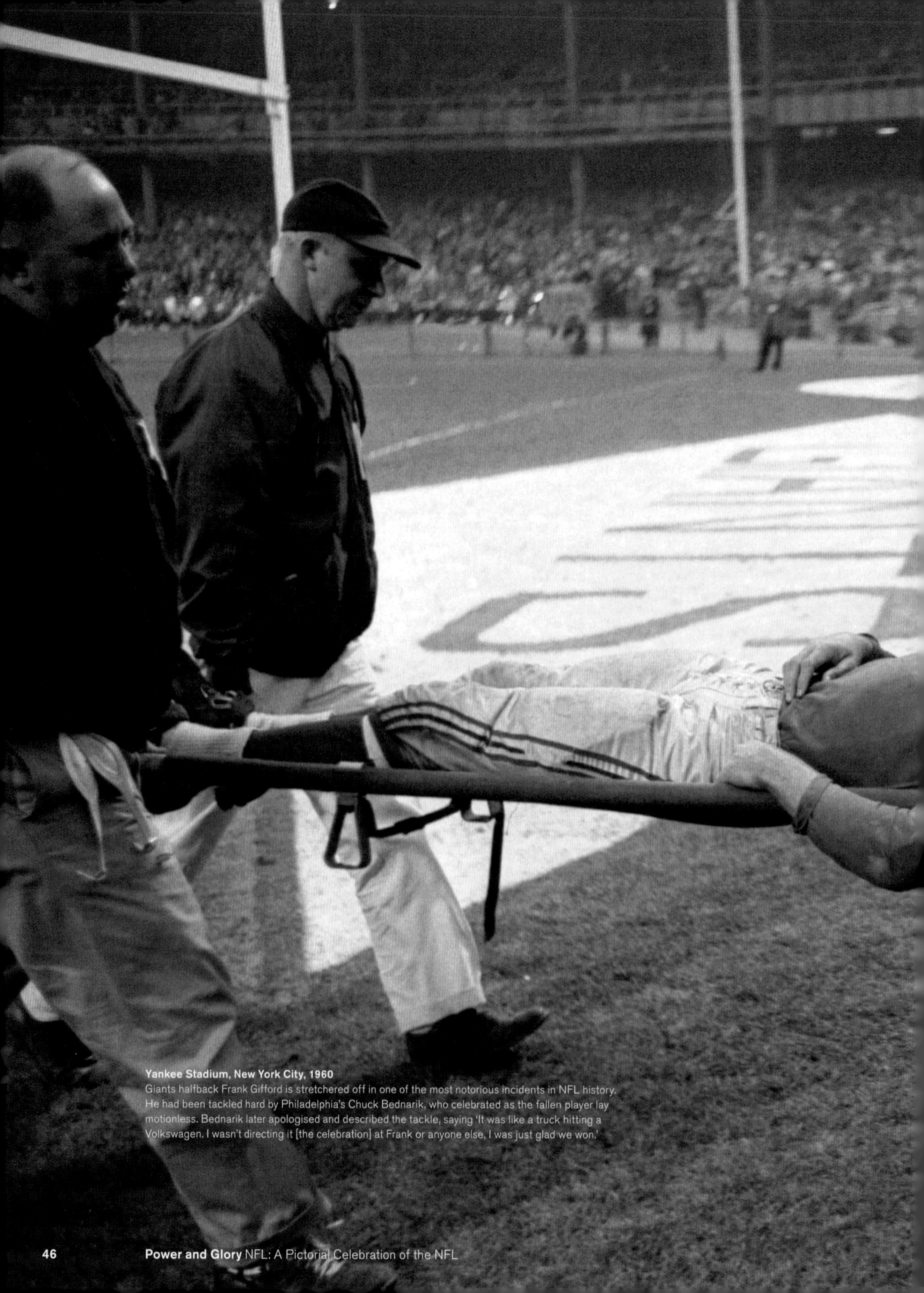

Yankee Stadium, New York City, 1960
Giants halfback Frank Gifford is stretchered off in one of the most notorious incidents in NFL history. He had been tackled hard by Philadelphia's Chuck Bednarik, who celebrated as the fallen player lay motionless. Bednarik later apologised and described the tackle, saying 'It was like a truck hitting a Volkswagen. I wasn't directing it [the celebration] at Frank or anyone else, I was just glad we won.'

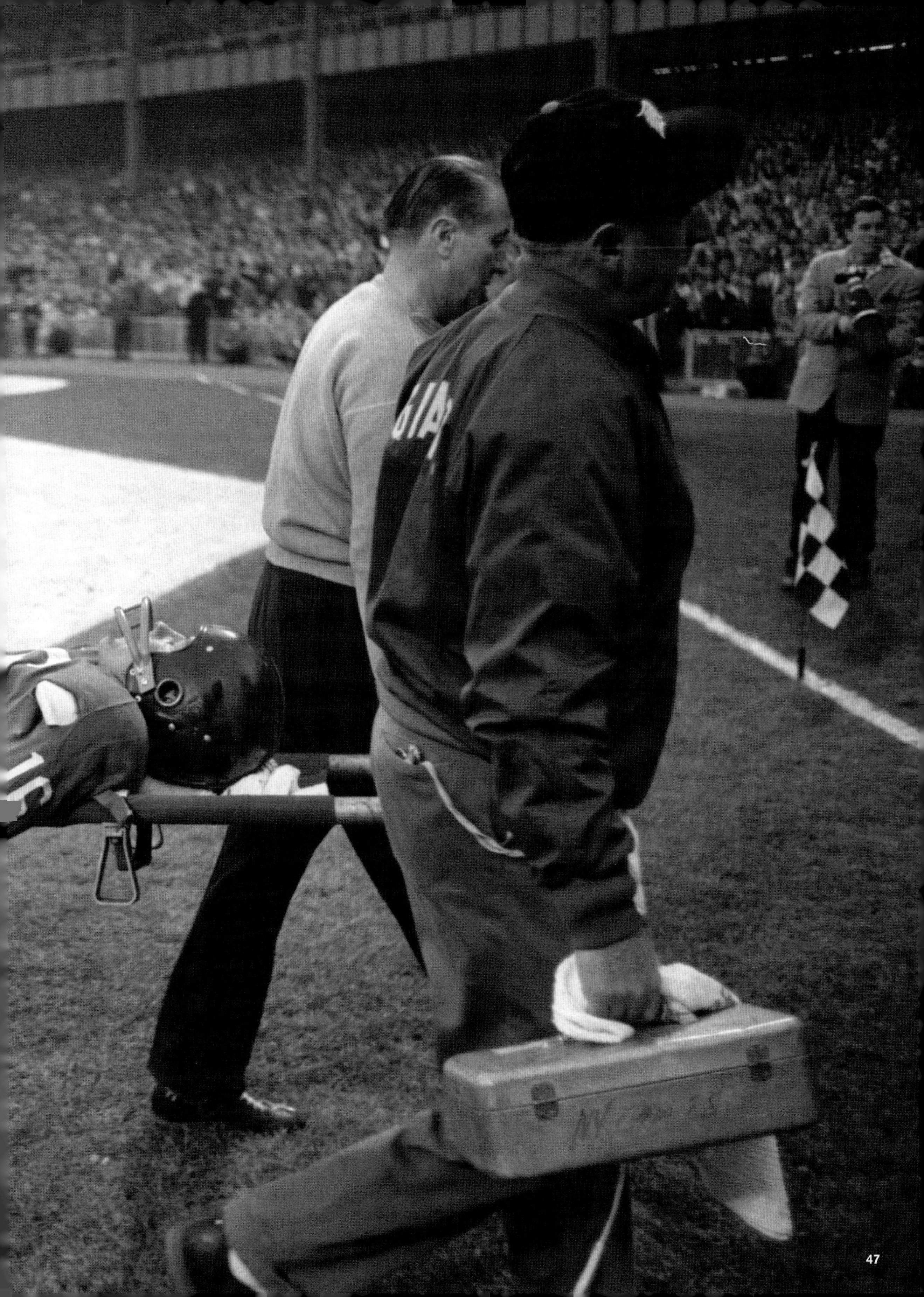

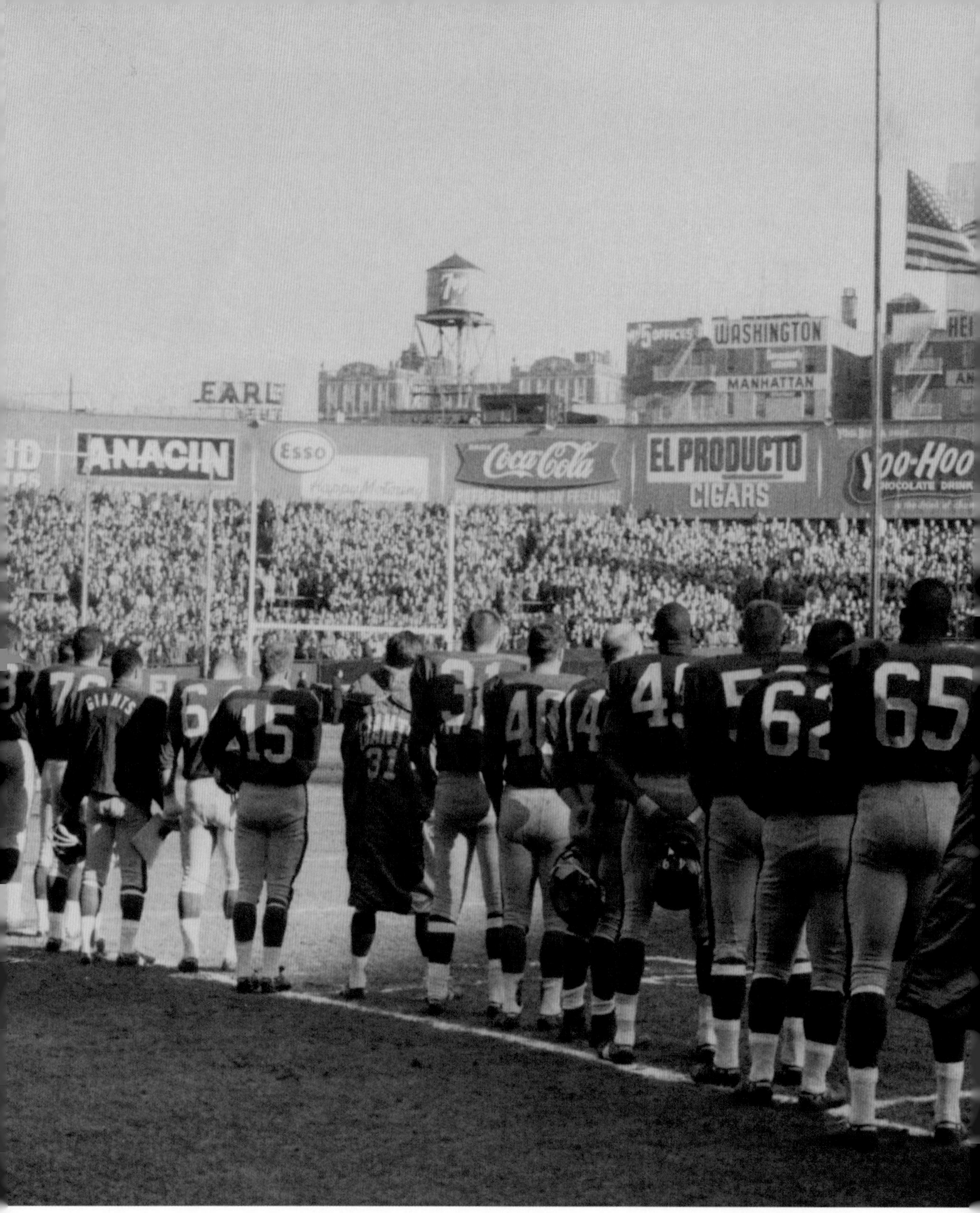
EARL
WASHINGTON
MANHATTAN
ANACIN
Esso
Coca-Cola
EL PRODUCTO
CIGARS
Yoo-Hoo
CHOCOLATE DRINK
GIANTS
15
62
65
GIANTS
31

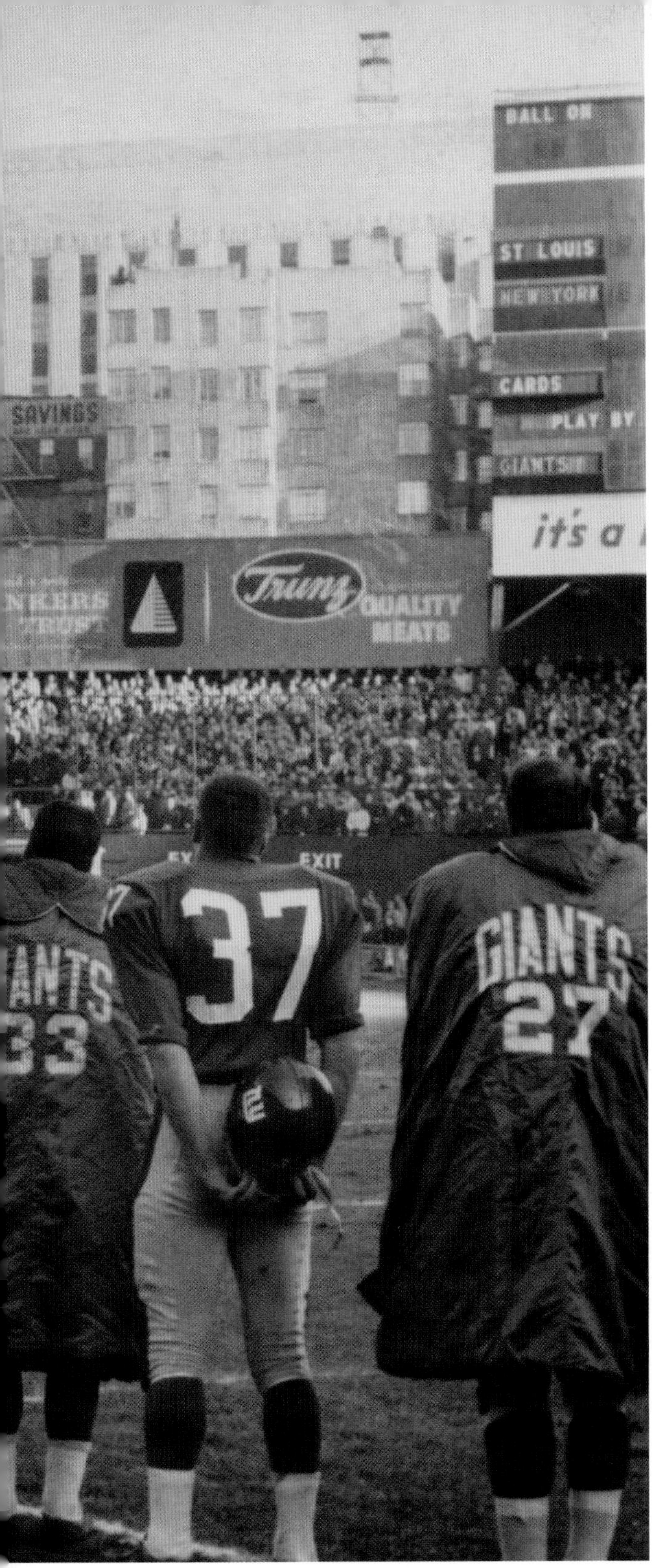

Yankee Stadium, New York City, 1963
A moment of reflection and prayer is held for President Kennedy, two days after he was assassinated.

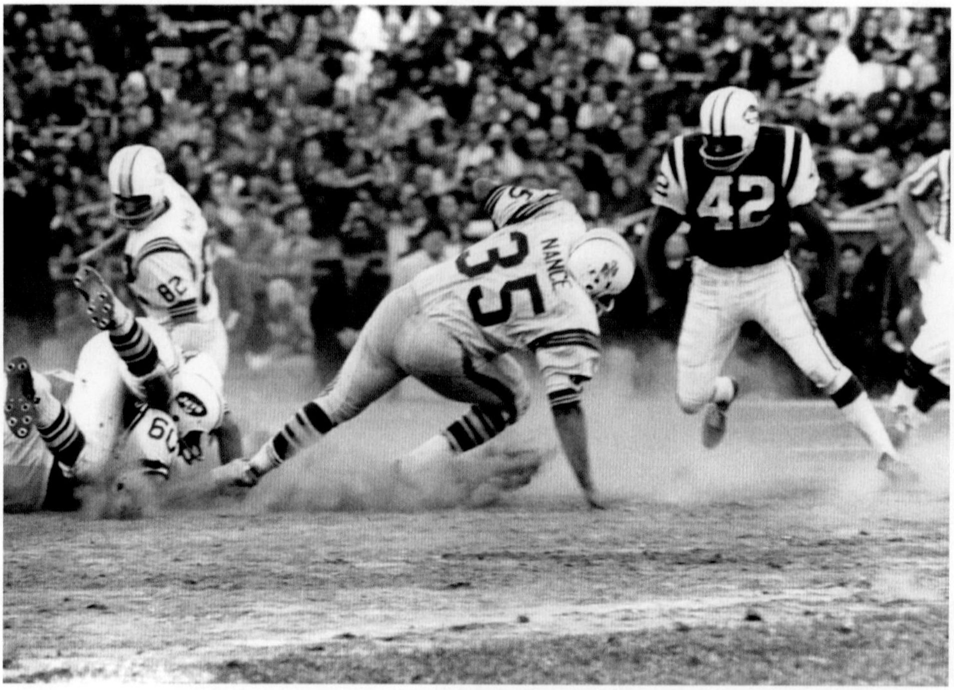

Fenway Park, Boston, 1965
The Boston Patriots fullback Jim Nance tries to keep his feet during a clash against the New York Jets.

Cleveland legend Jim Brown looks on from the sidelines.

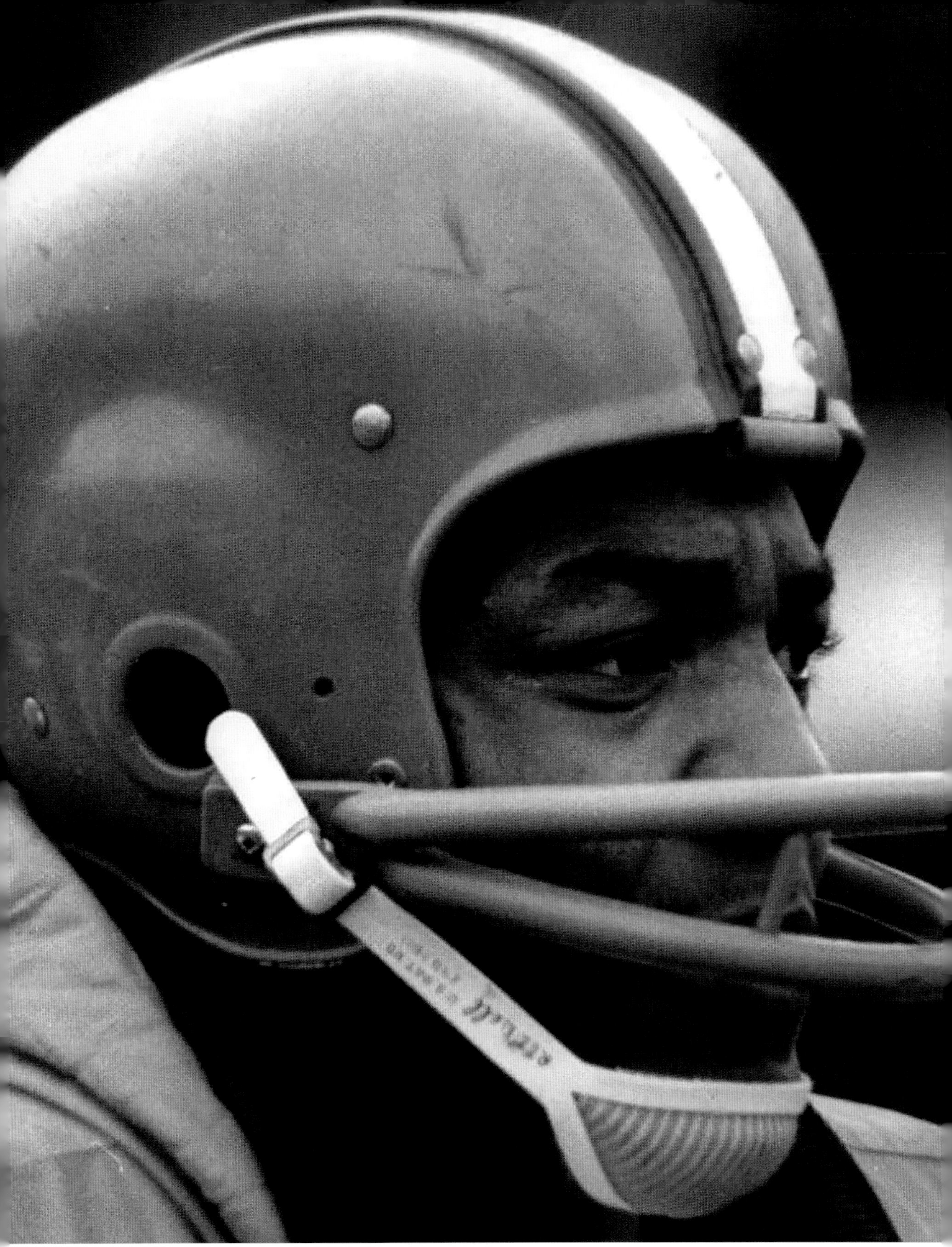

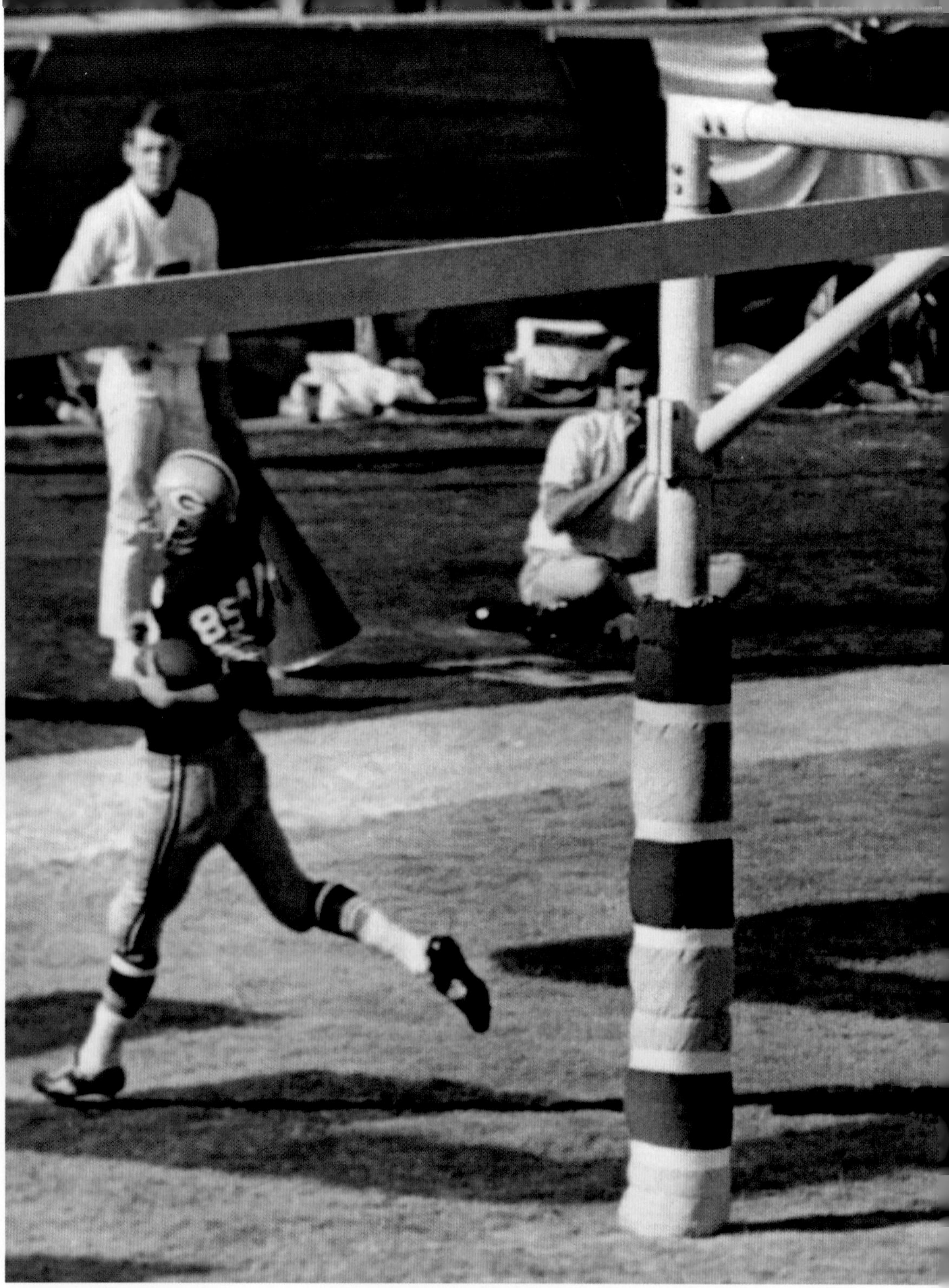

Los Angeles Coliseum, 1967, Los Angeles
The first ever Super Bowl. The Green Bay Packers' Max McGee scores against the Chiefs in a 35-10 victory, as the Packers become the first team to win a Super Bowl.

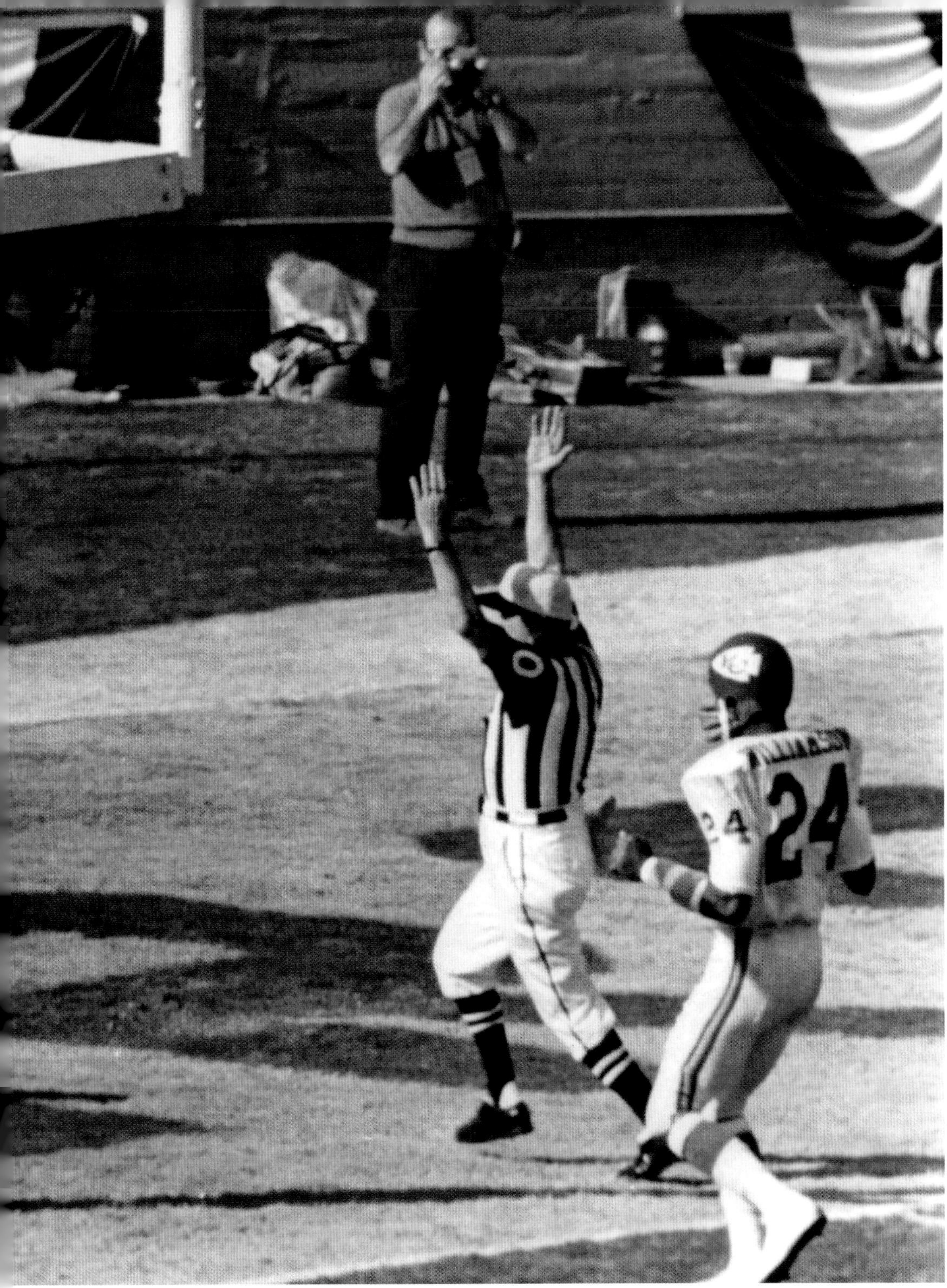
24
24

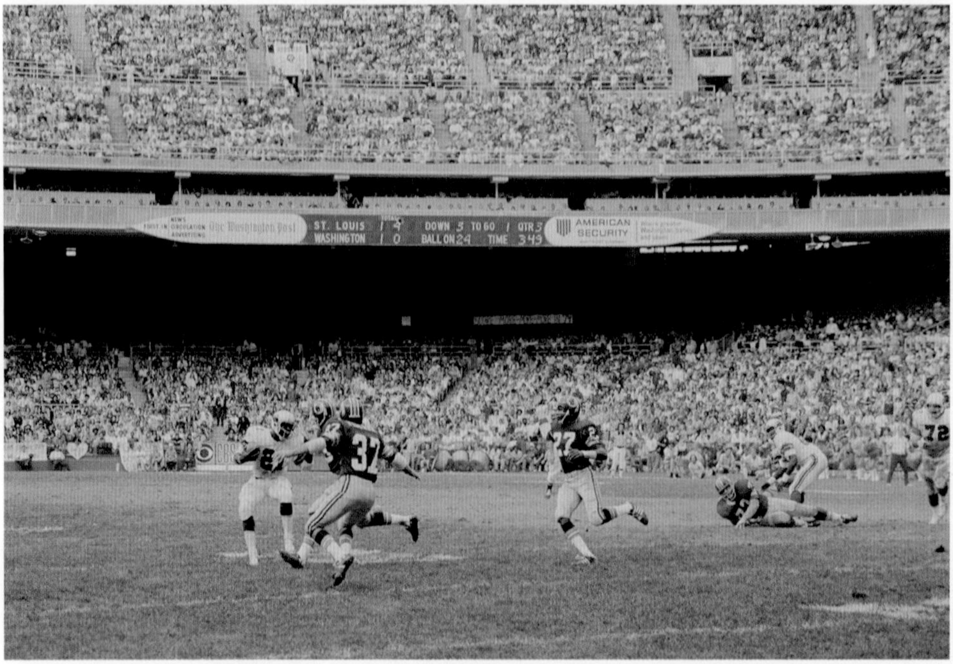

RFK Stadium, Washington DC, 1974
The St. Louis Cardinals take on Washington, as the scoreboard reads that the home team are leading 14-10.

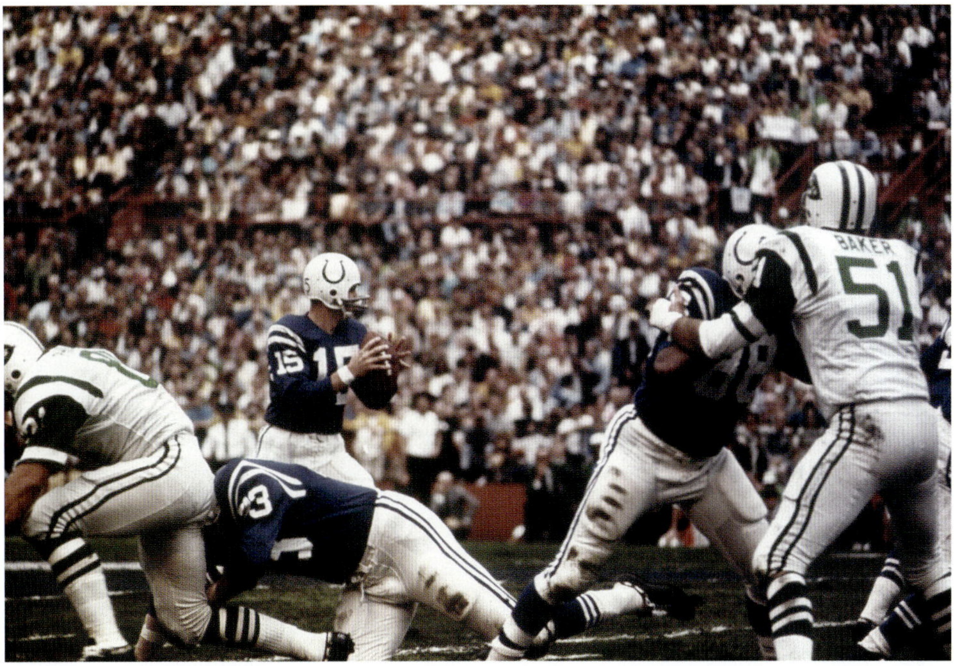

Orange Bowl, Miami, 1969
Super Bowl 3, the Colts quarterback Johnny Unitas looks for an opening against the Jets. New York would win, in what is still considered one of the great upsets in Super Bowl history.

Denver Broncos: Est. 1959

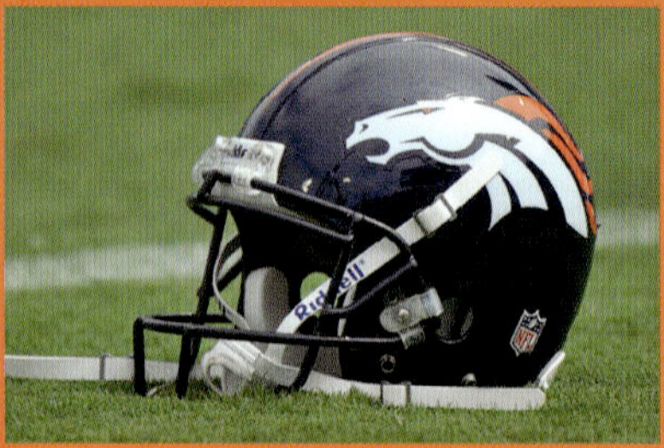

AFC West Champions: (15) 1977, 1978, 1984, 1986, 1987, 1989, 1991, 1996, 1998, 2005, 2011, 2012, 2013, 2014, 2015

AFC Conference Champions: (8) 1977, 1986, 1987, 1989, 1997, 1998, 2013, 2015

Super Bowl titles: (3) 1997, 1998, 2015

Super Bowl record: 3-5

In the 1997 season Denver got to the Super Bowl for a fifth time, but the past had not been kind to them. If they failed to win that match then they would have surpassed Minnesota and Buffalo's unwanted Super Bowl record of 0-4, and go to 0-5. In the 1977 season they lost to the Dallas Cowboys in Super Bowl 12. In the 1986 season they beat Cleveland in the AFC Championship game and lost to the New York Giants in the Super Bowl. In the 1987 season they beat Cleveland in the AFC Championship game and lost to Washington in the Super Bowl. In the 1989 season they beat Cleveland in the AFC Championship game and lost to San Francisco in the Super Bowl. Masters at beating Cleveland for the AFC title but failures in the Super Bowl was the Denver narrative up until the late 1990s, not to mention that all four defeats were lost by wide margins – with the overall score in all four games being 163-50.

For Super Bowl 32 Denver took on Green Bay, a game that starred two legendary quarterbacks in Brett Favre and John Elway. Elway had tasted defeat four times, while Favre had won the Super Bowl the year before. The Packers were strong favourites (with a predicted winning margin of 14 points) and things looked ominous for Denver when Favre threw a touchdown on Green Bay's first possession. However, the Broncos were determined to break their Super Bowl losing streak and fought back to take the lead. With only three minutes remaining the match was tied at 24-24, then Terrell Davis rushed in for the winning touchdown; even though earlier in the game the running back had temporarily lost his vision to an injury. Finally, Denver were champions, and then the following season Elway's Broncos became only the sixth team to win consecutive titles, this time beating the Atlanta Falcons 34-19 and Denver's Super Bowl record was looking better at 2-4.

The Broncos played their first season in 1960, and it wasn't until 1973 that they registered a winning campaign. In contrast, since getting to the 1977 Super Bowl they have only registered 11 losing seasons (five of those being in the last five years at the time of publication); and today they are recognised as one of the most successful teams in the league's history. When Denver won the Super Bowl in the 2015 season they joined an elite group that included eight other teams who had won it three times or more. Not that many people gave them a chance to beat the free-scoring Carolina Panthers who were favourites to win Super Bowl 50 by 5.5 points. Former Giants defensive end Osi Umenyiora was one of few people to tip the Broncos to beat Carolina due to the cliché of great defences winning championships; a cliché that's true.

The Broncos team also had the advantage of experiencing Super Bowl fever two years earlier when they were thrashed by Seattle. Although that had been a horrible one-sided beatdown, it gave the team an advantage over Carolina as they had already experienced the crazy week-long build-up to the big game. In contrast, Carolina quarterback Cam Newton, who had been so lethal that season, looked overwhelmed and like a cat caught in the headlights. He was eaten up by the Broncos' defence and sacked seven times with Von Miller named as MVP. The win gave legendary quarterback Peyton Manning a second Super Bowl ring. He was past his best by this point, but since moving to Denver from Indianapolis in 2012 Manning had cemented his place as a modern great and retired at the very top

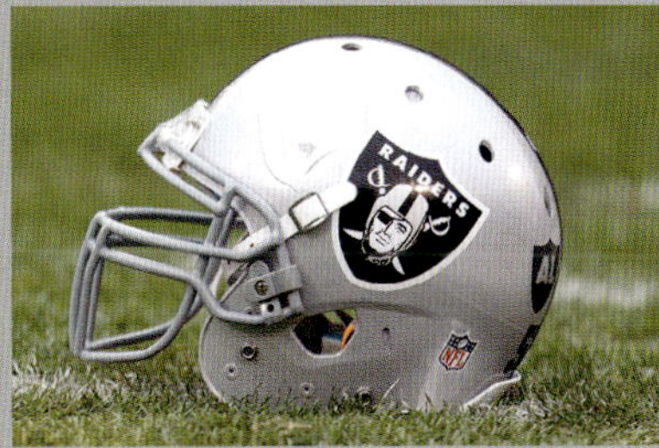

AFC West Champions: (12) 1970, 1972, 1973, 1974, 1975, 1976, 1983, 1985, 1990, 2000, 2001, 2002

AFL Champions: (1) 1967

AFC Conference Champions: (4) 1976, 1980, 1983, 2002

Super Bowl titles: (3) 1976, 1980, 1983

Super Bowl record: 3-2

Las Vegas Raiders: Est. 1960

Former names: Oakland Raiders (1960–1981, 995–2019); Los Angeles Raiders (1982–1994)

The Raiders competed in Super Bowl 2 in the 1967 season, but lost heavily against Green Bay; not that losing would become a Raiders tradition until many years later. Between 965 and 2002 the Raiders only registered six losing seasons. Joe Madden coached the team from 1969 to 978 and was never on the end of one losing campaign. n ten seasons under Madden, Oakland failed to make the post-season on just two occasions, as well as competing n six AFC Championship games, finally getting over he line in the 1976 season by beating the formidable Pittsburgh Steelers and getting to Super Bowl 11 to face he Minnesota Vikings. Oakland were favourites and took a 6-0 lead into half-time which the Vikings never recovered rom. The final score was 32-14 and Madden's Raiders had inally won the big one, to cement their legacy as one of the great teams of the era.

A year later the Raiders lost the AFC Championship game to Denver, but they were back in the Super Bowl in the 1980 season and up against Philadelphia. Tim Flores had taken over as Oakland head coach and the Eagles were slight favourites to win by three points. Up to this point no wild card team had won the Super Bowl and the Raiders put an end to that trend by beating Philly 27-10.

The early 1980s was a time when signs started appearing in the stands from fans pleading 'Save Our Raiders'. The nightmare of relocation was upon the relatively small city in the Bay area of Northern California and the team were heading south to Los Angeles. They found immediate success in the 1983 season and won Super Bowl 18 against defending champions Washington in a one-sided beatdown that ended 38-9. The Raiders, with three Super Bowl titles to their name, were now second only to Pittsburgh for overall wins; however to date the 1983 season was their last Super Bowl success.

The team returned to Oakland in 1995 and made it back to the Super Bowl in the 2002 season where they would lose 48-21 to Tampa Bay. Success was drying up and from 2003, they would go a painful 13 straight seasons without registering one winning season; a total contrast to the Raiders' winning culture created decades earlier. Worse was to follow if you were a fan from Oakland; of all the NFL relocations, the most significant and saddest for the league as a whole was the second move from Oakland, this time to Las Vegas in 2019. The NFL voted unanimously in favour of relocation and the media applauded, instead of questioning the ethics of such a decision. The talk among pundits centred on how exciting it would be to have a team in Vegas, as opposed to sticking up for the fans in the home city that made the Raiders unique.

The move was a depressing statement from the NFL which signified that there is no longer any room in the league for anything that is a bit rough around the edges. Oakland was raw, from the stadium to the fans who were the most flamboyant, craziest and passionate – with the 'Black Hole' end the nearest thing the NFL had to soccer's ultras. What a contrast it is in Las Vegas; in the 2021 season when they played Kansas, it seemed like half the stadium were Chiefs fans which is an unthinkable scenario in Oakland. Dining tables at pitchside where rich fans watch the games has replaced one of the most unique fanbases and this has made the NFL a far less interesting spectacle.

Kansas City Chiefs: Est. 1959

Former name: Dallas Texans (1960–1962)

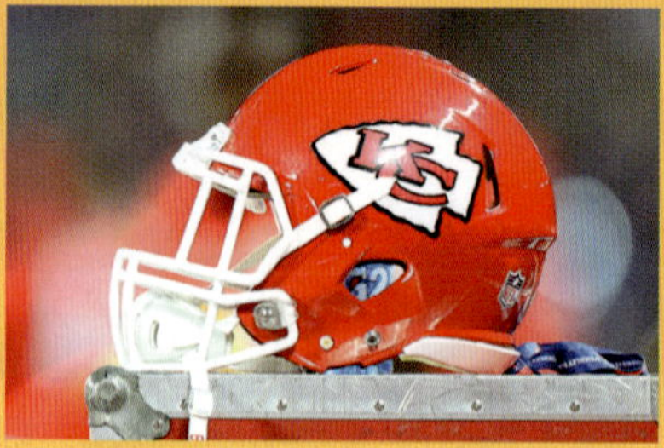

AFC West Champions: (12) 1971, 1993, 1995, 1997, 2003, 2010, 2016, 2017, 2018, 2019, 2020, 2021

AFL Champions: (3) 1962, 1966, 1969

AFC Conference Champions: (2) 2019, 2020

Super Bowl titles: (2) 1969, 2019

Super Bowl record: 2-2

Lamar Hunt was a businessman who had tried to purchase the NFL's Chicago Cardinals in the late 1950s. His failure to do so set in motion the very creation of the AFL, the 1960s rival of the NFL and the league that saw the emergence of the current AFC teams. Hunt's original plan was to relocate the Cardinals to his hometown of Dallas, and when that never transpired, he applied to the NFL to form a new club; however the application was refused and a new NFL team in Dallas called the Cowboys was already being formed. Hunt therefore created the Dallas Texans, who played in red and white and their first season was in 1960 in the American Football League, which he also created.

In their third season the Texans won the AFL Championship with a victory over state rivals the Houston Oilers. Despite his desire to have a team in Dallas, Hunt was now of the opinion that the city wasn't big enough for two teams, and the mayor of Kansas Harold Roe Bartle, whose nickname was 'The Chief', persuaded him to relocate to Missouri in 1963, so the Kansas City Chiefs were born.

When they won the 1966 AFL title, something new and very different was set to follow. Plans had been made for the winner of the AFL to play in a showpiece game against the NFL champions, in this case the Green Bay Packers. Lamar Hunt was an influential figure in these plans and had come up with the title 'Super Bowl' which was a name inspired by an elastic glitter ball for kids called 'Super Ball'. The Packers beat Kansas 35-10, but the first half had been competitive and the Chiefs were given respect for their performance at a time when the NFL was considered the superior of the two leagues.

The AFL's New York Jets won Super Bowl 3, but the view was still that the AFL was inferior; a perception that ended when Kansas City made it to Super Bowl 4 and defeated the NFL's Minnesota Vikings who before the game were favoured to win by 13 points. This victory for Kansas meant that the Super Bowl record between the AFL and the NFL was now 2-2; and when the two leagues merged into one Kansas were pitted in the AFC West, but decline would follow and between 1974 and 1988 Kansas only recorded two winning seasons.

Despite appearing in two of the first four Super Bowls, it would be a long and frustrating wait until the next one. Super Bowl 54, played in February 2020, was a classic and one of the last major sporting events to take place before the world was turned on its head due to the Covid-19 pandemic. Kansas City versus San Francisco would be the last NFL game played before a sold-out crowd until September 2021.

In the 2018 season, a unique and emerging new quarterback, Patrick Mahomes, had so nearly got his team to Super Bowl 53, narrowly losing to Tom Brady's New England in the AFC Championship game. Kansas made it to Super Bowl 54 but were trailing 20-10 with just over six minutes on the clock. Mahomes then stepped up to prove his greatness at the age of just 24 and threw two touchdowns for his side to take the lead. In the dying moments, a third touchdown was scored and the Chiefs had won the game with 21 unanswered points to claim their second Super Bowl, 50 years since the last one, in what stands as the widest margin between a team repeating Super Bowl glory.

LA Chargers: Est. 1959

Former name: San Diego Chargers (1961–2016)

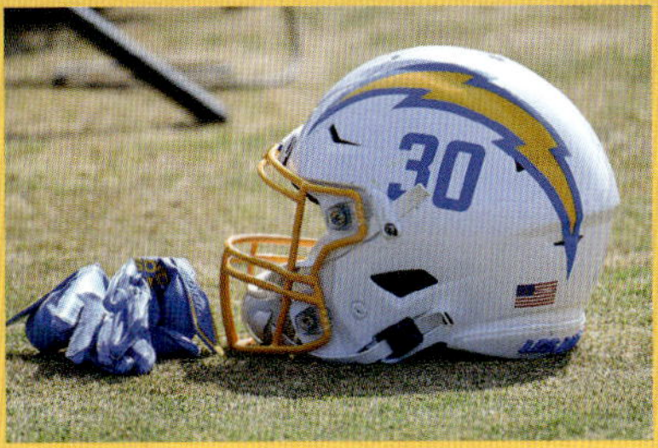

AFC West Champions: (10) 1979, 1980, 1981, 1992, 1994, 2004, 2006, 2007, 2008, 2009

AFL Championships: (1) 1963

AFC Conference Champions: (1) 1994

Super Bowl record: 0-1

The Chargers were founded in LA and the name was inspired by the roar of 'charge' from the local University team along with the sound of a bugle, which is still heard at Chargers games today.

After only one year in LA the team was relocated to San Diego and by the 1963 season, they won the AFL Championship in what today is the one and only time that the Chargers have been crowned champions of the entire league they were participating in. When the 'Bolts' joined the NFL after the 1970 AFL merger, they would not register a winning season until 1978; however a strong team was emerging by the end of the decade. In seasons 1980 and 1981 San Diego were just one win away from a Super Bowl appearance, but would lose the AFC Championship game two years in a row. In 1981 they lost 27-7 to Cincinnati, and a year earlier it had been a tighter game against the Oakland Raiders but the Chargers still came up short at 34-27.

Between seasons 1983 and 1991 San Diego only registered one winning record. However, in the 1994 campaign San Diego were back in the AFC Championship game, this time against the Pittsburgh Steelers. With just over five minutes to go they were trailing 13-10, then quarterback Stan Humphries threw a 43-yard touchdown to wide receiver Tony Martin, and the Chargers were in the Super Bowl for the first – and to date the only – time. It was South California versus North California for Super Bowl 29 and their opponents San Francisco were heavily favoured to win by 18.5 points, the second largest points prediction in Super Bowl history. The Chargers making it this far had been a surprise as their squad was in transition and had 22 new players on the roster; the 49ers being heavy favourites turned out to be a fair prediction and, in the end, the winning margin was by 23 as San Francisco put 14 points on the board in each of the first three quarters and won 49-26.

If Chargers owner Dean Spanos were to run for mayor of San Diego against Ming the Merciless, then Ming would win by a landslide. Spanos had tried to gain planning permission and public funds for a new downtown stadium. As per usual when NFL owners don't get what they want from the city, they decide to relocate somewhere else. The team had played at the Qualcomm Stadium since 1967 (known then as the San Diego Stadium). The ground was demolished in 2020 as the Chargers had been gone from San Diego for four years and were once again the LA Chargers, as they had been in 1960. The move came at the same time as the Rams decided to return to LA and this has been both a problem and a solution for the Chargers relocation.

On the plus side, the two teams have used their resources to share a brand-new stadium in the city outskirts. However, the Chargers have been mocked for their lack of support ever since moving to Los Angeles. In the first few years of being in LA they played their home games at a 30,000-capacity soccer stadium which fell short of NFL rules of a minimum capacity of 50,000. Even so, the Chargers couldn't sell it out and relied on away fans to fill the spaces. Home games felt like away games and the team suffered. Talk and speculation centred around going back to San Diego where they had a solid fanbase who wanted them back; however that scenario never transpired and the future will be in LA.

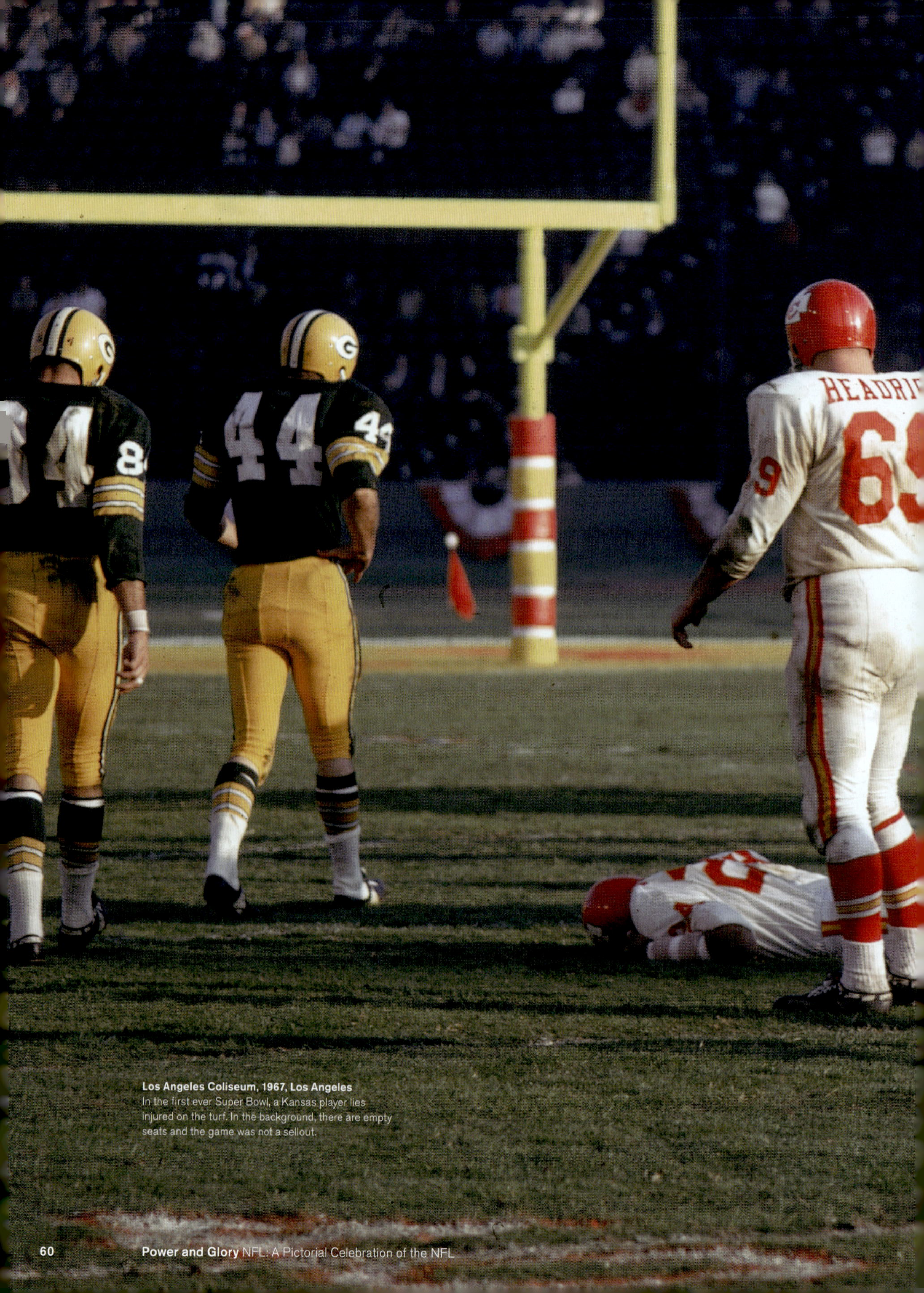

Los Angeles Coliseum, 1967, Los Angeles
In the first ever Super Bowl, a Kansas player lies injured on the turf. In the background, there are empty seats and the game was not a sellout.

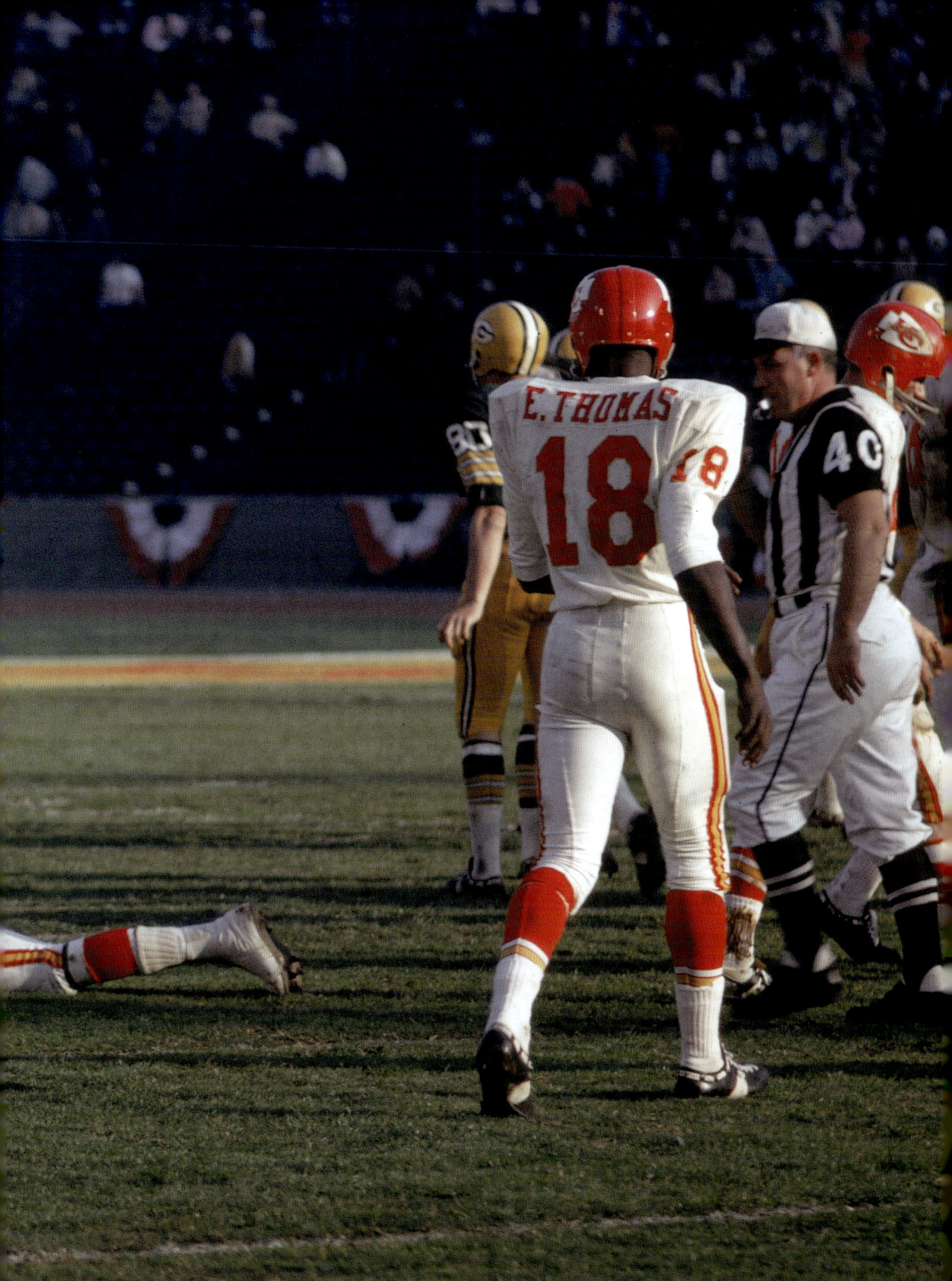
E.THOMAS
18
18
40
80

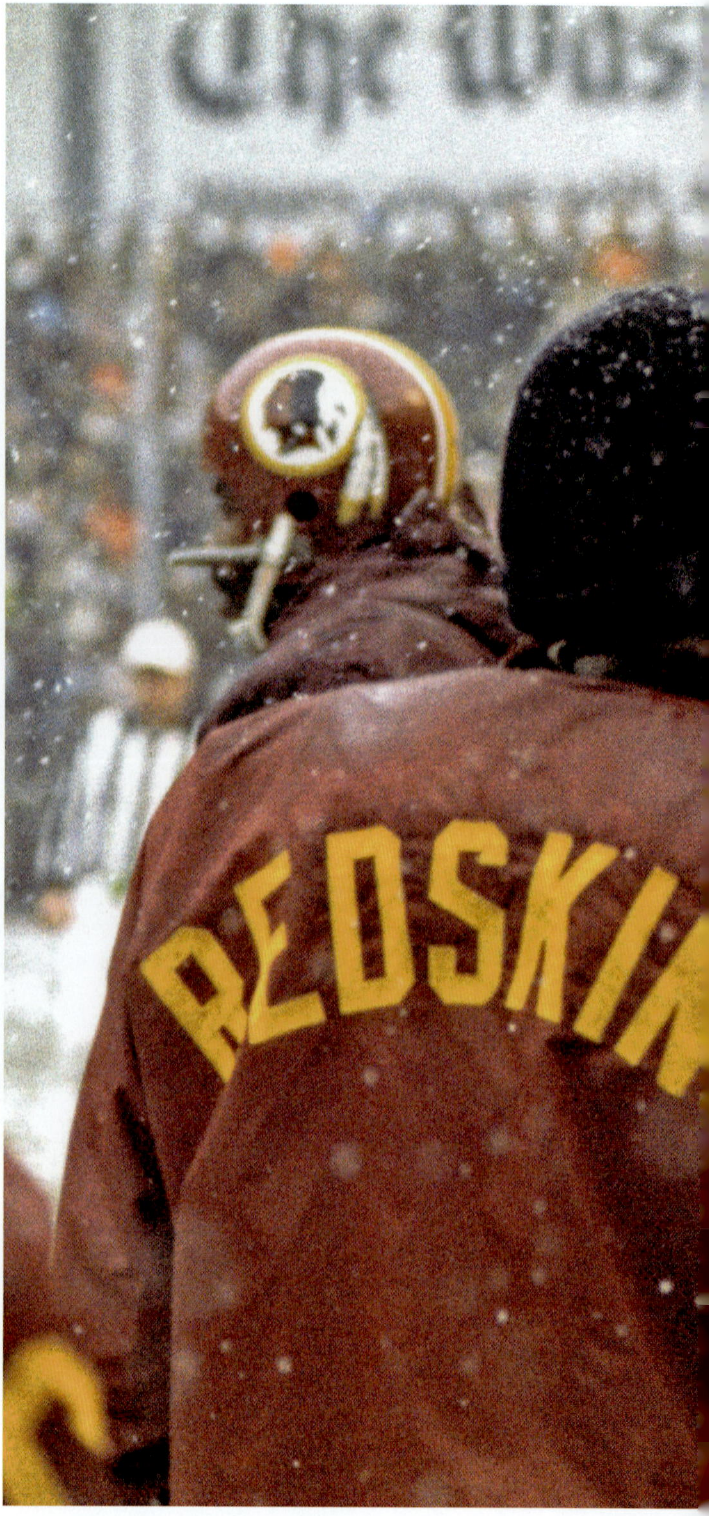

RFK Stadium, Washington DC, 1973
Three quarterbacks in discussion during a snowy game against Philadelphia. Sam Wyche (centre), Sonny Jurgensen (left) and Billy Kilmer (right).

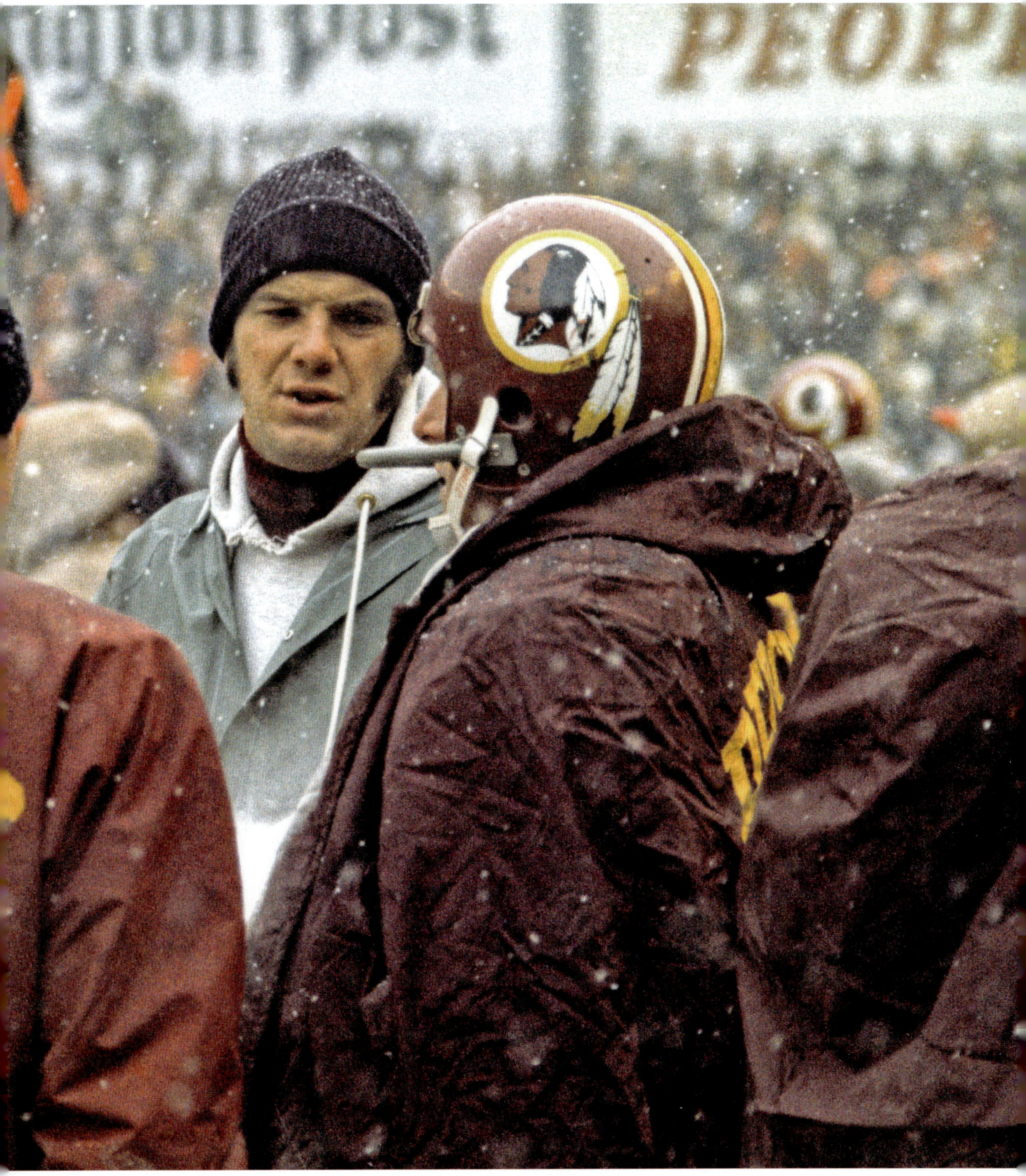

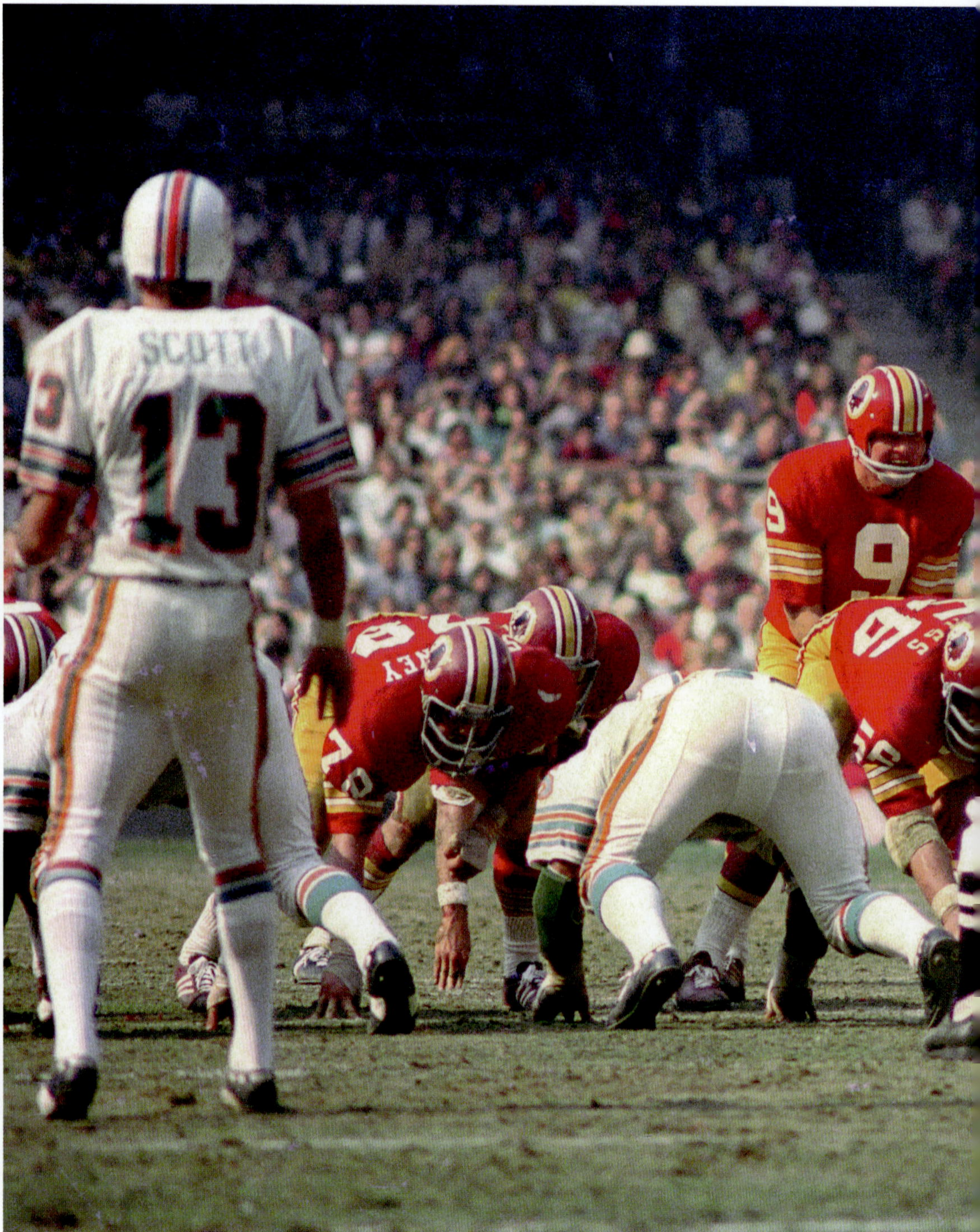

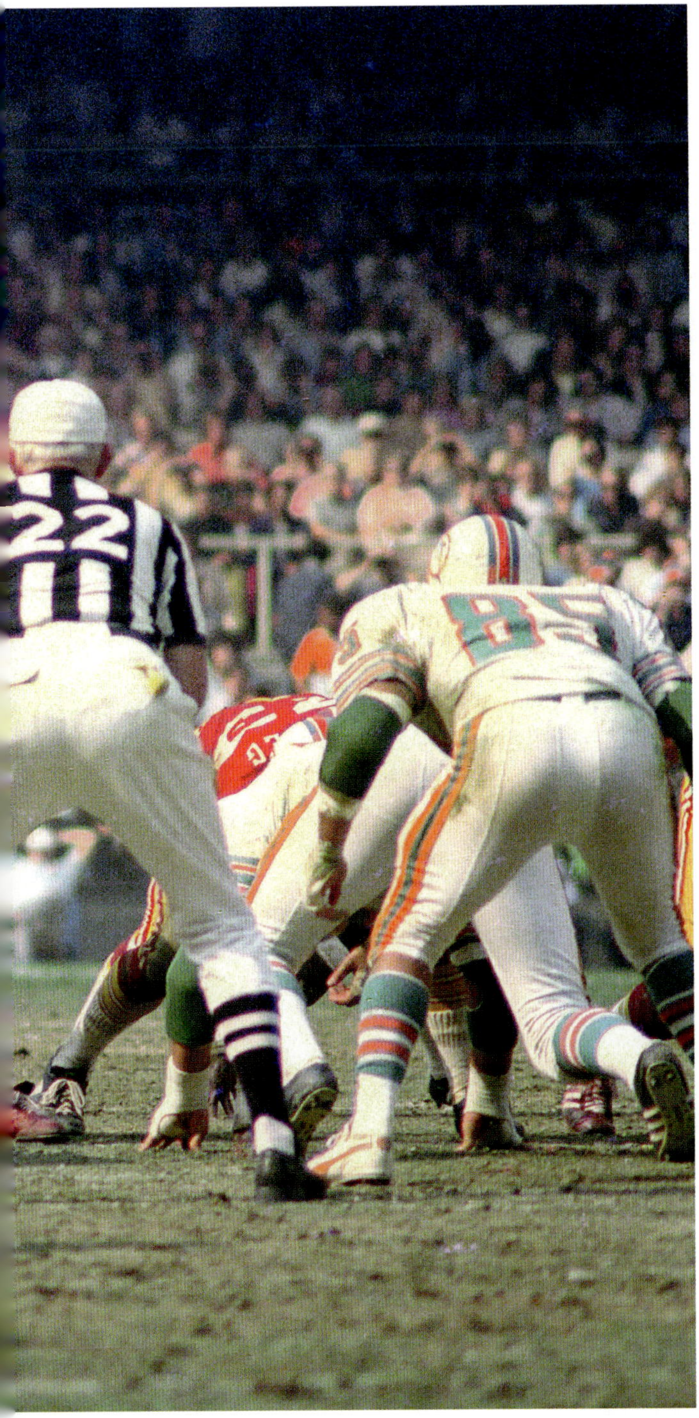

RFK Stadium, Washington DC, 1974
Washington quarterback Sonny Jurgensen calls signals as he prepares to take the snap against Miami.

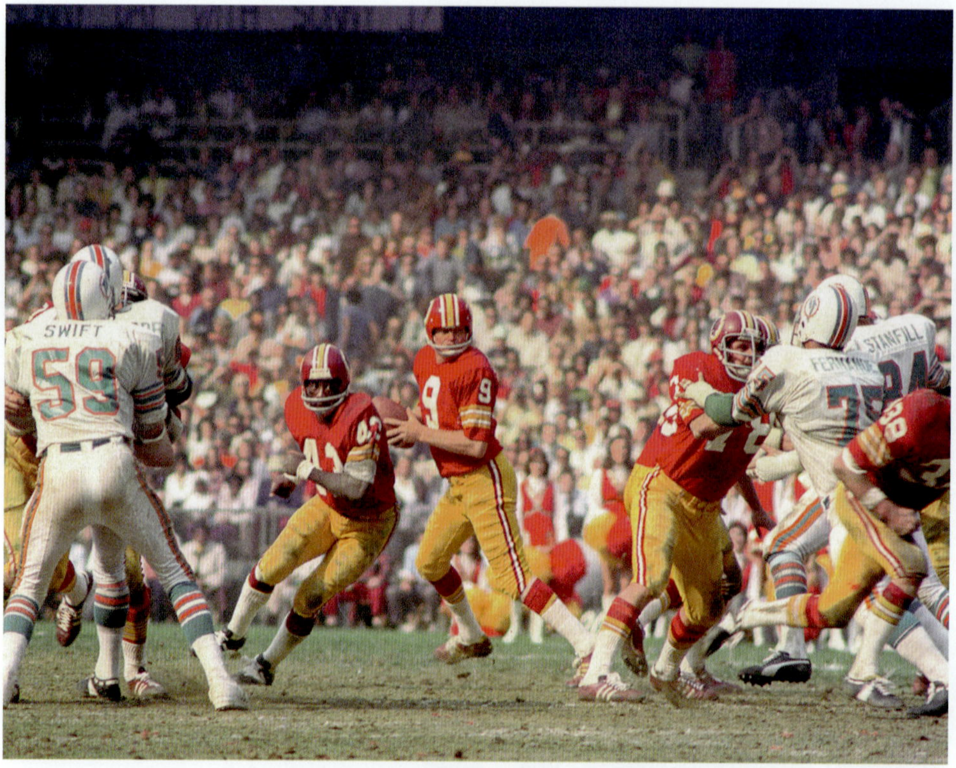

RFK Stadium, Washington DC, 1974
Washington quarterback Sonny Jurgensen in action against Miami.

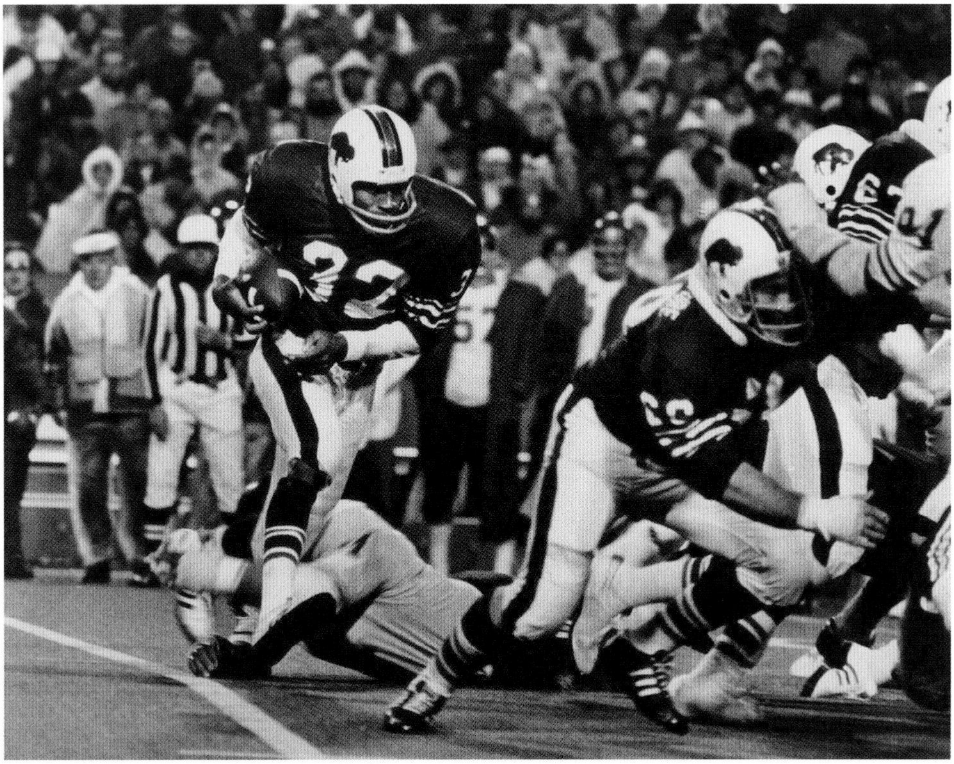

Buffalo Bills running back OJ Simpson carries the ball during a game in 1975
Two seasons earlier, Simpson became the first player to rush for more than 2,000 yards in a single season.

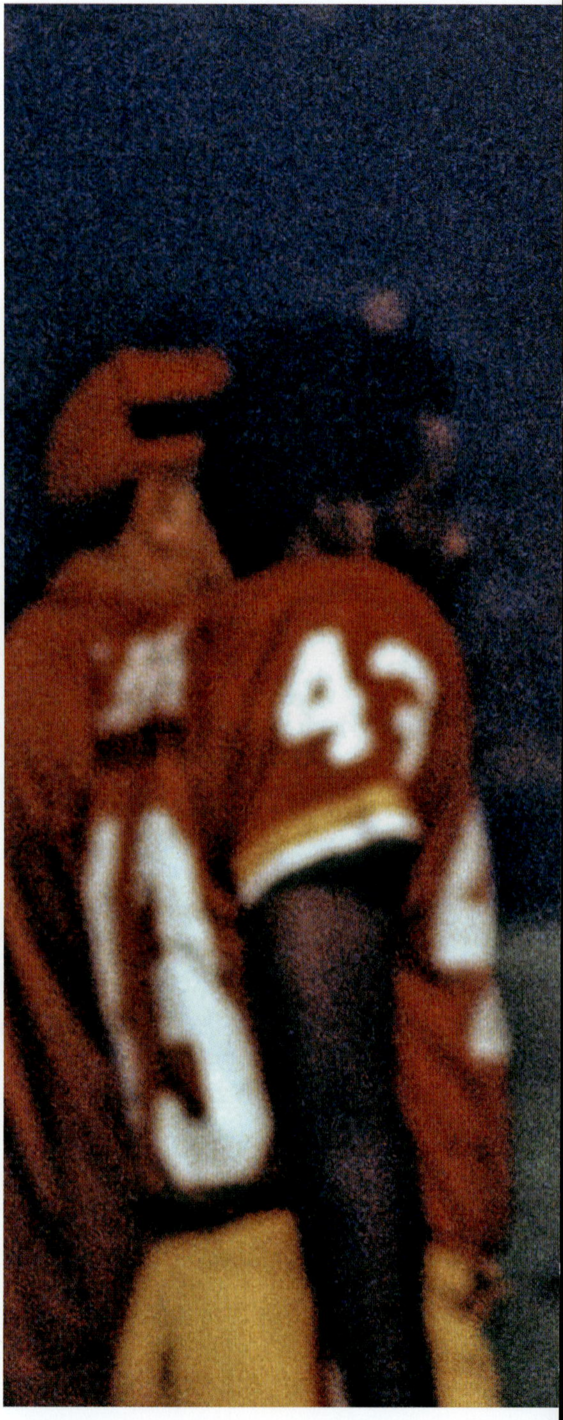

RFK Stadium, Washington DC, 1973
Washington quarterback Sonny Jurgensen on the sideline during a game versus the Baltimore Colts.

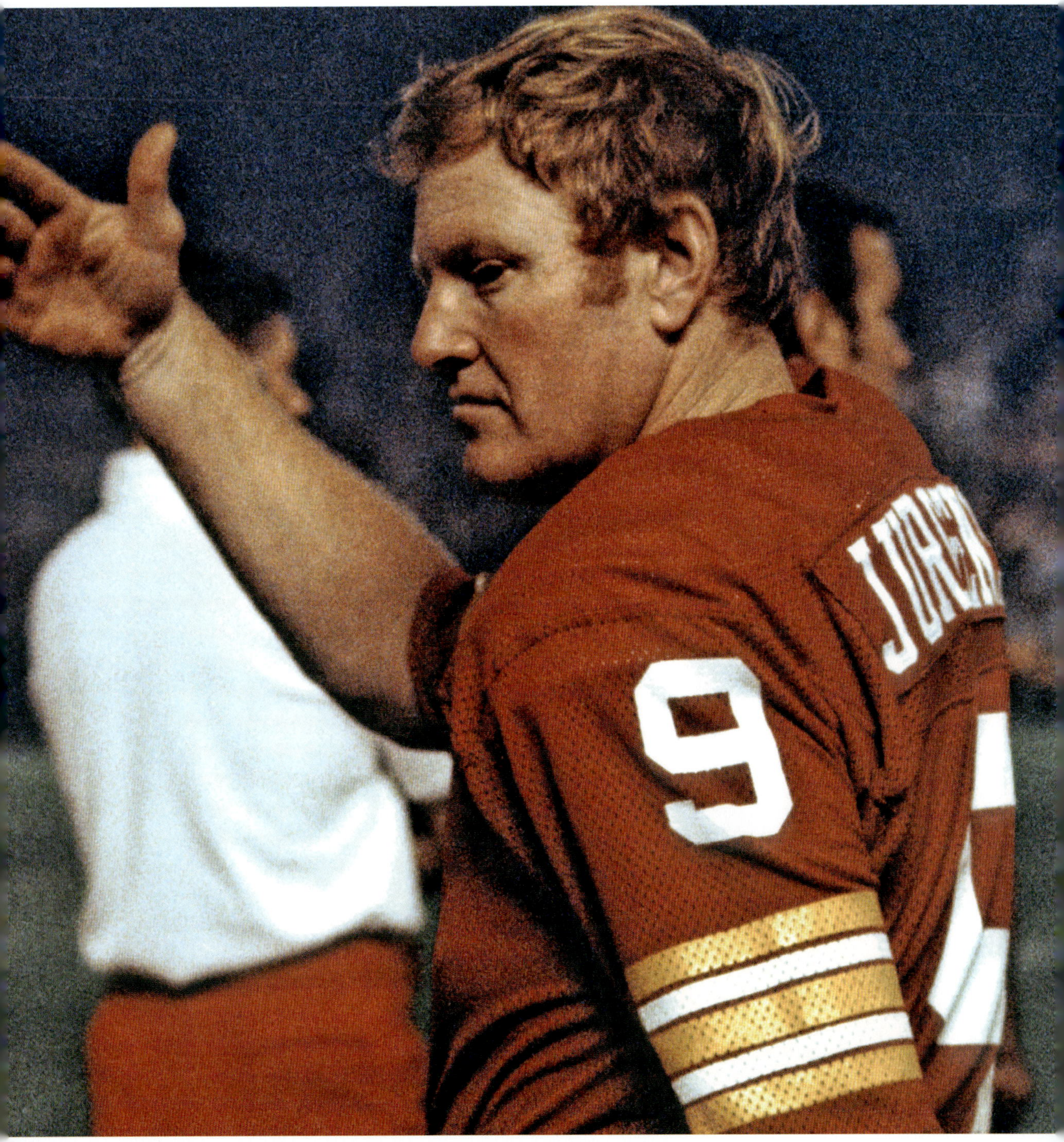
9

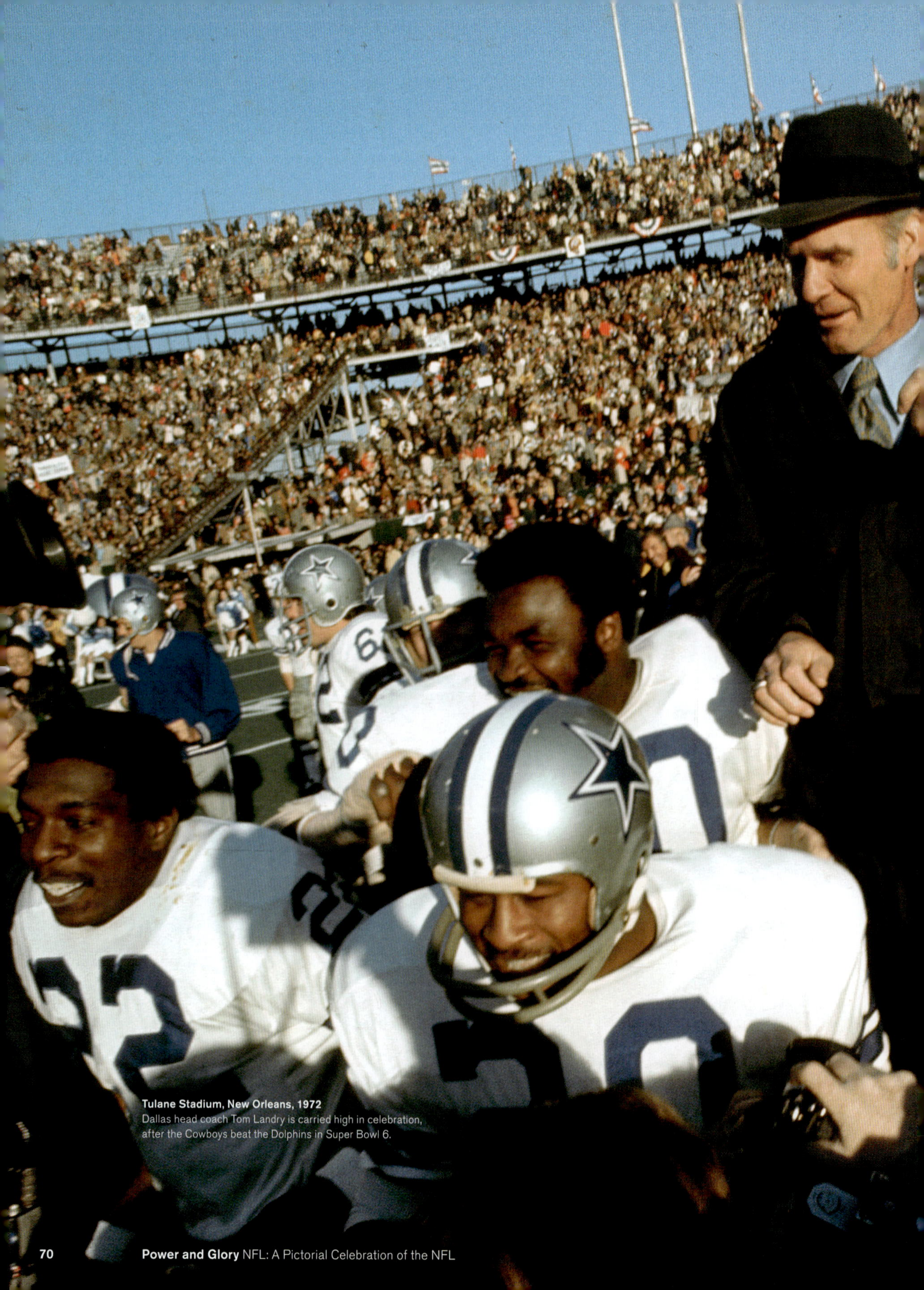

Tulane Stadium, New Orleans, 1972
Dallas head coach Tom Landry is carried high in celebration, after the Cowboys beat the Dolphins in Super Bowl 6.

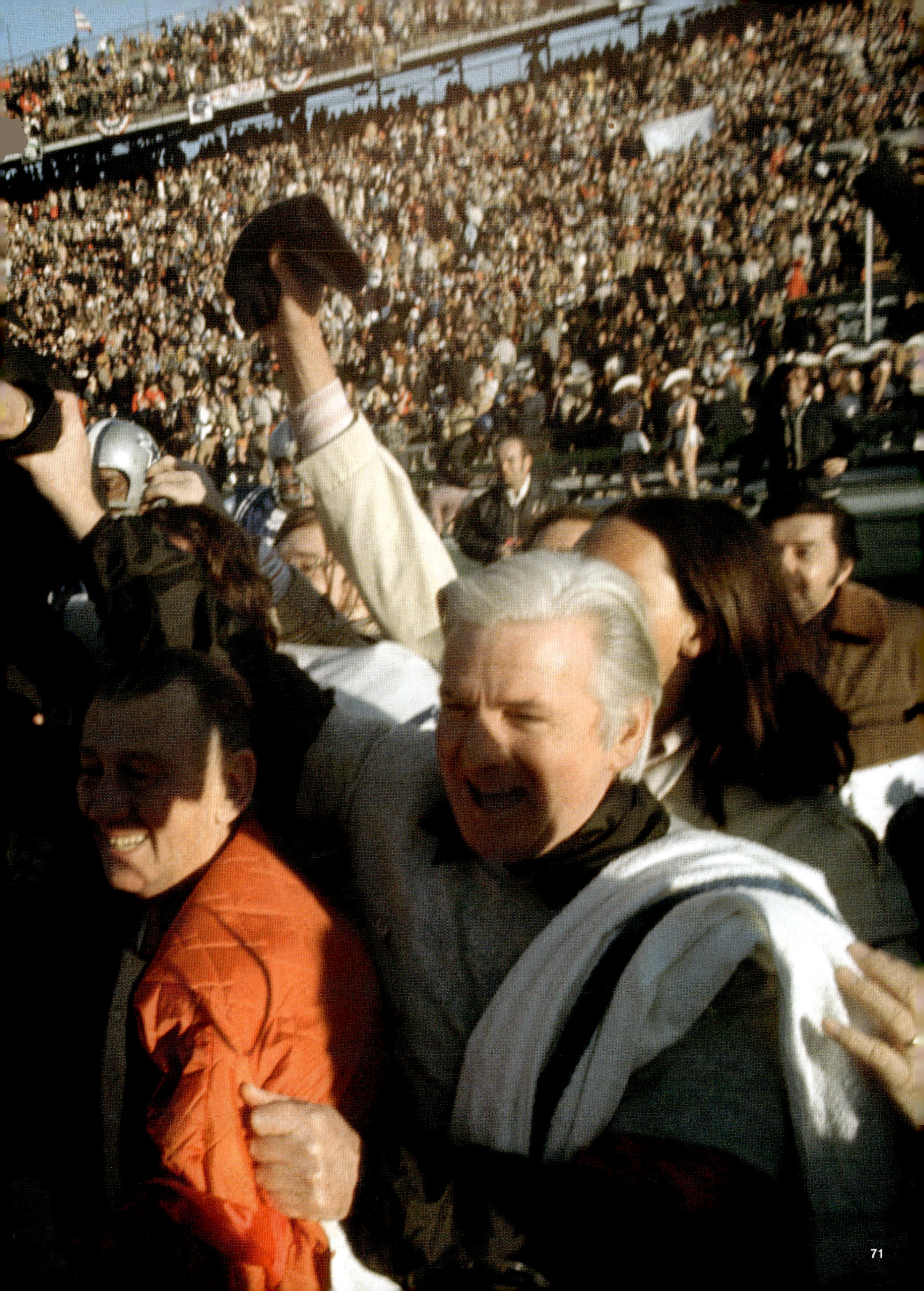

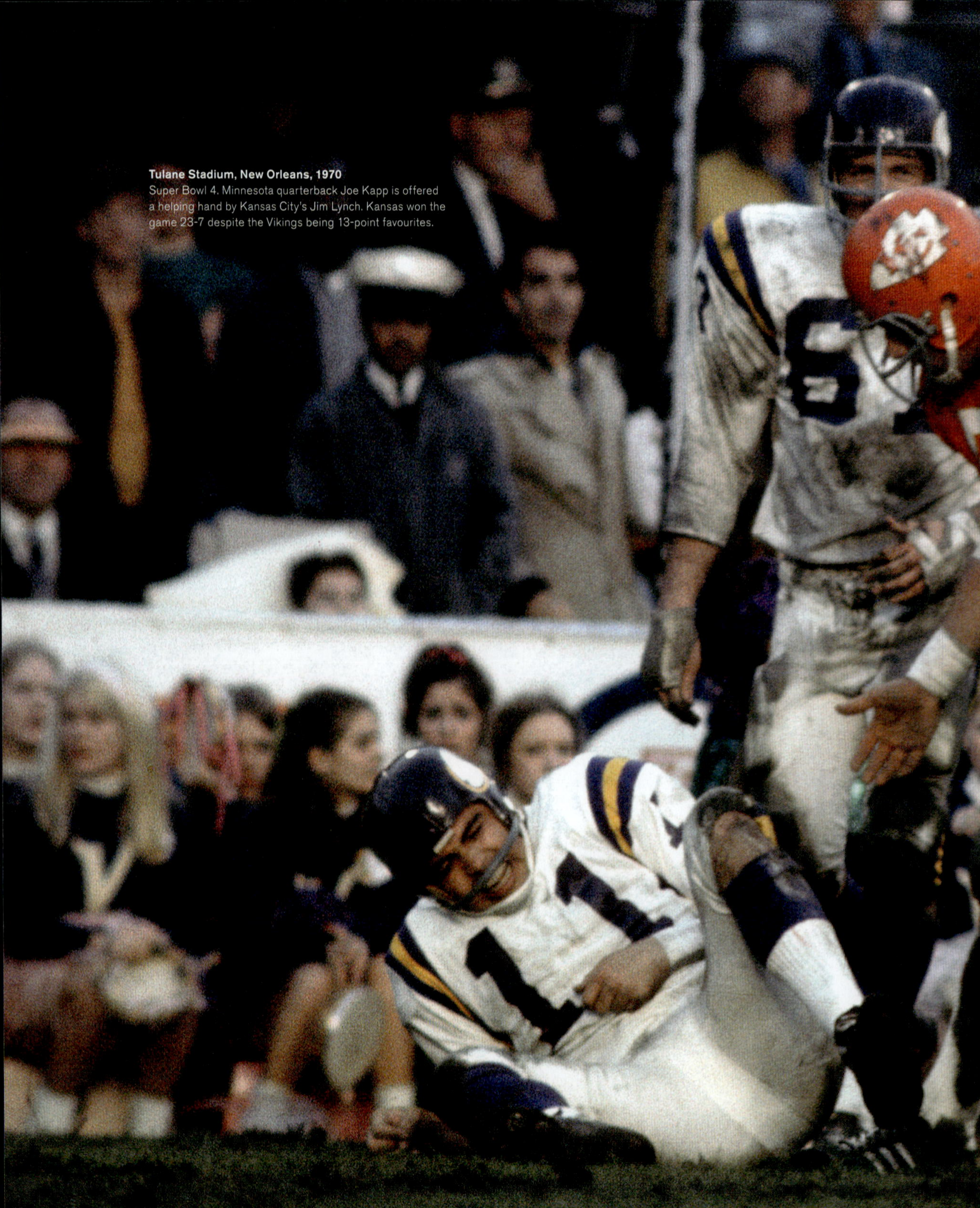

Tulane Stadium, New Orleans, 1970
Super Bowl 4. Minnesota quarterback Joe Kapp is offered a helping hand by Kansas City's Jim Lynch. Kansas won the game 23-7 despite the Vikings being 13-point favourites.

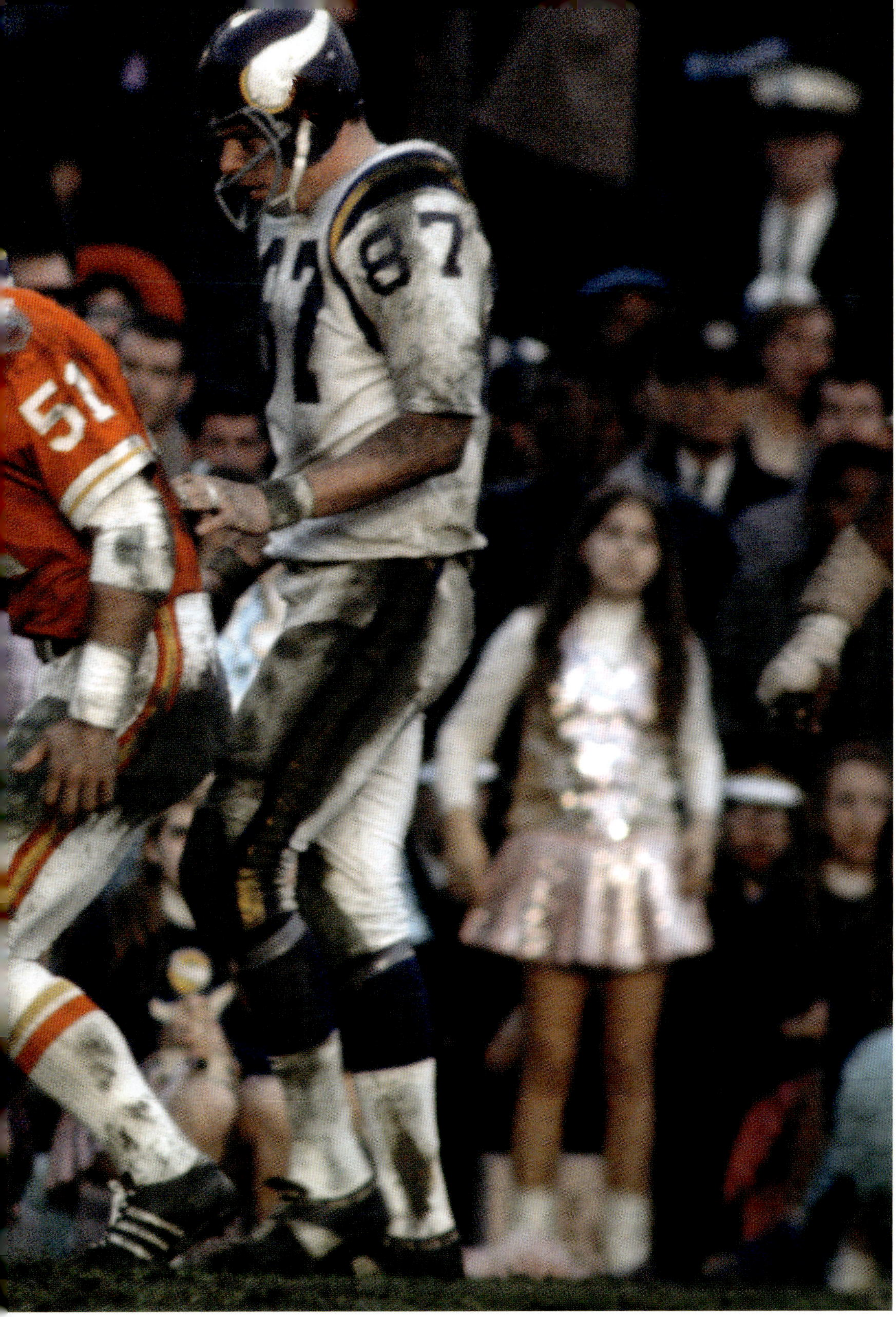

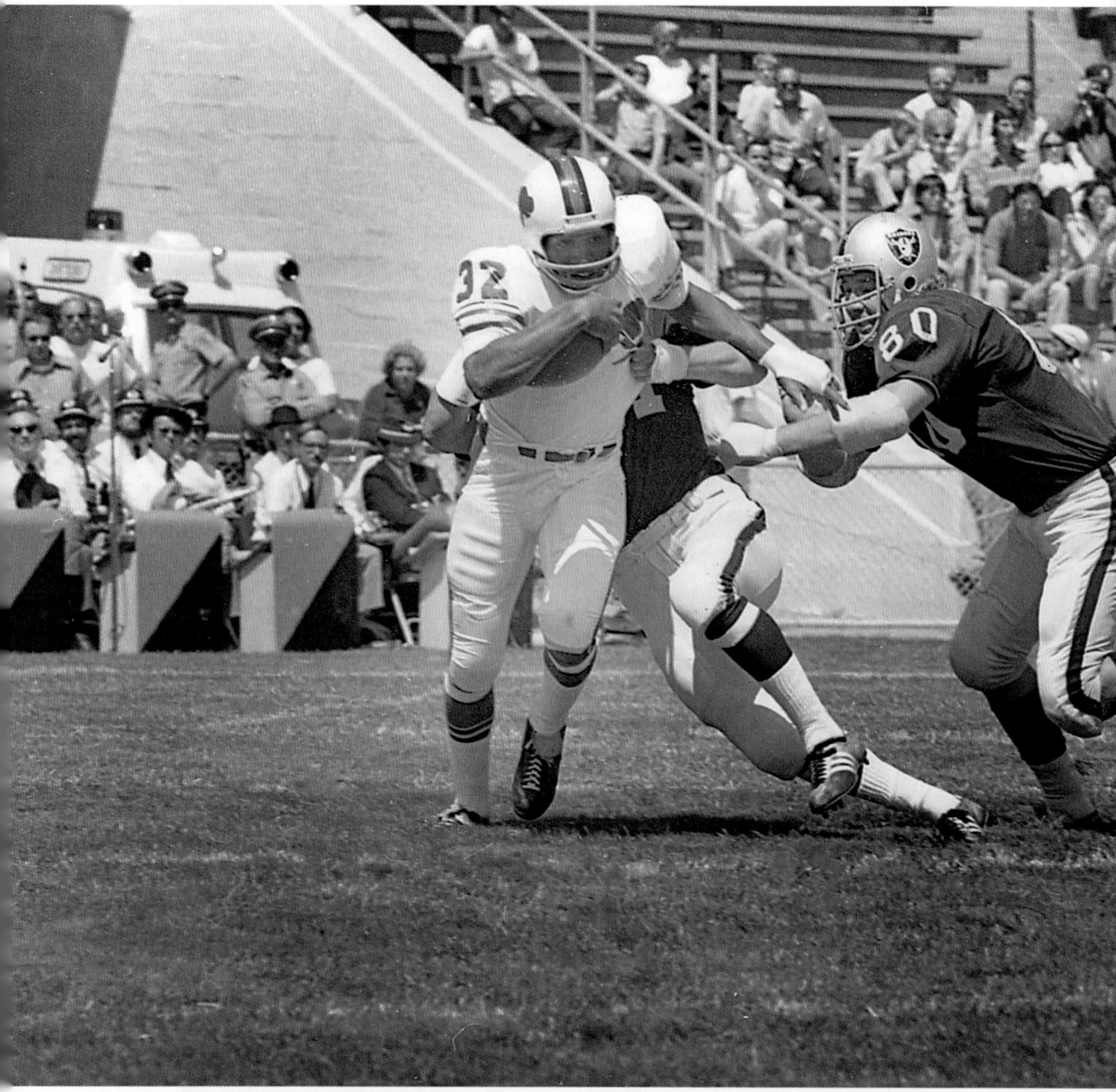

University of California's Berkeley Stadium, Berkeley, 1973
OJ Simpson rushes with the ball, against the Oakland Raiders.

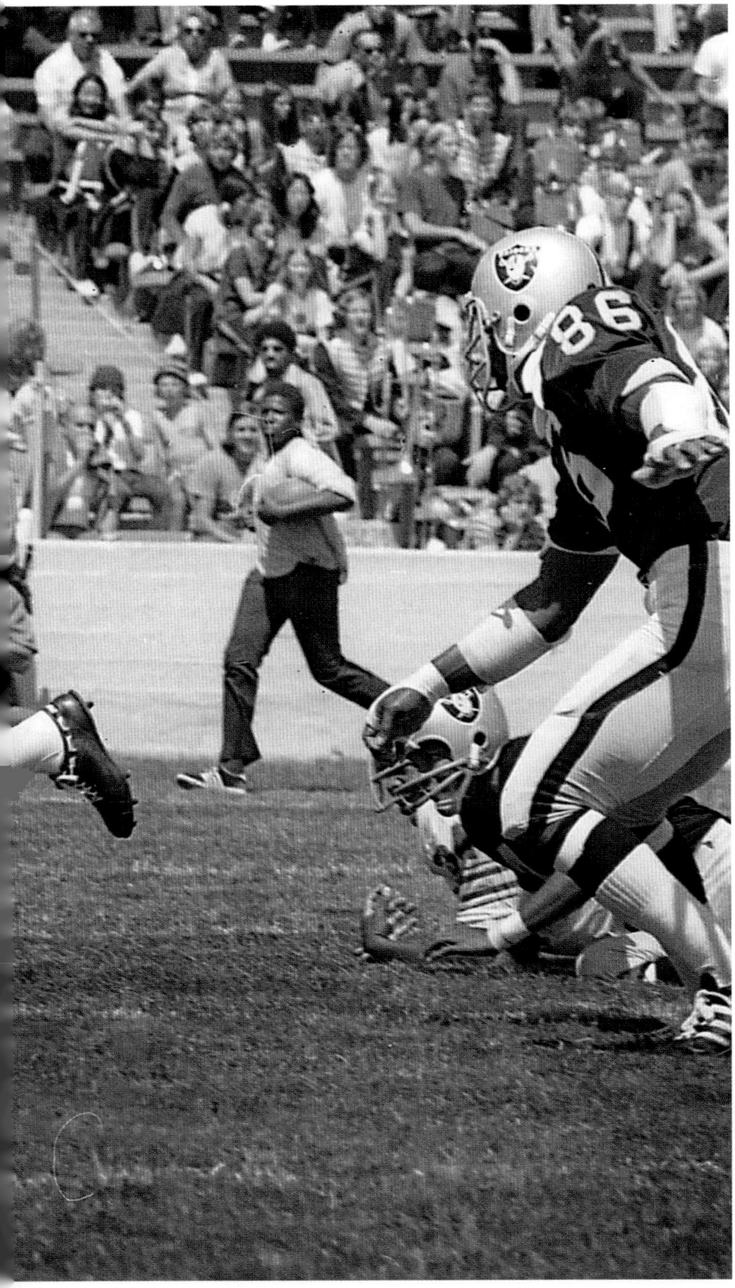
86

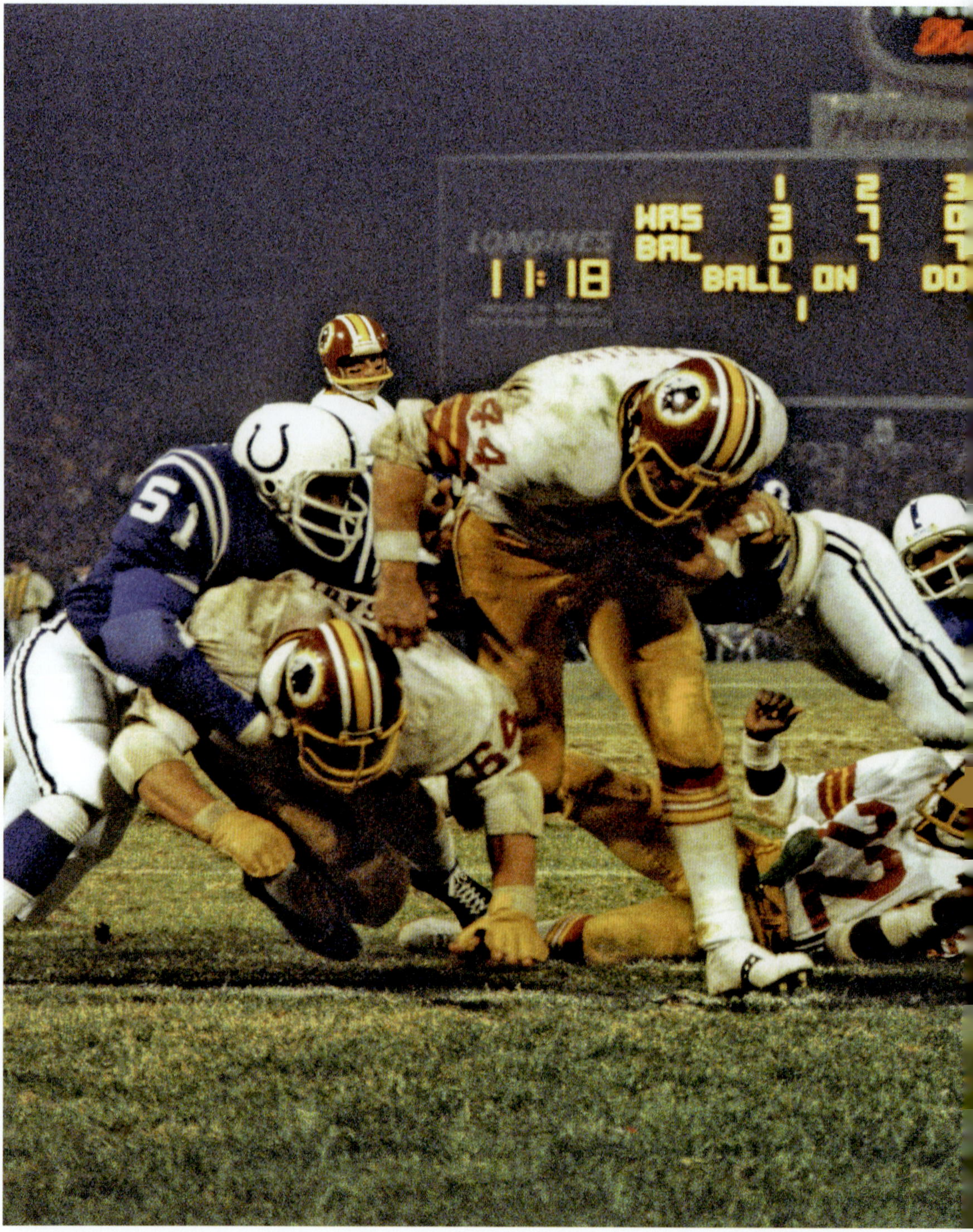

1 2
WAS 3 7
BAL 0 7
11:18
BALL ON

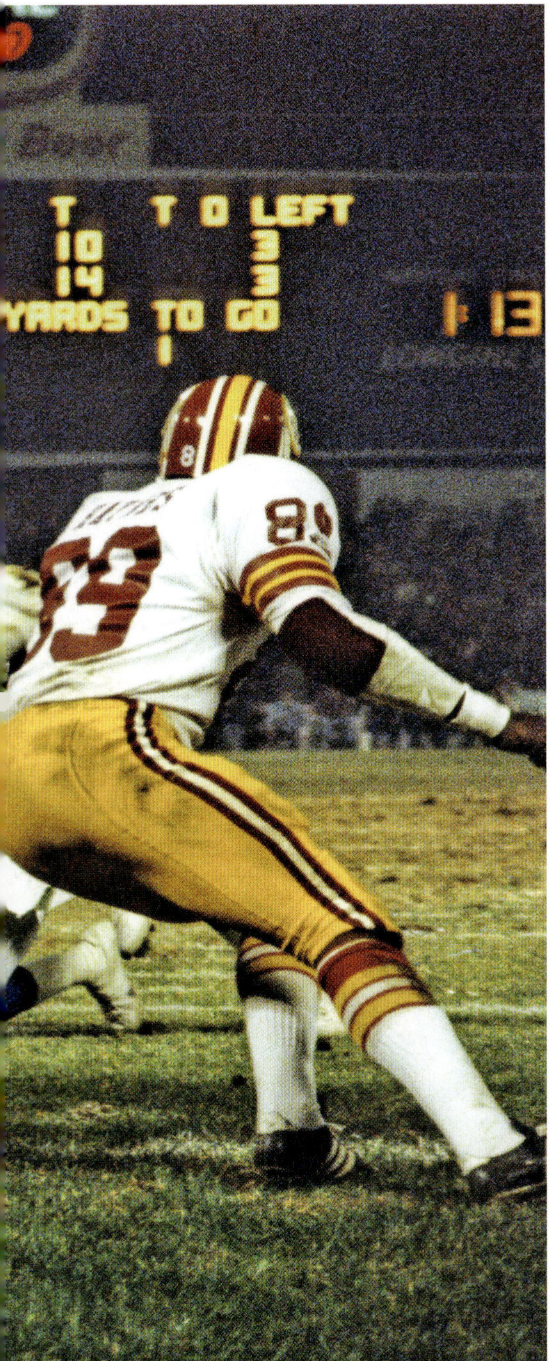

Memorial Stadium, Baltimore, 1978
Washington running back John Riggins charges into the endzone, in a road game against the Colts.

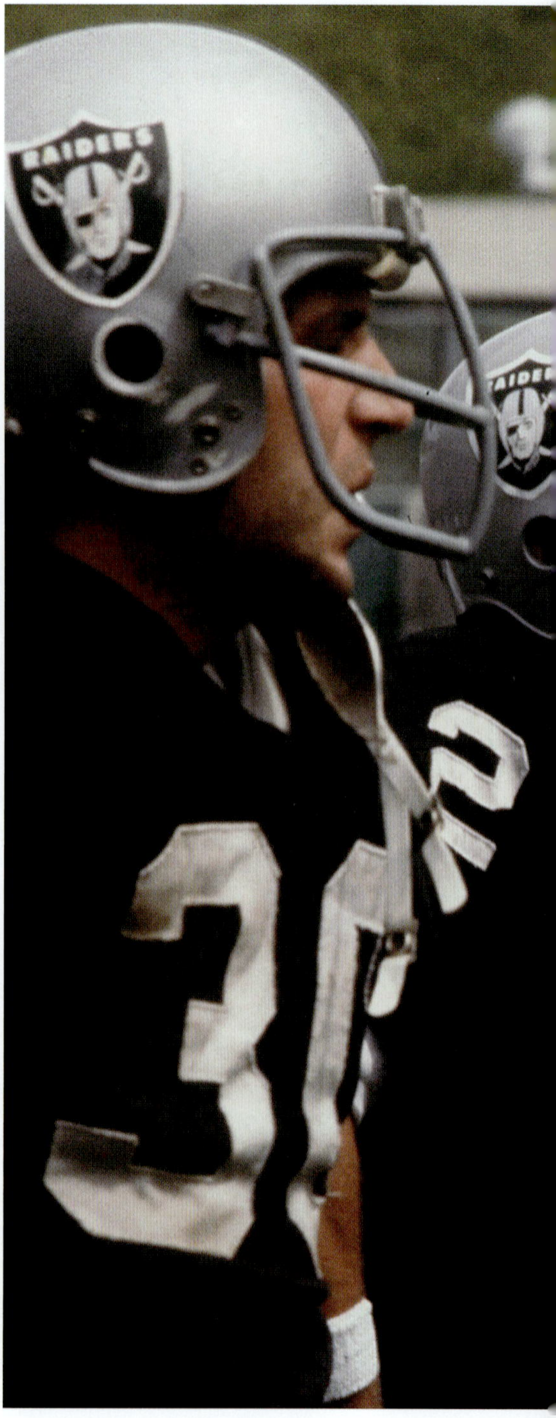

Oakland Coliseum, Oakland, 1976
Legendary coach John Madden during the 1976 season, which would end with his Raiders finally winning a Super Bowl. Madden never registered one losing season during his ten years in charge of Oakland.

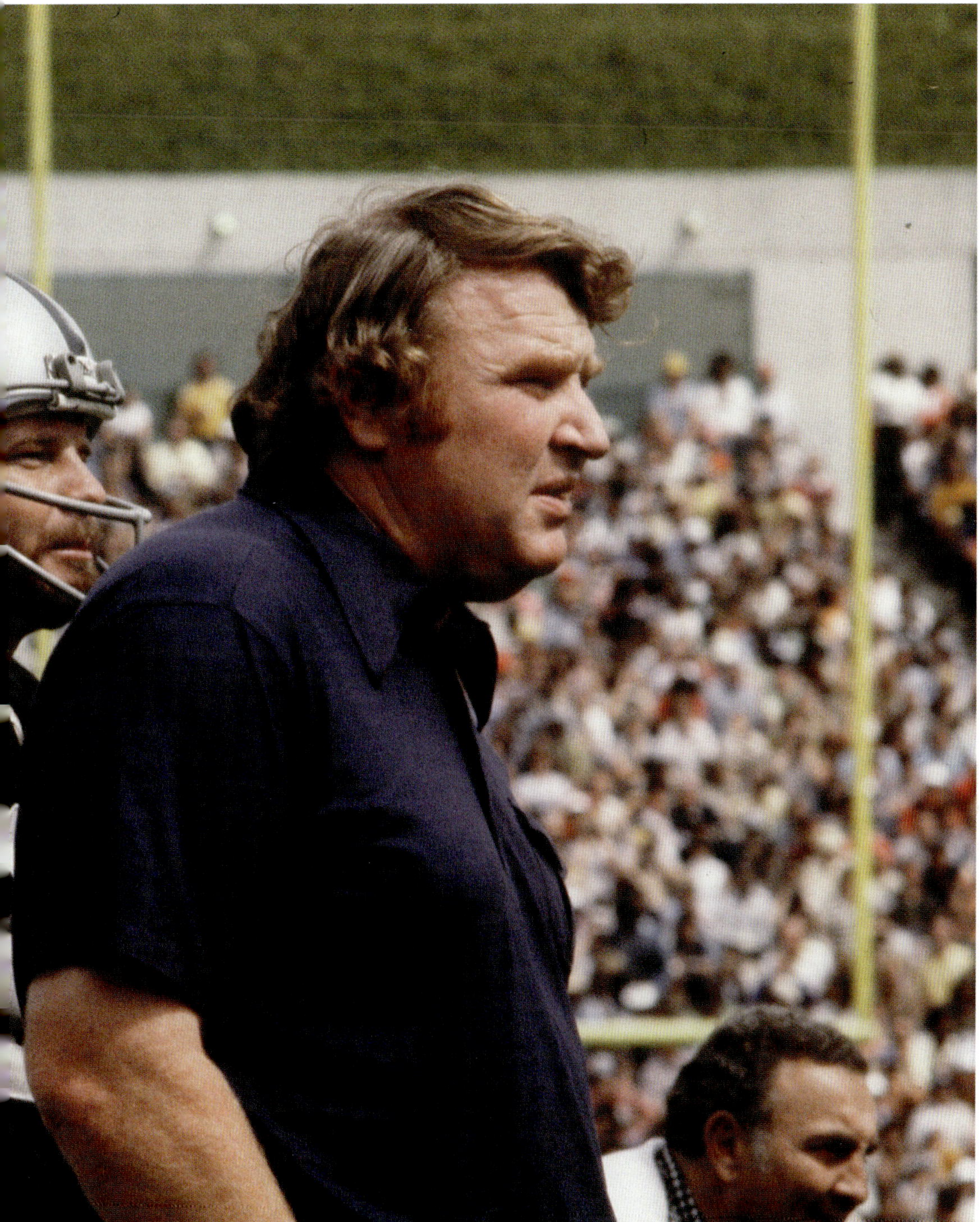

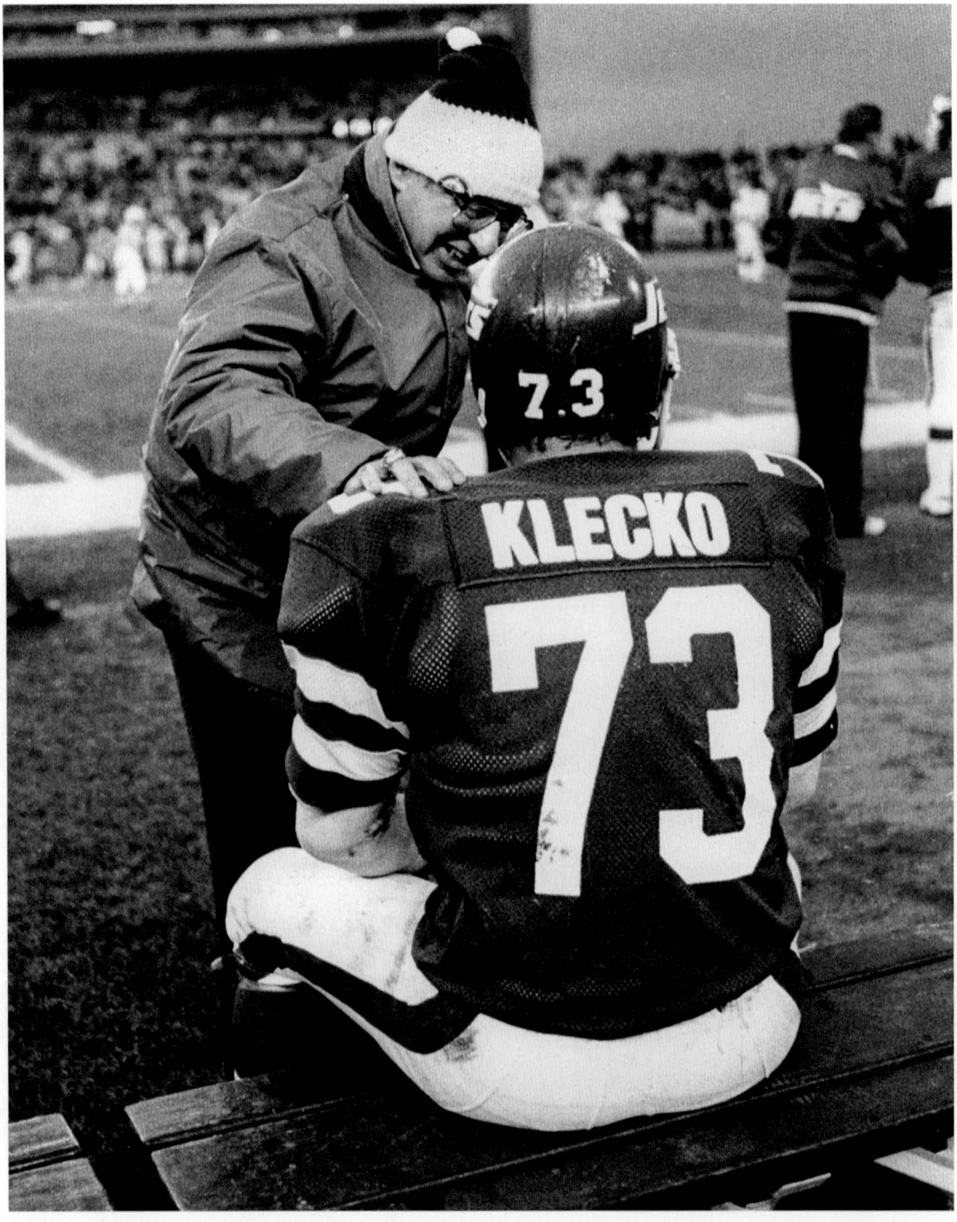

Shea Stadium, New York City, 1978
Doctor James Nicholas examines Jets players on the sidelines.

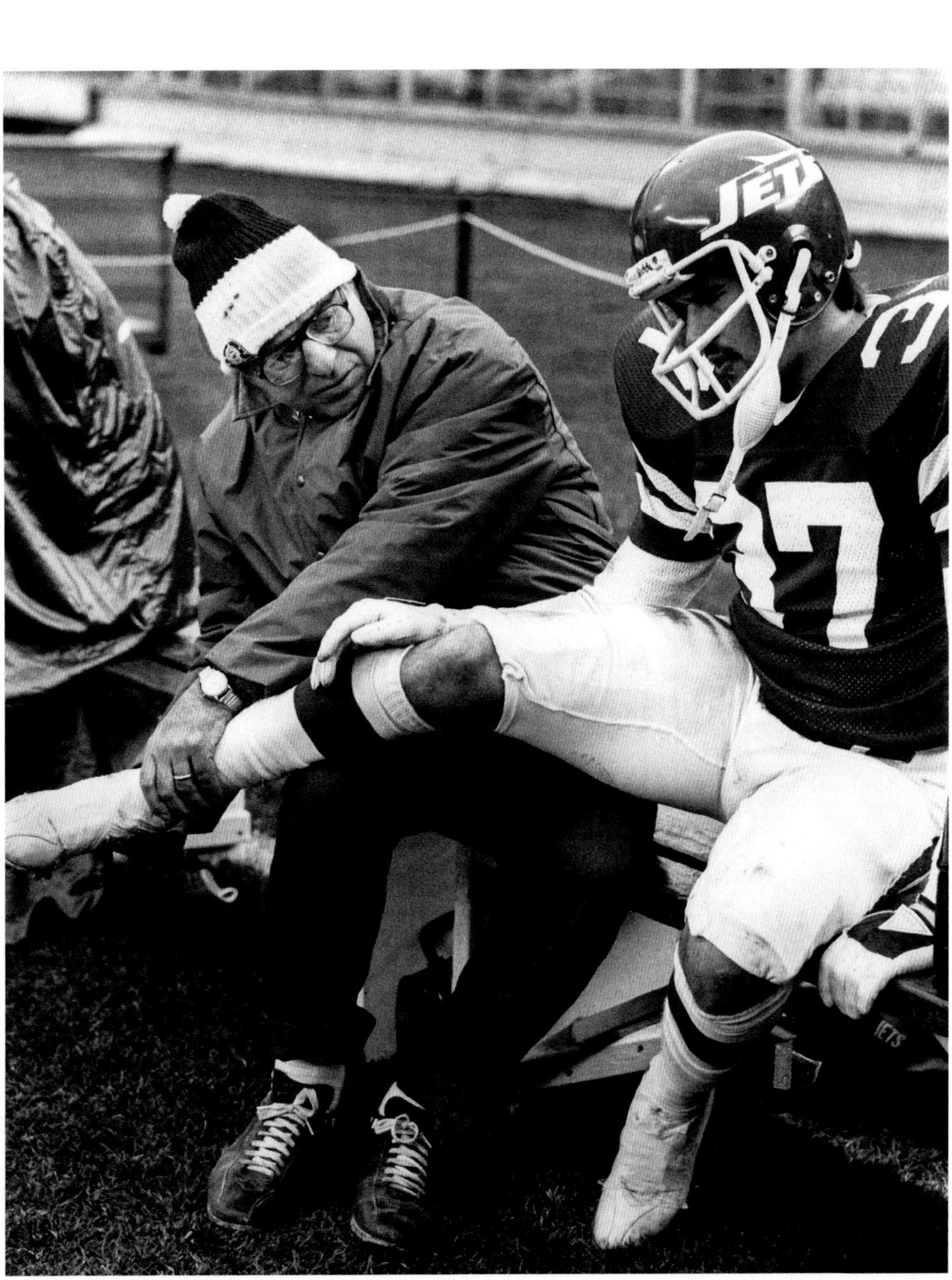
JETS
37

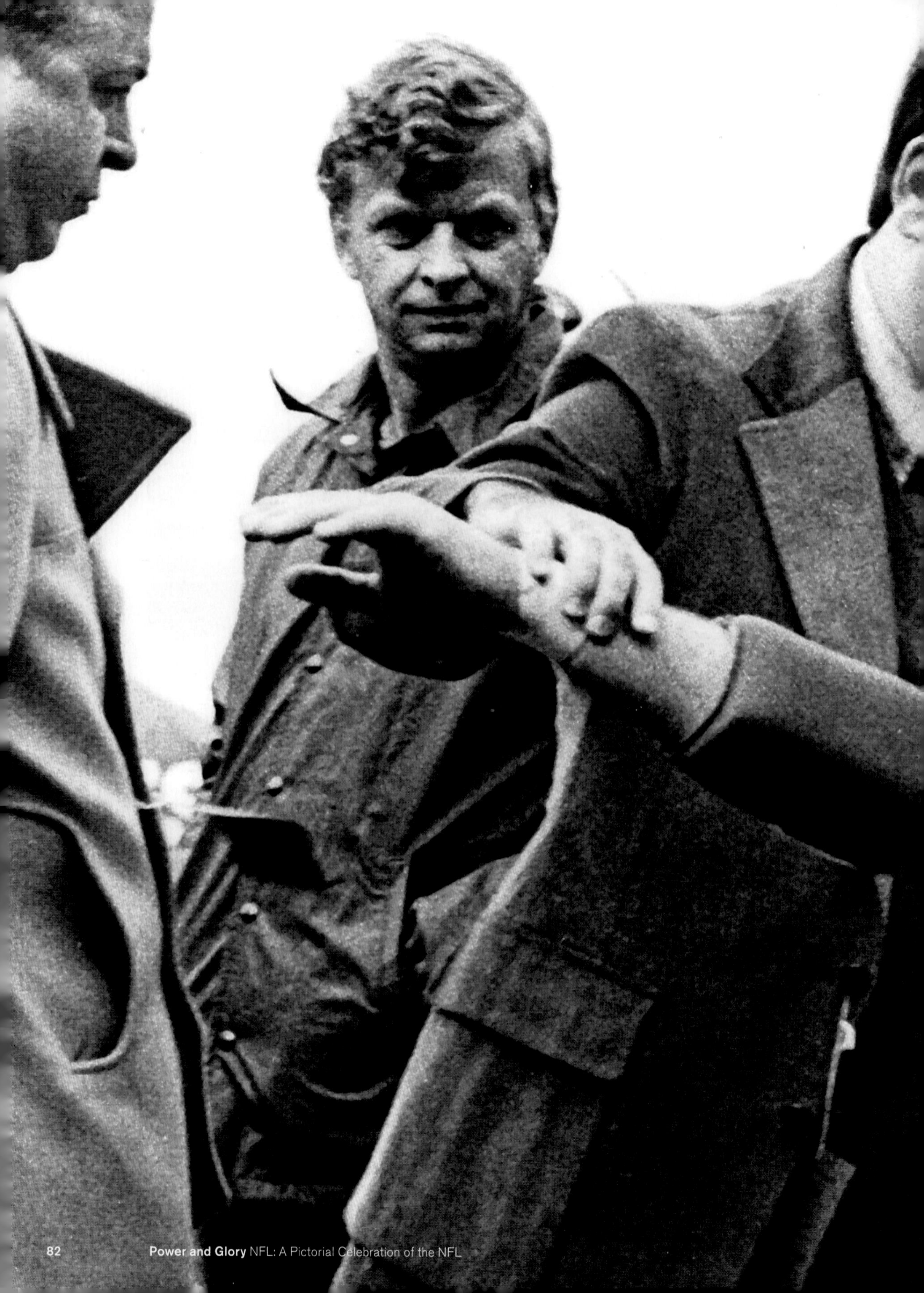

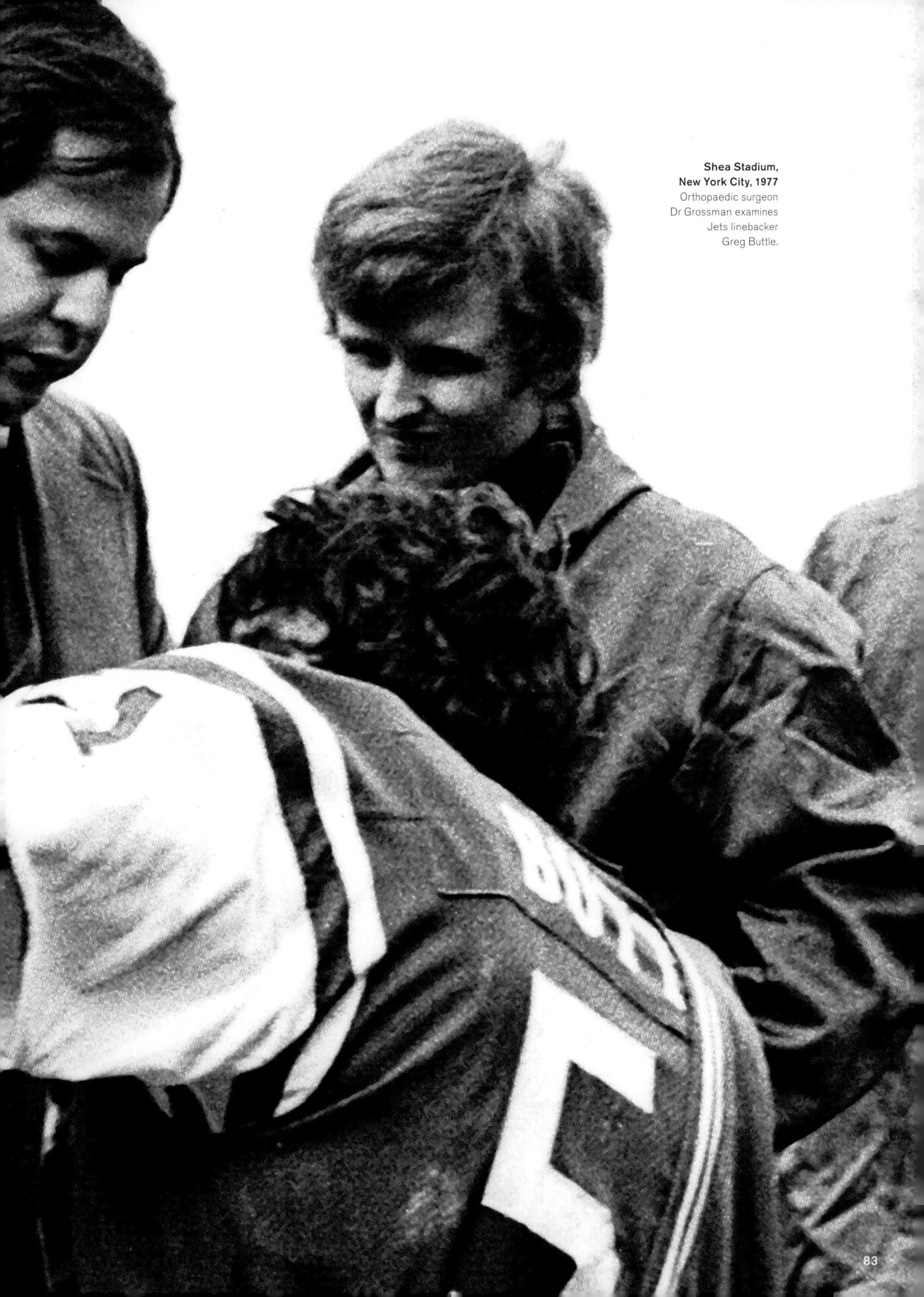

Shea Stadium, New York City, 1977
Orthopaedic surgeon Dr Grossman examines Jets linebacker Greg Buttle.

Cleveland Browns: Est. 1944

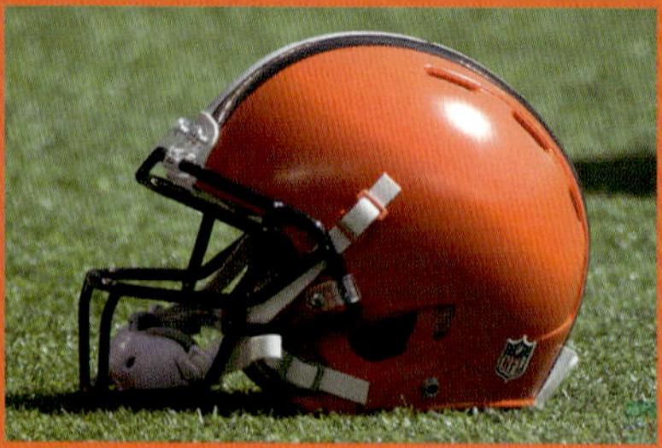

AFC Central Champions: (6) 1971, 1980, 1985, 1986, 1987, 1989

AAFC Champions: (4) 1946, 1947, 1948, 1949

NFL Champions pre-Super Bowl: (4) 1950, 1954, 1955, 1964

Super Bowl record: 0-0

No fanbase has suffered quite like the Browns have in he last two decades, yet no set of supporters are more optimistic and more ready to see their team win. Despite gaining a reputation for losing, the faithful of Cleveland saw victory in the face of ultimate defeat.

A core principle in this book has been to never refer o teams as a 'franchise' or 'organisation' as is the trend rom the media. 'Franchise' is a cold and soulless term to describe these teams, all of which are such a fundamental part of their regions. Cleveland without the Browns is a ragedy and in turn the NFL doesn't work without them. The city nearly lost its team forever when in 1996 owner Art Modell relocated them to Baltimore to form the Ravens. Cleveland took legal action and the compromise was that the Baltimore Ravens would take the spot of the Browns, acquire the playing roster, but the branding/naming and their heritage remained in Cleveland, and n a few years the Browns would be allowed to return. Cleveland's message was simple, 'You ain't getting id of us that easy, see you again in three years!'

Despite gaining a reputation for losing, when you consider overall history, then they have won more NFL championships than most teams, even if they were all prior to the NFL/AFL 1970 merger. On top of our NFL championships that Cleveland won between 1950 and 1964, they also won four AAFC titles in a row between 1946 and 1949. The AAFC was a legitimate rival to the NFL but folded at the end of the decade, so the Browns joined the NFL and won the championship in their debut season, highlighting that heir teams who won AAFL titles could stake a claim to being the best team in football.

By the 1960s this club was a standard-bearer for success and glory; for winning the major honours, and they also had the league's biggest star in the running back Jim Brown, a contender today for the NFL's most influential player. The 1980s saw a strong Cleveland Browns and they made it to the post-season seven times in the decade, including three AFC Championship games, but on all three occasions they lost o the Denver Broncos. The closest of these three games was in the 1986 season when Cleveland lost to an overtime field goal. In the 2020 season they also came close to getting to another AFC Championship game, but narrowly lost to Kansas City.

Browns fans didn't dwell; it had been a massive relief to have made it to the play-offs as well as beating Pittsburgh in the wild card game. It had been 18 years since their last post-season, and only a few years earlier they had gone two seasons with a combined record of played 32 lost 31. In the 2017 season, when they lost every game, Browns fans held a parade in honour of the perfect 0-16 record as one fan said, 'It's not easy to lose every game of the season, but we did it.'

The Browns are named after Paul Brown, who co-founded and coached the team, and they are the only NFL club with no logo on the helmet. The tradition, spirit and image of the club has been an equaliser or the lack of success this millennium. What has compounded the misery of recent years is that since the AFC Central became the AFC North in 2002, the Browns have not registered one divisional championship. Draft picks have been wasted, promising quarterbacks have amounted to being huge disappointments; however, the 'dawg pound' are still as passionate as ever and ready to see Cleveland prevail.

Cincinnati Bengals: Est. 1967

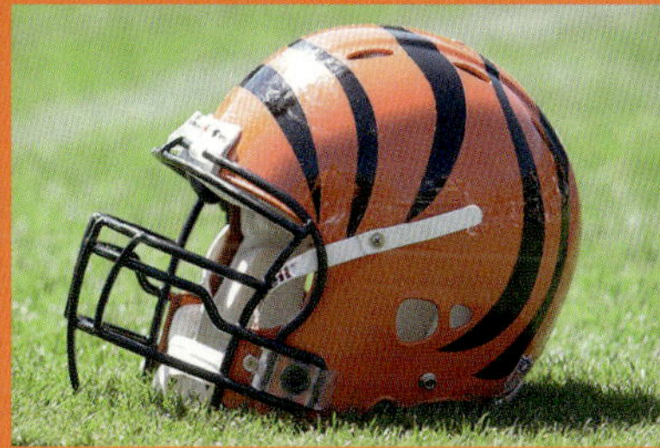

AFC Central Champions: (5) 1970, 1973, 1981, 1988, 1990

AFC North Champions: (5) 2005, 2009, 2013, 2015, 2021

AFC Conference Champions (3): 1981, 1988, 2021

Super Bowl record: 0-3

n 1963 the Cleveland Browns sacked their founder and head :oach Paul Brown, in a move that would play a part in the oundation of the Cincinnati Bengals. In 1967 the AFL ıpproved the application of Ohio's newest team and they vere pitted in the AFL West division despite being in the ıorth-east of the country. Of the two NFL teams Paul 3rown helped create, one is named after him and the other ıamed their current ground after him as the Bengals play n the Paul Brown Stadium, which at the time of writing is ›ne of only three NFL stadiums left that isn't named after a :ommercial brand.

Brown branded his new team in the same colours as ıis former club in Cleveland, and was initially sceptical of he Bengals (named after a famous white Bengal tiger in Cincinnati Zoo) joining the young AFL as he ;aw the league as a weaker competitor to the older and established NFL, where he had won titles with Cleveland. He stated, 'I didn't pay $10m to play in the AFL.' However, with a merger of the two leagues ›n the cards joining the AFL was the best way back into the NFL.

Brown coached the Bengals for eight seasons with the team getting to the play-offs three times n the 1970s. They never won a play-off game until the 1981 season when they beat Buffalo in the livisional match. Then in the next game they beat San Diego 27-7 and they were in a Super Bowl to ace San Francisco who were headed by the young Joe Montana. Like the Bengals this was the 49ers' irst Super Bowl, and they took a 20-0 lead into half-time. Cincinnati were facing a record interval deficit ınd they also created a second Super Bowl record, as the team who gained the most yards in the game ·et ended up losing.

The Bengals made a return to the Super Bowl in the 1988 season, and once again their opponent vas Montana's San Francisco. By this point the 49ers had notched up another Super Bowl victory in 984 and wanted a third win to seal their dynasty status. The Bengals needed a win to be champions or the first time, and with only three minutes and ten seconds left on the clock they were leading 16-13. 'he game had been tight, but Montana threw a pass into the endzone with just 34 seconds remaining ınd the Bengals would not be seen at another Super Bowl for 33 years.

The NFL prides itself on parity which is summed up perfectly by Cincinnati making it to Super Bowl 56 in the 2021 season. They hadn't registered a winning season for five years. In 2019 and 2020 they ıad a record of played 32 won six, so by the start of the 2021 season nobody would have predicted that he Ohio team in tiger helmets would make it to the final game. Improvement was expected, as young ıuarterback Joe Burrow had shown much promise in his rookie season, but at the start of 2021 the 3engals were rated fourth from last in the betting. The bookies' favourites were the Kansas City Chiefs ınd in the AFC Championship game they were expected to beat the Bengals, despite Burrow and co. ;urprising everyone by getting this far. A field goal won the game for Cincinnati in overtime and it was ›ff to LA to play the Rams. Leading 20-17 with a couple of minutes remaining, history could have been lifferent if a harsh penalty against Cincinnati wasn't called when the Rams were on third down, but LA ook advantage and scored late on. The Bengals had lost their third Super Bowl.

Pittsburgh Steelers: Est. 1933

Former names: Pittsburgh Pirates (1933–1939); Phil-Pitt 'Steagles' (1943); Card-Pitt (1944)

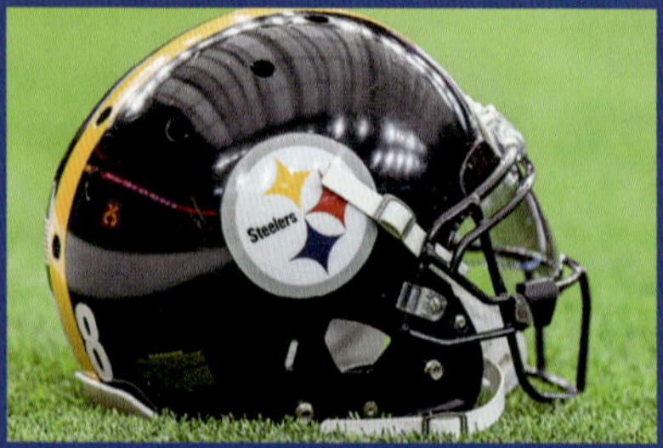

AFC Central Champions: (15) 1972, 1974, 1975, 1976, 1977, 1978, 1979, 1983, 1984, 1992, 1994, 1995, 1996, 1997, 2001

AFC North Champions: (9) 2002, 2004, 2007, 2008, 2010, 2014, 2016, 2017, 2020

AFC Conference Champions: (8) 1974, 1975, 1978, 1979, 1995, 2005, 2008, 2010

Super Bowl titles: (6) 1974, 1975, 1978, 1979, 2005, 2008

Super Bowl record: 6-2

Reputations can change over time. In the early years of the 1970s the Pittsburgh Steelers were the oldest team in the league to have never been crowned as NFL champions. The team had made one play-off appearance in 1947 where they lost to their Pennsylvania rivals, the Philadelphia Eagles. Only a few years earlier both teams had been merged into one team known as the 'Steagles' or Phil-Pitt, a contender for the worst name in NFL history until a year later when Pittsburgh merged with the Chicago Cardinals to become Card-Pitt. Both mergers were attributed to the loss of players who had gone to fight in the Second World War.

By the end of the 1970s the Steelers would be viewed differently; no longer an unsuccessful team with an unremarkable history. The 1979 season saw them crowned Super Bowl champions for the fourth time, a record that no other team was close to. Led by quarterback Terry Bradshaw and a ruthless defence known as the 'Steel Curtain', the 1970s Pittsburgh Steelers are in the conversation for the NFL's greatest ever dynasty. The 'Steel Curtain' are also in the conversation for best defence of all time.

Although Pittsburgh didn't get to the Super Bowl in the 1976 season, with Bradshaw injured, the defence got them to the AFC Championship match due to only allowing the opposition an average of 3.1 points per game in the last nine fixtures of the regular season. They registered an incredible five shut-outs (clean sheets), three of which were in consecutive games. The Steelers' first Super Bowl win came in the 1974 season against Minnesota Vikings, who were on the end of their third Super Bowl loss. If losing can become a habit then so can winning and the following season the Steelers became the third team in history to win back-to-back Super Bowls with a 21-17 defeat of the Dallas Cowboys. Three years later, Pittsburgh were back to once again face Dallas, which would mark the first time there would be a rematch of a previous Super Bowl, and whoever won would set a record of being the first team to achieve three overall wins. In a tight game Bradshaw would throw four touchdowns and be named MVP in a 35-31 victory. A year later the Steelers were back for Super Bowl 14 to face the LA Rams, but were trailing 19-17 going into the final quarter. The 'black and gold' scored two touchdowns to win the game and once again Bradshaw was named MVP.

It would be a while before Pittsburgh would be back in the Super Bowl and when they did make it in the 1995 season, they were beaten by Dallas in a second rematch. It was a pivotal game as it took the Cowboys to five overall Super Bowl wins; a record they shared with San Francisco. The only thing to do for the former holders was get back ahead and Pittsburgh did just that by adding two more Super Bowl titles in the first decade of the millennium to reclaim the record. Quarterback Ben Roethlisberger led the team to victory against the Seattle Seahawks in the 2005 season, then against Arizona in 2008 in a thrilling game that was won by a touchdown with just 35 seconds remaining. Mike Tomlin became the youngest head coach to win a Super Bowl and is currently the longest-serving head coach in the NFL.

Baltimore Ravens: Est. 1996

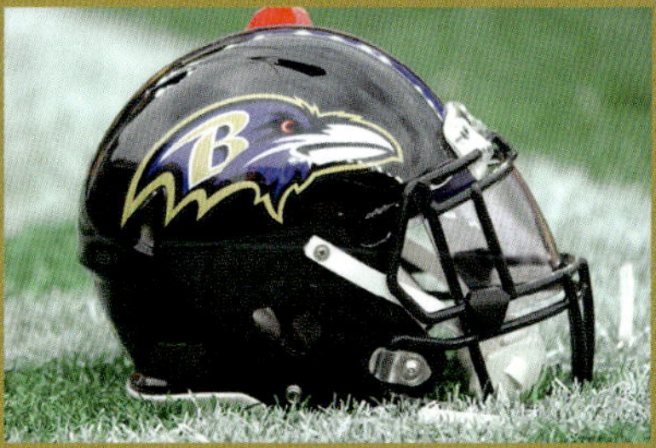

AFC North Champions: (6) 2003, 2006, 2011, 2012, 2018, 2019

AFC Conference Champions: (2) 2000, 2012

Super Bowl titles: (2) 2000, 2012

Super Bowl record: 2-0

One of the reasons the Ravens have no substantial history is because the relocation of the Browns to Baltimore caused such a protest from Cleveland that the Ravens were not allowed to claim the Ohio team's heritage. This makes the Baltimore Ravens fairly unique among the teams who have been relocated, as officially this is a new team founded in 1996.

The Ravens have had to find other credible links to history. The logo on the helmet is of course the bird itself, but unlike other NFL teams, Baltimore also has a crest for the jersey which has the look of an English and European soccer badge. The crest is based on the state flag of Maryland which derives from a coat of arms of the English politician who founded the state, George Calvert, the 1st Baron Baltimore, who died in 1632.

Baltimore's marching band are legendary and perhaps the most celebrated in the NFL. They date back to 1947 and were known as the Colts Marching Band, until the team was relocated to Indianapolis, although the group stayed in Baltimore to become known as 'The band that would not die'. Owner Art Modell, who moved the Browns to Baltimore in 1996, had asked permission from Indianapolis to take back the 'Colts' name from them, which would reinvent the Baltimore Colts while Indianapolis would have to undergo a rebranding and naming process. Indianapolis unsurprisingly kept their name so via focus group input and newspaper phone polls the name Ravens was chosen over other choices that included Americans, Marauders, Mustangs and Railers. The Bulldogs had been a popular choice among fans polled, but that name was never put into the final ballot, in which 33,748 fans sent their vote into a newspaper and Ravens was the clear winner.

If you have no history, then one consolation is to be incredibly successful in just a short period of time, and the Ravens have done exactly that. At the age of four they were Super Bowl winners, then repeated that success in the 2012 season. Super Bowl 35 in the 2000 season was a one-sided beatdown. Baltimore allowed the New York Giants just 152 yards of offence in a 34-7 win which was the seventh overall largest margin of victory in a Super Bowl. In the 2012 season when Baltimore faced San Francisco, it was a tighter affair and nicknamed the 'Har-bowl' as John Harbaugh coached the Ravens while his brother Jim coached the 49ers. To add to 'Harbaugh-fest', Jim's son Jay was on the same touchline as John and was part of the coaching team for the Ravens. The 49ers had a 5-0 Super Bowl record and were one win away from equalling Pittsburgh's record of six overall wins, but Baltimore came out strong and were 21-6 ahead at half-time due to three touchdown passes from Joe Flacco. They had also tried an outrageous play involving the now legendary kicker Justin Tucker when, after faking the field goal, Tucker took hold of the ball and charged round the left side of the scrum towards the endzone before he was stopped and possession was lost on downs.

The second half could not have started better; from the kick-off Jacoby Jones caught the ball in his own endzone and charged 108 yards for a touchdown to make the score 28-6. Not long afterwards the lights in the stadium went out, giving the game the title of 'The Blackout'. When the lights came back on San Francisco were re-energised and by the end there were only three points separating the sides, but the Ravens' defence held firm and the new team in Baltimore would be double Super Bowl winners at the age of just 17.

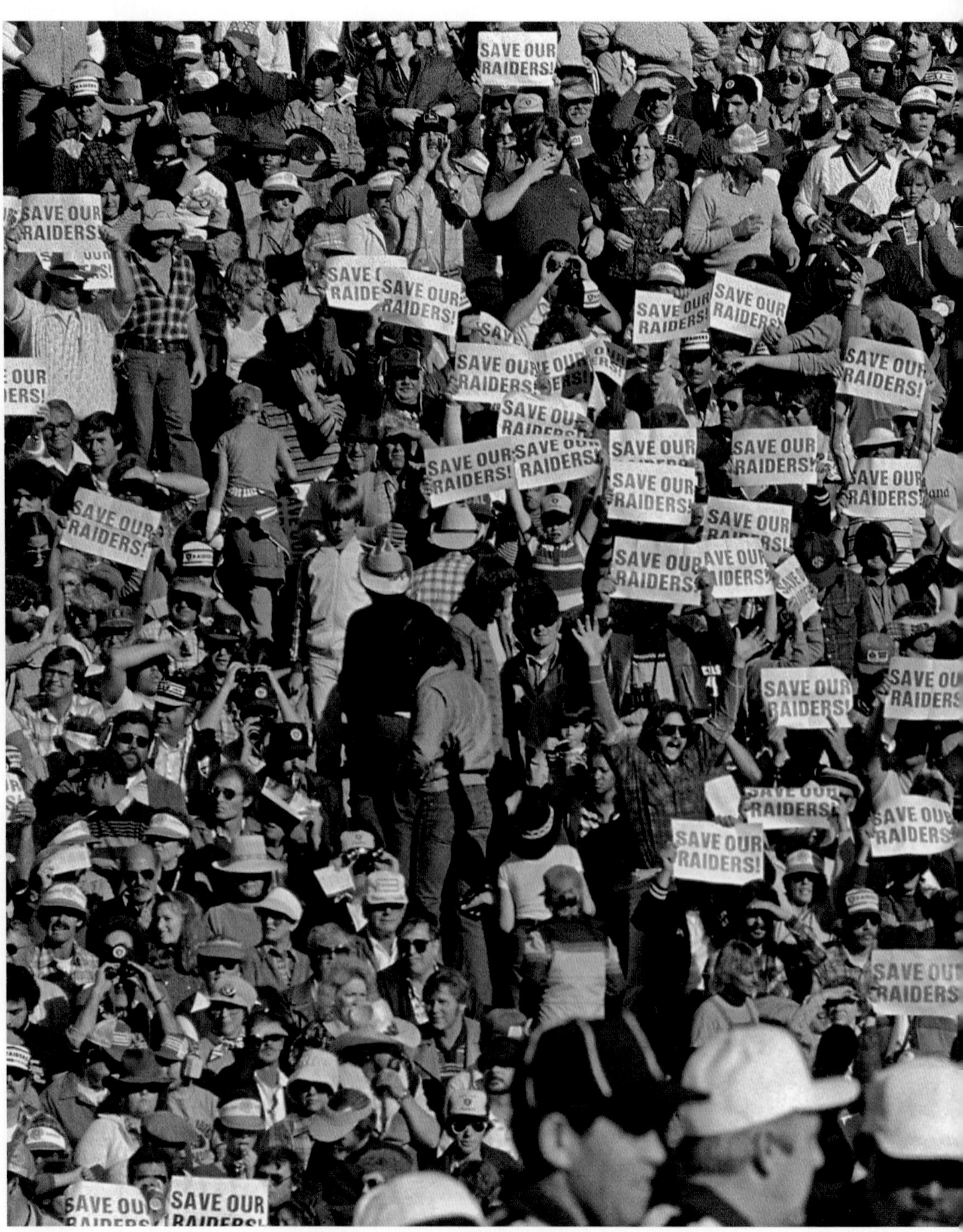
SAVE OUR RAIDERS!
SAVE OUR RAIDERS!
SAVE OUR RAIDERS!
SAVE OUR RAIDERS!
SAVE OUR RAIDERS!

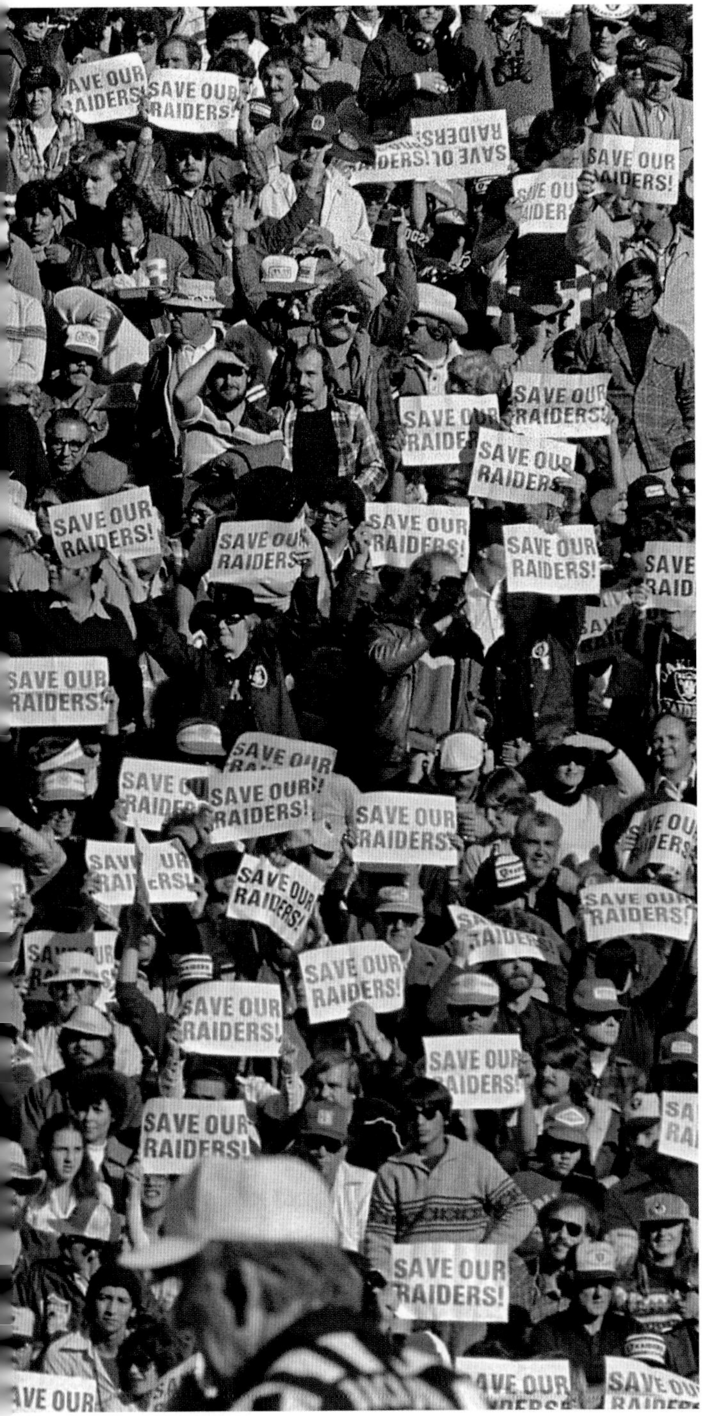

Oakland Coliseum, Oakland, 1980

During a game versus the Dallas Cowboys, Oakland Raiders fans plead with owner Al Davis not to relocate the team to Los Angeles. The team won the Super Bowl that year, and by the 1982 season the Raiders had been relocated to LA.

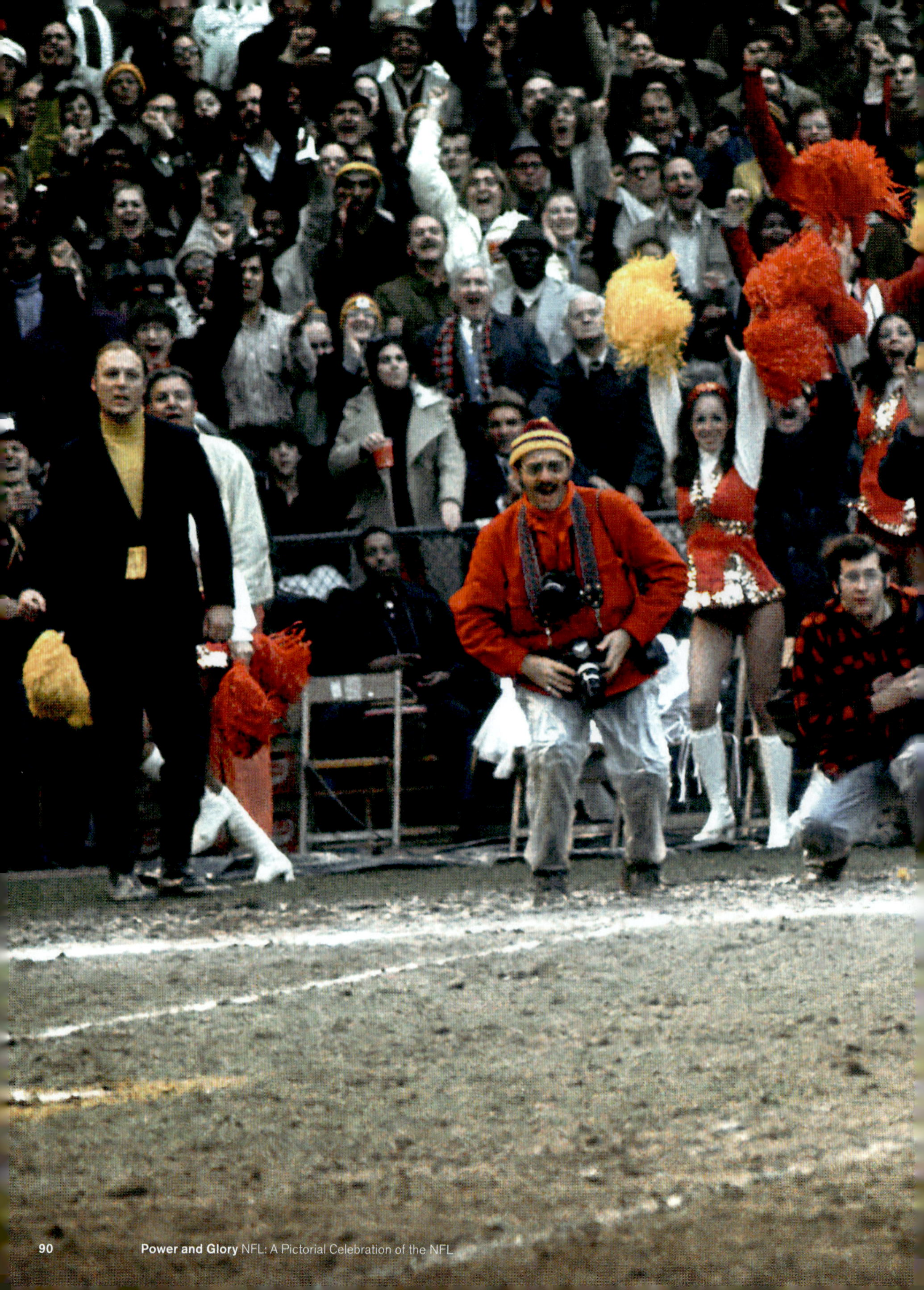

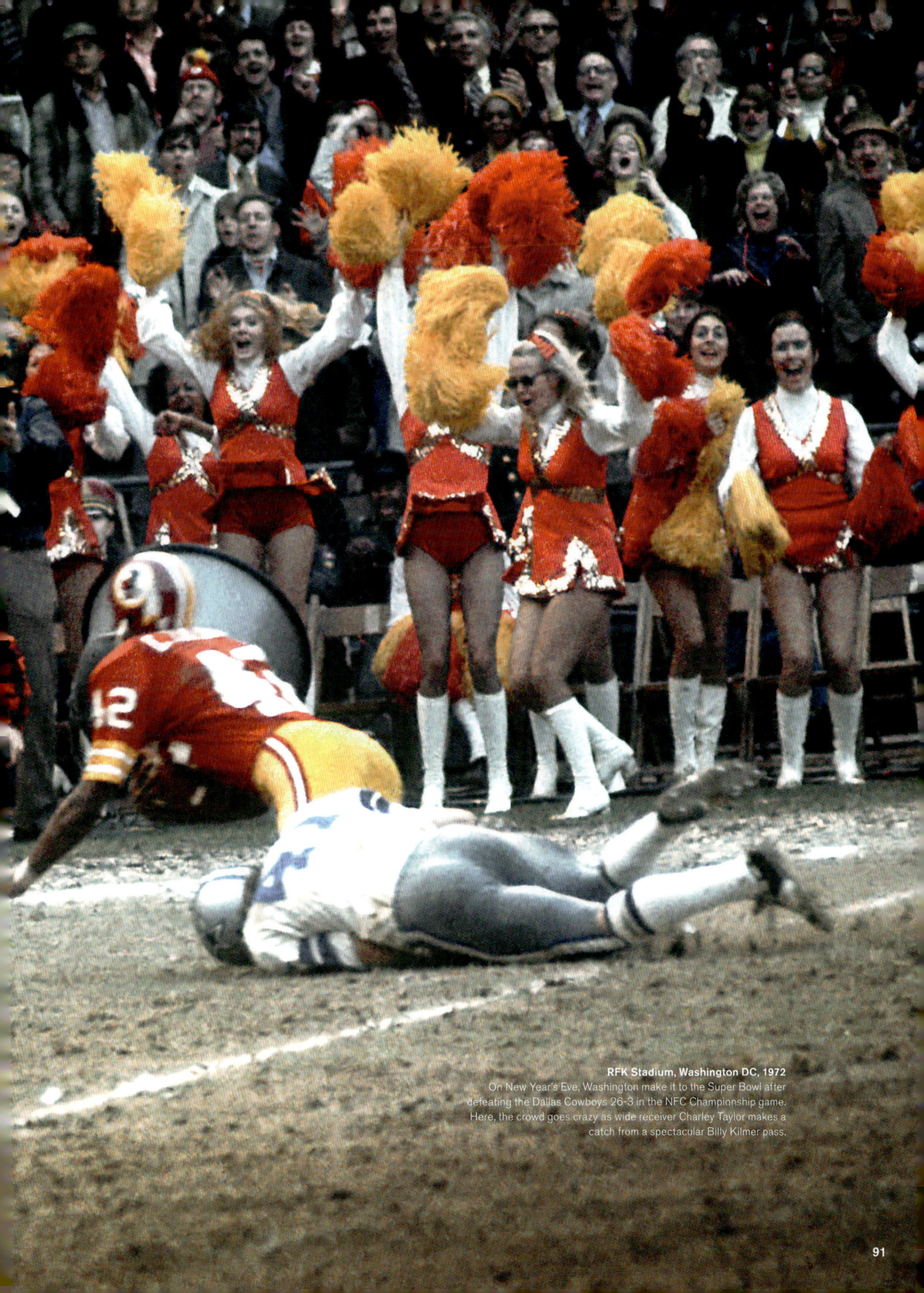

RFK Stadium, Washington DC, 1972

On New Year's Eve, Washington make it to the Super Bowl after defeating the Dallas Cowboys 26-3 in the NFC Championship game. Here, the crowd goes crazy as wide receiver Charley Taylor makes a catch from a spectacular Billy Kilmer pass.

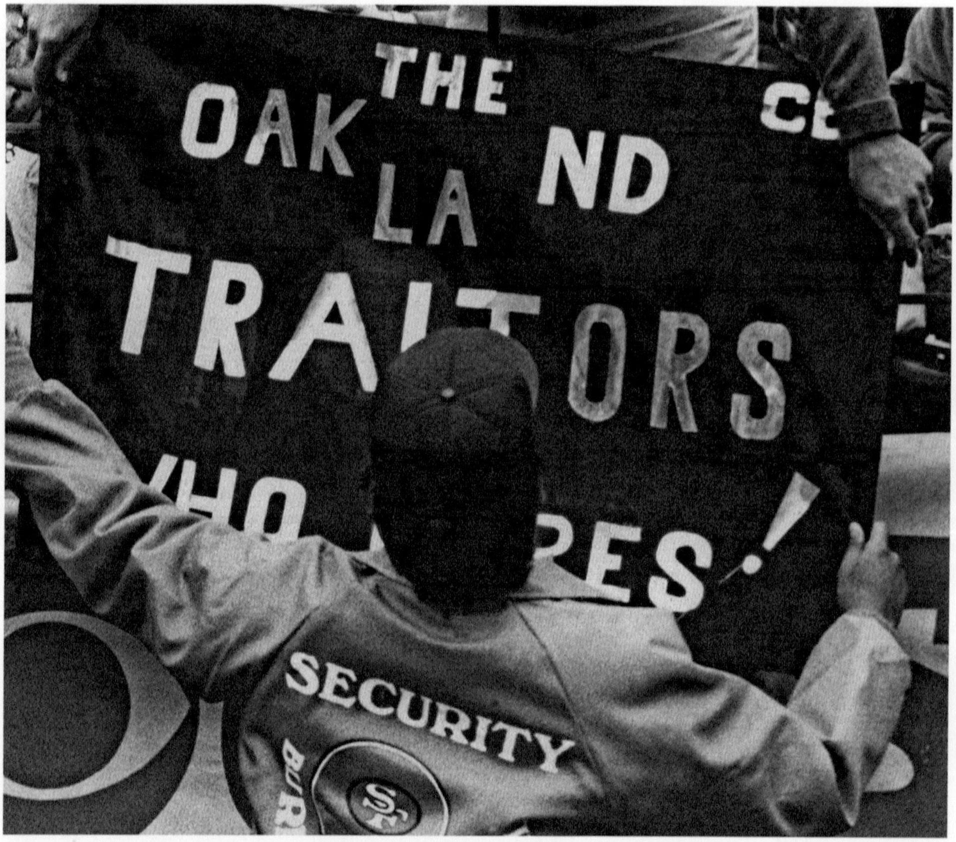

Candlestick Park, San Francisco, unspecified date after 1981
San Francisco security staff try and remove a protest banner from a Raiders fan disgusted at the team's move from Oakland to Los Angeles.

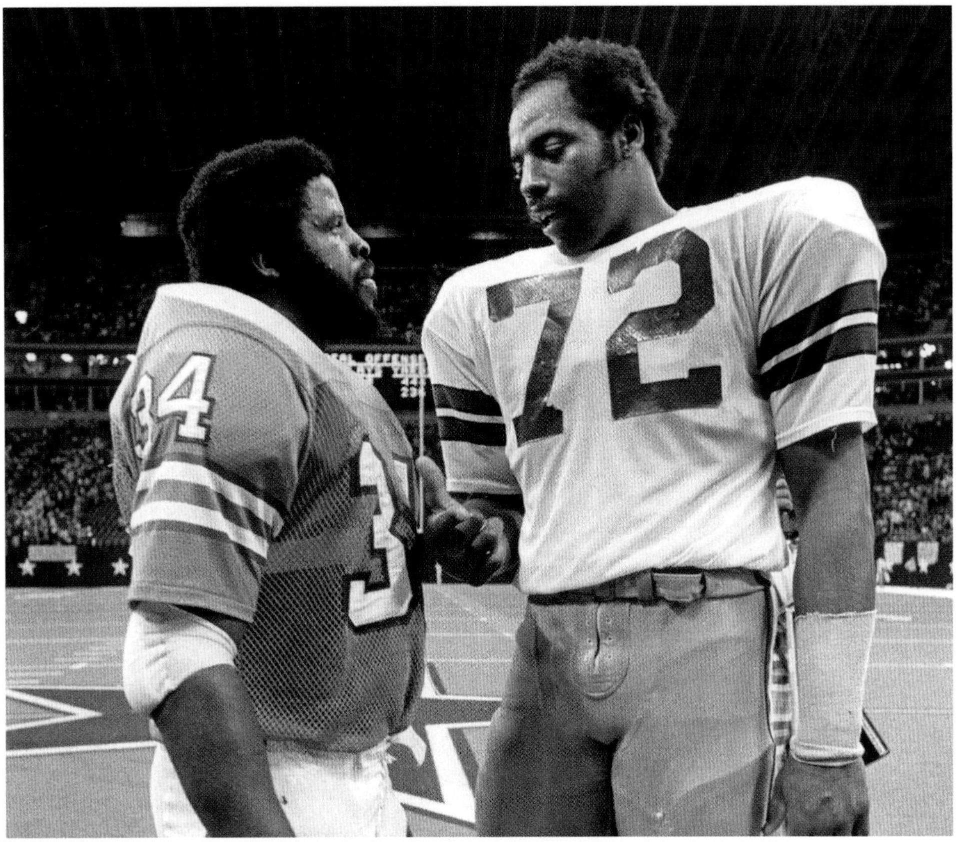

Texas Stadium, Dallas, date unspecified
The Dallas Cowboys defensive end Ed 'Too tall' Jones chats with the Houston Oilers running back Earl Campbell.

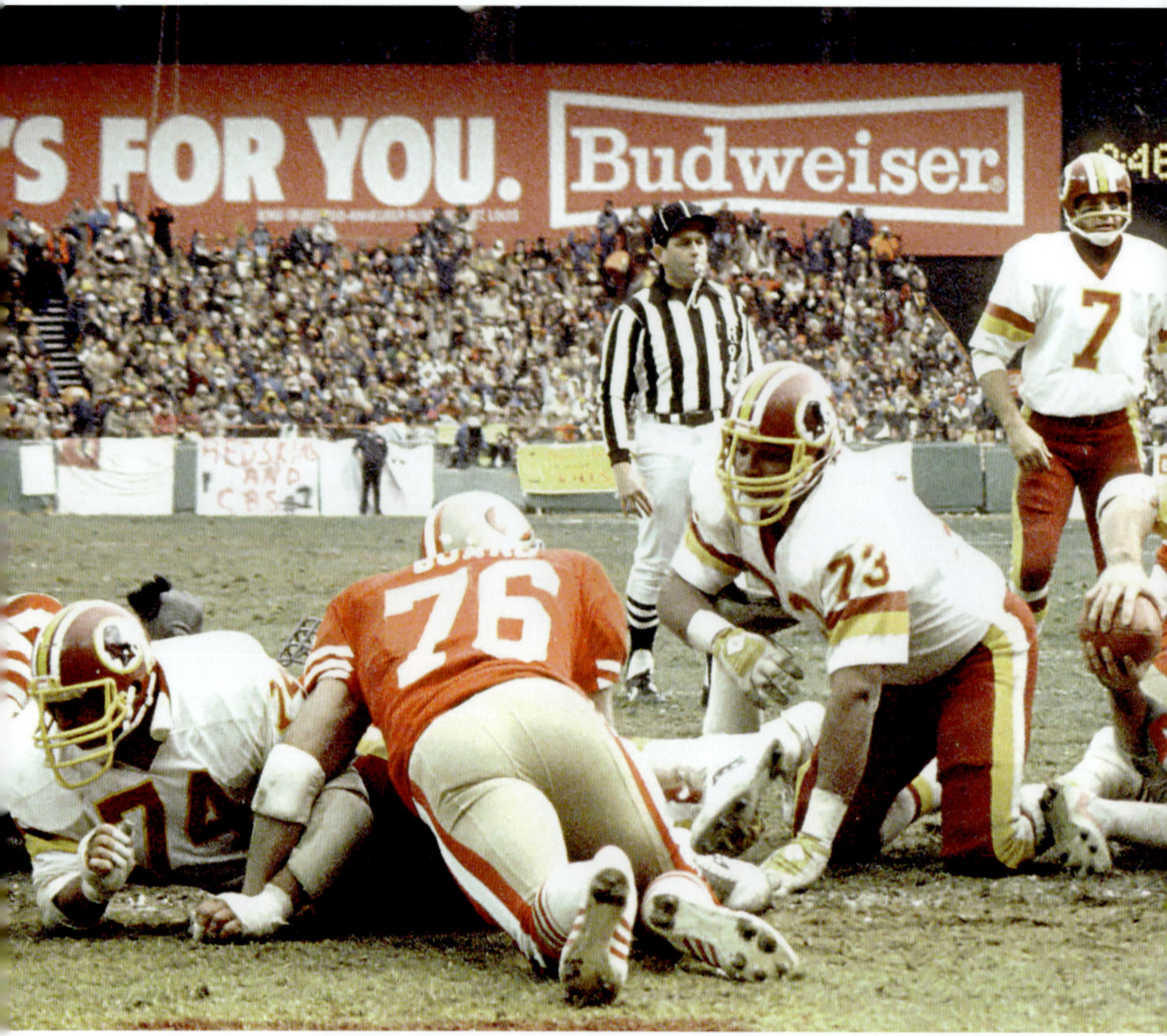

RFK Stadium, Washington DC, 1984
Redskins running back John Riggins scores a touchdown as Washington defeat San Francisco in the NFC Championship game, to book a place in the Super Bowl.

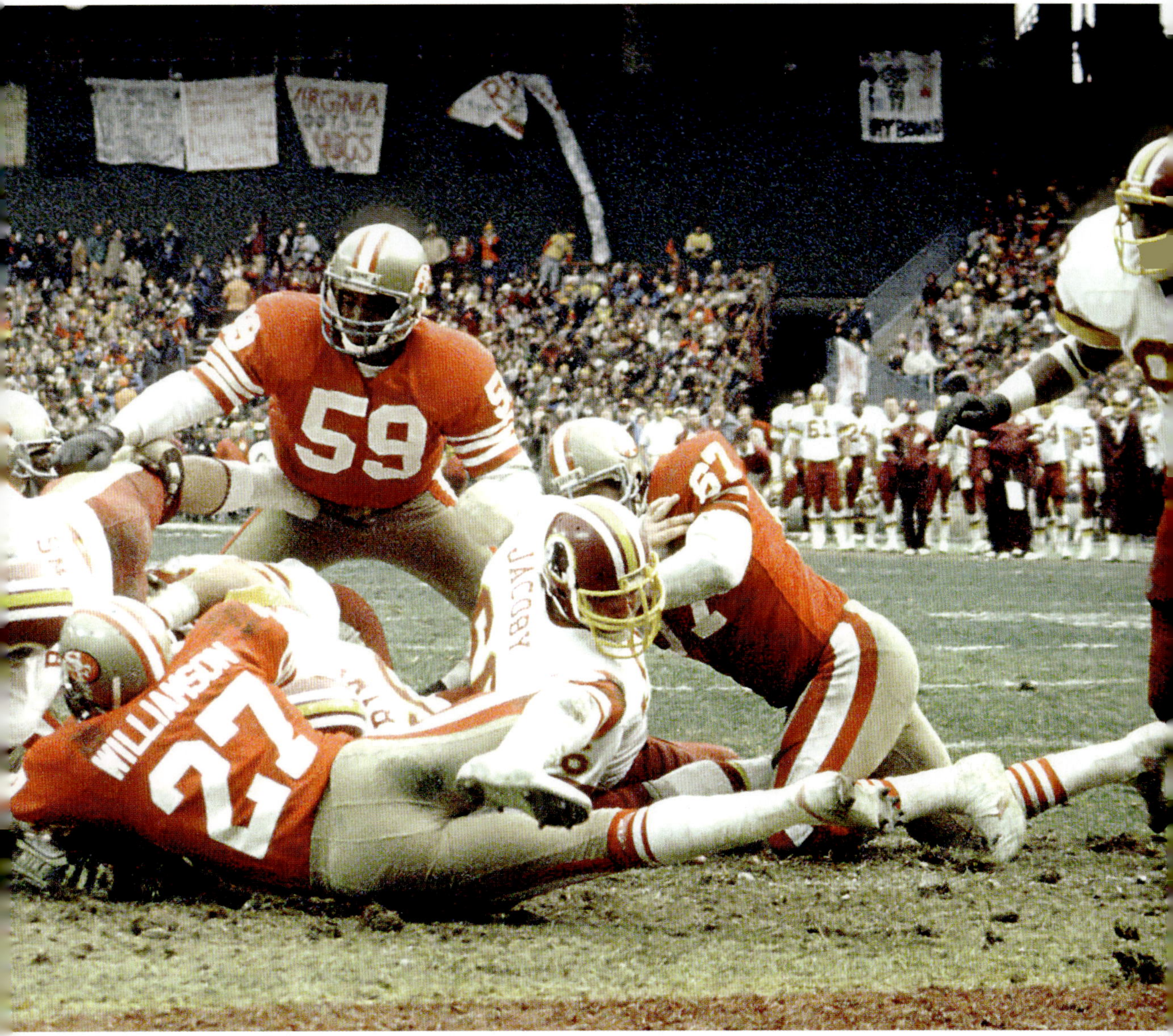
59
JACOBY
27
67

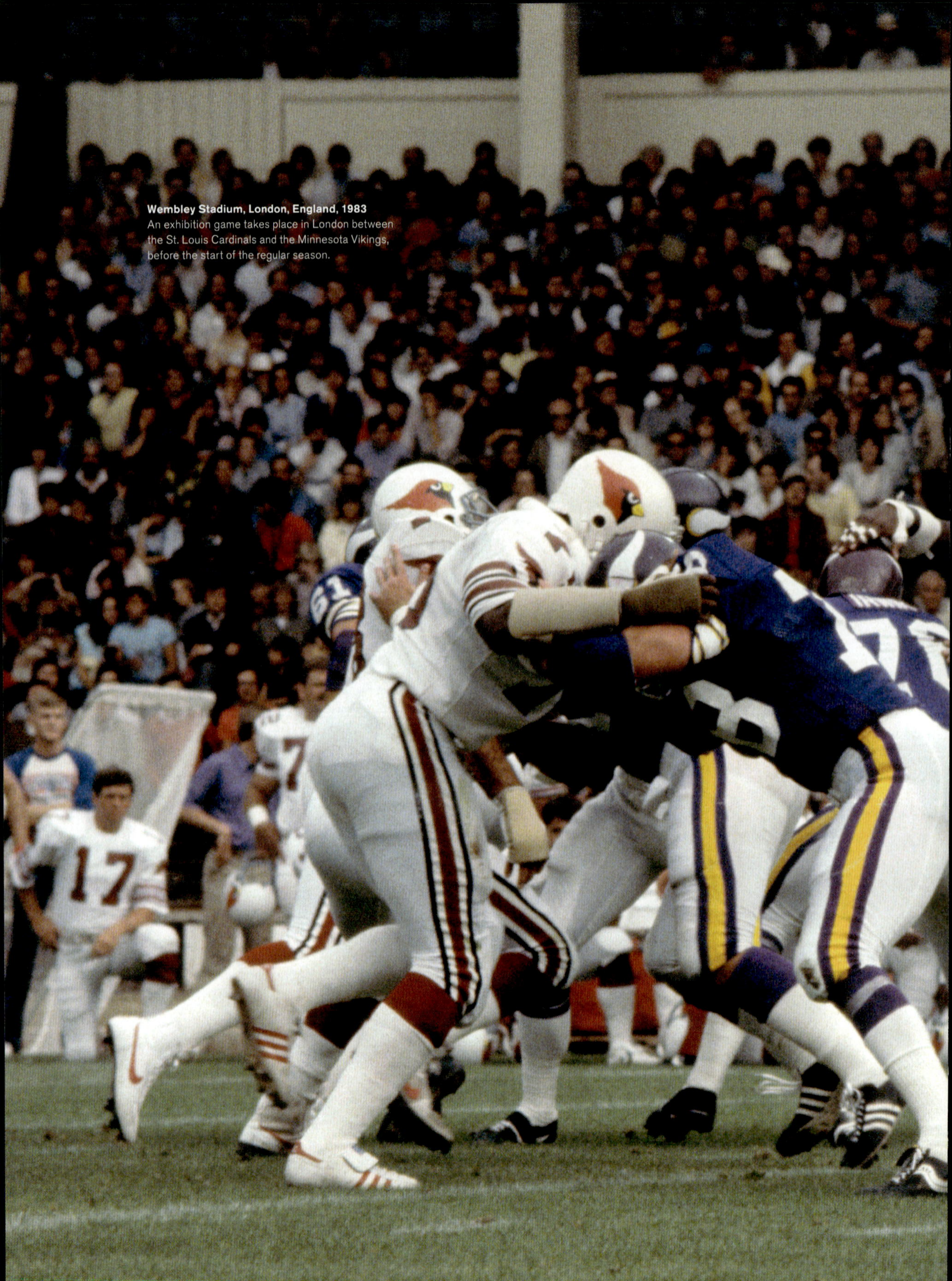

Wembley Stadium, London, England, 1983
An exhibition game takes place in London between the St. Louis Cardinals and the Minnesota Vikings, before the start of the regular season.

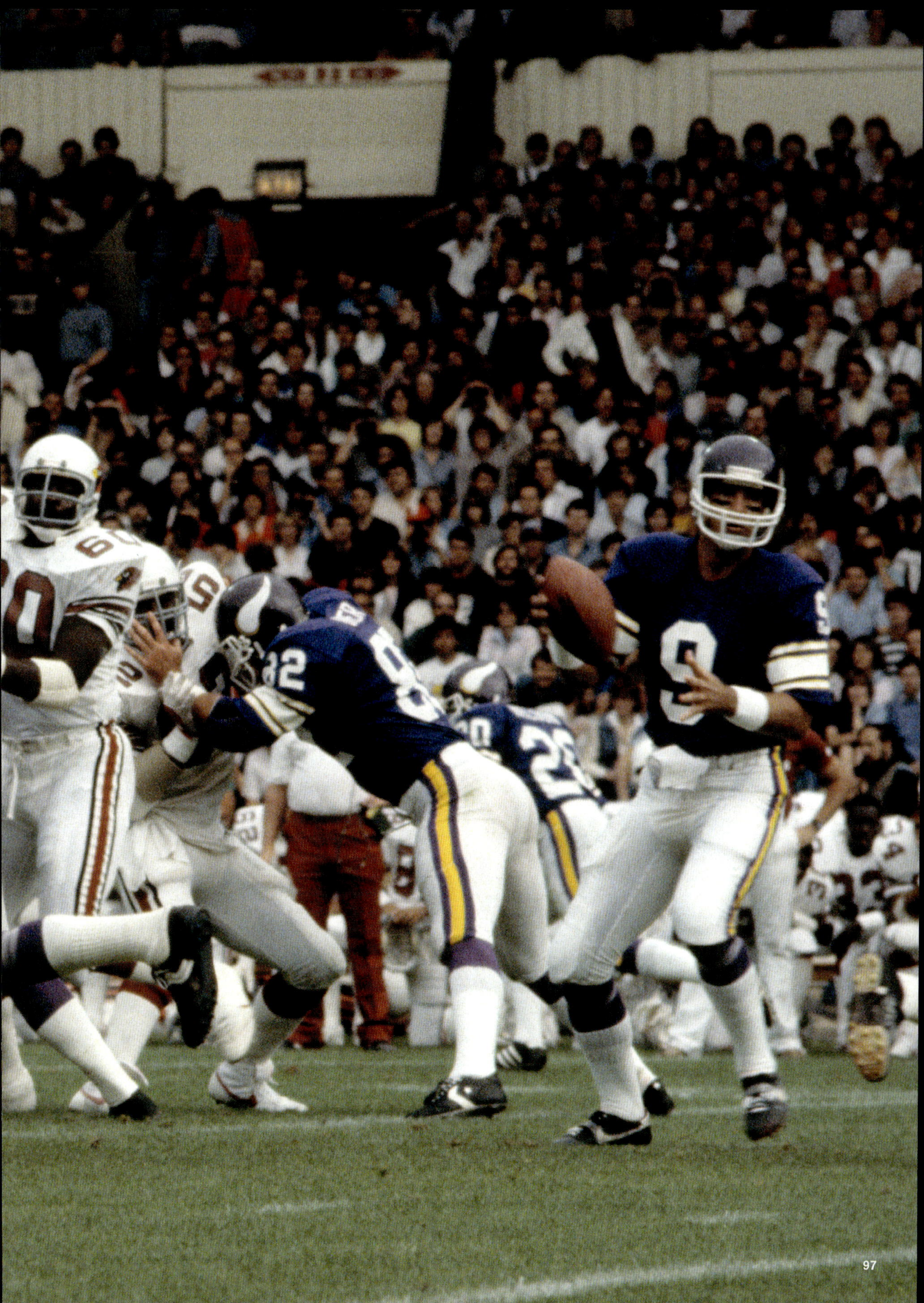

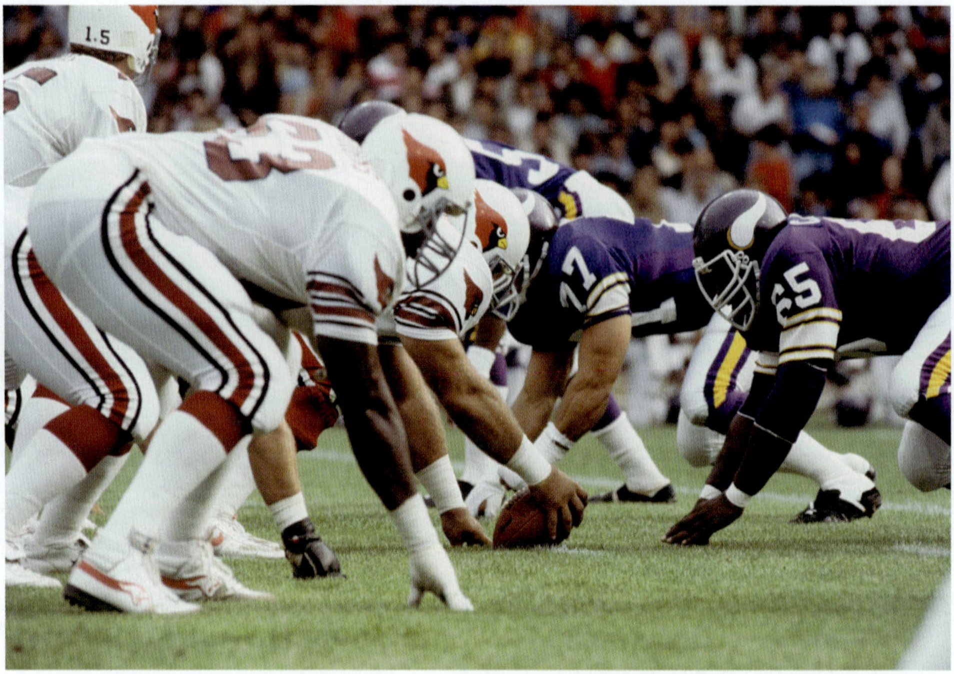

Wembley Stadium, London, England, 1983
During the same exhibition game, the St. Louis offence is preparing for a snap.

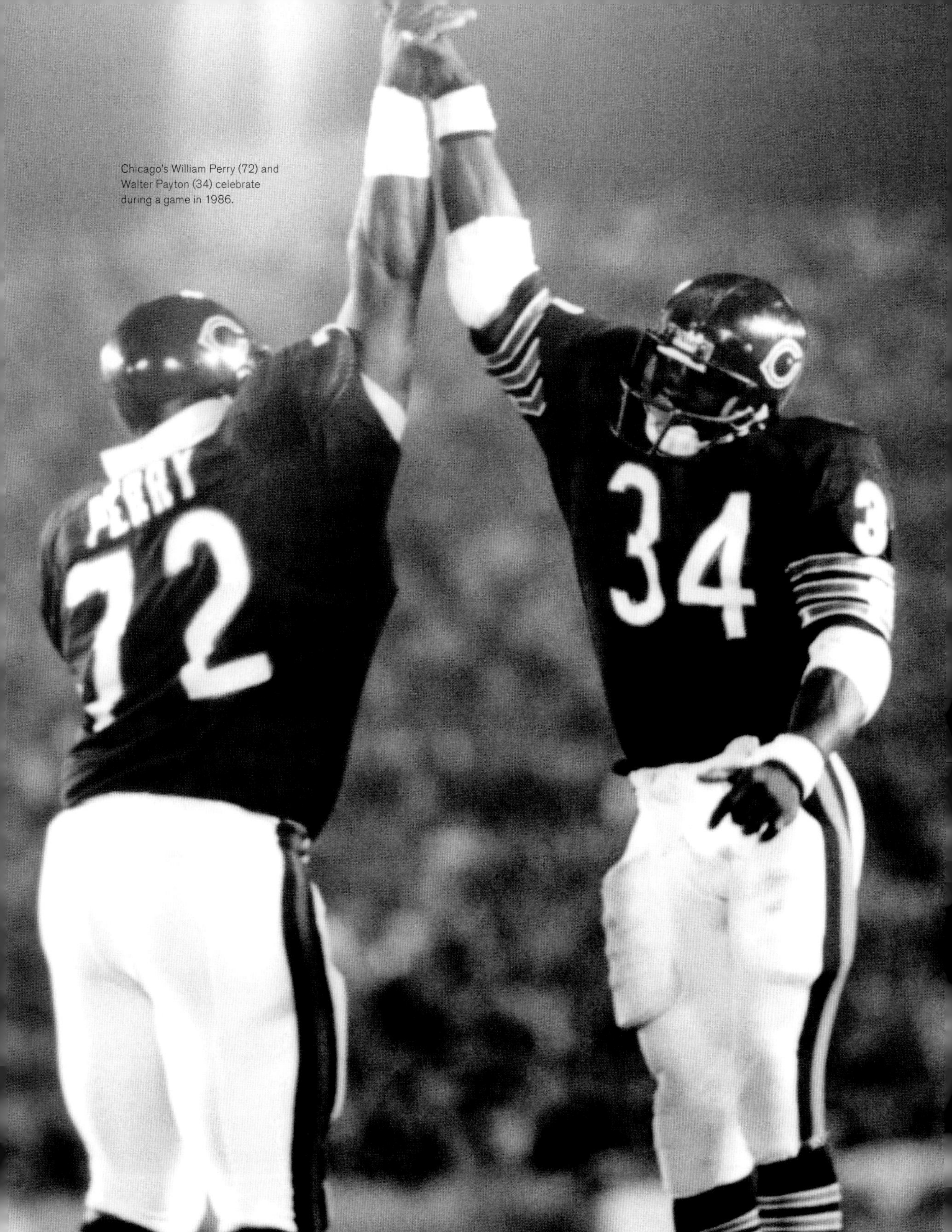

Chicago's William Perry (72) and Walter Payton (34) celebrate during a game in 1986.

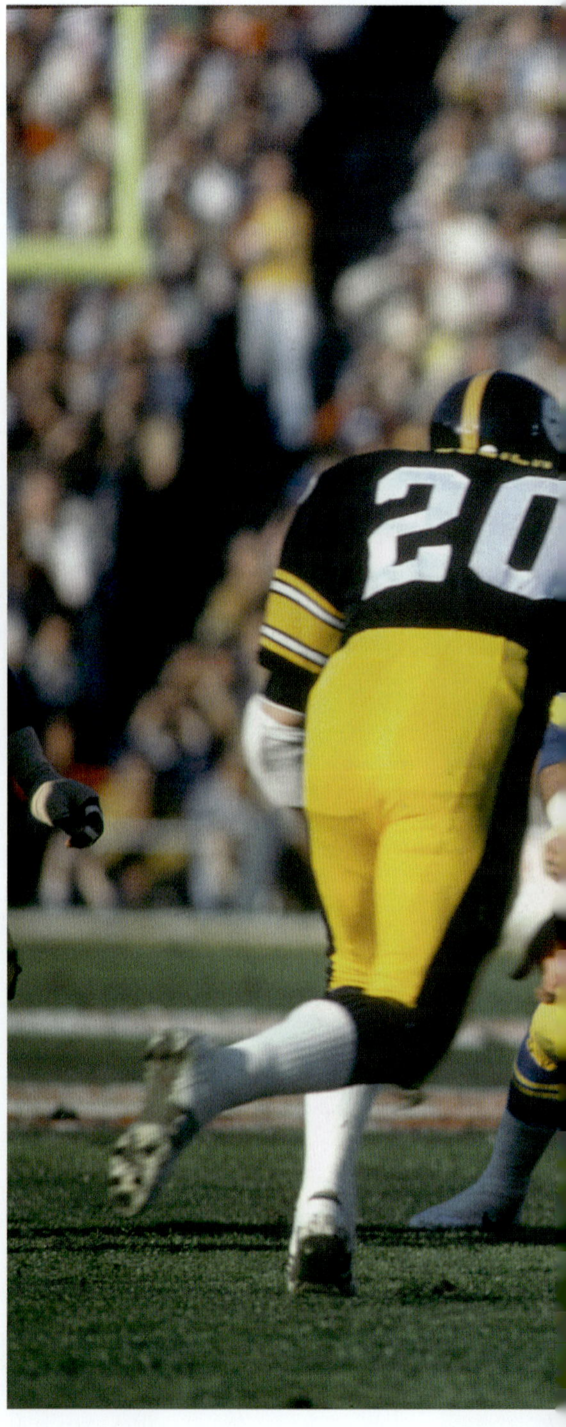

Rose Bowl, Pasadena, 1980
Pittsburgh's Terry Bradshaw in action against the LA Rams in Super Bowl 14. The Steelers won the game 31-19 to become the first team to win four Super Bowl championships.

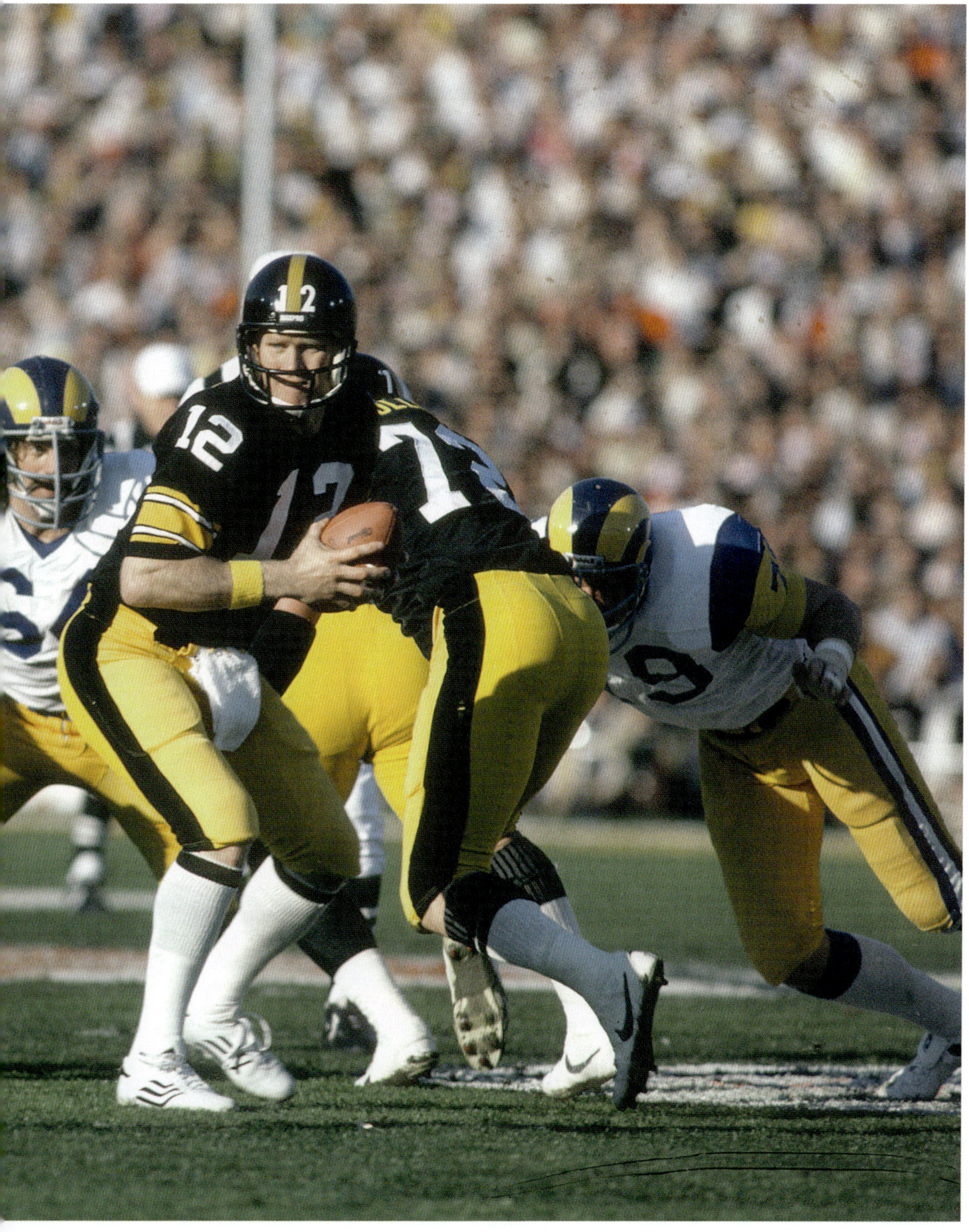

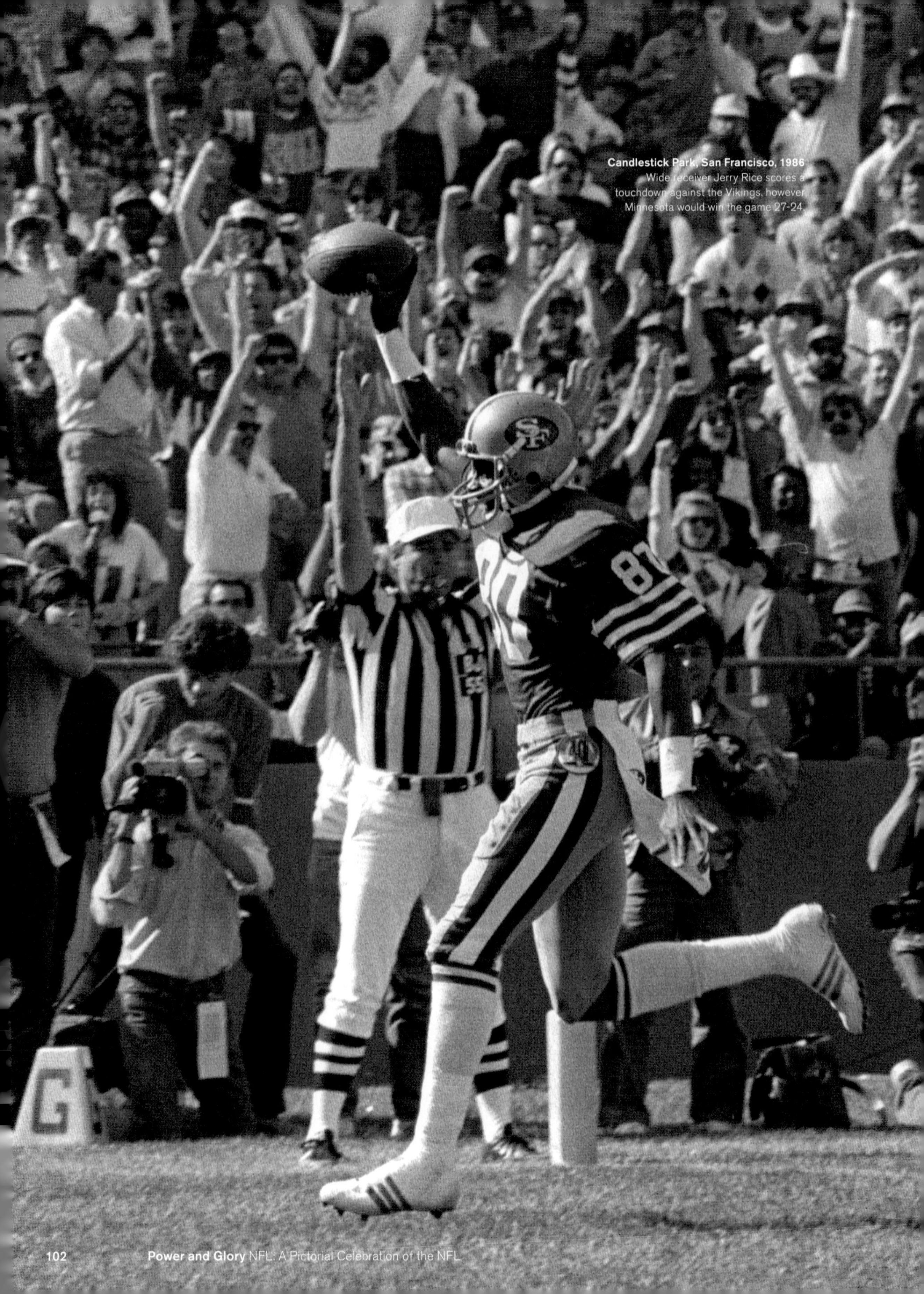

Candlestick Park, San Francisco, 1986
Wide receiver Jerry Rice scores a touchdown against the Vikings, however Minnesota would win the game 27-24.

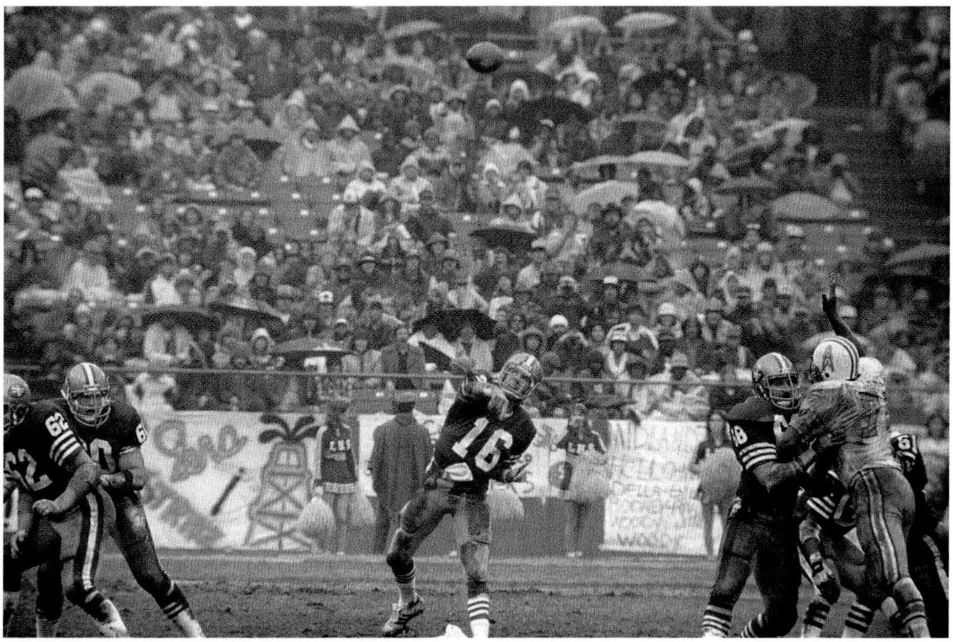

Candlestick Park, San Francisco, 1981
Joe Montana fires in a long ball in a game against the Oilers as the rain pours down.

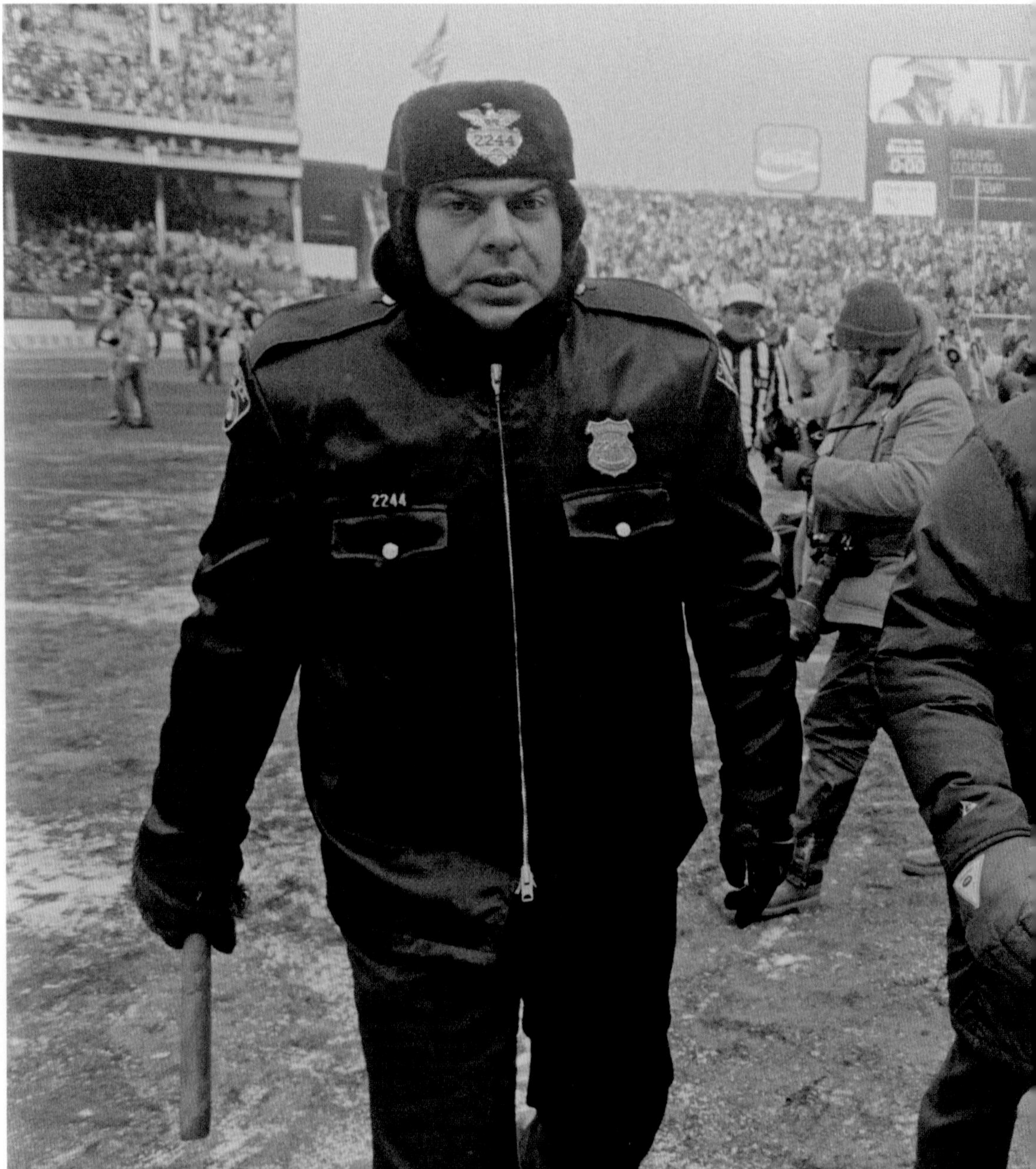

Cleveland Municipal Stadium, Cleveland, 1981
Browns coach Sam Rutigliano leaves the field in disappointment, after his team loses the divisional play-off against the Oakland Raiders. This was the coldest game played since the 1967 ice bowl between Green Bay and Dallas.

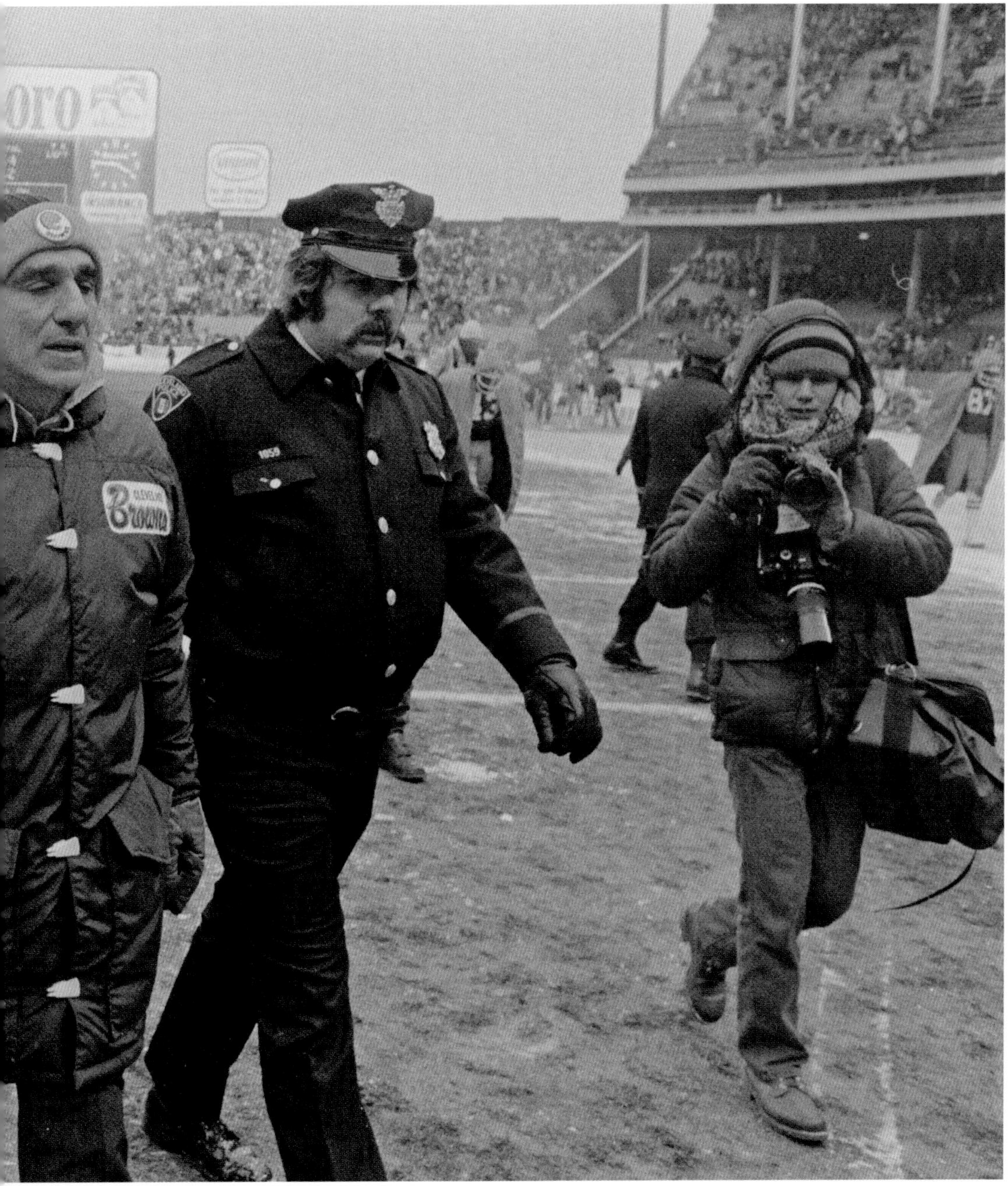
Browns

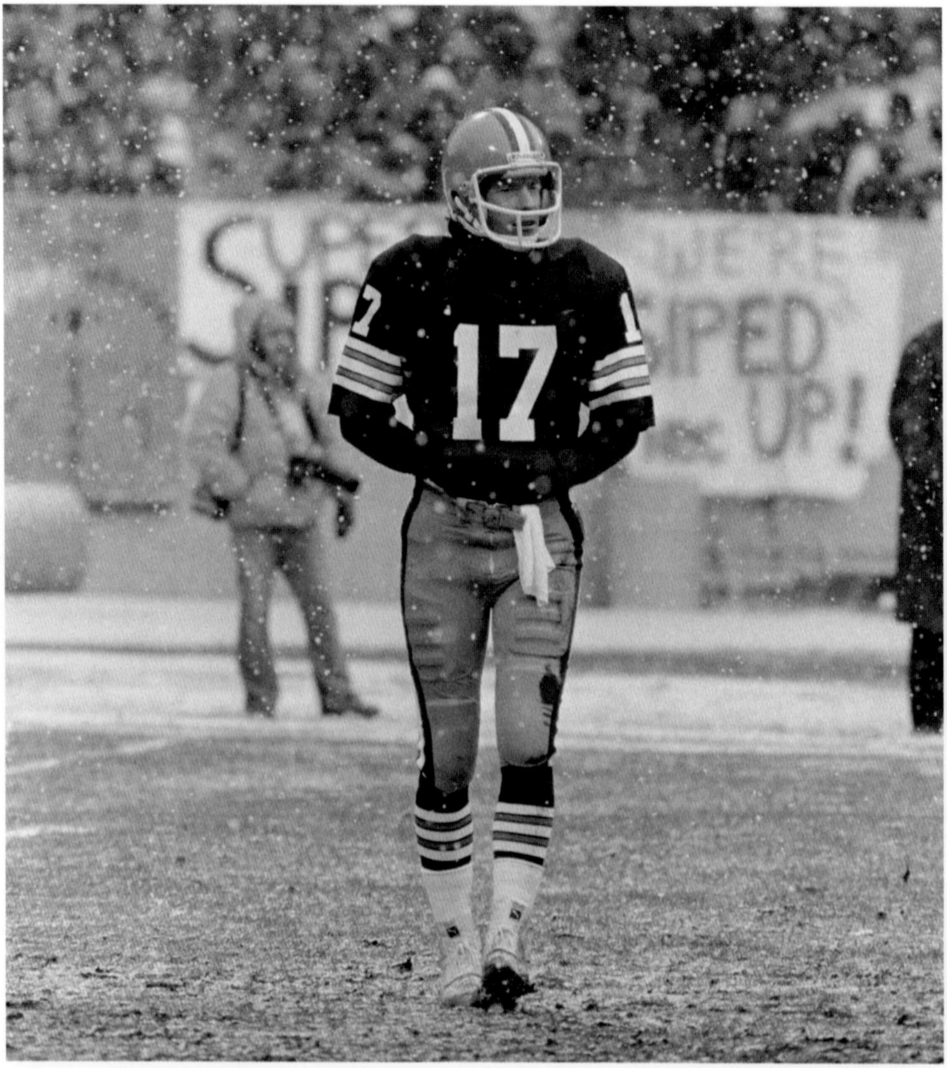

Cleveland Municipal Stadium, Cleveland, 1980
Browns quarterback Brian Sipe tries to keep his hands warm during a regular season game in December.

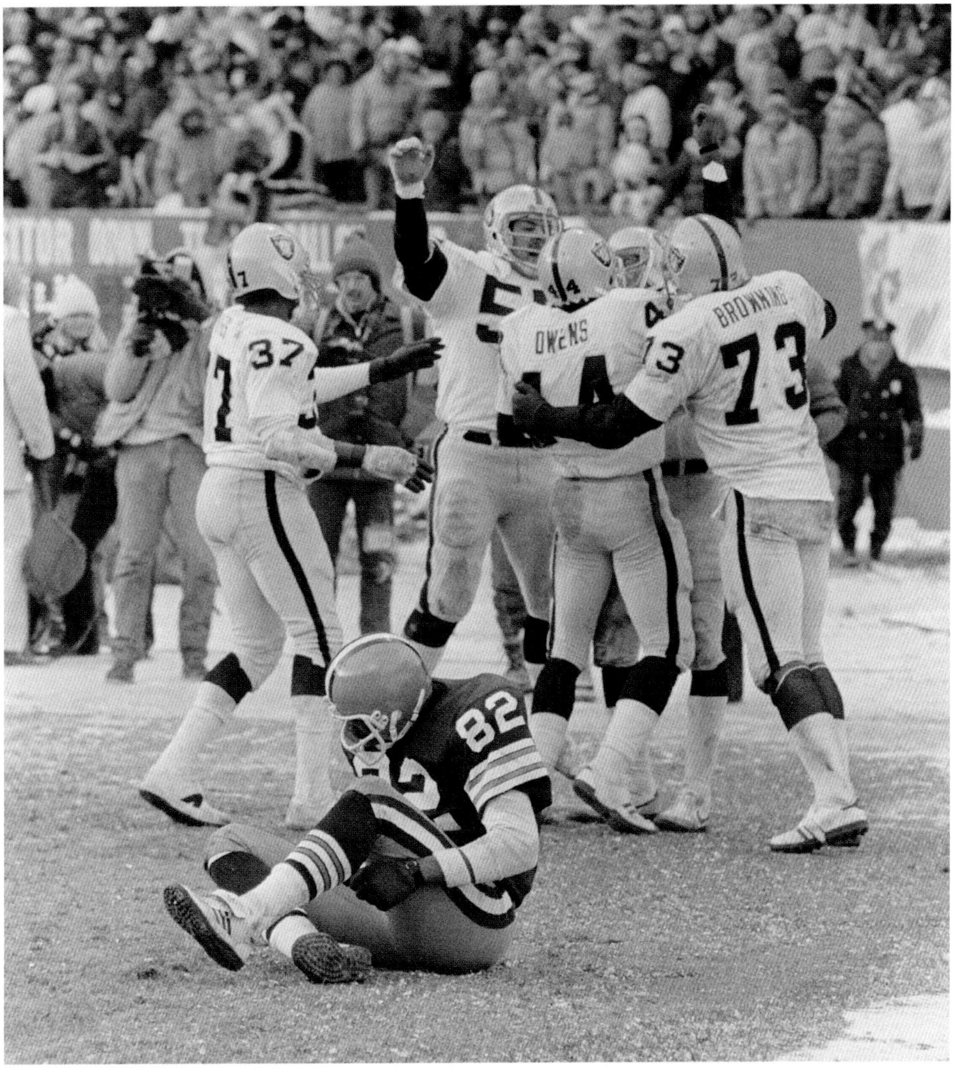

Cleveland Municipal Stadium, Cleveland, 1981
Browns receiver Ozzie Newsom sits on the floor dejected, after the Raiders make a crucial interception in the last seconds in the divisional play-off.

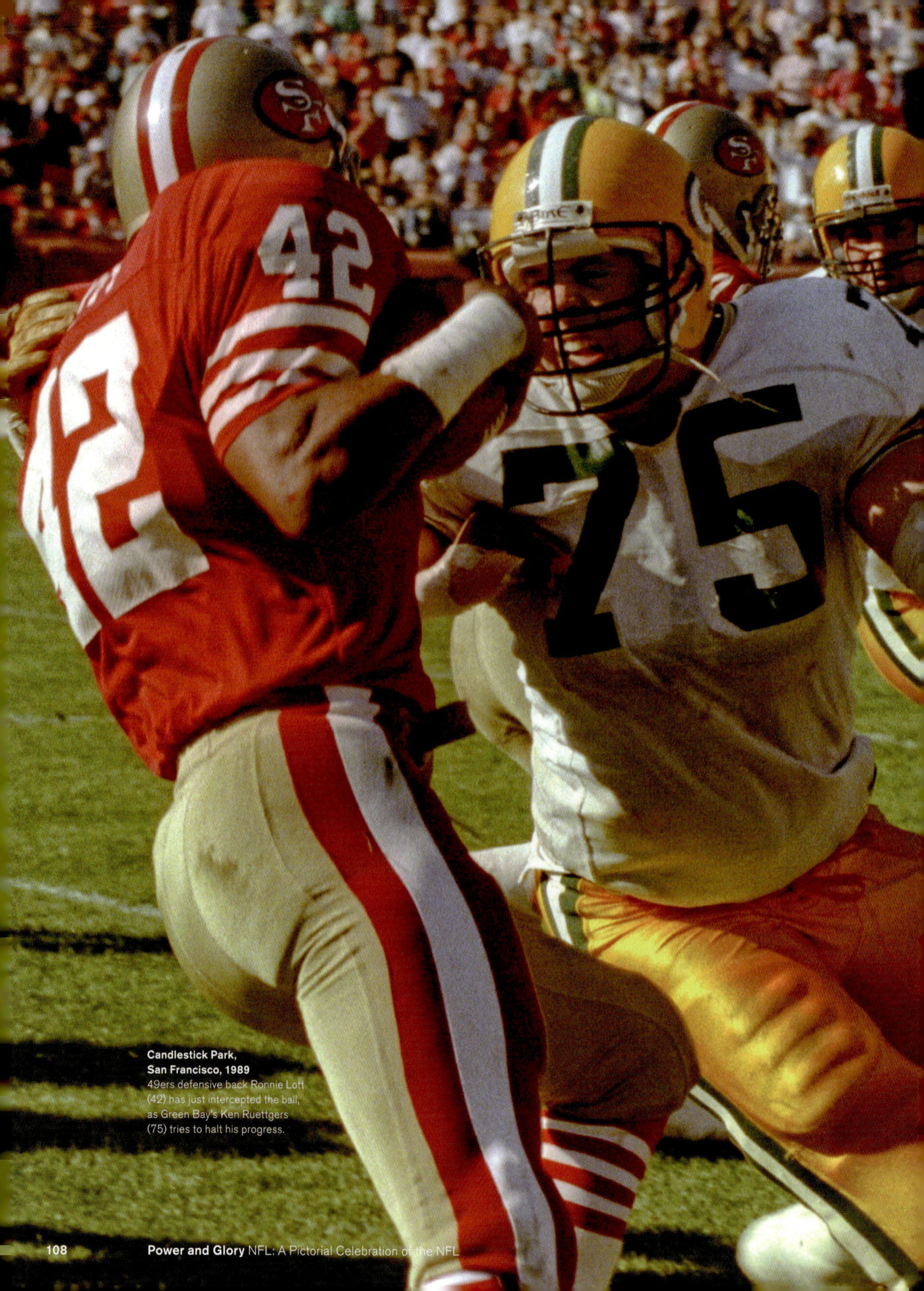

Candlestick Park, San Francisco, 1989
49ers defensive back Ronnie Lott (42) has just intercepted the ball, as Green Bay's Ken Ruettgers (75) tries to halt his progress.

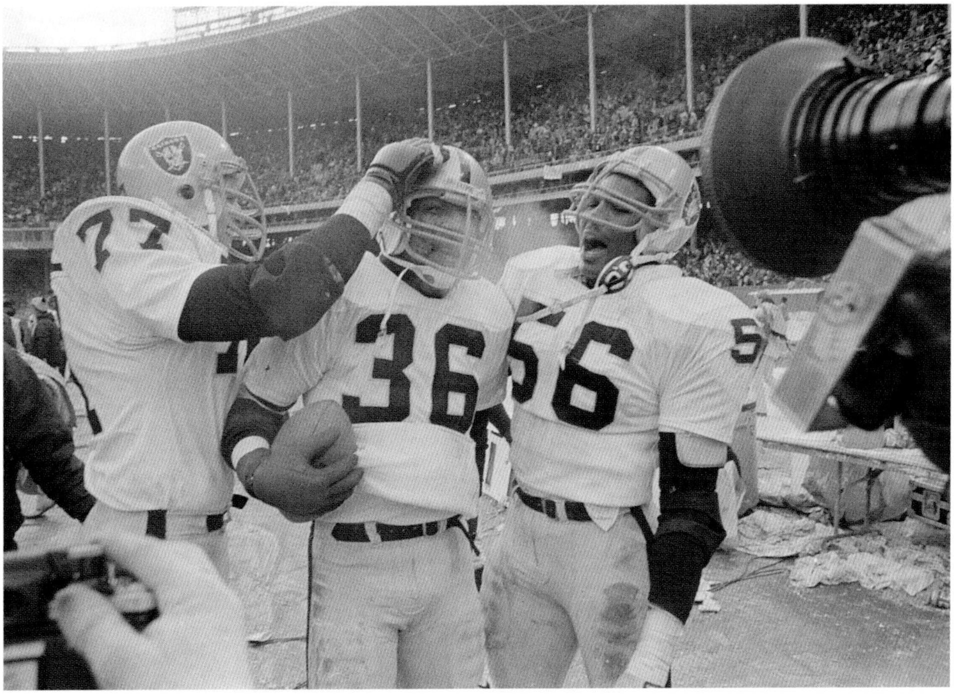

Cleveland Municipal Stadium, Cleveland, 1981
Raiders players celebrating the game-winning interception are Joe Campbell (left), Mike Davis (centre) and Steve Sylvester (right).

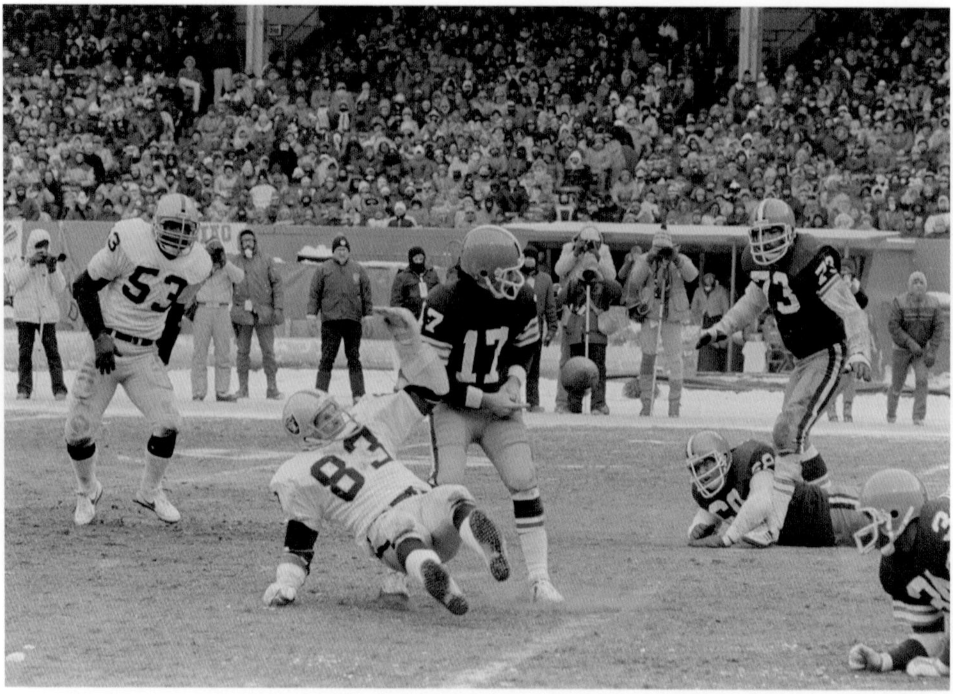

Cleveland Municipal Stadium, Cleveland, 1981
In the 'ice-bowl 2' divisional play-off against the Raiders, there is panic as Browns quarterback Brian Sipe has the ball taken out of his hands.

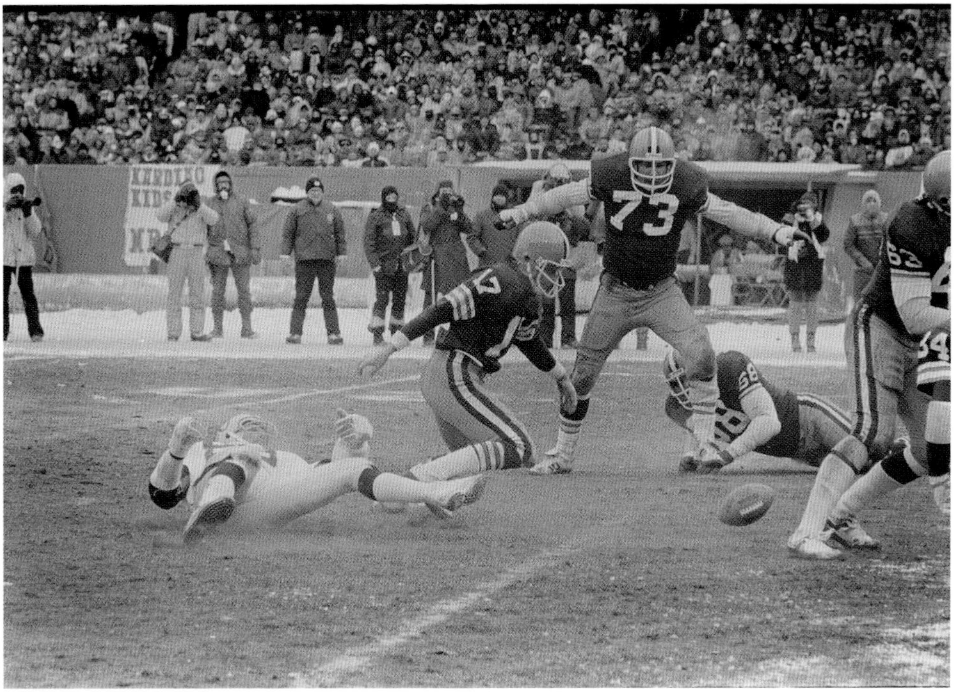

Tennessee Titans: Est. 1959

Former names: Houston Oilers (1960–1996); Tennessee Oilers (1997–1998)

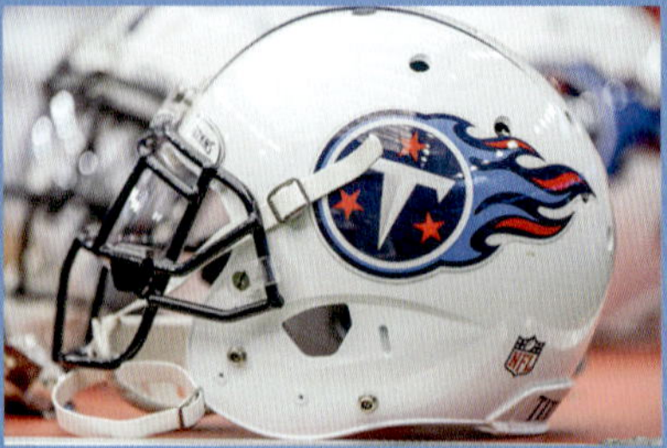

AFC Central Champions: (3) 1991, 1993, 2000

AFC South Champions: (4) 2002, 2008, 2020, 2021

AFC Conference Champions: (1) 1999

AFL Champions: (2) 1960, 1961

Super Bowl record: 0-1

Things started off well for the Houston Oilers, winning the first two championships of the newly formed AFL in 1960 and 1961, then in 1967 they became the first team in football to play in an indoor domed stadium when they moved into the Houston Astrodome. They wouldn't repeat the success of their first two seasons in existence, although they would make ten play-off appearances beyond the 1970 NFL/AFL merger. Seven of these post-season appearances came in consecutive years between 1987 and 1993 but the team could never get over the line to compete in the AFC Championship game for the first time since the 1979 season.

The biggest regret they will have in this time was a crazy loss at Buffalo in a game simply known as 'The Comeback'. Houston went 35-3 ahead early into the third quarter and the disgusted home fans left the stadium en masse; the game was surely over. By the end of the third quarter the Bills had put 28 unanswered points on the board as the fans scrambled to get back into the stadium. The Oilers lost 41-38 and had to suffer the indignity of being on the end of the biggest comeback in NFL history.

The Oilers had a very distinguishable image, with their derrick logo being one of the most unique in the NFL. Despite the Astrodome having been regenerated, the owner wanted the city to fund a new stadium which was difficult given loss of oil revenue in recent years. Eight hundred miles away in Tennessee they were prepared to build a new stadium and a controversial relocation was announced. The fans of Houston were disgusted and boycotted the final season. In the last Oilers game just 15,000 showed up.

The Tennessee team kept the Oilers name until becoming the Titans in 1999 and the colours changed to a darker blue. This felt like an entirely new club, with the paperwork stating the ownership being the most significant link between the Oilers and the Titans. They first played in Memphis but disappointing crowd numbers led to a move to Nashville.

Like the Oilers, one of the most defining games of the Titans' history was against Buffalo, but this time the result was very different. If a game warrants a title then you know it's special, and on this occasion the 'Music City Miracle' is one of the greatest comebacks in play-off history, due to the fact that Buffalo took the lead with just 15 seconds left on the clock. From the kick-off Frank Wycheck passed the ball sideways to Kevin Dyson who ran it into the endzone for the win, as the crowd went ballistic in a way rarely seen today due to more corporate environments. The Bills protested that it was a forward pass but the touchdown stood. This moved the Titans on to a divisional play-off against the Colts which they won 19-16.

The Titans would then do what the Oilers couldn't, and they made it to the ultimate showpiece by beating Jacksonville in the AFC Championship game. Super Bowl 34 against St Louis Rams remains one of the most dramatic endings where the margin of glory and despair came down to inches. Whoever won this Super Bowl would do so for the first time in their history and with six seconds remaining the Titans had one last play on the Rams' ten-yard line, one touchdown away from levelling. The ball was caught by Dyson but he was tackled on the one-yard line. He stretched his arm out but

Indianapolis Colts: Est. 1953

Former names: Baltimore Colts (1953–1984)

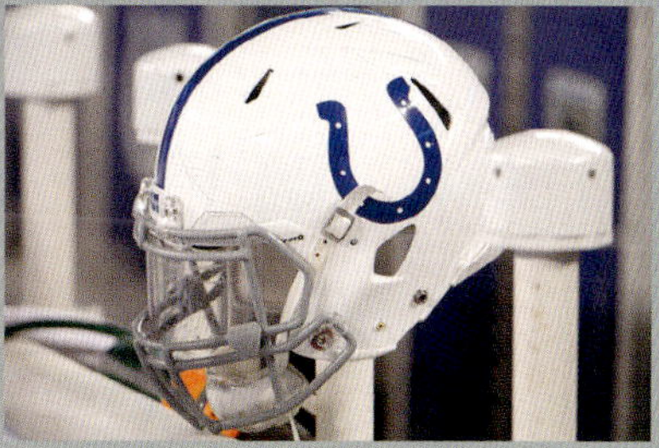

AFC East Champions: (6) 1970, 1975, 1976, 1977, 1987, 1999

AFC South Champions: (9) 2003, 2004, 2005, 2006, 2007, 2009, 2010, 2013, 2014

AFC Conference Champions: (3) 1970, 2006, 2009

NFL Champions pre-1970 NFL/AFL merger: (3) 1958, 1959, 1968

Super Bowl titles: (2) 1970, 2006

Super Bowl record: 2-2

The Colts have now spent more years in Indianapolis than Baltimore; however when the move was made in 1984, the Baltimore team had already notched up four NFL championships including one Super Bowl. They were one of the marquee teams in the league, yet owner Robert Irsay had a dispute with the Baltimore authorities and moved the team to Indianapolis in one of the most notorious relocations in NFL history. In the middle of the night, 15 trucks filled with the club's assets (all taking separate routes to avoid suspicion) was all it took to change the sporting landscape for two separate cities.

The Memorial Stadium in Baltimore required a major upgrade but the city's mayor insisted that the money would have to come from private finances (i.e. the Colts themselves) and that the state simply didn't have the funds to justify burdening the taxpayer. Indianapolis on the other hand were willing to invest public money; meanwhile legendary Colts quarterback Johnny Unitas was so disgusted at the move that he disowned the club, and today his statue stands outside the stadium of the Baltimore Ravens (though some will point out that the Ravens did the same thing to Cleveland!).

The Colts went to Super Bowl 3 in 1969 and lost to the Jets in one of the NFL's biggest upsets. The AFL would then merge with the NFL, and two separate conferences were formed; the NFC with the older more established teams, and the AFC with the newer teams. To make the numbers of each conference even, the Colts, Browns and Steelers agreed to join the AFC. Super Bowl 5 was the first one post the merger, as the NFC's Dallas Cowboys played the AFC's Colts. In the fourth quarter, the Colts trailed 13-6 before scoring a touchdown to level. The game became known as the 'blunder bowl' due to the amount of errors; Baltimore themselves would give away seven turnovers which is a record for a winning team in a Super Bowl. Not that they cared, and with five seconds remaining on the clock they became champions courtesy of a field goal.

The Colts name and branding comes from a famous annual horse race in Baltimore called the Preakness Stakes. There are links to the Ohio team called the Dayton Triangles, suggesting that the Colts are actually over 100 years of age, and played the first ever NFL game which was a 14-0 victory over the Columbus Panhandles (yes, Panhandles; NFL teams didn't have to be named after scary animals in 1920). Dayton played in the APFA, which would become the NFL, but the Triangles left for New York and their franchise spot would eventually be owned by the Dallas Texans in 1952. Then in 1953 all the Texans' assets including the players were transferred to Baltimore and a new team emerged. Although the Colts officially were founded in 1953, it is clouded, and both the Dayton Triangles and Dallas Texans played in the Colts' famous white and blue colours.

The golden era for the Colts in Indianapolis came between seasons 2006 and 2009 when legendary quarterback Peyton Manning took the team to two Super Bowls. In 2009 they were beaten by the New Orleans Saints despite leading in the fourth quarter 17-16. A few years earlier, by 2006 the team had gone 36 years with no Super Bowl appearance and things didn't start well when the Chicago Bears scored after just 14 seconds – the earliest touchdown in Super Bowl history. 'Indy', however, regrouped, Manning led his team to victory and the Colts had won the Super Bowl again, this time as Indianapolis.

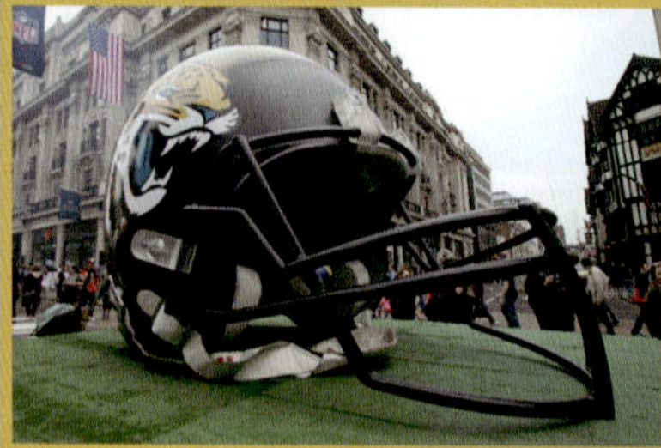

AFC Central Champions: (2) 1998, 1999

AFC South Champions: (1) 2017

Super Bowl record: 0-0

Jacksonville Jaguars: Est. 1993

f the Jacksonville Jaguars were a human being, they came out the womb running but then spent their teenage years lying on a bed playing computer games while binging on junk food. They were founded in 1993 and played their first NFL season in 1995, in the AFC Central with Pittsburgh, Cleveland, Cincinnati, and Tennessee. The first battle they had was with the car manufacturer Jaguar who had claimed that the club's leaping cat logo was too similar to theirs.

On the field things looked pretty good; after just one year in the league Jacksonville were one game away from the Super Bowl, but would lose the AFC Championship game 20-6 to New England. By 1999 the Florida team had already notched up four seasons that saw them in the play-offs, indicating that the Jaguars were going to be a major force in the NFL. The team returned to the play-offs in seasons 2005 and 2007 and by this point were in a different division. Along with Tennessee, they had been moved from the AFC Central to the newly formed AFC South as the NFL introduced the Houston Texans in the 2002 expansion, meaning there would be eight divisions of four teams.

After not registering a winning season in nine years, the 2017 Jaguars turned the tide and got as far as the AFC Championship game where they would again meet New England for a place in the Super Bowl. Quarterback Blake Bortles was seen as a weak link in the side, but the Jags had a strong running back in Leonard Fournette and a defence that specialised in turnovers, leading to the nickname 'Sacksonville'. Despite New England being strong favourites, Jacksonville were 20-10 ahead early into the fourth quarter. At this point the much-maligned Jacksonville Jaguars being in the Super Bowl was a very real possibility; however Tom Brady led his team to a 24-20 win and Jacksonville remain one of four clubs to have never been to a Super Bowl.

Instead of building on the momentum of 2017, the Jaguars went back to losing and registered the worst record in the league twice in a row in 2020 and 2021. The one bright spot of such a bad record was that they were able to get the number one draft pick two years in a row which meant the acquisition of the much sought-after quarterback Trevor Lawrence.

Perhaps the most standout part of the Jags' recent history is their association with the International Series of games played at London's Wembley Stadium. Since their first appearance in 2013, they have played every London series since, but it didn't start off too well with the Jags losing in their first two London games. In 2015 Buffalo came to Wembley, which was slowly becoming Jacksonville's second home, but they needed a win to get the UK NFL fanbase onside. Jacksonville took a 27-3 lead but Buffalo came back in the second half and went 31-27 ahead late into the final quarter. It looked like the Jags' London nightmare would continue but right at the end Bortles threw to Allen Hurns who made a spectacular flying catch in the endzone. After eight games in London, the Jaguars' record is 4-4 which is better than their average; although one worrying factor for fans located in Jacksonville is the constant speculation that the team could be relocated to London, as the fanbase in the UK has grown massively off the back of these games. The concept of franchising doesn't really go down well outside of the US, and recently it would appear more likely that the NFL would probably favour expanding to more teams, than to move a team from one country to another.

Houston Texans: Est. 1999

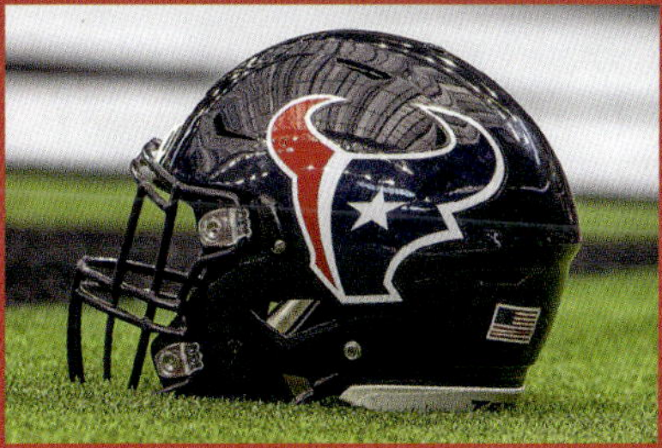

AFC South Champions: (6) 2011, 2012, 2015, 2016, 2018, 2019

Super Bowl record: 0-0

A void was left in Houston in the 1990s, when the city's established NFL team the Oilers rode off to Tennessee to be rebranded as the Titans. Meanwhile, the Cleveland Browns demanded a return to the NFL after being franchised to Baltimore to become the Ravens, after that city itself had also lost its team to Indianapolis in the franchise merry-go-round. The return of the Browns meant 31 teams in the NFL, an uneven number, therefore in order to create eight divisions of four teams, a new spot was up for grabs for a city to have an NFL team. Toronto and Los Angeles were in consideration; however, the final choice was Houston. Instead of playing in the indoor Houston Astrodome, like the Oilers had done, a new stadium was built holding 72,220. The branding and uniforms were also different making the Texans feel like a newly founded team, unlike a rebirth of an old one, in contrast to the Cleveland Browns who had returned as the same club.

Names that were considered for the new team in Houston included Bobcats, Stallions, Wildcatters and, most intriguing, Apollos, given the city's association with space exploration. Instead they chose a name that makes them the only team in the NFL in which the second name is related to an entire state, and it's also a name that had been used in the past. The Dallas Texans played one NFL season in 1952 in which they carried a 1-11 record. They were dissolved after that solitary season. Another team also called the Dallas Texans sprung up in 1960, and after three seasons in the AFL they became the Kansas City Chiefs. Given the history of the name, the Houston Texans have some degree of longevity, despite being the baby of the NFL.

Speaking of Dallas, one of the great missed opportunities in modern NFL is the lack of rivalry between the two teams of Texas due to being in different conferences. Since Houston's first NFL season in 2002, they have only played Dallas on five occasions with the Cowboys 3-2 ahead in the series of games. The last meeting between the two was in 2018 with the Texans winning from an overtime field goal. One intriguing factor of Houston being an AFC team, and Dallas being in the NFC, is that it makes an all-Texas Super Bowl one day possible.

Along with Jacksonville, Detroit, and Cleveland, the Texans have never made an appearance in the Super Bowl, although Houston and Jacksonville will point out that they have a short history, while Cleveland and Detroit are two of the NFL's oldest teams and have had more years to achieve glory. One standalone record that the Texans will want to lose is being the only team in the NFL never to have played in a conference championship game, where you are just the one win away from a Super Bowl appearance. They have had four chances to get to the AFC Championship game but were beaten in the divisional play-offs by Baltimore in season 2011, New England in seasons 2012 and 2016, and Kansas City in season 2019. To get to the divisional play-off against Kansas in the 2019 season, the Texans had to made a late comeback against a strong Buffalo side, despite being 16-0 down deep into the third quarter. In the entire first half they had managed just 62 yards, and due to an incredible fourth-quarter comeback won 22-19 in what will go down as the most thrilling post-season game in this club's short history.

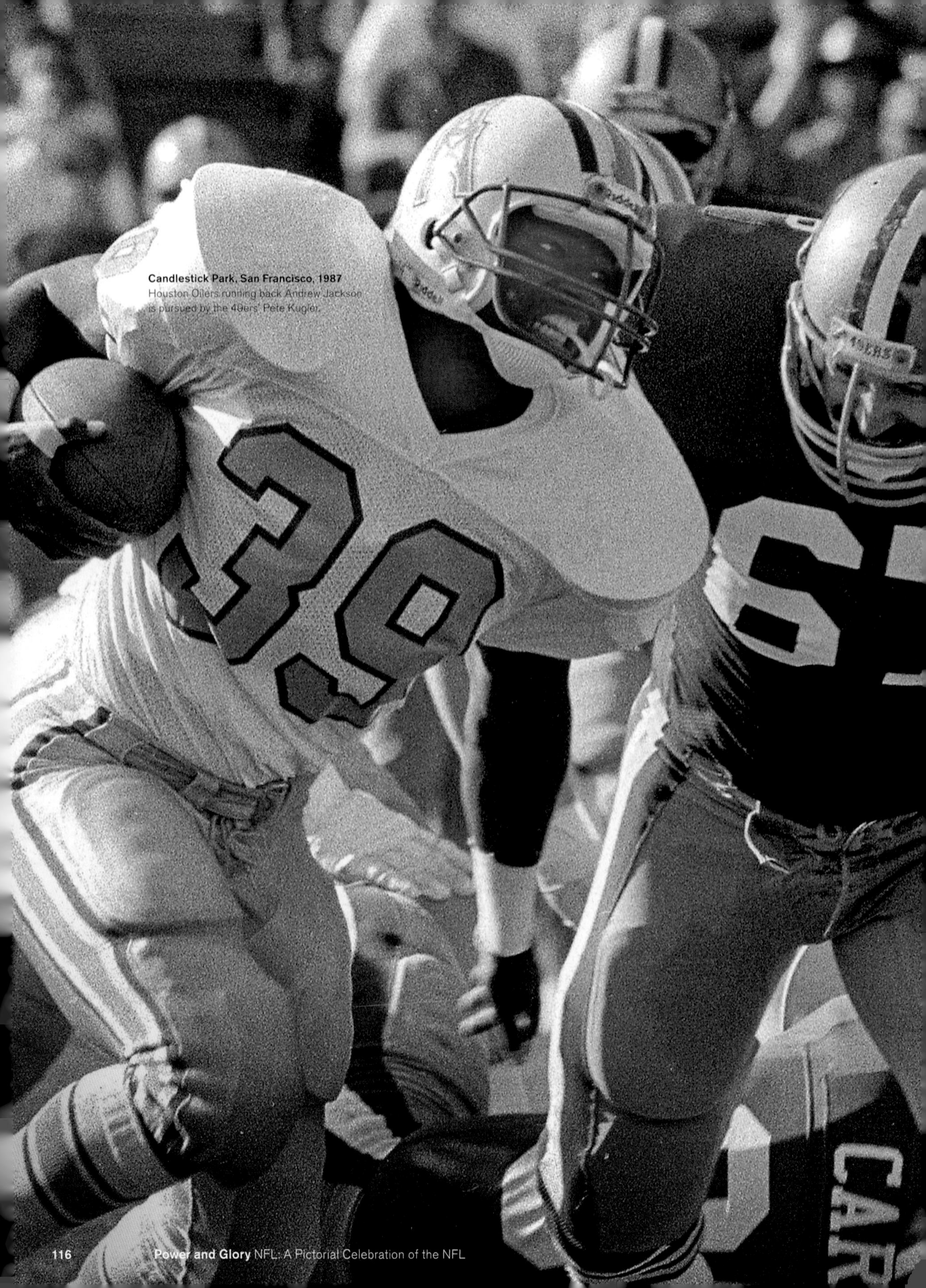

Candlestick Park, San Francisco, 1987
Houston Oilers running back Andrew Jackson is pursued by the 49ers' Pete Kugler.

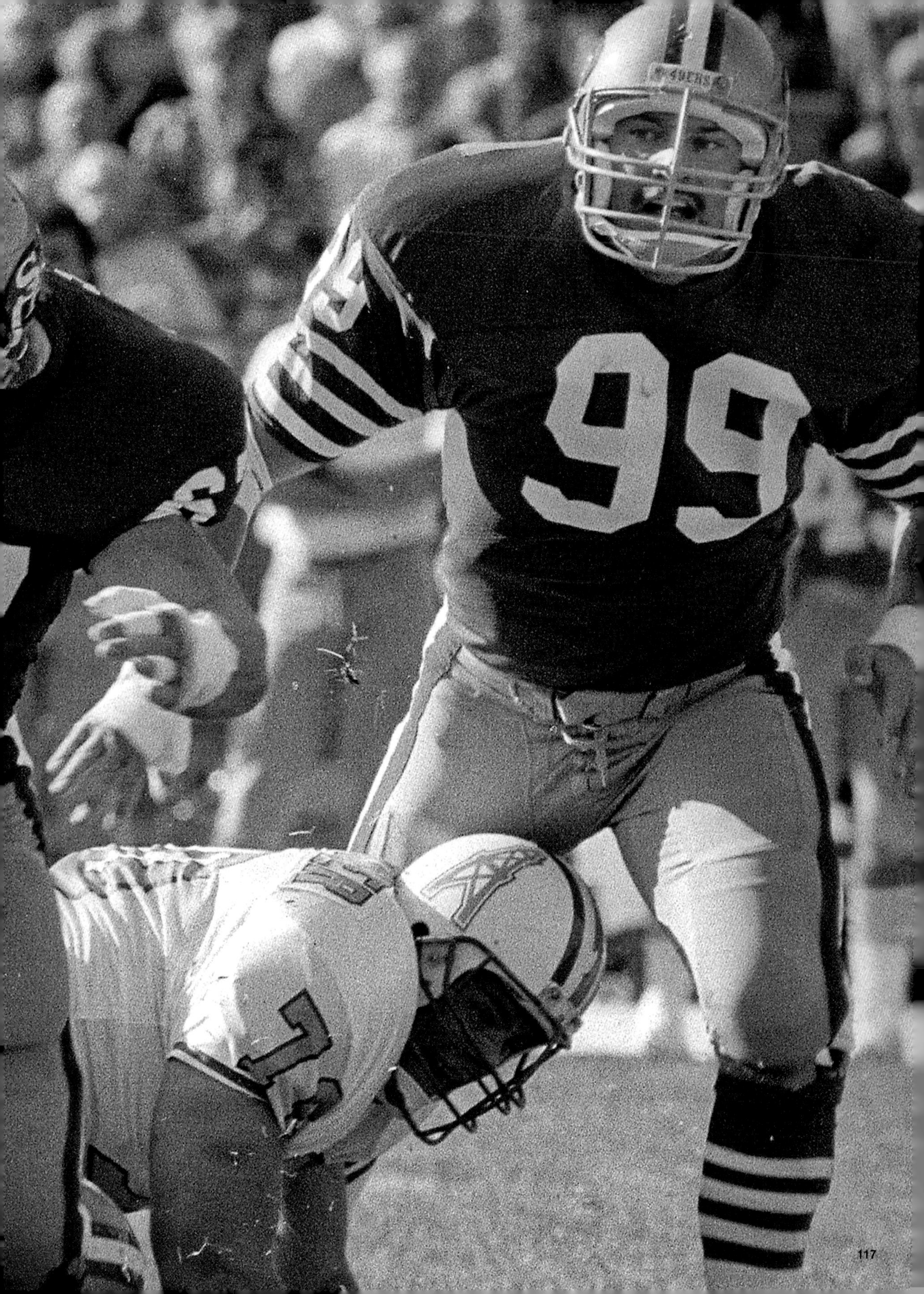

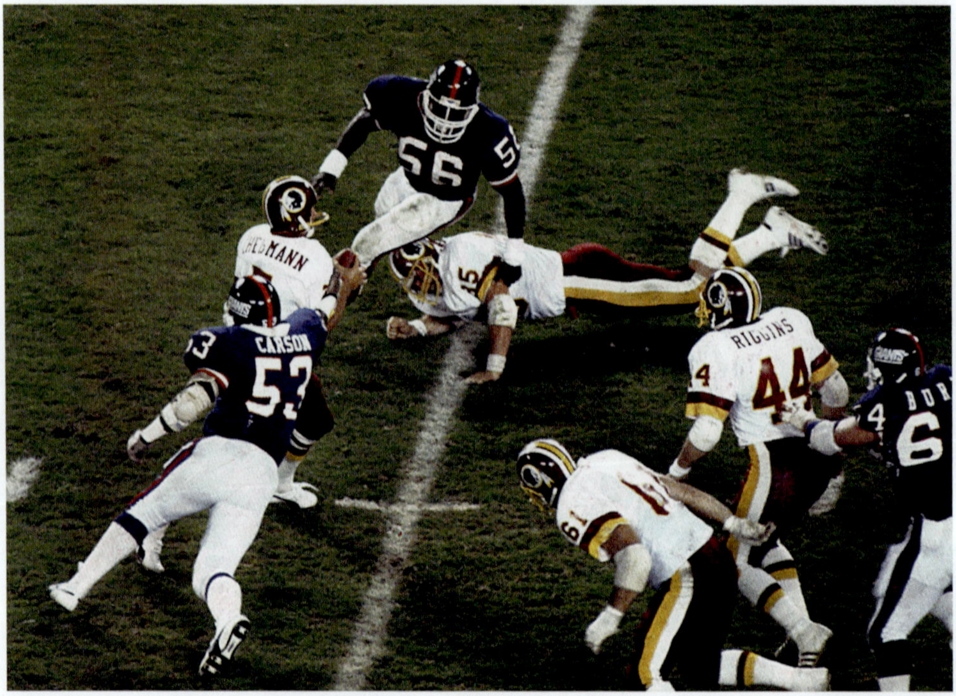

RFK Stadium, Washington DC, 1985
New York linebackers Lawrence Taylor (56) and Harry Carson (53) close in on Redskins quarterback Joe Theismann. The resulting impact broke Theismann's right leg and ended his career. The *Washington Post* described it as 'The hit that no one who saw it can ever forget.'

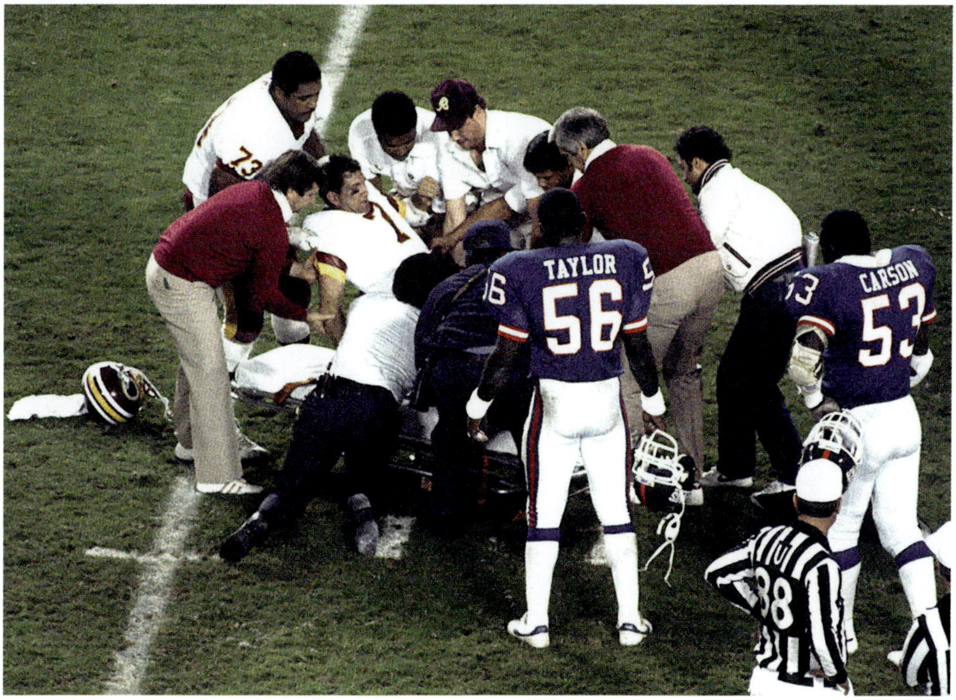
TAYLOR
56
CARSON
53

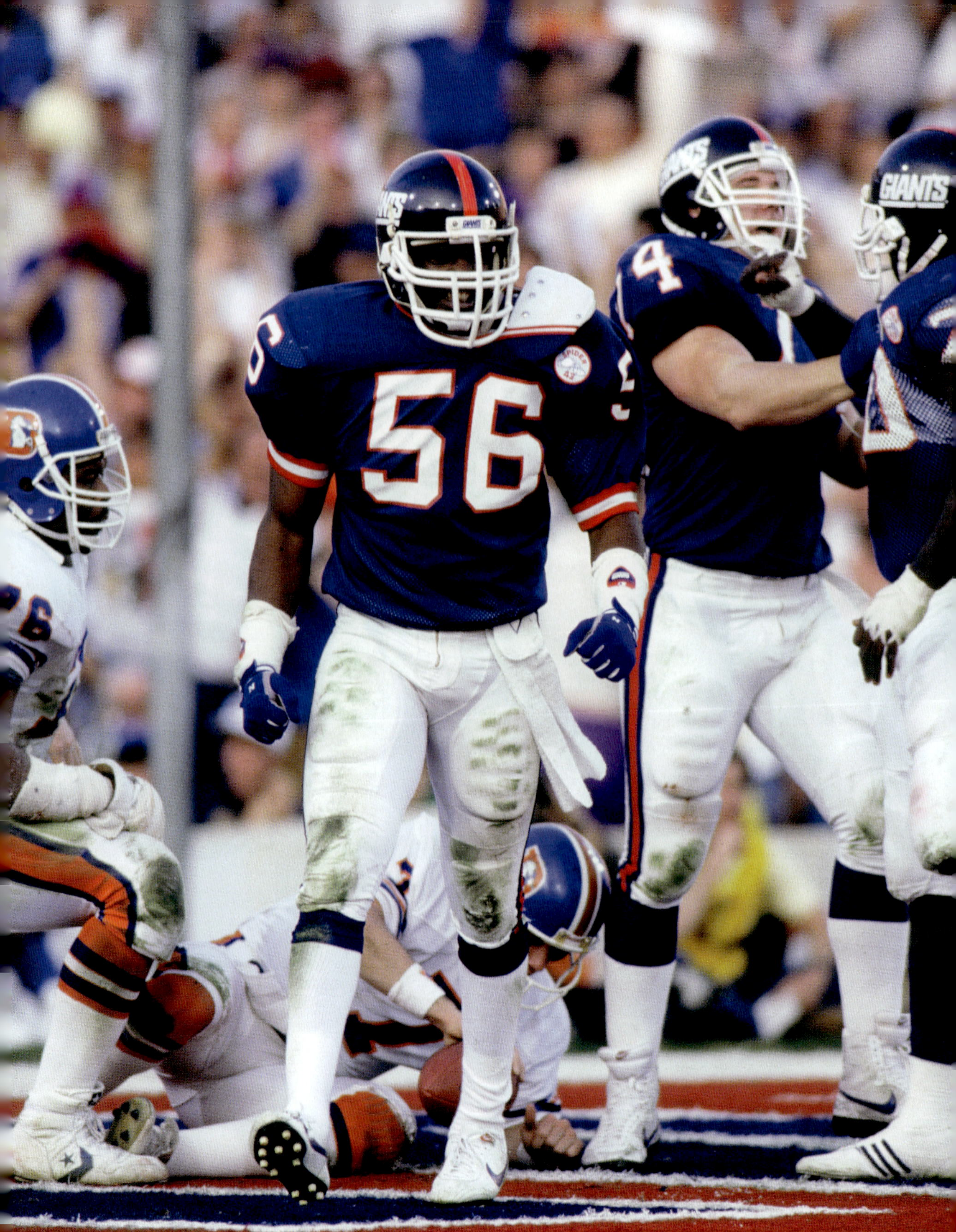
GIANTS
GIANTS
GIANTS
56

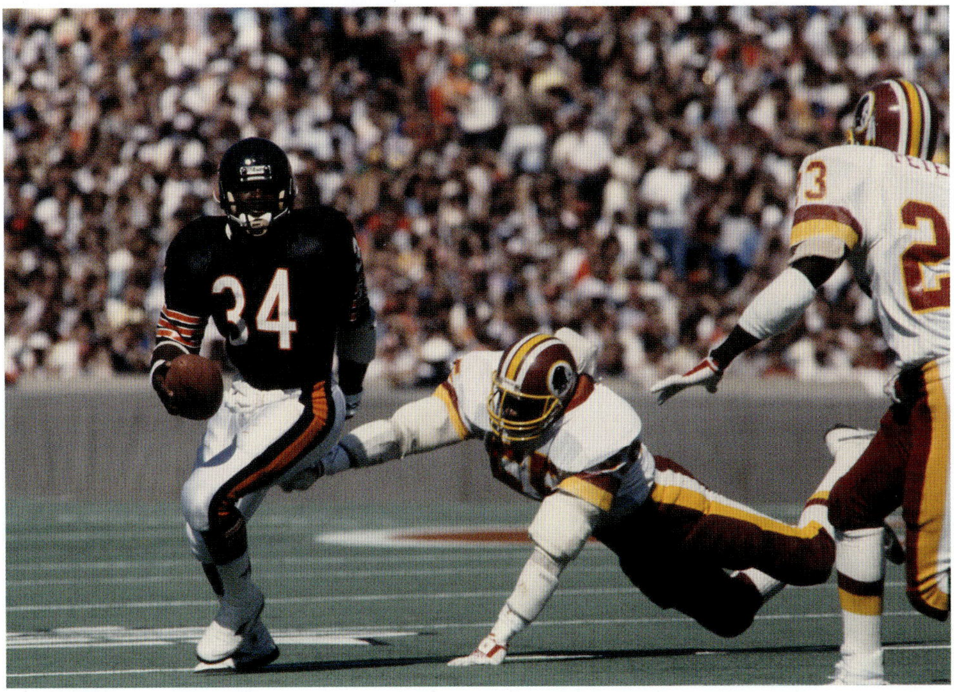

Rose Bowl, Pasadena, 1987
Super Bowl 21, Denver's John Elway is tackled in his own endzone resulting in a two-point safety for the Giants, as Lawrence Taylor (56) leads the celebrations.

Soldier Field, Chicago, 1985
The Bears' Walter Payton rushes with the ball in a regular season game against Washington, which Chicago won 45-10.

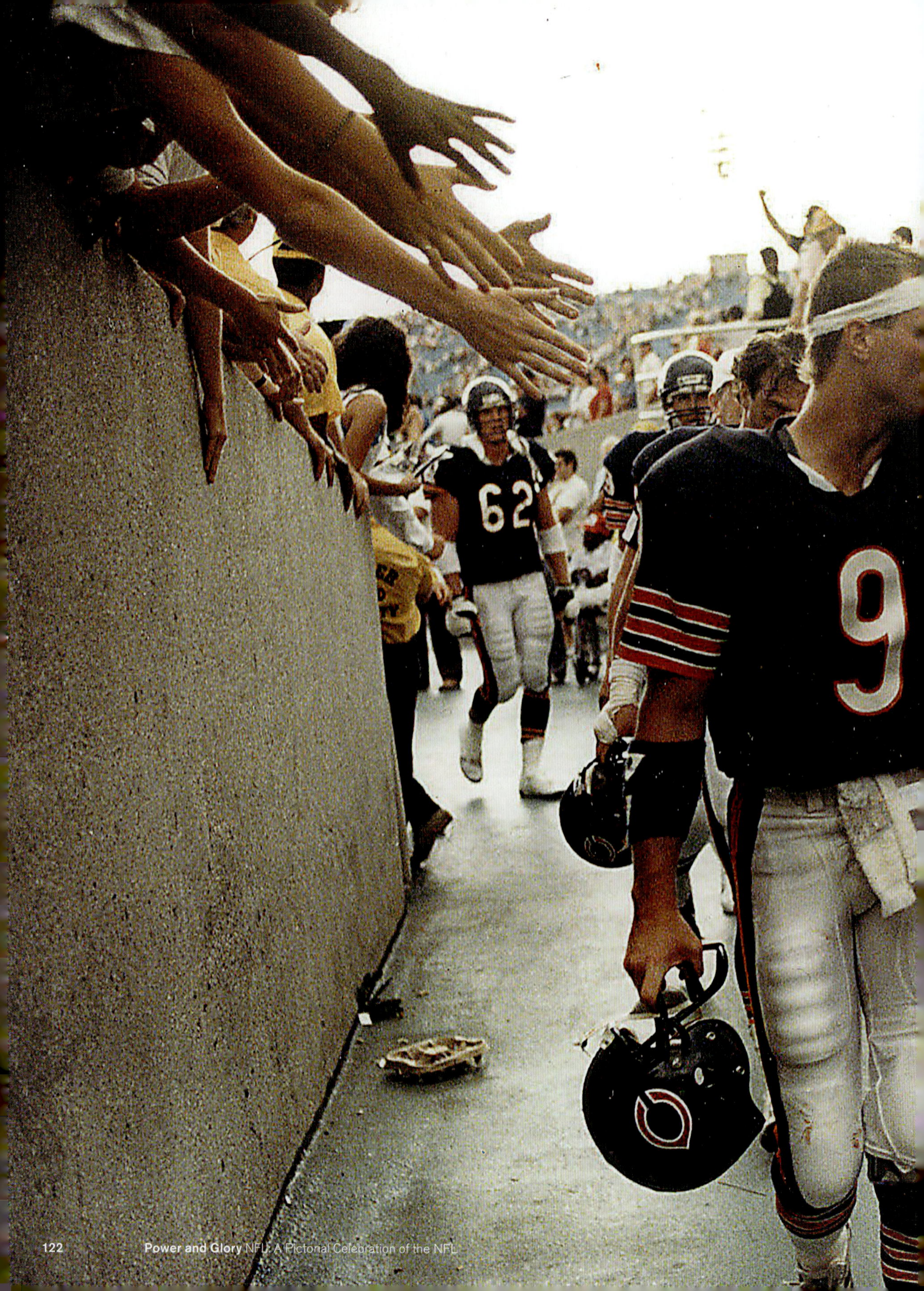
62
9

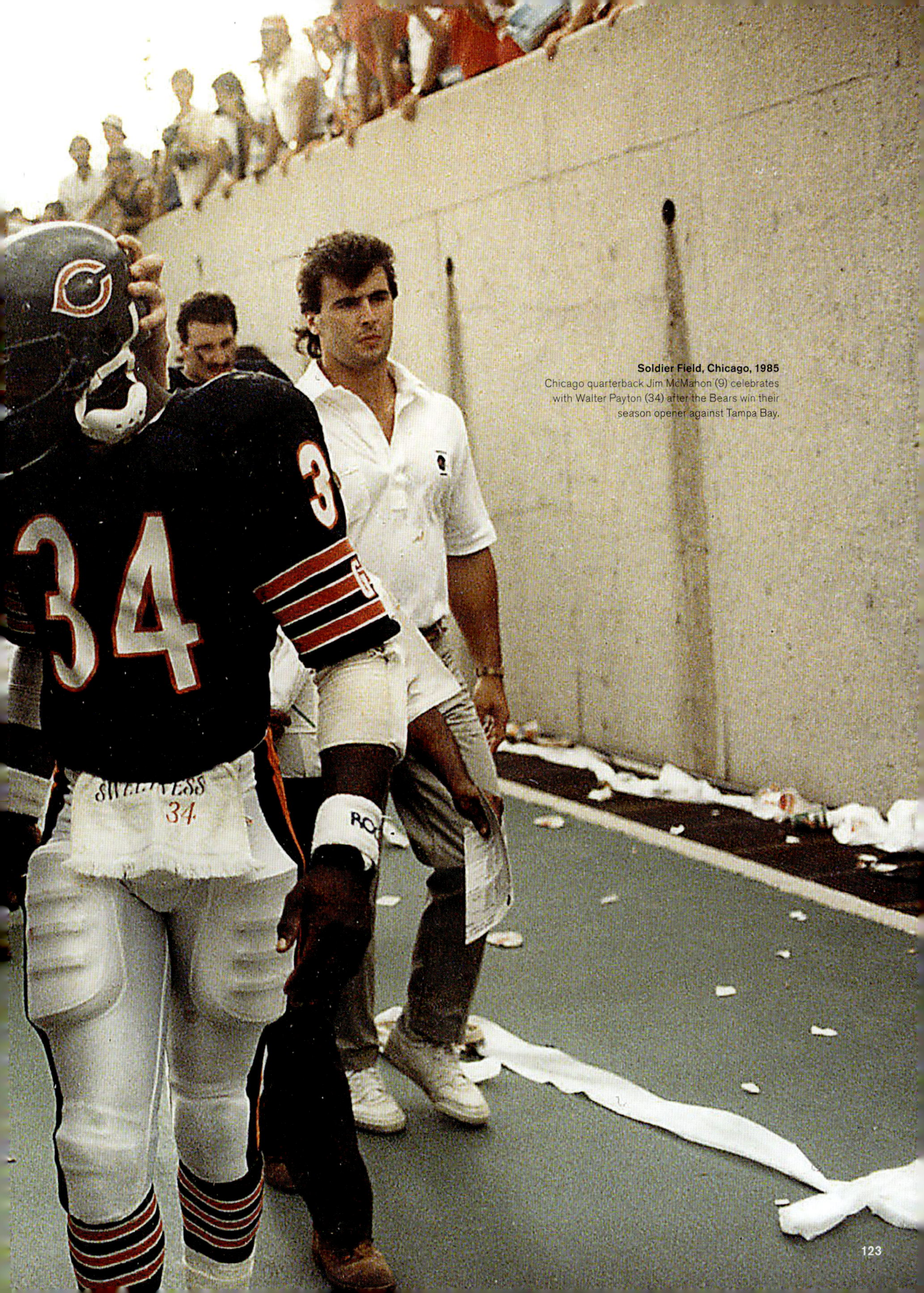

Soldier Field, Chicago, 1985
Chicago quarterback Jim McMahon (9) celebrates with Walter Payton (34) after the Bears win their season opener against Tampa Bay.

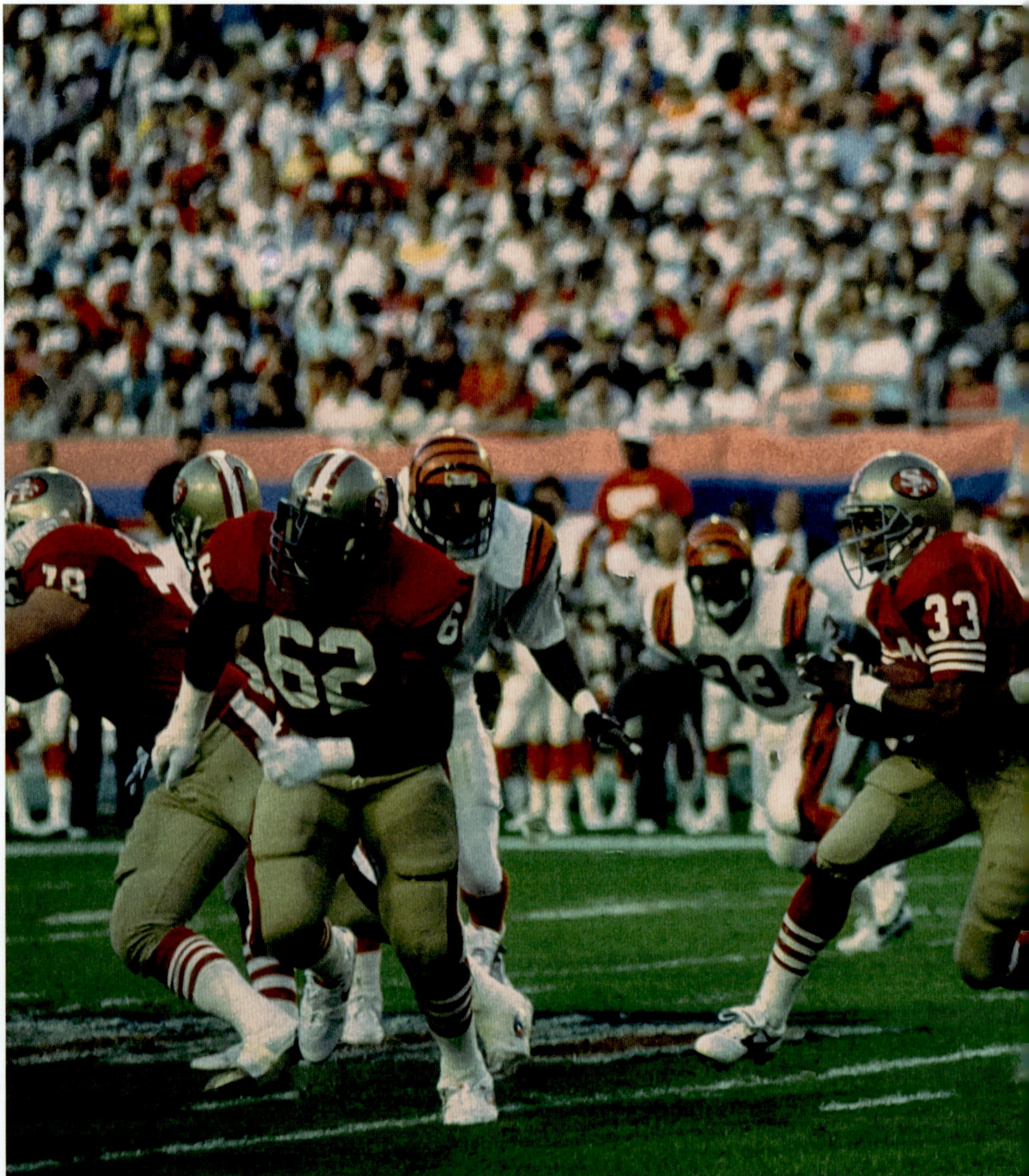

Joe Robbie Stadium, Florida, 1989
In Super Bowl 23, San Francisco quarterback Joe Montana (16) hands the ball off to Roger Craig (33) in a tight game against the Cincinnati Bengals which ended 20-16 to the 49ers.

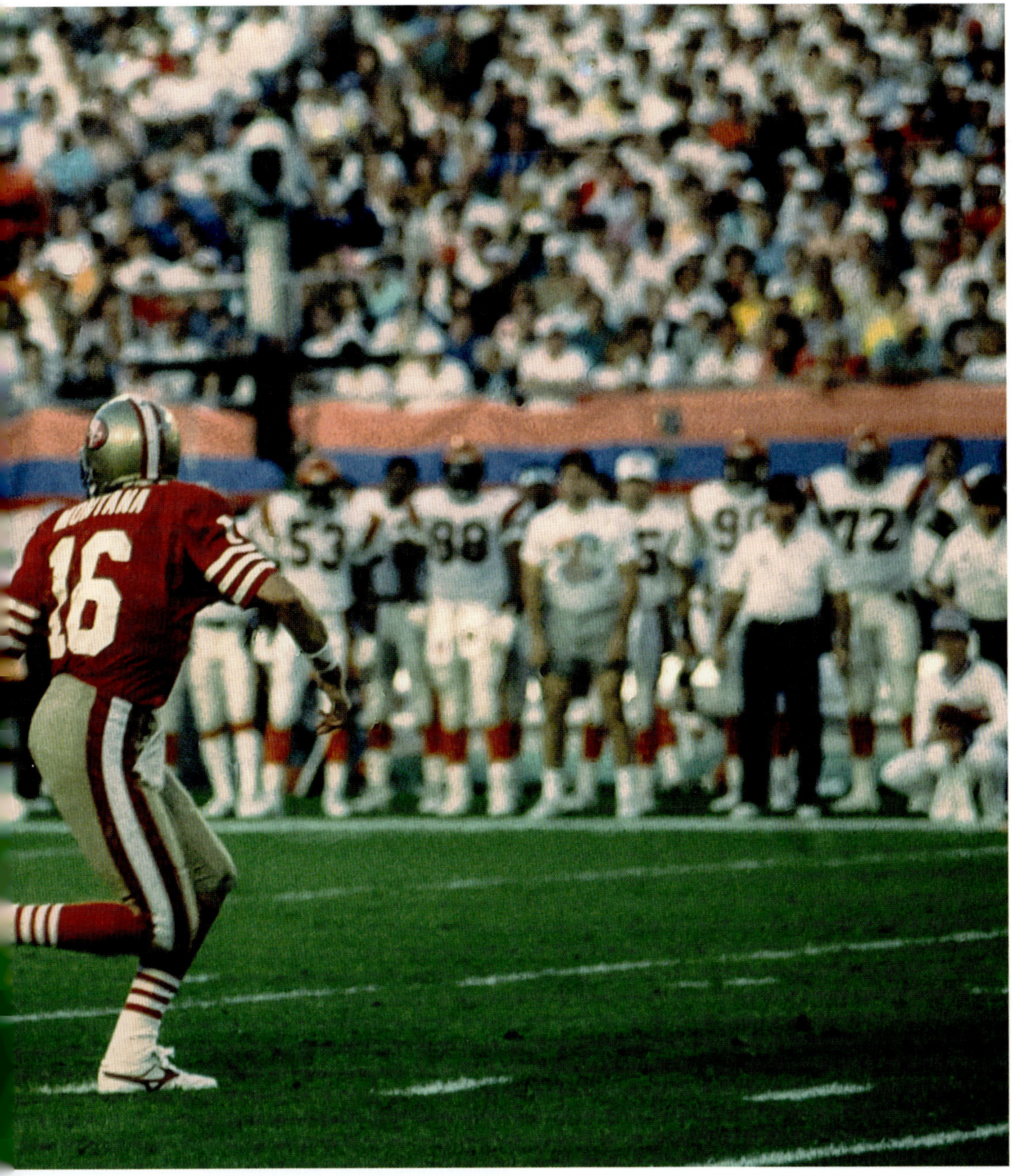
MONTANA
16
53
88
72

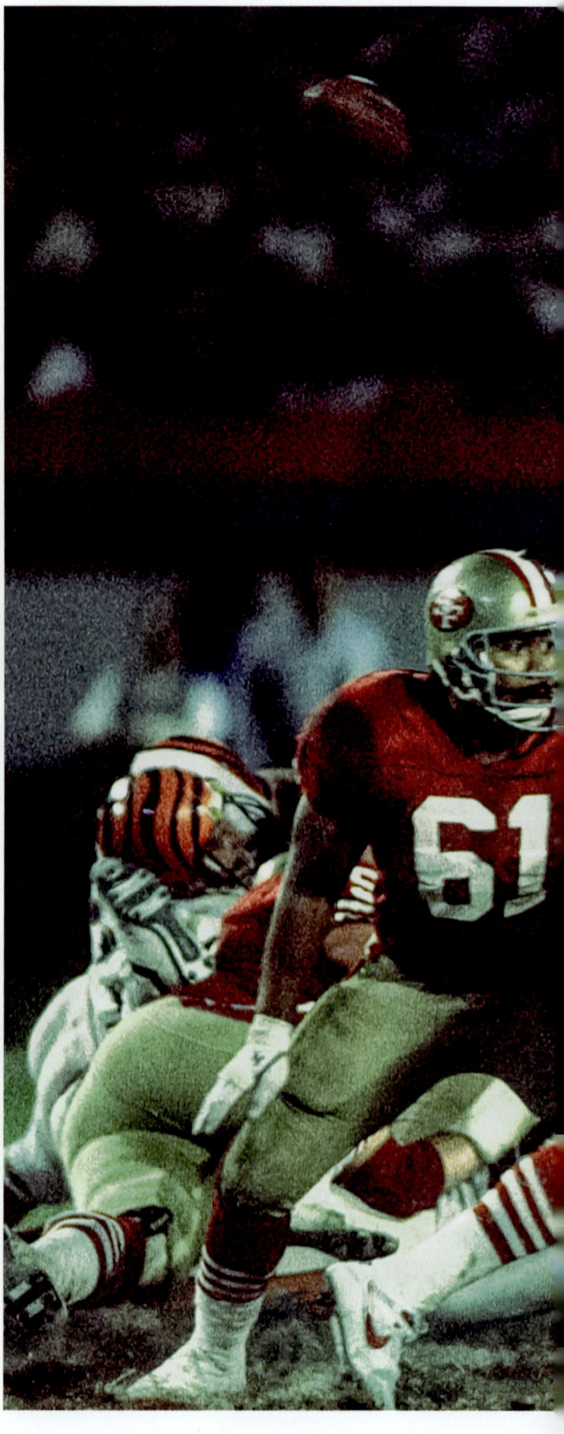

Joe Robbie Stadium, Florida, 1989
In Super Bowl 23, Joe Montana launches a pass, before the rush of the Bengals defence can stop him.

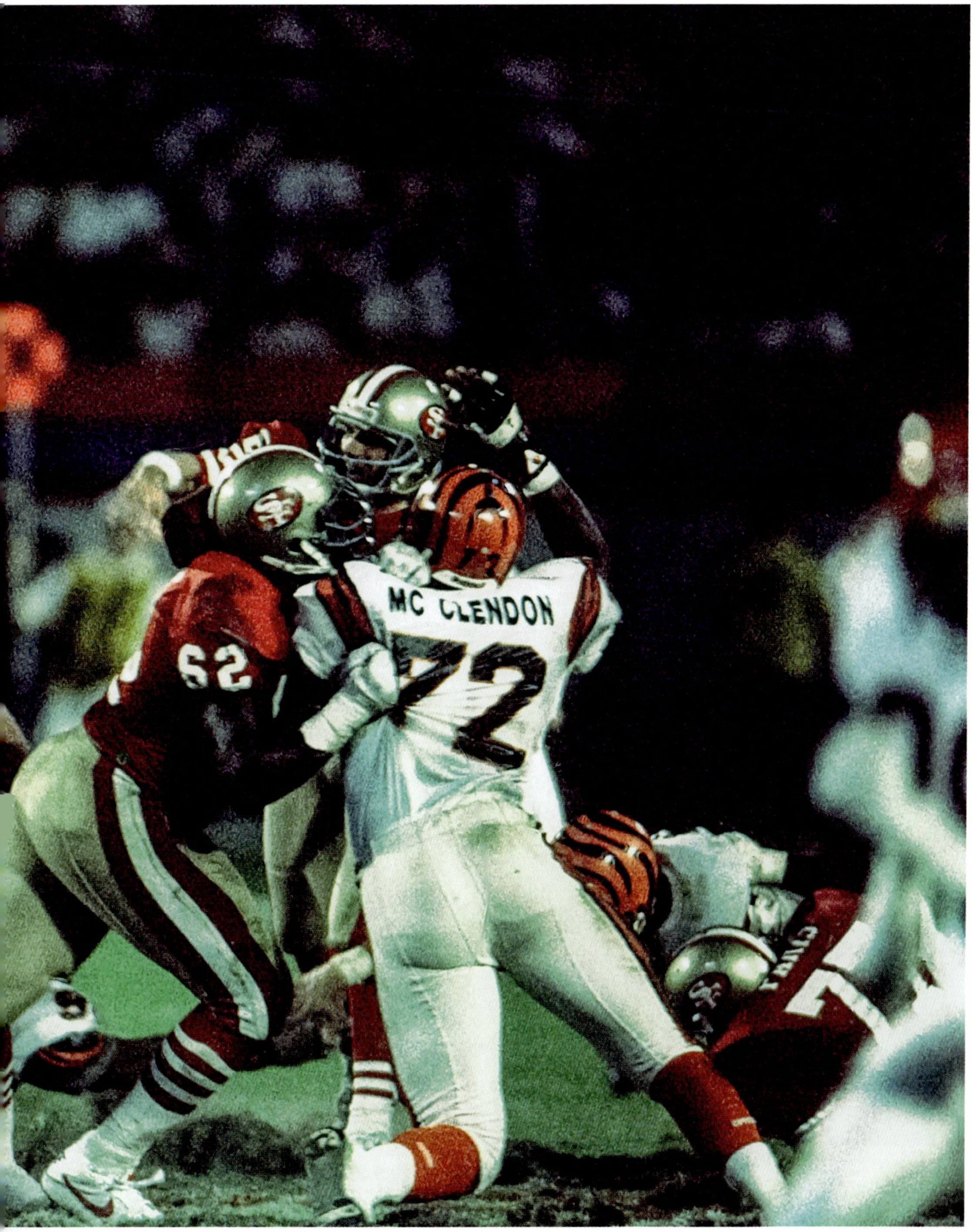
MC CLENDON
72
62

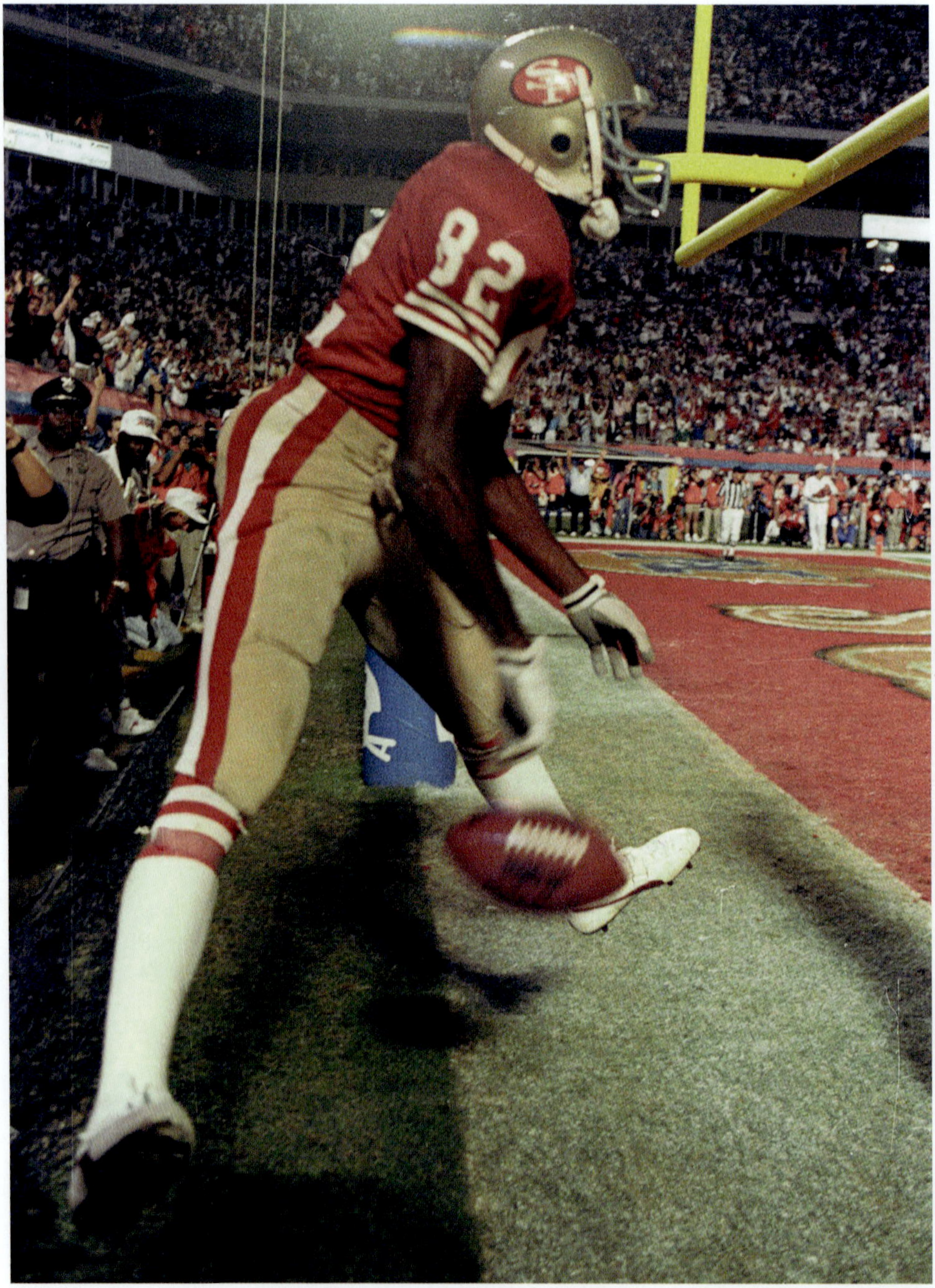

Joe Robbie Stadium, Florida, 1989
In Super Bowl 23, wide receiver Jon Taylor celebrates scoring the winning touchdown in the dying moments against Cincinnati.

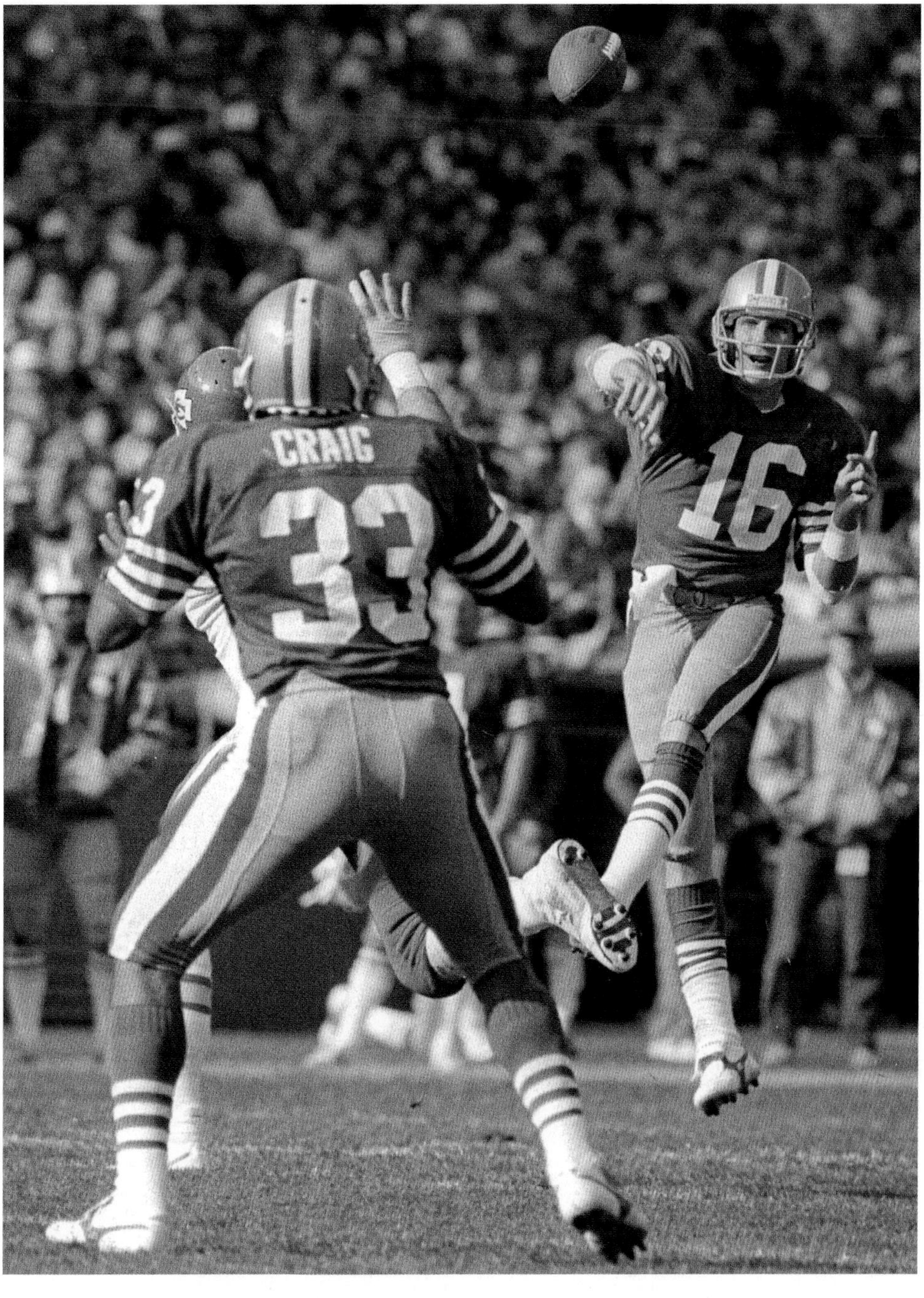

Candlestick Park, San Francisco, 1985
Joe Montana launches a pass to running back Roger Craig.

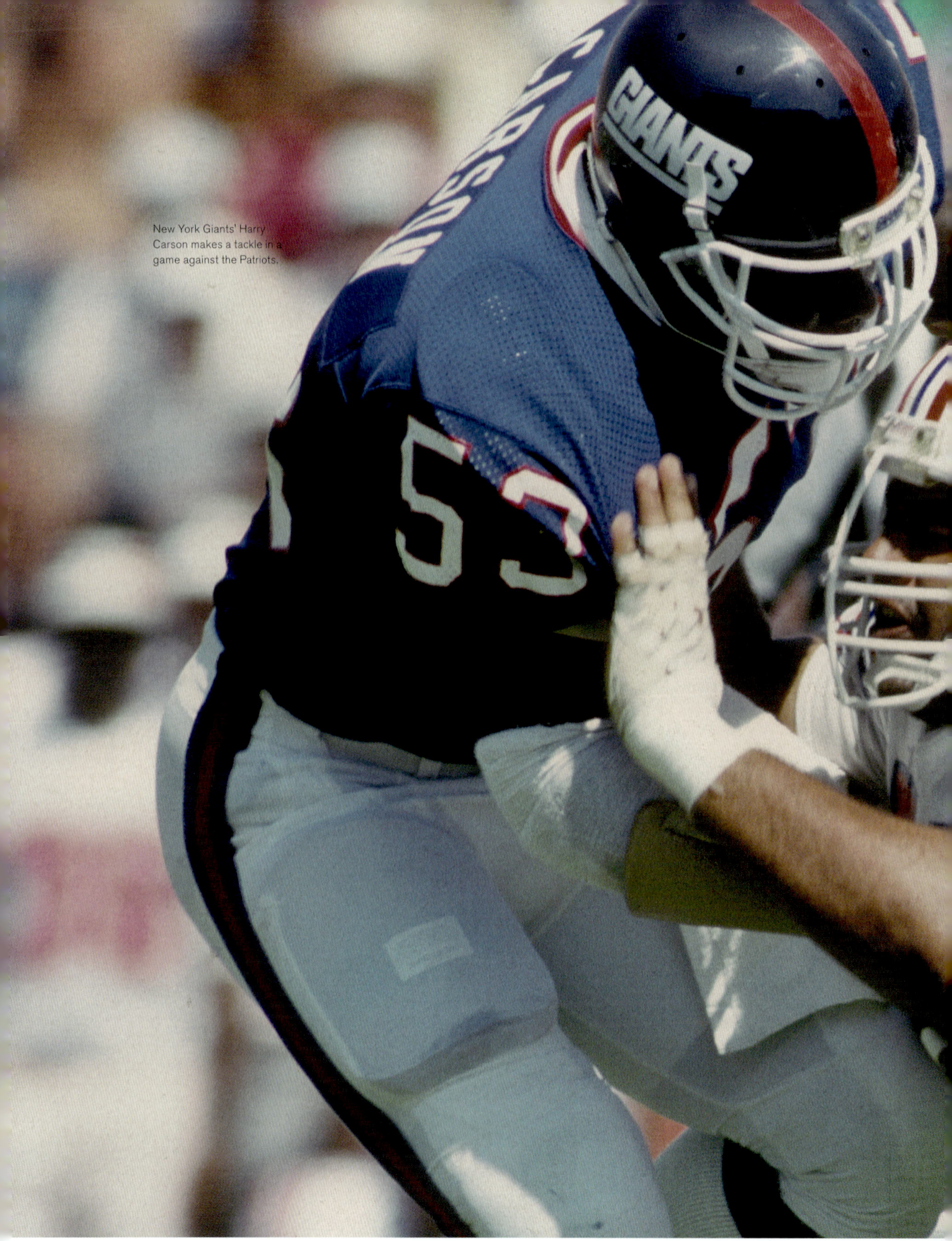

New York Giants' Harry Carson makes a tackle in a game against the Patriots.

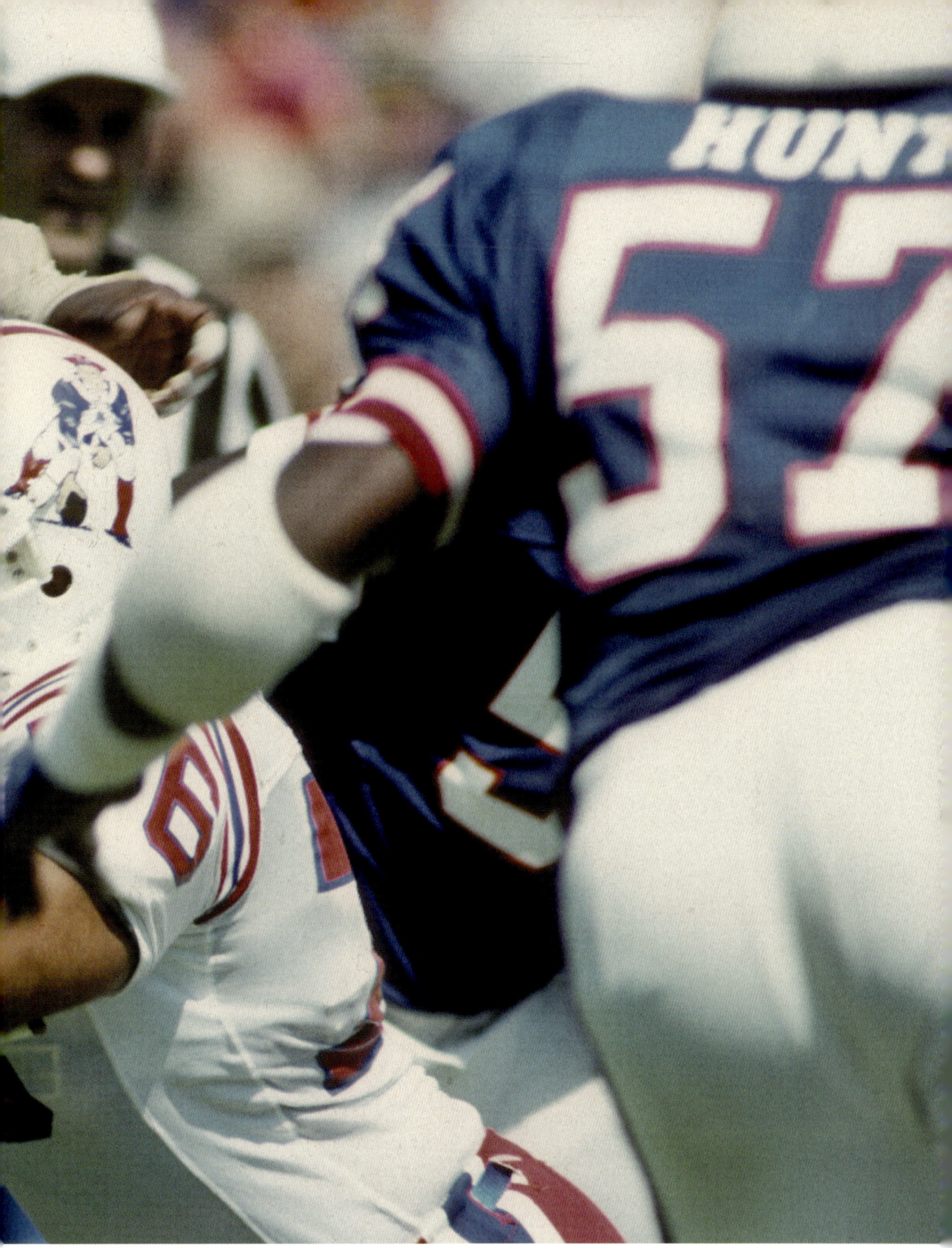
HUNT

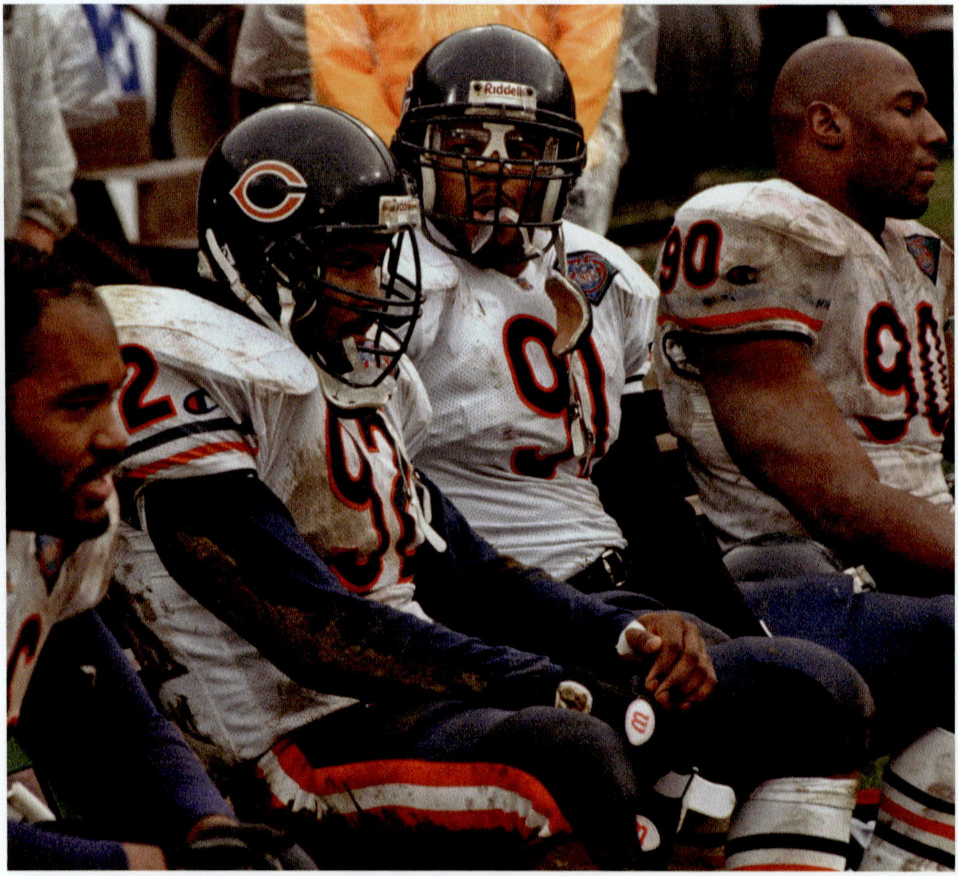

Candlestick Park, San Francisco, 1995
The Chicago bench take a breather. From left to right are Albert Fontenot, Barry Mitner, Myron Baker, and Alonzo Spellman.

Lambeau Field, Green Bay, 1998
Tennessee Oilers running back Eddie George makes no gain against the Green Bay Packers defence.

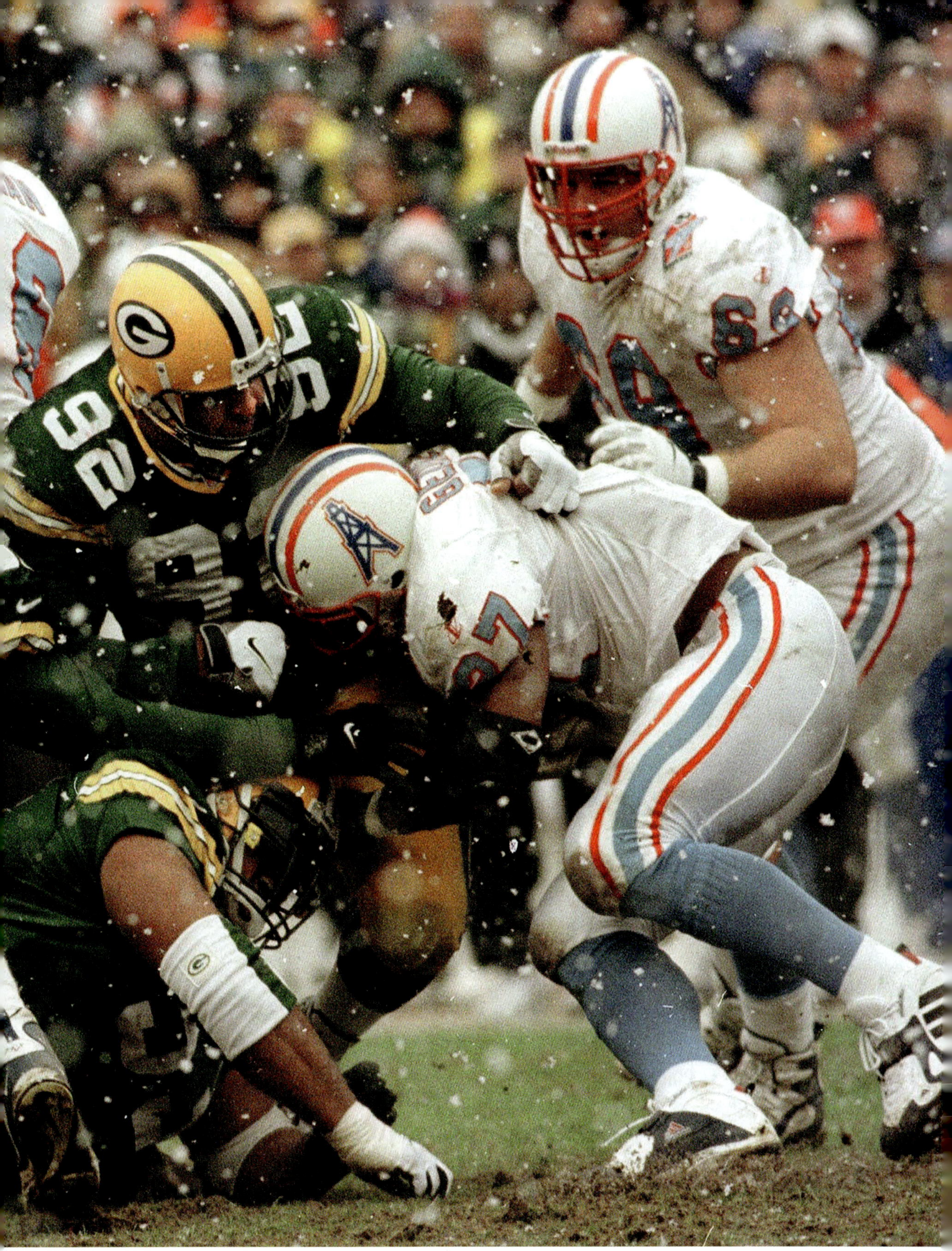

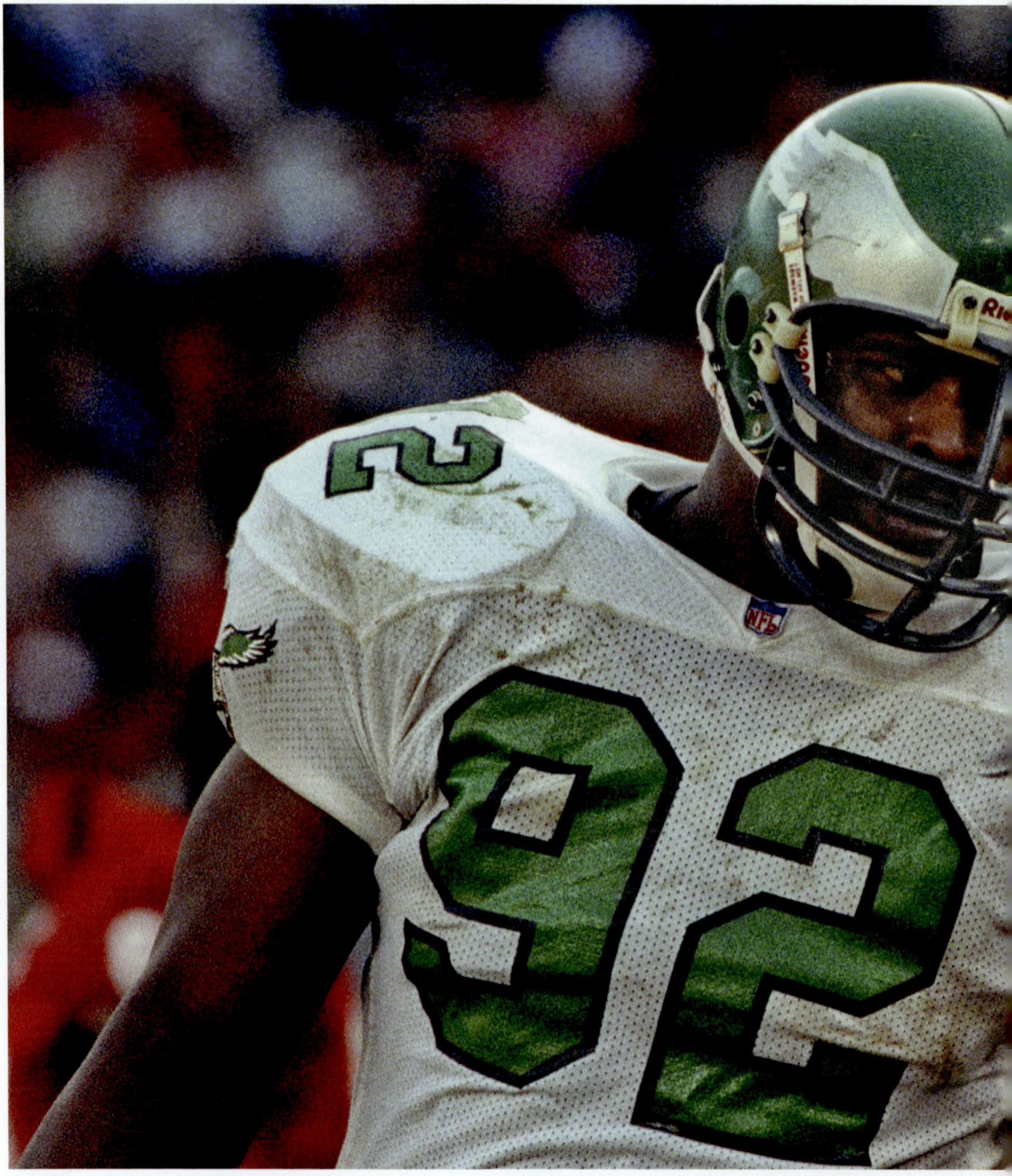

Candlestick Park, San Francisco, 1992
One of the last things that any quarterback wants is to be face to face with Philadelphia's Reggie White. The defensive end was a quarterback wrecking machine and sack specialist and here looks to be sending a warning to 49ers quarterback Steve Young.

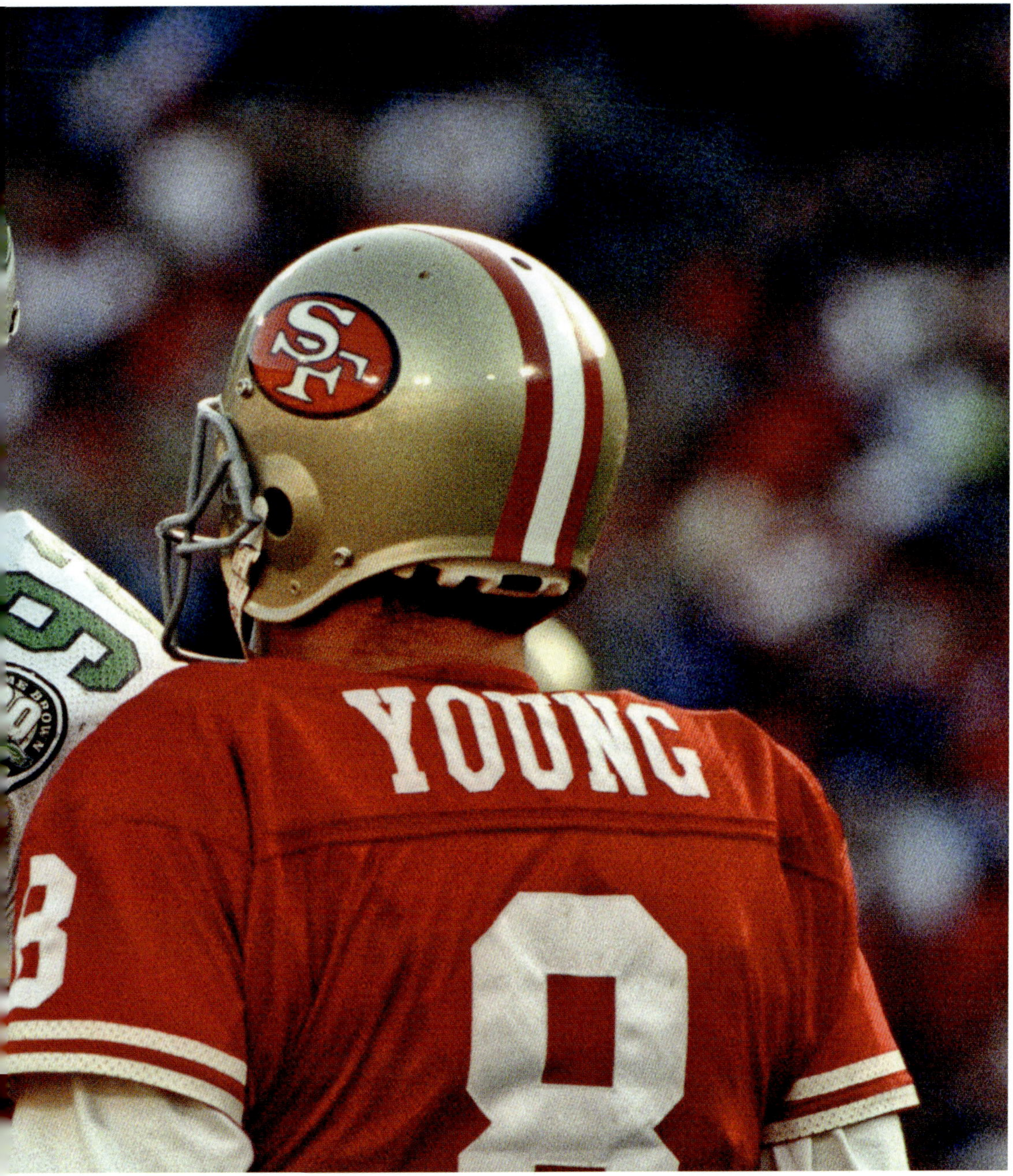
YOUNG

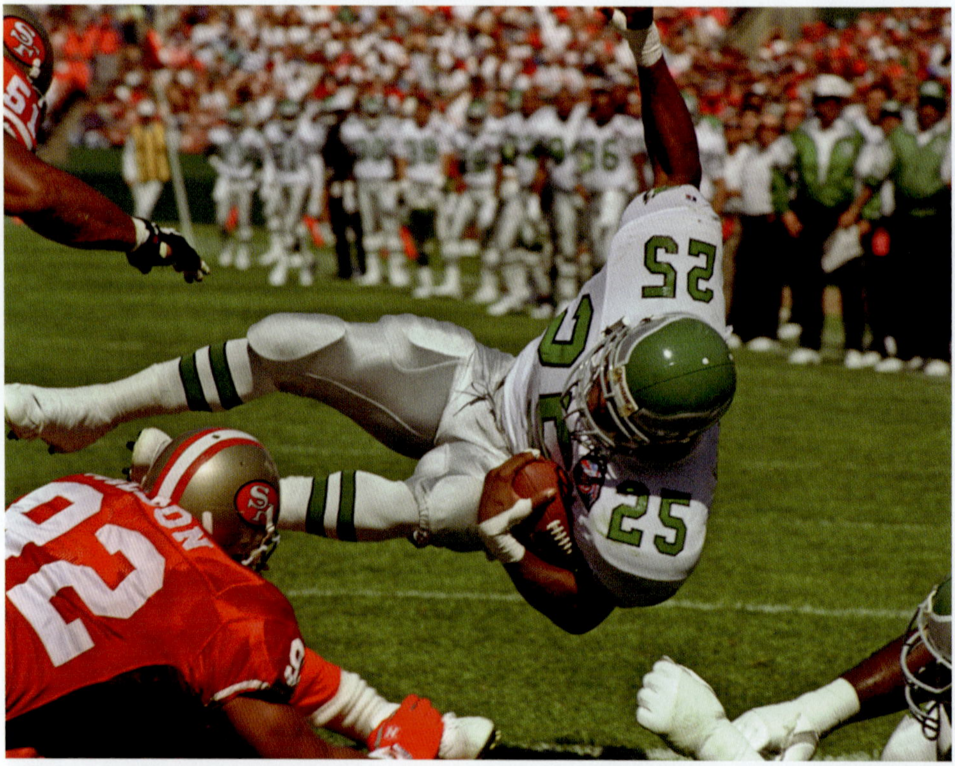

Candlestick Park, San Francisco, 1994
Philadelphia running back Charlie Garner attacks the 49ers defence during a 40-8 Eagles road win.

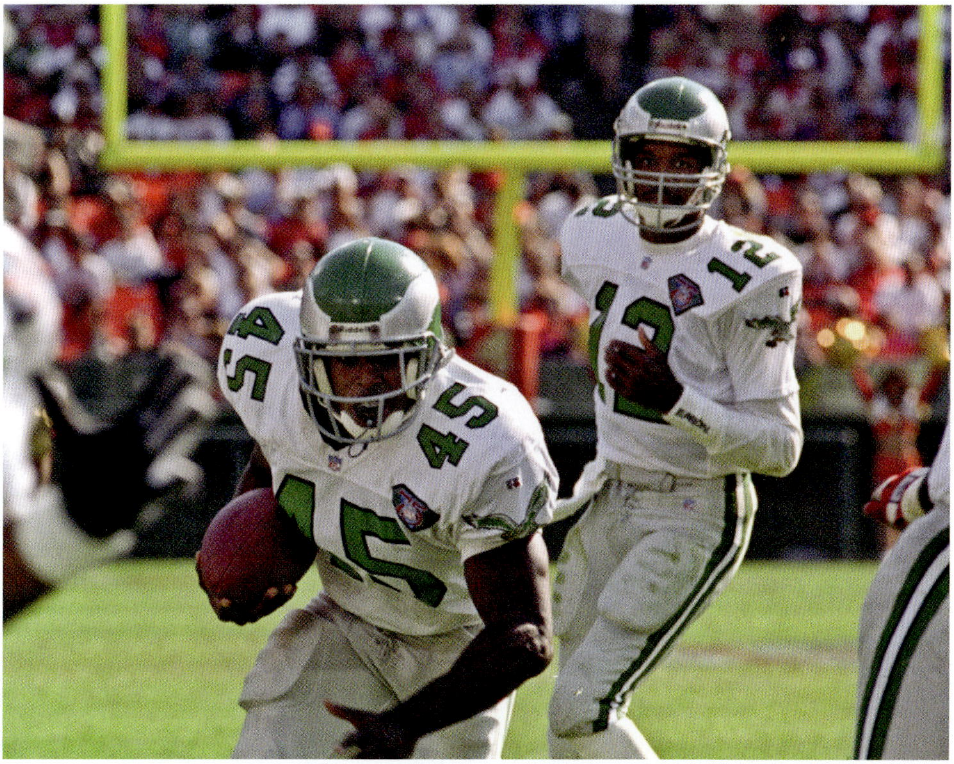

Candlestick Park, San Francisco, 1994
In the same game, Vaughn Hebron rushes with the ball, as quarterback Randall Cunningham looks on.

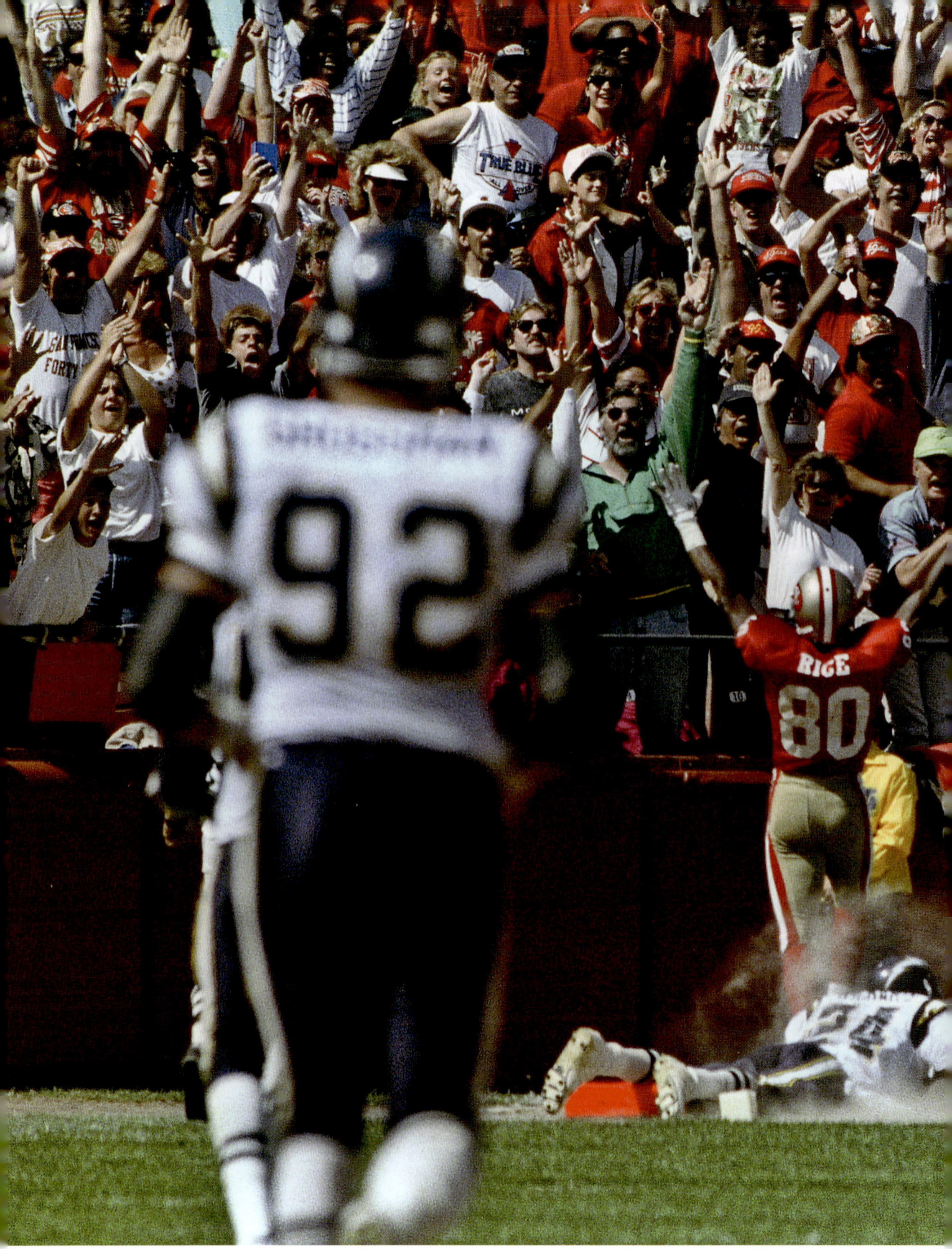
92
RICE
80

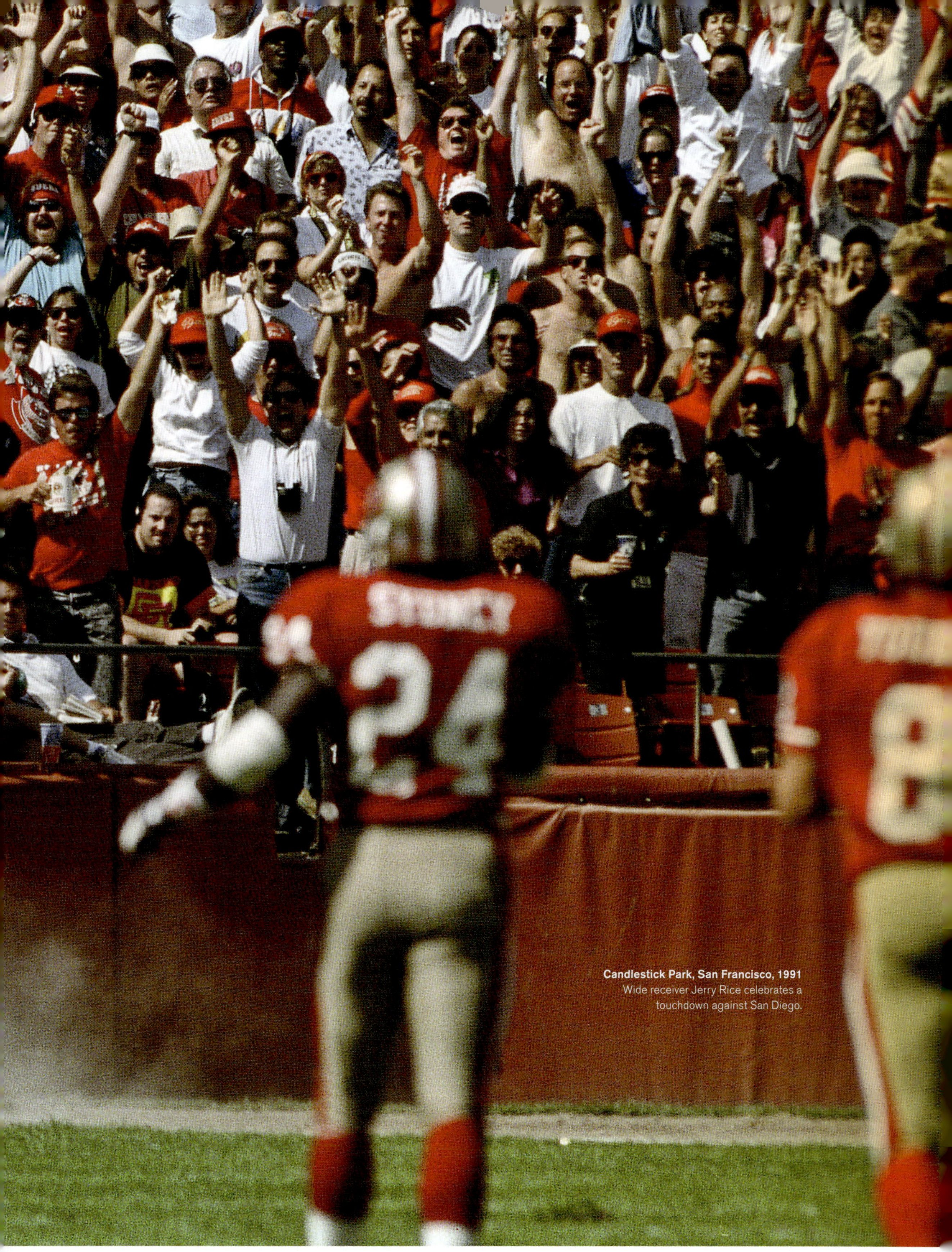

Candlestick Park, San Francisco, 1991
Wide receiver Jerry Rice celebrates a touchdown against San Diego.

Chicago Bears: Est. 1920

Former names: Decatur Stanleys (1920); Chicago Stanleys (1921)

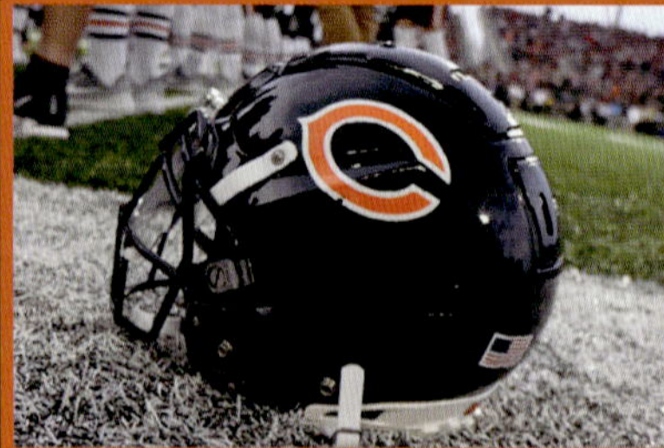

NFL Championships pre-1970 merger: (8) 1921, 1932, 1933, 1940, 1941, 1943, 1946, 1963

NFC Central Champions: (7) 1984, 1985, 1986, 1987, 1988, 1990, 2001

NFC North Champions: (4) 2005, 2006, 2010, 2018

NFC Conference Champions: (2) 1985, 2006

Super Bowl titles: (1) 1985

Super Bowl record: 1-1

The Bears' rivalry with the Green Bay Packers is perhaps the most notable in the NFL, given the longevity of the feud, and the fact that both teams were the standard-bearer for success in the NFL's early years. As recognition of this great rivalry, in 2019, the season that marked 100 years of the league, the NFL broke with their tradition of having the first game of the season feature the defending Super Bowl champions and instead scheduled the Bears to play the Packers, a statement saying this is the most significant fixture over the NFL's 100-year history.

A rivalry that has petered out in significance is the Bears versus the Cardinals, but when both teams were based in the same city it was known as the 'Battle of Chicago'. In the 1930s both teams played at the same stadium, Wrigley Field, home of baseball's Chicago Cubs (who inspired the name of the Bears), and both are the only two teams left in the league who have been ever present in the NFL since the first season in 1920 (when the NFL was known as the APFA). The Cardinals would move out of Chicago in 1959 and the Bears moved into Soldier Field in 1971; their current home and a stadium that is the oldest in the NFL and has been operational for various teams since 1924.

The Bears have won more NFL matches than any other team, including the biggest margin of all time when they thrashed the Redskins 73-0 in the 1940 NFL Championship game; they have more Hall of Fame players than any other team. However, despite past glories they could do with something to shout about in the modern era. Pre the 1970 NFL merger this was a team that, with the exception of Green Bay, had won more NFL Championships than anyone else; but after 56 Super Bowls the Bears have only two appearances to their name and the one win. However, the season they did win the Super Bowl, they did so with one of the sport's most celebrated teams and one that has five Hall of Fame players in Walter Payton, Jim Covert, Mike Singletary, Richard Dent, and Dan Hampton. The 1985 Bears even had their own hit single called 'The Super Bowl Shuffle' which got nominated for a Grammy in the R&B category. On the field, where things really counted, the team had registered a 15-1 record in the regular season with an overall points margin of 456-198. Led by coach Mike Ditka the defence was formidable and had not conceded one single point in the play-offs, beating the Giants 21-0 and the Rams 24-0. In the Super Bowl, the Patriots would manage to get on the scoresheet but were obliterated 46-10 as the Bears finally broke their duck, and won their first NFL Championship since 1963.

In the UK, American football was becoming big at the same time the Bears won Super Bowl 20, and so they acquired a huge British fanbase that has been evident on the two occasions Chicago have played in the International Series in London. The name William 'The Refrigerator' Perry became a household name and the huge defensive tackle even played occasionally in offence, helping out running back Walter Payton as well as scoring some touchdowns of his own. Perry's most famous touchdown came in Super Bowl 20. The Bears are all about history and as he charged through to the Patriots' endzone the commentator said, 'Another Super Bowl record, the first refrigerator to score.'

Detroit Lions: Est. 1930

Former names: Portsmouth Spartans (1930–1933)

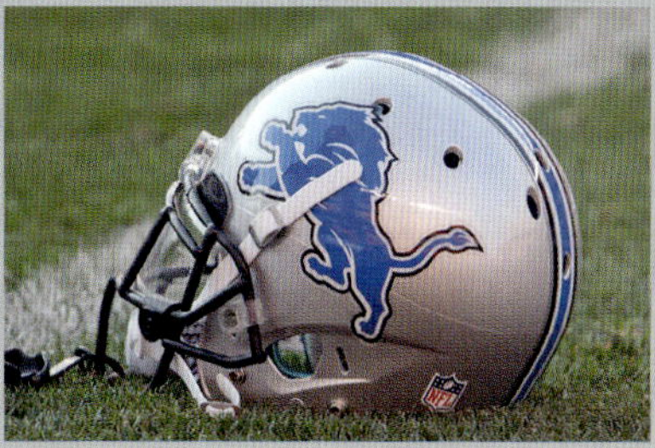

NFL Championships pre-1970 merger: (4) 1935, 1952, 1953, 1957

NFC Central Champions: (3) 1983, 1991, 1993

Super Bowl record: 0-0

With no Super Bowl appearance, no NFC North title, and only 12 post-seasons since the 1970 NFL/AFL merger, nobody can ever accuse a Detroit Lions fan of being a glory hunter. Things started off fairly well, and after only five years the Lions were NFL champions after beating the New York Giants in the 1935 Championship game. At this time they had been in Detroit for just two years, after starting out in the little city of Portsmouth, Ohio. Detroit's baseball team were called the Tigers so the football team became Lions.

The golden era was in the 1950s when the team brought home three NFL Championships to Motor City. Their quarterback for all three championships won during the 1950s was Bobby Layne, though he was injured for the final games of the 1957 season. He was traded to Pittsburgh in 1958, and in what became known as 'the curse of Bobby Layne' it was claimed that he said the Lions would not win again for 50 years; though many question whether Layne actually said this, as it wasn't published at the time, and is something that probably became an urban myth as Detroit struggled in the years ahead.

The closest the Lions have come to the Super Bowl was in the 1991 season when they made their sole appearance in the NFC Championship game. To get there they did something they have only ever done once in post-1970 NFL/AFL merger history which was to win a play-off game. They beat Dallas 38-6 in the divisional play-off, although in the NFC Conference Championship game they would lose 41-10 to Washington. The 1990s saw Detroit make it to six post-seasons, but since the start of the new century they have only been to the play-offs three times.

Two things are guaranteed on Thanksgiving: turkey, and the Detroit Lions playing at home. On every Thanksgiving the team in blue and silver will be on at midday to play a divisional rival, as 'America the Beautiful' gets sung before kick-off. It's one of the most unique traditions in sport and first started in 1934. Owner George A. Richards had links to radio networks and so 94 stations affiliated to NBC broadcast the game, which brought in much-needed revenue to the Lions who were only a few years old, struggling to attract fans, and losing money. Since 1934 the only time that the Lions have not played on Thanksgiving was during the Second World War, and their overall record is 37-43-2, with the Green Bay Packers the team they have played the most Thanksgiving fixtures against.

One of the most unusual incidents in the NFL happened during a Lions home game in 1997 and highlights the change of social demographic among the fans, as the league has become more corporate in recent years. Fans still make noise today, but in the Pontiac Silverdome in 1997 the crowd were so loud and energised that they got told off by the match official! The New York Jets were on first down and took a time-out because they couldn't communicate due to the noise (which is the very point of home advantage). When the game resumed the official stopped play before the Jets made a snap and warned the Detroit fans, 'We need quiet so that we can get a play.' That didn't work! The fans booed even louder, and so the referee warned the fans that their team would be charged with a time-out if they didn't quieten down. This bizarre incident can be viewed on YouTube and in the comments section one person simply says, 'I still can't believe this actually happened. And it would only happen to the Lions too!'

Green Bay Packers: Est. 1919

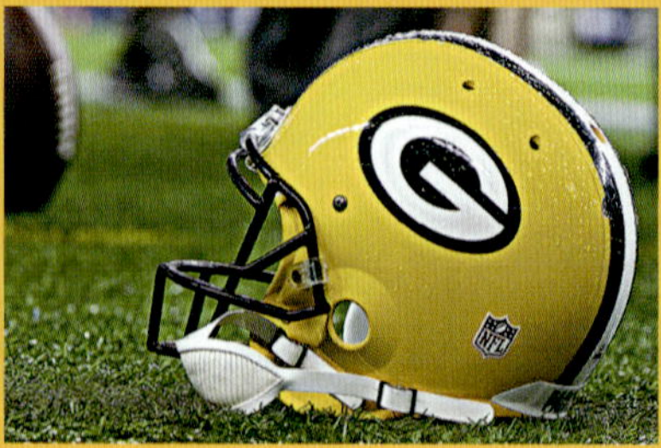

NFL Championships pre-1970 merger: (11) 1929, 1930, 1931, 1936, 1939, 1944, 1961, 1962, 1965, 1966, 1967

NFC Central Champions: (4) 1972, 1995, 1996, 1997

NFC North Champions: (12) 2002, 2003, 2004, 2007, 2011, 2012, 2013, 2014, 2016, 2019, 2020, 2021

NFC Conference Champions: (3) 1996, 1997, 2010

Super Bowl titles: (4) 1966, 1967, 1996, 2010

Super Bowl record: 4-1

At over 100 years of age, Green Bay are a contradiction to the NFL. In a league of big-city teams and billionaire owners, the Packers stand alone as a 'not-for-profit' club without a single owner, and the one team who are located in a small town. The Packers have more owners and members than Green Bay has in population; 361,300 fans have shares in the club, in a town that is home to 104,777 people, and one that gets freezing in winter. Despite this, the team in a little town in Wisconsin have built up a huge fanbase that stretches across America and beyond and they have won more NFL titles than any other team. With four Super Bowls to their name they have also won a further 11 NFL Championships in the days before the 1970 NFL/AFL merger.

The Packers' current home, Lambeau Field – opened in 1957 and the oldest continuously used NFL stadium – is named after Earl 'Curly' Lambeau who founded the club with George Whitney Calhoun. They received free kits and equipment from the Indian Packing Company, on the condition that the team was named after them; and the team's first nickname was the 'Indian Packers'.

By 1929 Green Bay were NFL champions for the first time, and would win a further eight titles before being part of the game that would change the American sporting landscape forever – Super Bowl 1. Coach Vince Lombardi saw his NFL team beat the AFL's Kansas City Chiefs 35-10 at the Los Angeles Memorial Coliseum in January 1967. A marching band and a trumpet player were the half-time show, and the average price of a ticket was $12. The NFL were relieved that the Packers won heavily as they were desperate to prove their league was far superior to the AFL. Lombardi's Packers were back the following year to face the Oakland Raiders and once again won heavily, 33-14. In the following two Super Bowls the AFL teams won and so Green Bay would remain the only NFL team that reigned superior over the AFL. Due to these two wins, they will always have an association with any Super Bowl played as the current trophy is named after Vince Lombardi, who died in 1970 aged 57.

The 1970s and 1980s saw Green Bay get to the play-offs just twice. In the 1990s quarterback Brett Favre came on to the scene, and after a difficult start in the 1992 season he battled adversity and cemented his place as the starting quarterback. By the 1996 season he was a Super Bowl winner as Green Bay beat New England 35-21 for their first championship since 1967.

While Favre was still a starter, the Packers acquired a young quarterback called Aaron Rodgers in one of the most bizarre NFL drafts. Rodgers was the number one draft pick in 2005 and was expected to go to San Francisco, yet the 49ers turned him down as did a whole host of other teams. Eventually Green Bay picked him and, in the years to follow Rodgers produced a standard of performance that has led him to being in the conversation as one of the greatest quarterbacks to have ever played the game; his crowning moment coming in Super Bowl 45 with a 31-25 win over the Pittsburgh Steelers. Rodgers and Green Bay are desperate for one more Super Bowl glory; for Rodgers the two rings will seal his legacy, and for the team as a whole they would have equalled the same amount of wins that their NFC rivals Dallas and San Francisco have.

Minnesota Vikings: Est. 1960

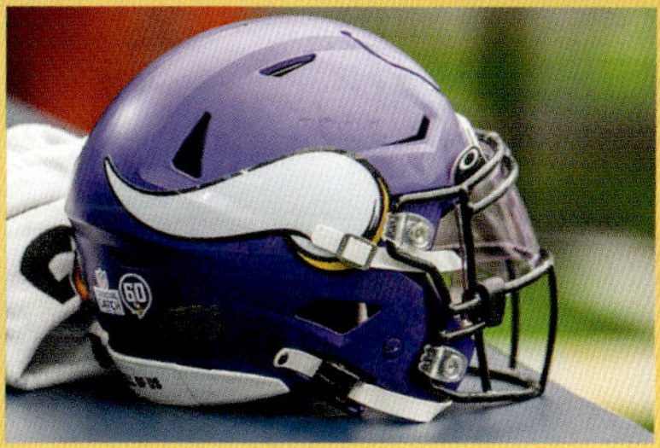

NFL Championships pre-1970 merger: (1) 1969

NFC Central Champions: (14) 1970, 1971, 1973, 1974, 1975, 1976, 1977, 1978, 1980, 1989, 1992, 1994, 1998, 2000

NFC North Champions: (4) 2008, 2009, 2015, 2017

NFC Conference Champions: (3) 1973, 1974, 1976

Super Bowl record: 0-4

The Vikings are perennial contenders; they have made the post-season on 30 occasions and have one of the better win percentages in the NFL. However, a significant part of Vikings history is losing when it matters – with their record in the Super Bowl being one of trauma. By the conclusion of the 1976 season, they had been to more Super Bowls than any other team in history – the only problem was they lost each one. The first defeat, in Super Bowl 4, was the biggest surprise as NFL teams were considered superior to AFL teams, and the Vikings were favoured by the bookies to win by 13 points. Instead, Kansas beat them 23-7 and the NFL then merged with the AFL.

The Vikings were back in the big game in the 1973 season to play the Dolphins in Super Bowl 8. They wouldn't score until the fourth quarter, by which point they were already losing 24-0. The following season, the Vikings were once again kings of the NFC Conference, but second best to the AFC, this time losing 16-6 to the legendary 1970s Pittsburgh Steelers. As it was the year before, Minnesota wouldn't get on the scoresheet until the final quarter, by which time the game was already lost. Two seasons later a familiar pattern emerged: Minnesota dominated the NFC Central division, won the NFC Conference, and lost another Super Bowl, this time to the Oakland Raiders by a score of 32-14. For their third Super Bowl in a row, Minnesota had failed to get on the scoresheet for the entire first half. Coach Bud Grant had taken the Vikings to all four Super Bowl appearances and the team have not been back since. To compound the pain, they have lost six NFC Championship games in seasons 1977, 1987, 1998, 2000, 2009, and 2017, not winning a single one during that period.

Upon foundation in 1960, the Vikings were supposed to have joined the newly formed AFL. However the NFL had 13 teams, and liked the Minnesota territory and so offered the Vikings the spare place. Along with the Raiders and the Patriots, they are the only team in the NFL to feature a human as the club's logo (Washington having changed logo in recent years). The name was inspired through the high percentage of Minnesota's population being descended from Scandinavian ancestry.

The Vikings now play in a new indoor arena, but in the first 20 years of their existence they played outdoors in one of the coldest sporting environments in the United States, leading them to move into the indoor Metrodome between 1982 and 2013. Not that having an indoor arena is a guarantee of conquering the Minneapolis weather and in 2010 the domed roof collapsed due to the amount of snow on top of it. Before moving into the current stadium, the Vikings played a season in the home of the local college team and their final outdoor home fixture was played against Seattle in one of the coldest games ever played in the NFL; the steam coming from the mouths of the players visible even from a wide camera angle.

Indoor stadiums are a double-edged sword – everyone prefers the warm, but bad-weather games in rain, snow and minus temperatures have always made for an incredible spectacle and showcased American football as a sport for warriors. This wild-card game against Seattle in the 2015 season was a metaphor for the Vikings' fortunes over the years. They could have won the game with a close-range field goal in the last second, but it was missed by Blair Walsh and Minnesota fell short.

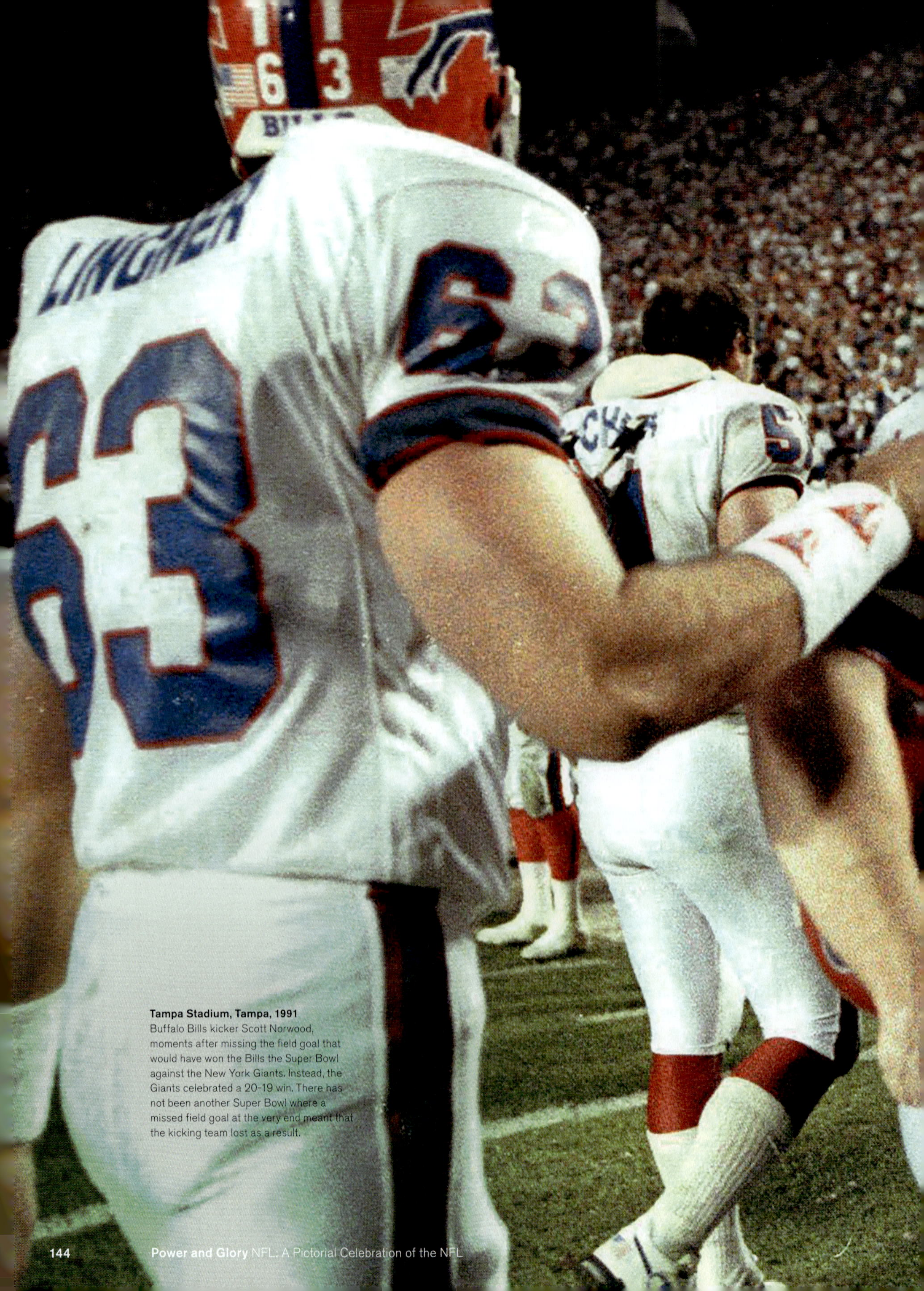

Tampa Stadium, Tampa, 1991
Buffalo Bills kicker Scott Norwood, moments after missing the field goal that would have won the Bills the Super Bowl against the New York Giants. Instead, the Giants celebrated a 20-19 win. There has not been another Super Bowl where a missed field goal at the very end meant that the kicking team lost as a result.

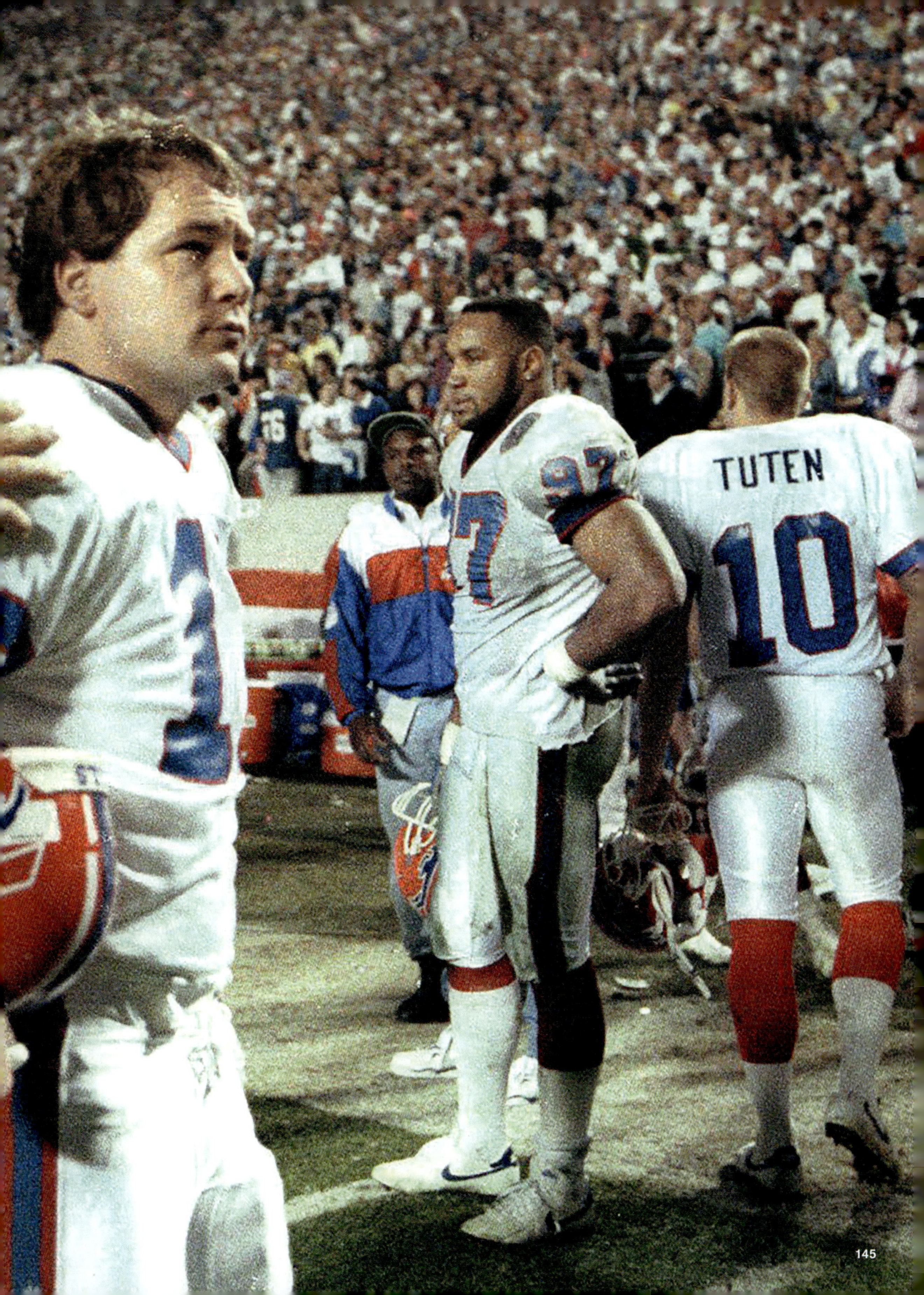
TUTEN
10
97

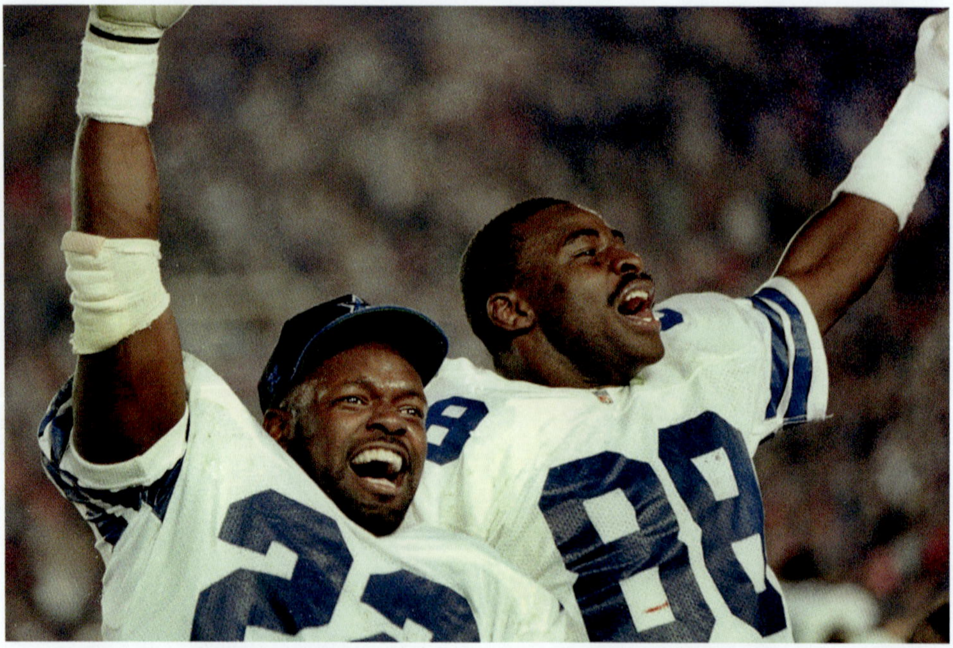

Rose Bowl, Pasadena, 1993
Dallas have just beaten the Buffalo Bills in Super Bowl 27, by a score of 52-17. Emmitt Smith (left) and Michael Irvin (right) celebrate.

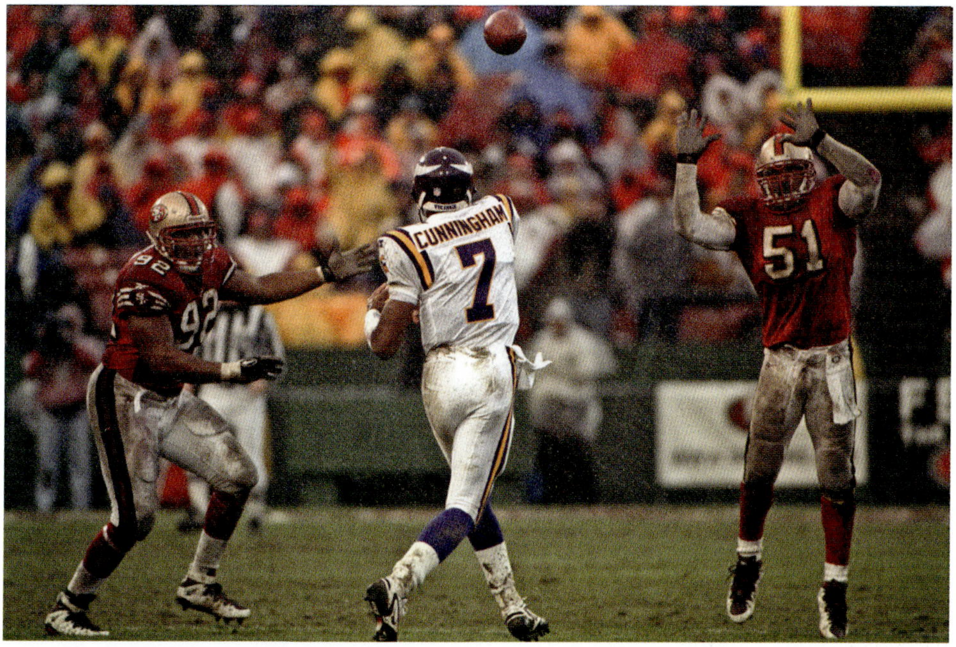

Candlestick Park, San Francisco, 1997
Minnesota quarterback Randall Cunningham throws while being pursued by 49ers defensive end Roy Barker (92) and linebacker Ken Norton (51).

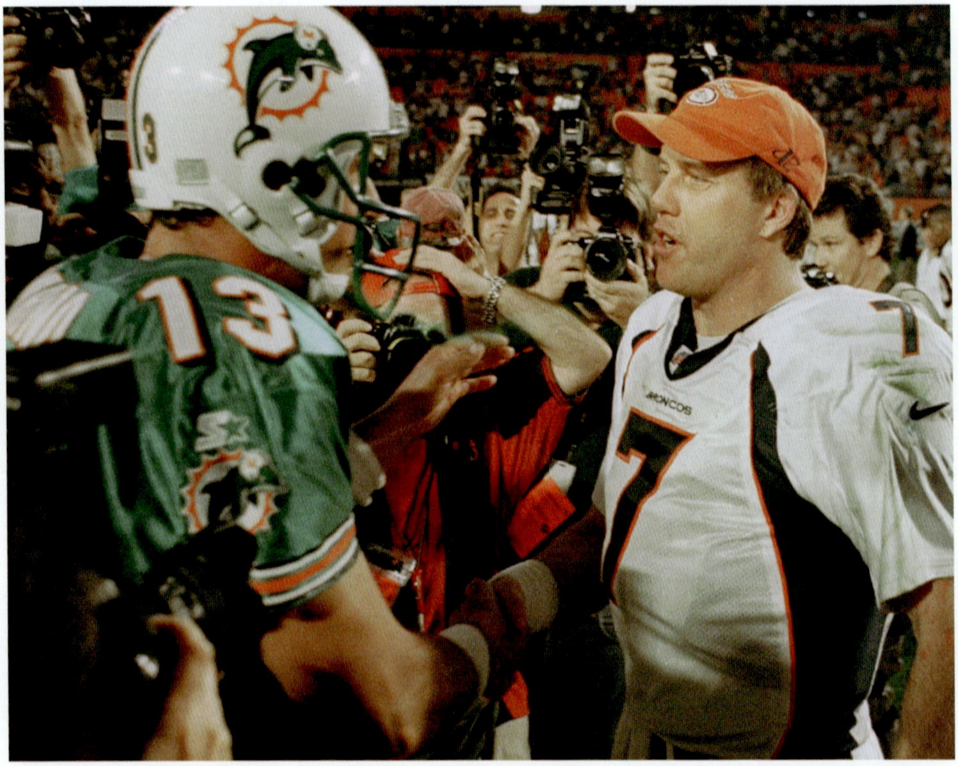

Pro Player Stadium, Miami, 1998
Two quarterback legends shake hands at the end of the game, Miami Dolphins' Dan Marino (left) and Denver's John Elway (right).

Sun Devil Stadium, Temple, 1996
In Super Bowl 30, Dallas and Pittsburgh prepare for a snap. The winner would equal San Francisco's record of five Super Bowl wins, and Dallas came out on top 27-17.

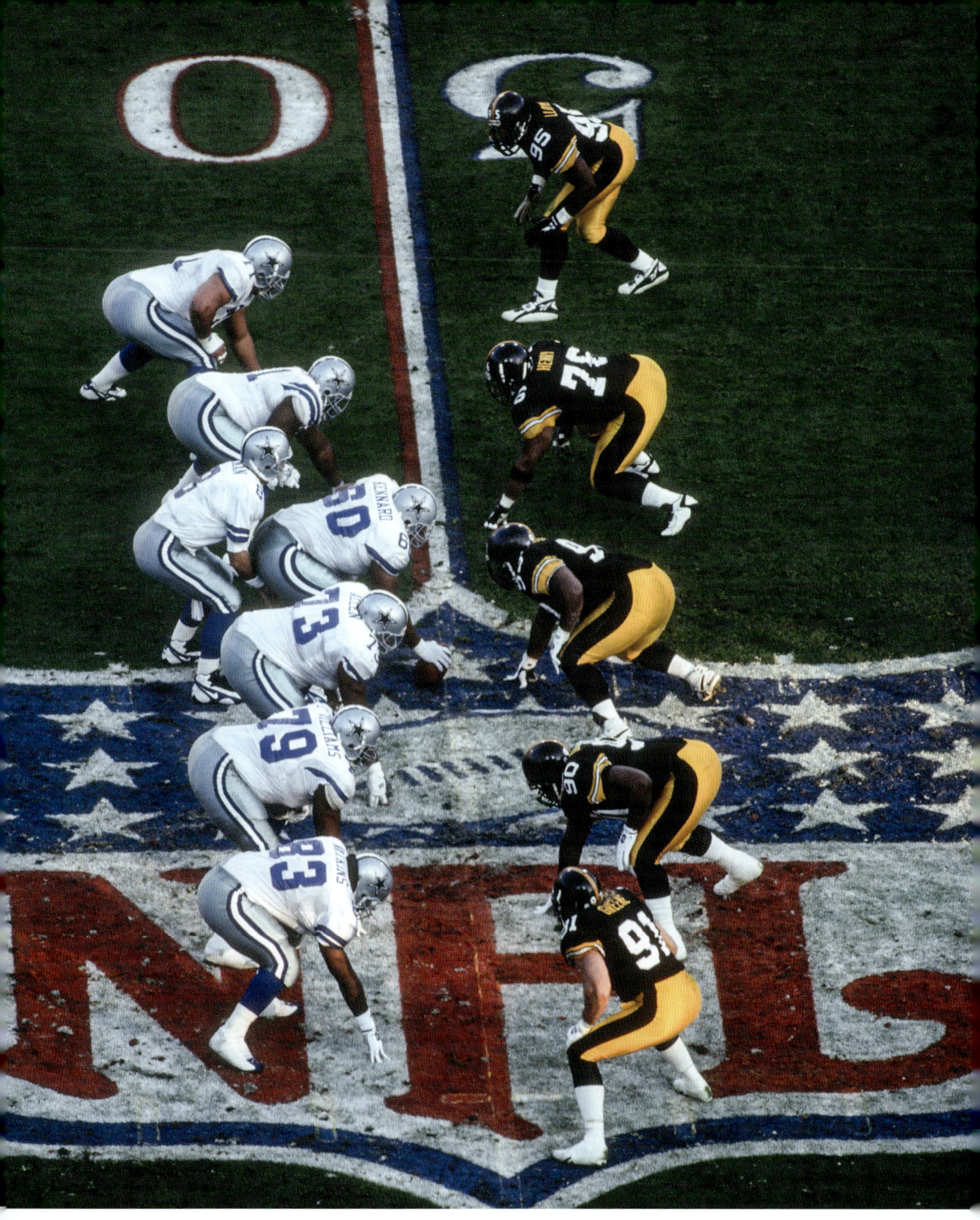
KENNARD

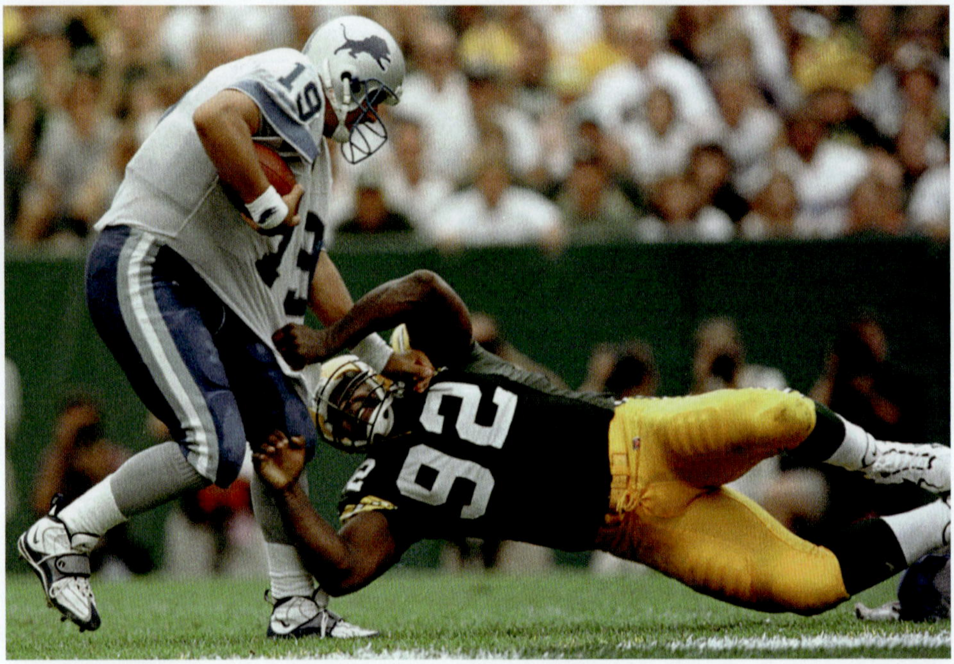

Lambeau Field, Green Bay, 1998
Green Bay Packers defensive end Reggie White does what he does best, which is making life miserable for quarterbacks. In this case, Lions quarterback Scott Mitchell is caught by the 'Minister of Defence'.

Candlestick Park, San Francisco, 1993
Jerry Rice does what he does best, which is scoring touchdowns. In this game the 49ers beat their state rivals the Rams 40-17.

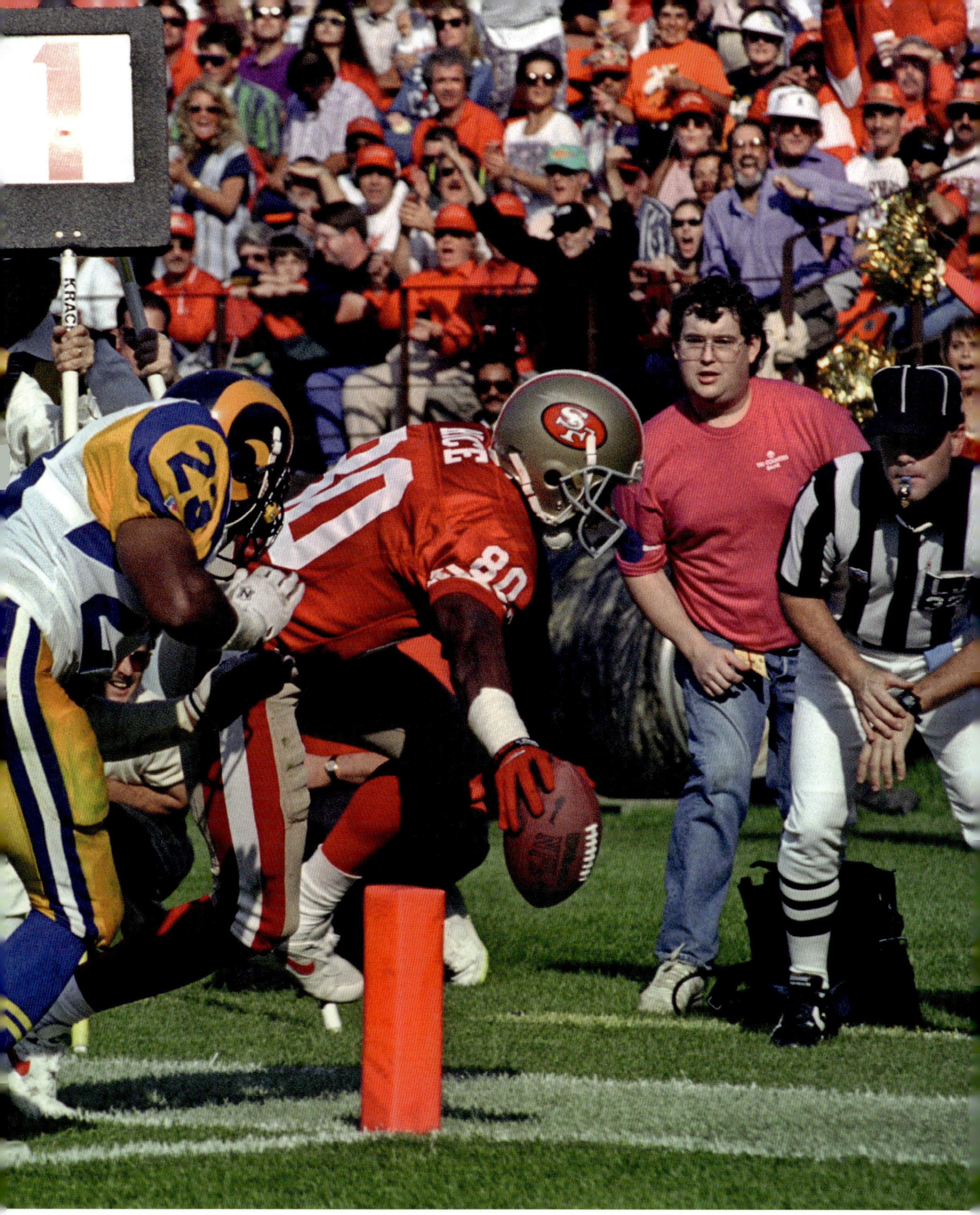
1
80

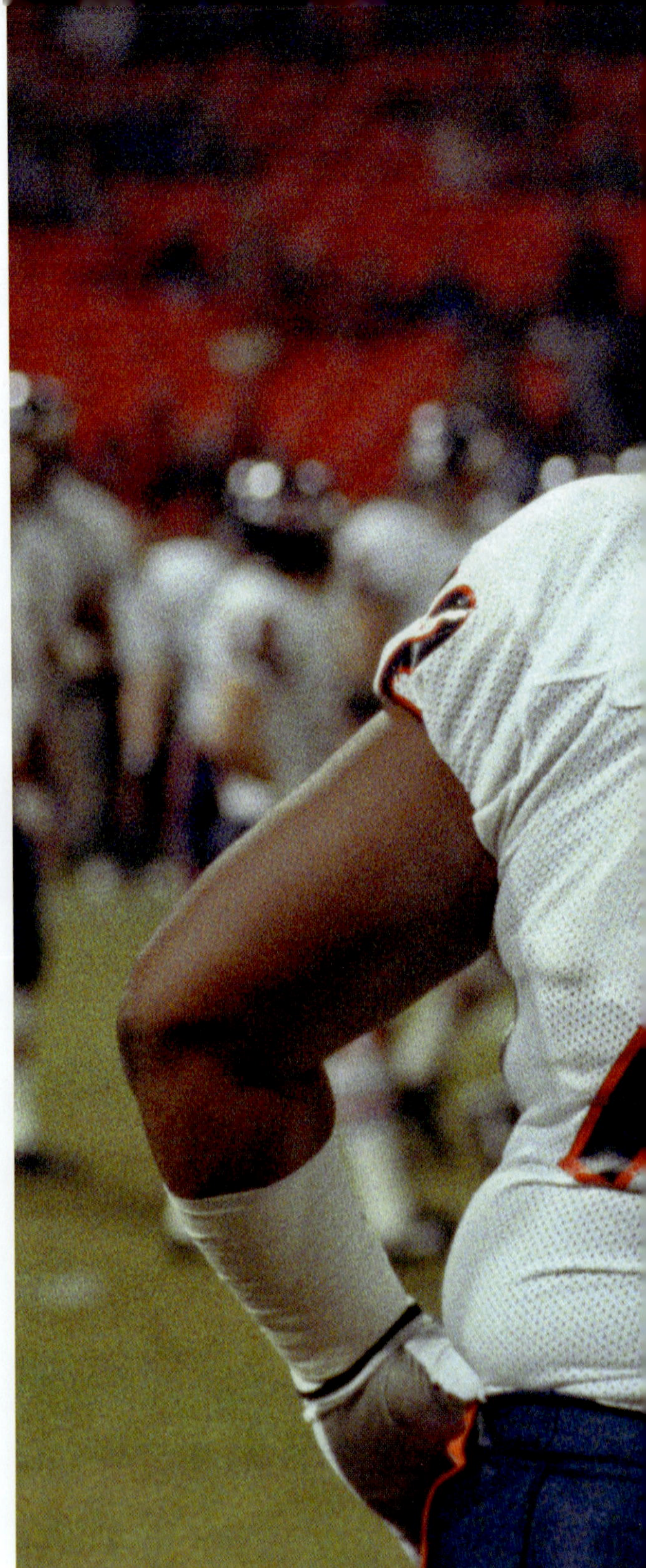

Candlestick Park, San Francisco, 1991
Chicago Bears defensive end Richard Dent (95) talks with defensive tackle William 'The Refrigerator' Perry (72).

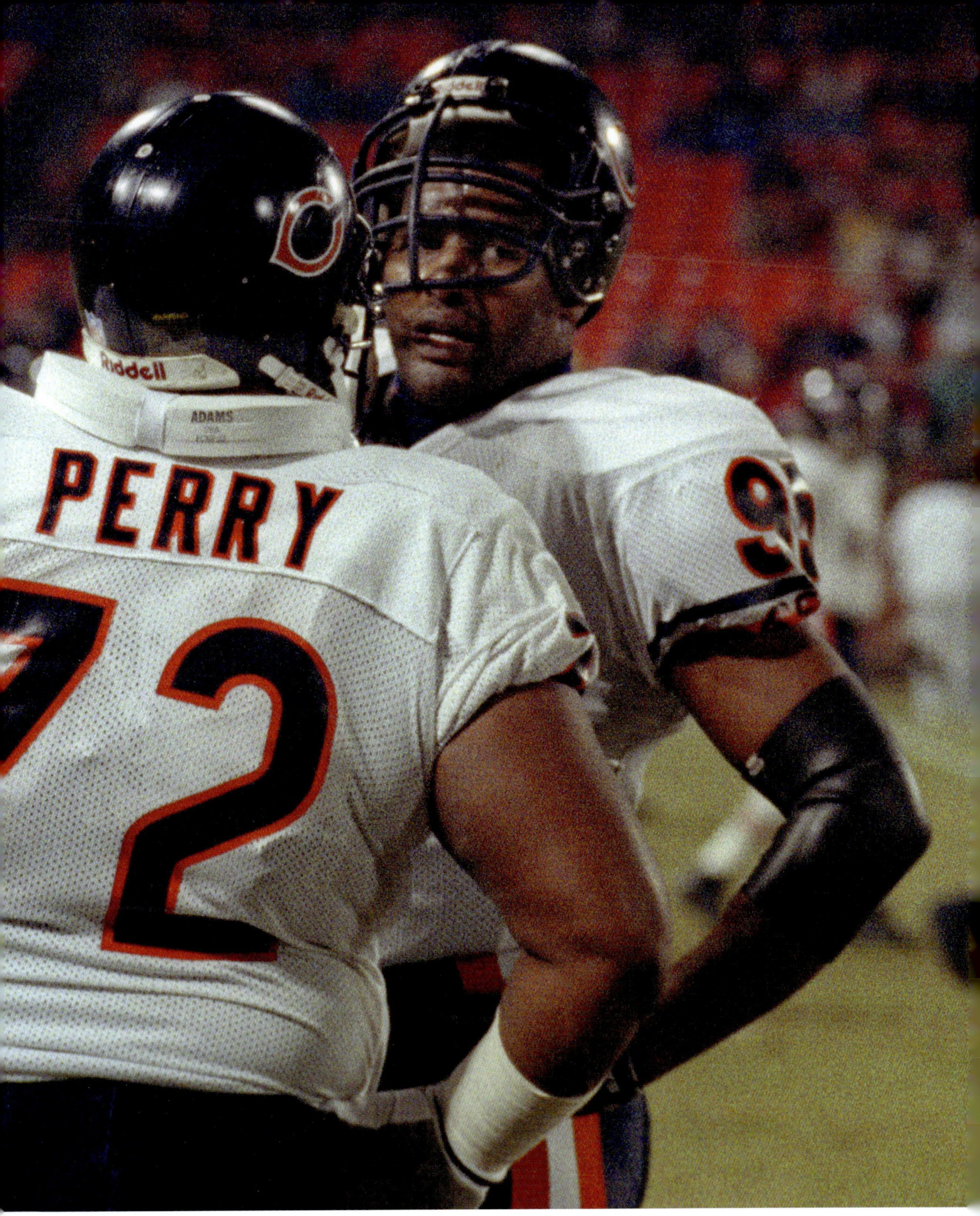
PERRY
72
Riddell

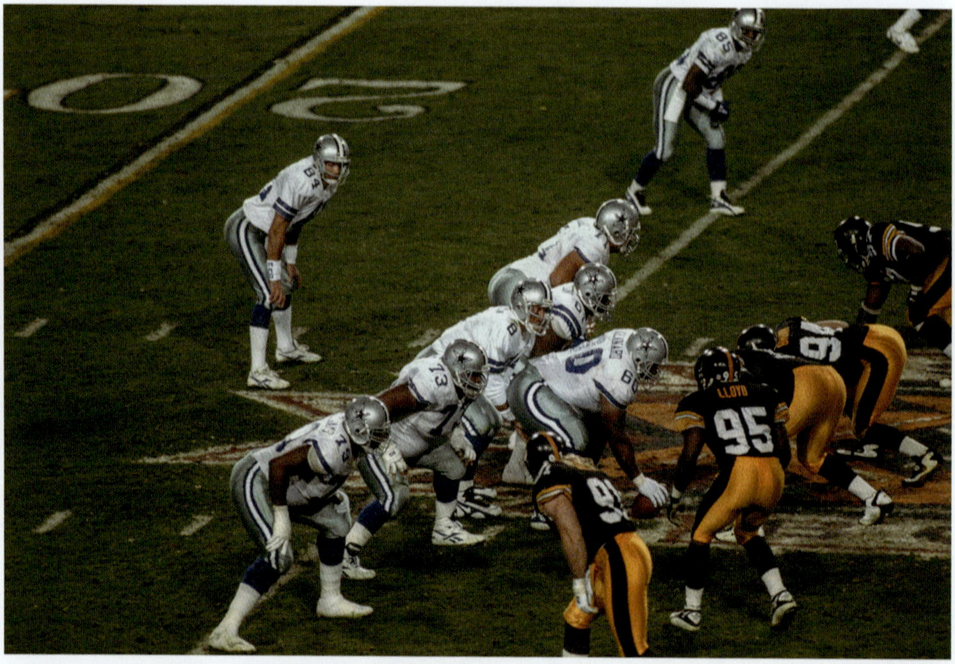

Sun Devil Stadium, Temple, 1996
Super Bowl 30, Dallas quarterback Troy Aikman prepares for a snap against Pittsburgh. The Steelers before this game had never lost a Super Bowl, but after this game their record would change to 4-1.

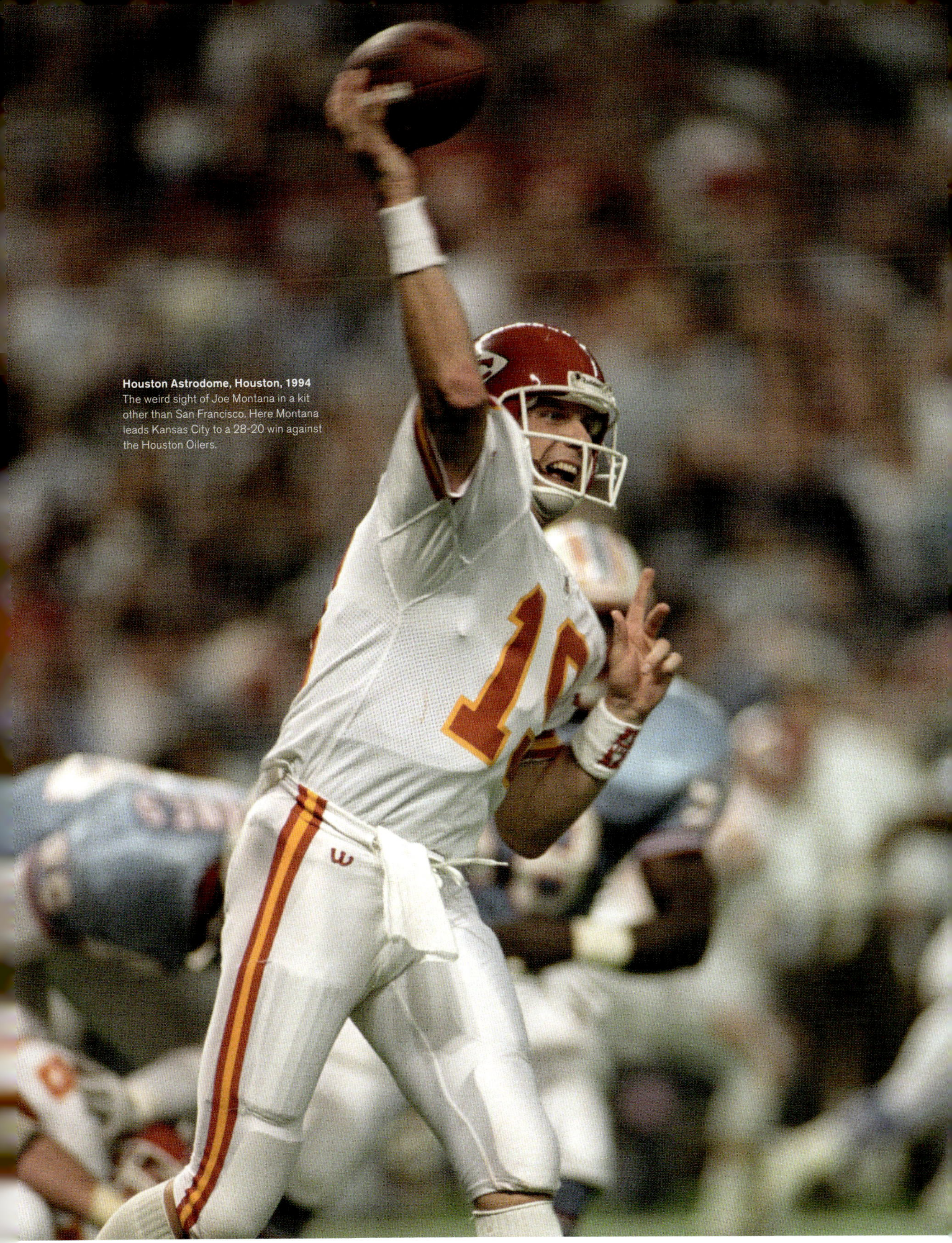

Houston Astrodome, Houston, 1994
The weird sight of Joe Montana in a kit other than San Francisco. Here Montana leads Kansas City to a 28-20 win against the Houston Oilers.

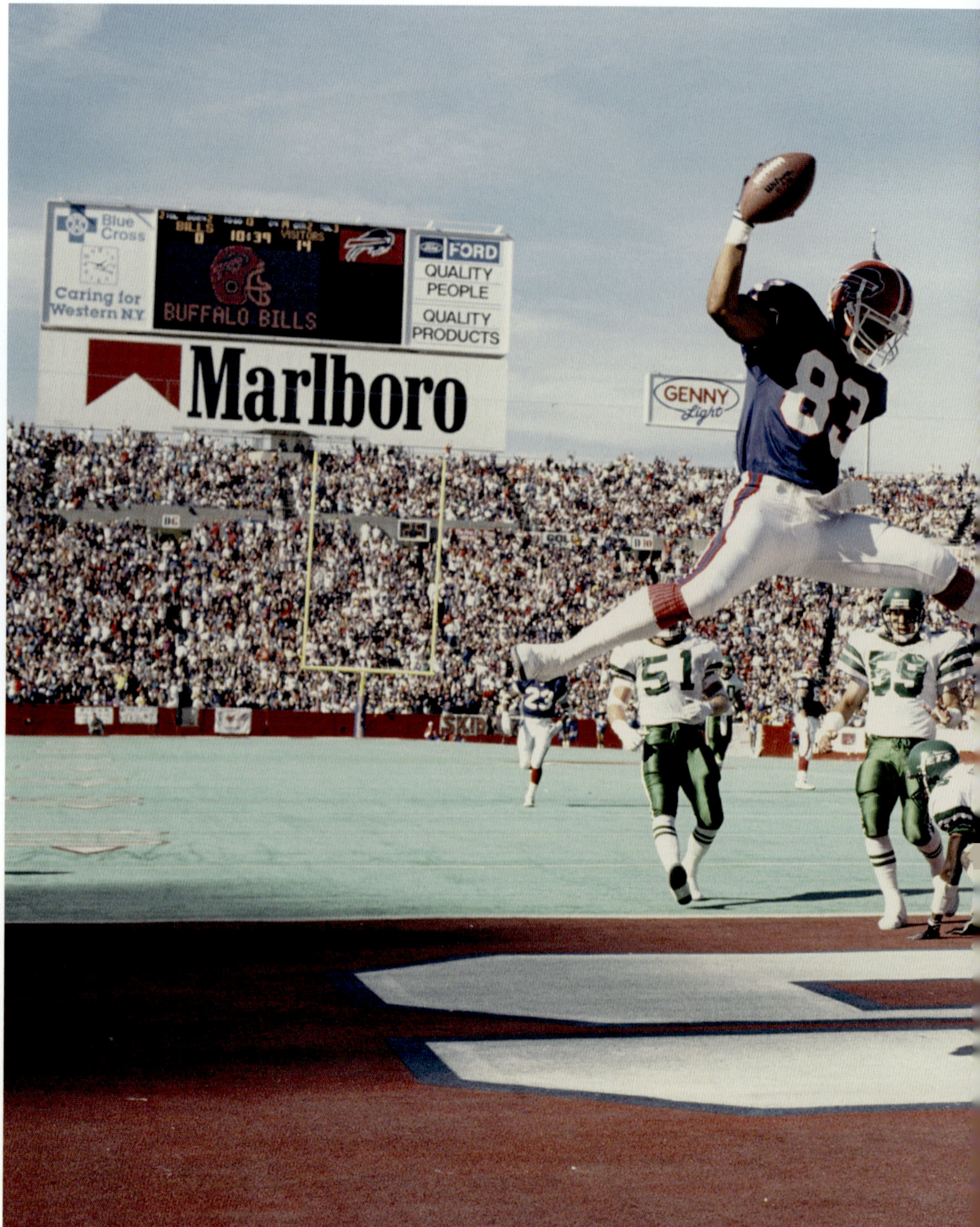
Blue Cross
Caring for Western NY
BILLS
0
10:39
VISITORS
14
BUFFALO BILLS
FORD
QUALITY PEOPLE
QUALITY PRODUCTS
Marlboro
GENNY Light

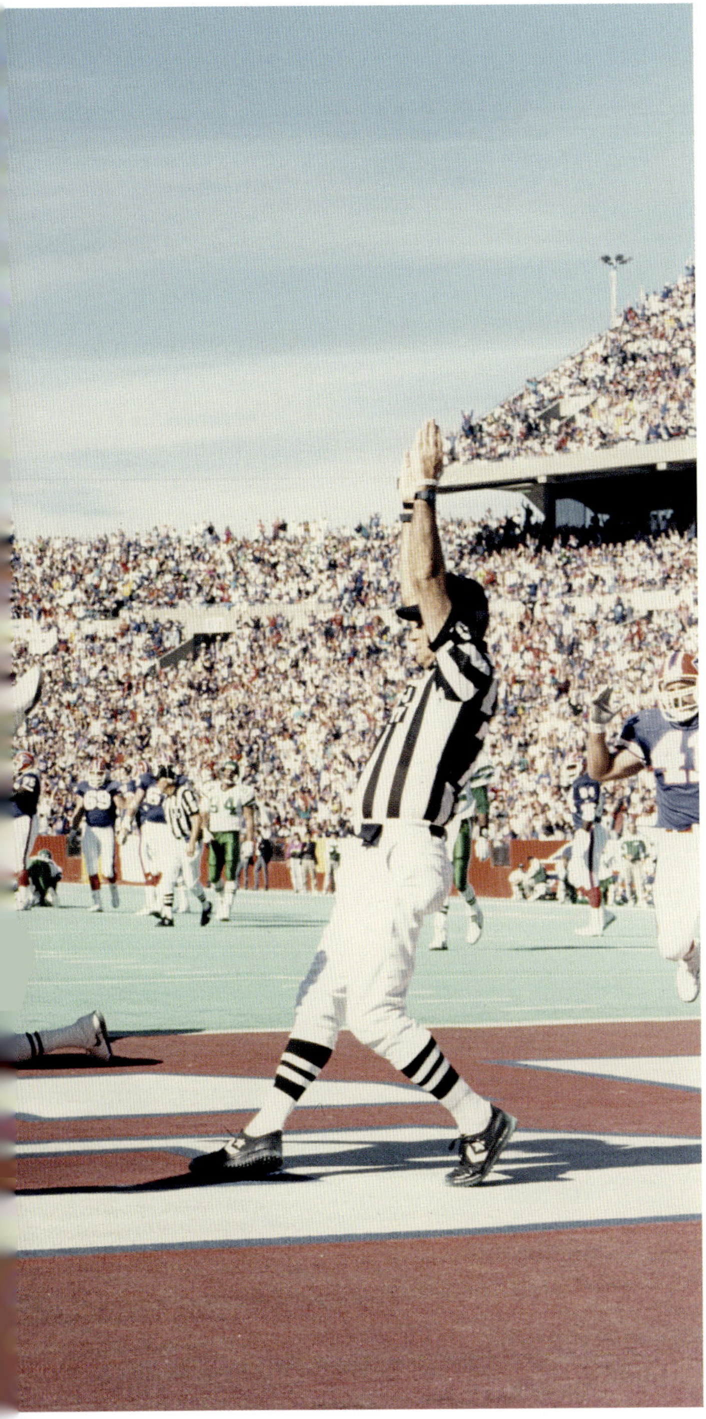

Rich Stadium, Buffalo, 1990
Bills wide receiver Andre Reed celebrates scoring a touchdown against AFC East rivals the New York Jets. In the background the scoreboard tells us that the visitors were leading 14-0 before the touchdown.

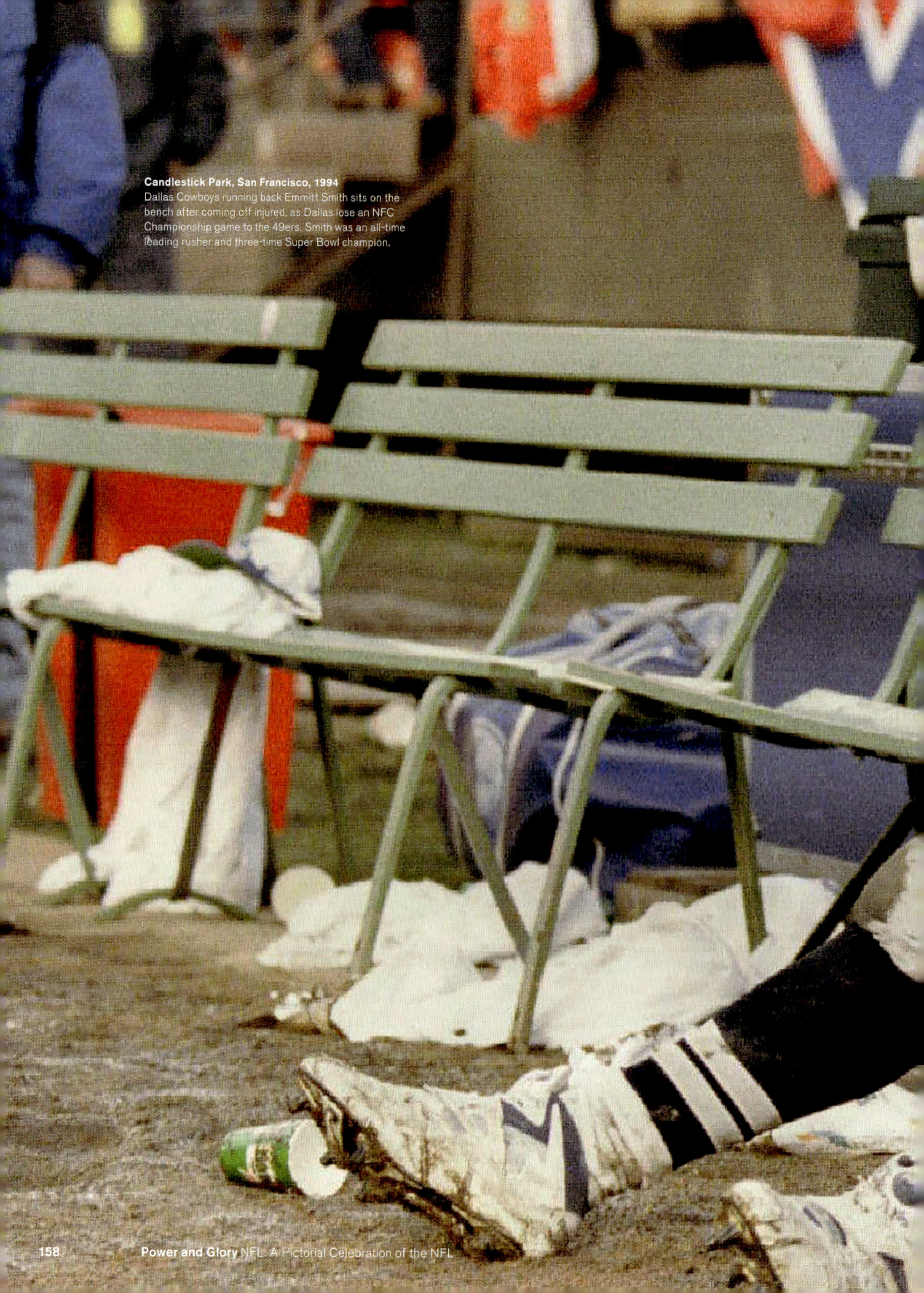

Candlestick Park, San Francisco, 1994
Dallas Cowboys running back Emmitt Smith sits on the bench after coming off injured, as Dallas lose an NFC Championship game to the 49ers. Smith was an all-time leading rusher and three-time Super Bowl champion.

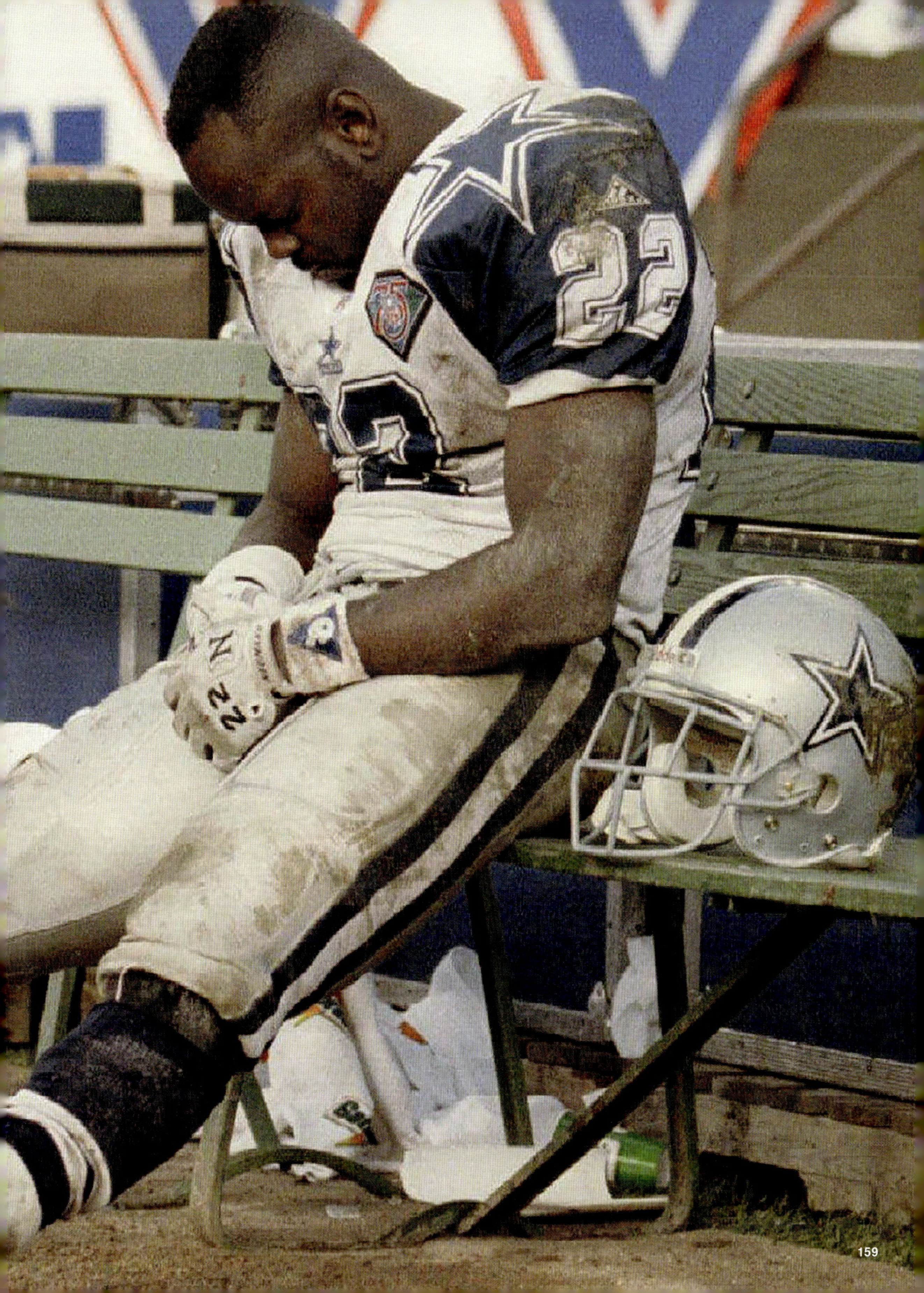
22

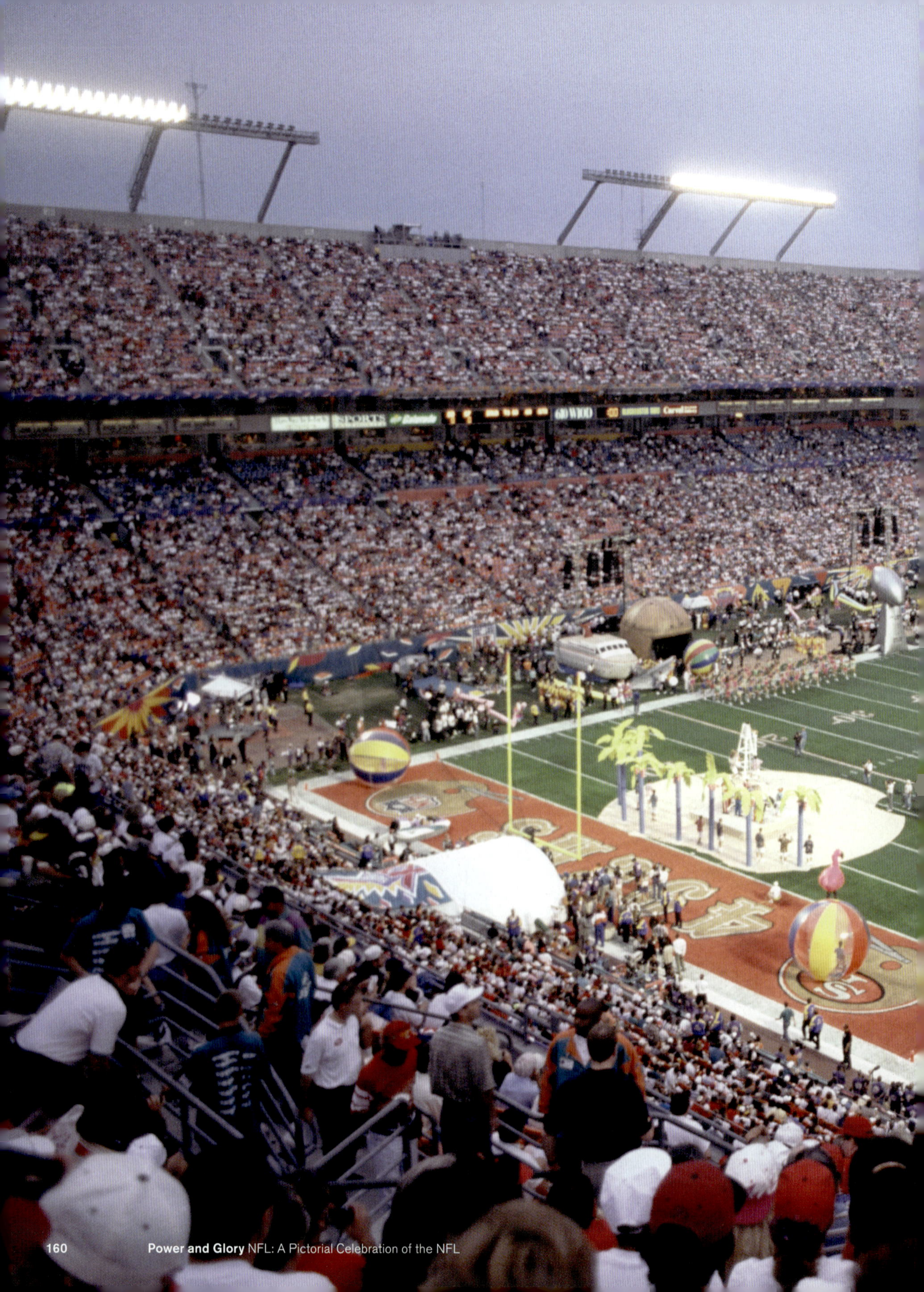

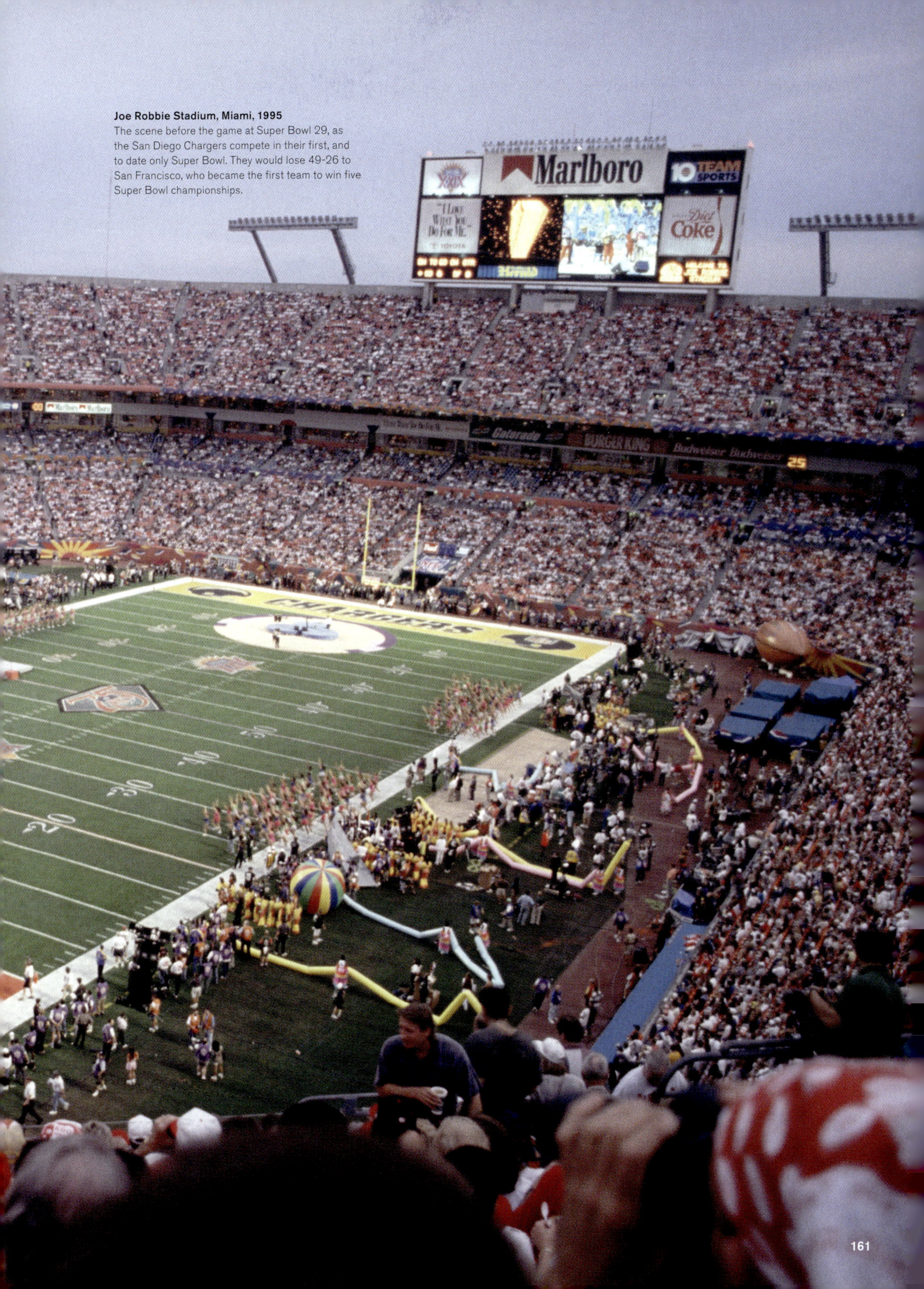

Joe Robbie Stadium, Miami, 1995
The scene before the game at Super Bowl 29, as the San Diego Chargers compete in their first, and to date only Super Bowl. They would lose 49-26 to San Francisco, who became the first team to win five Super Bowl championships.

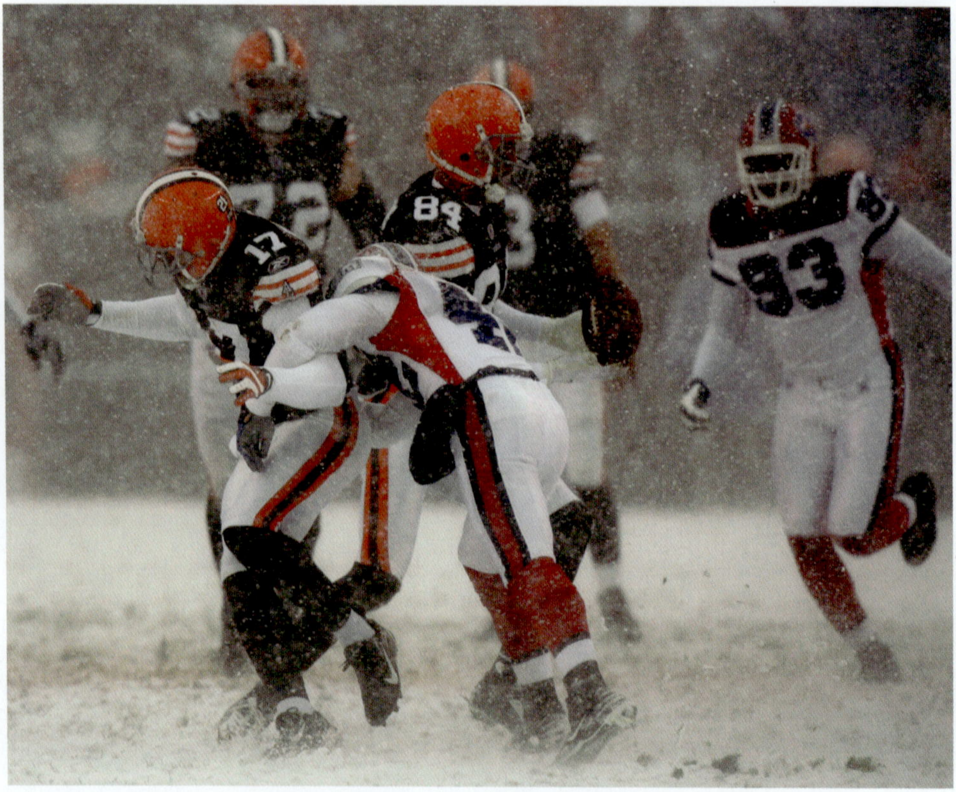

Cleveland Browns Stadium, Cleveland, 2007
Buffalo take on Cleveland in a winter wonderland setting. The Browns won 8-0.

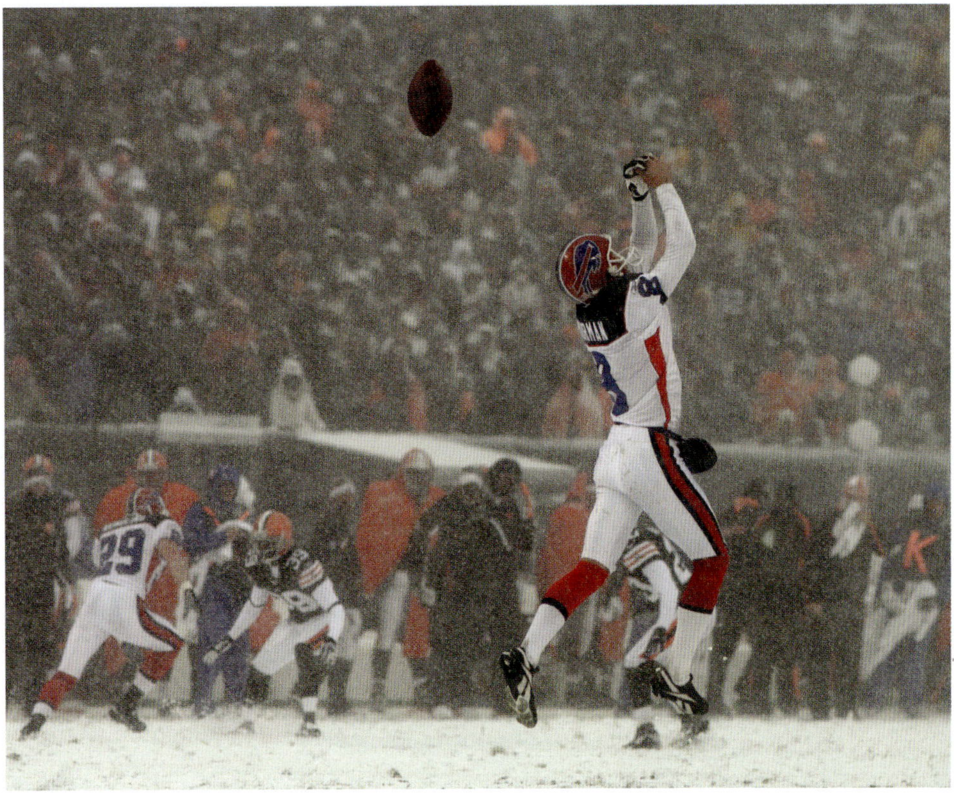

Cleveland Browns Stadium, Cleveland, 2007
A snap goes over the head of Buffalo Bills punter Brian Moorman, as the snow falls in Cleveland.

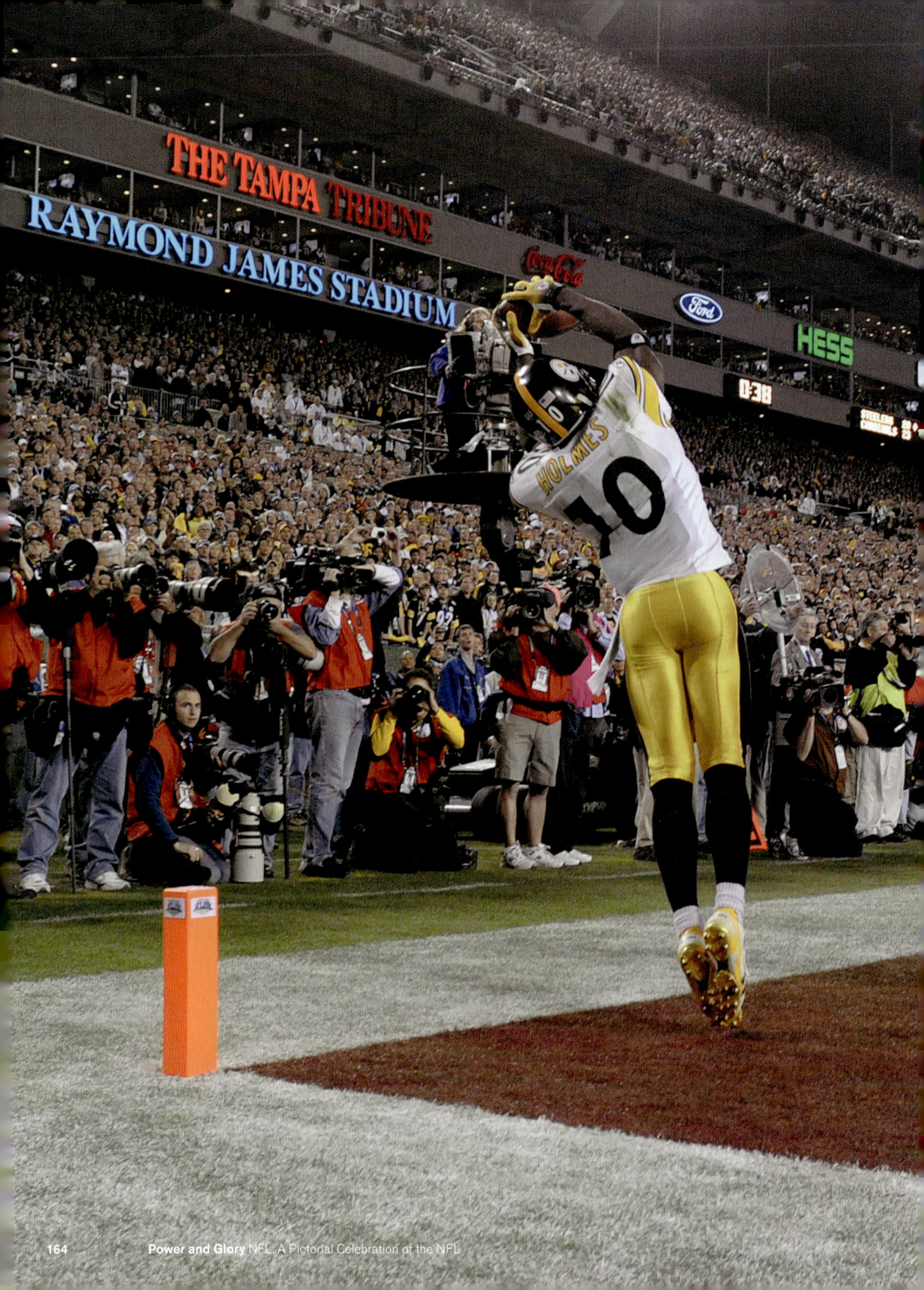
THE TAMPA TRIBUNE
RAYMOND JAMES STADIUM
Coca-Cola
Ford
HESS
0:38
HOLMES
10

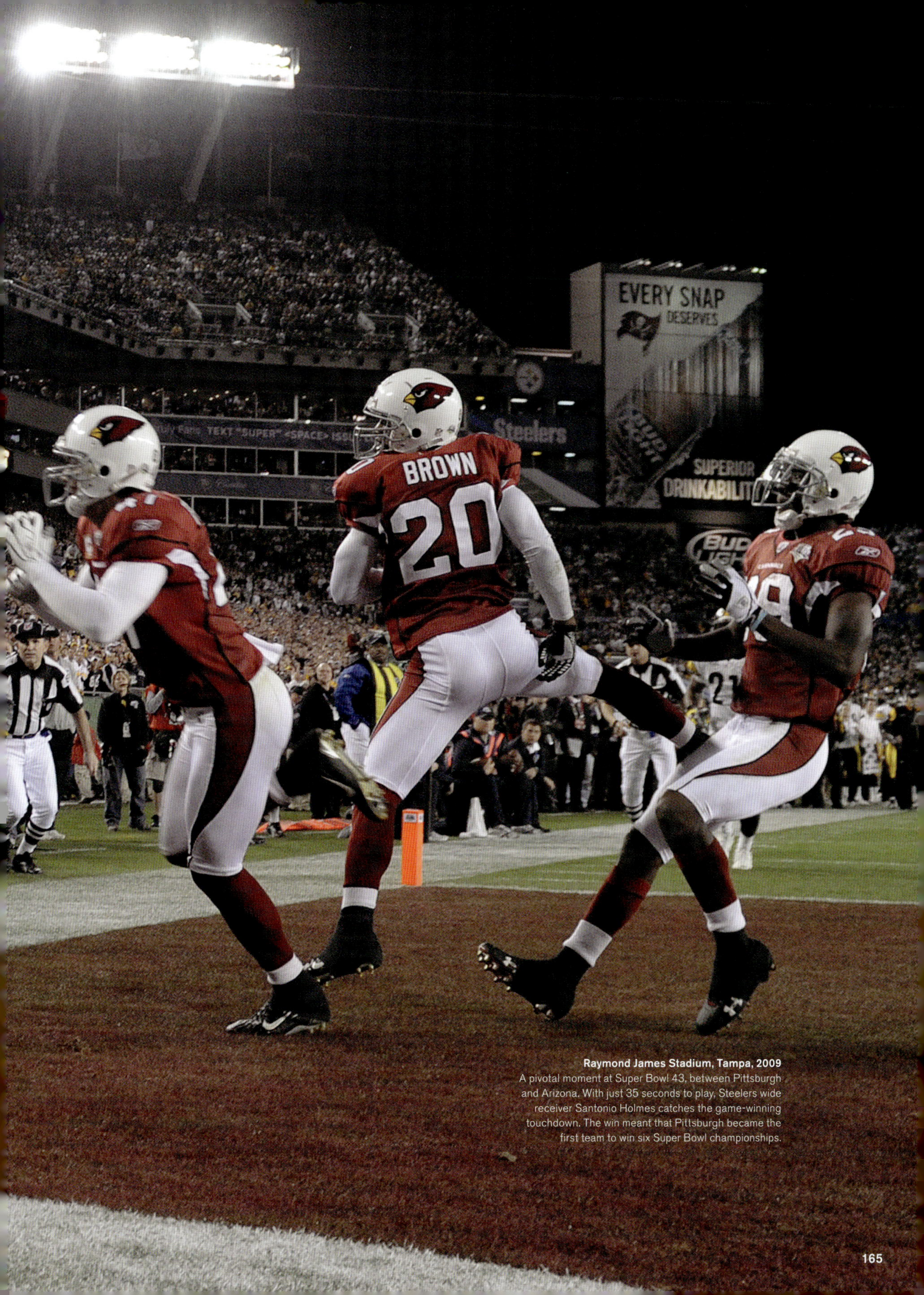

Raymond James Stadium, Tampa, 2009
A pivotal moment at Super Bowl 43, between Pittsburgh and Arizona. With just 35 seconds to play, Steelers wide receiver Santonio Holmes catches the game-winning touchdown. The win meant that Pittsburgh became the first team to win six Super Bowl championships.

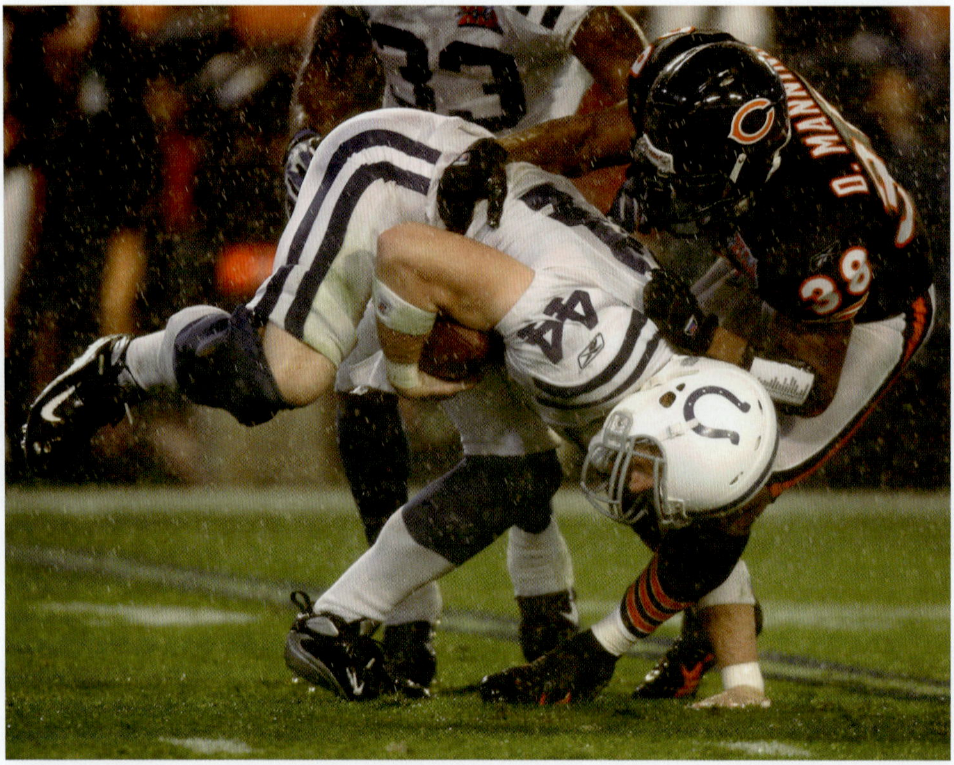

Dolphins Stadium, Miami, 2007
A rain storm occurs during the second quarter at Super Bowl 41. Here the Colts' Dallas Clark is tackled by Chicago's Daniel Manning.

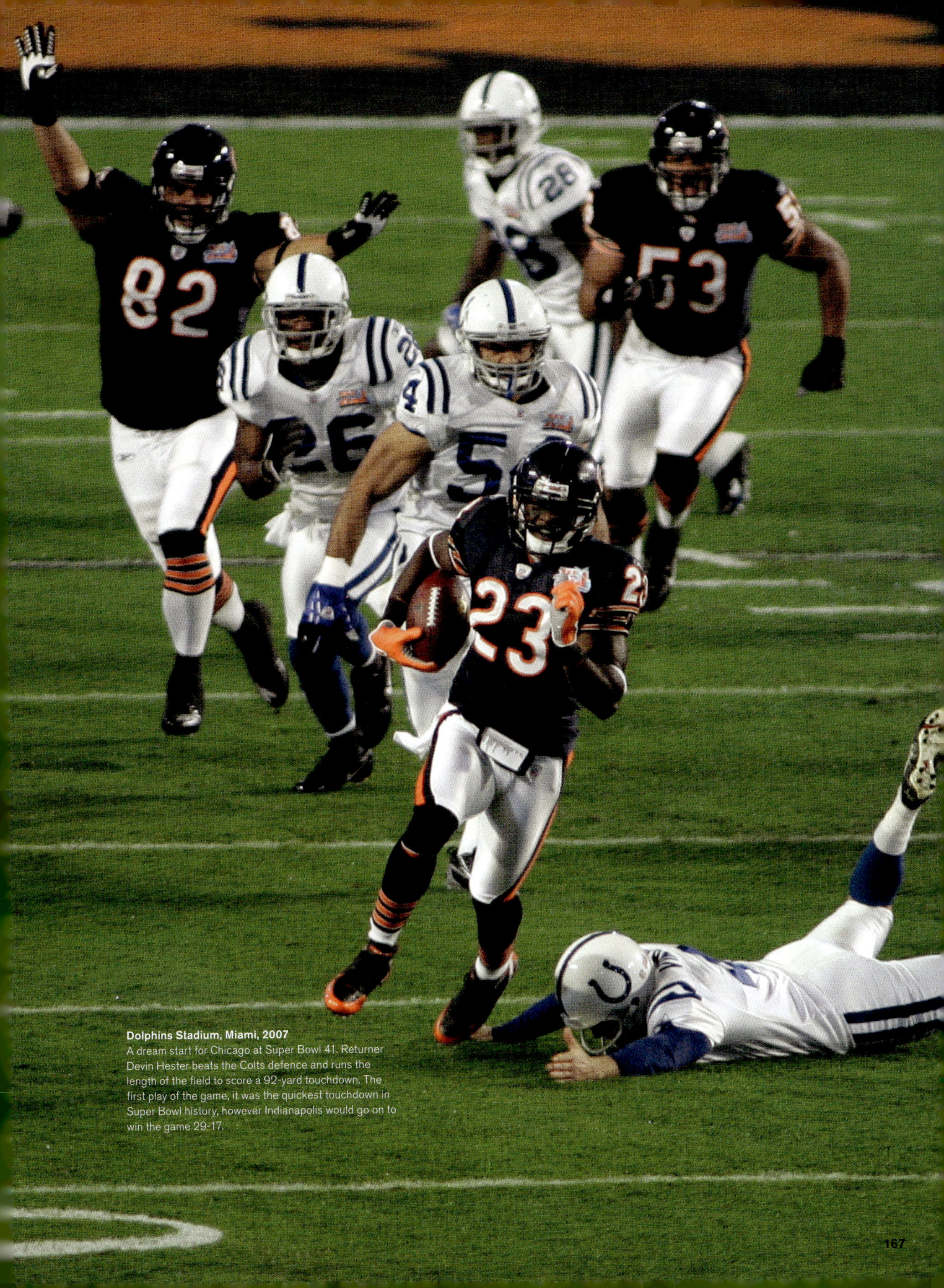

Dolphins Stadium, Miami, 2007
A dream start for Chicago at Super Bowl 41. Returner Devin Hester beats the Colts defence and runs the length of the field to score a 92-yard touchdown. The first play of the game, it was the quickest touchdown in Super Bowl history, however Indianapolis would go on to win the game 29-17.

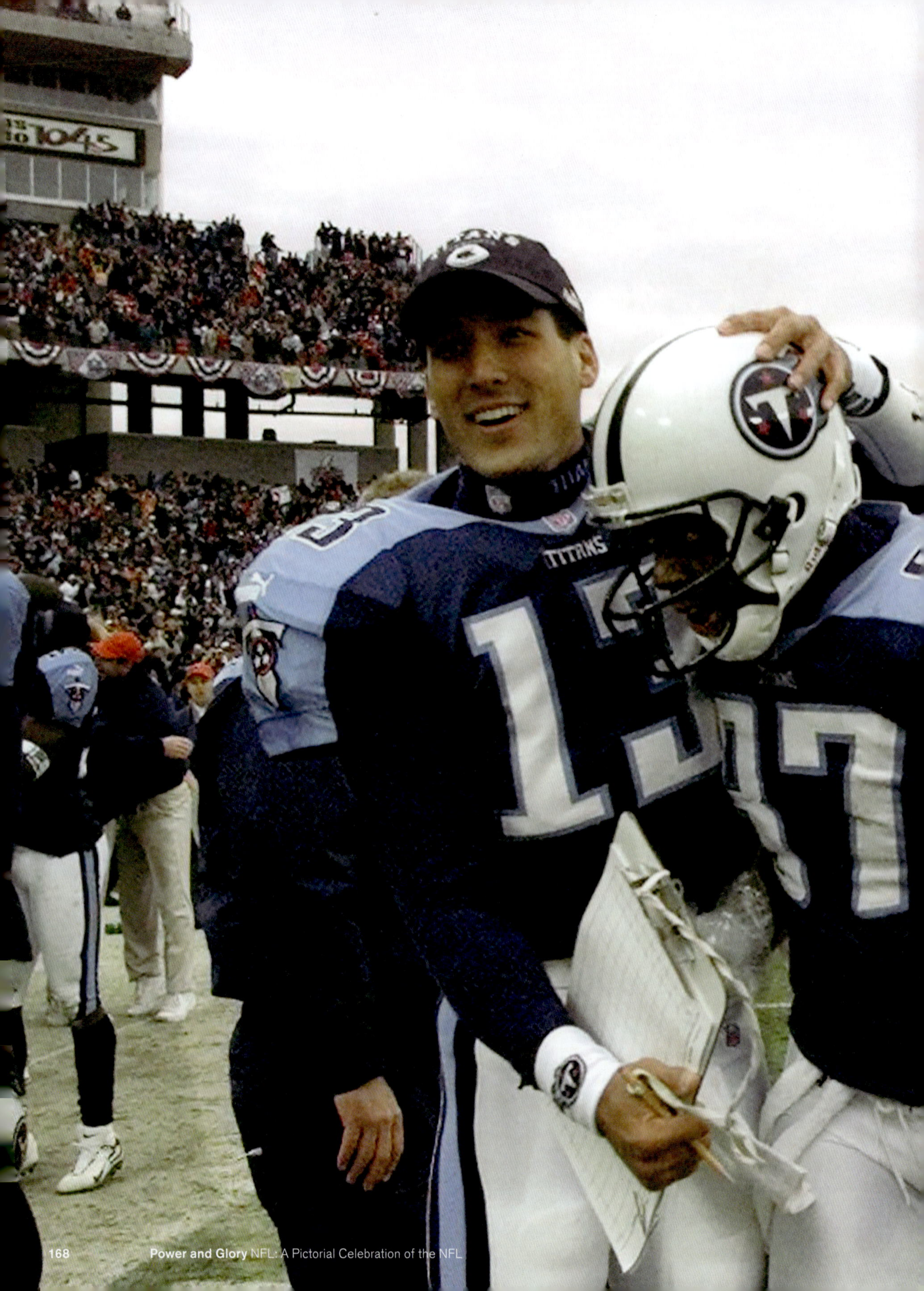

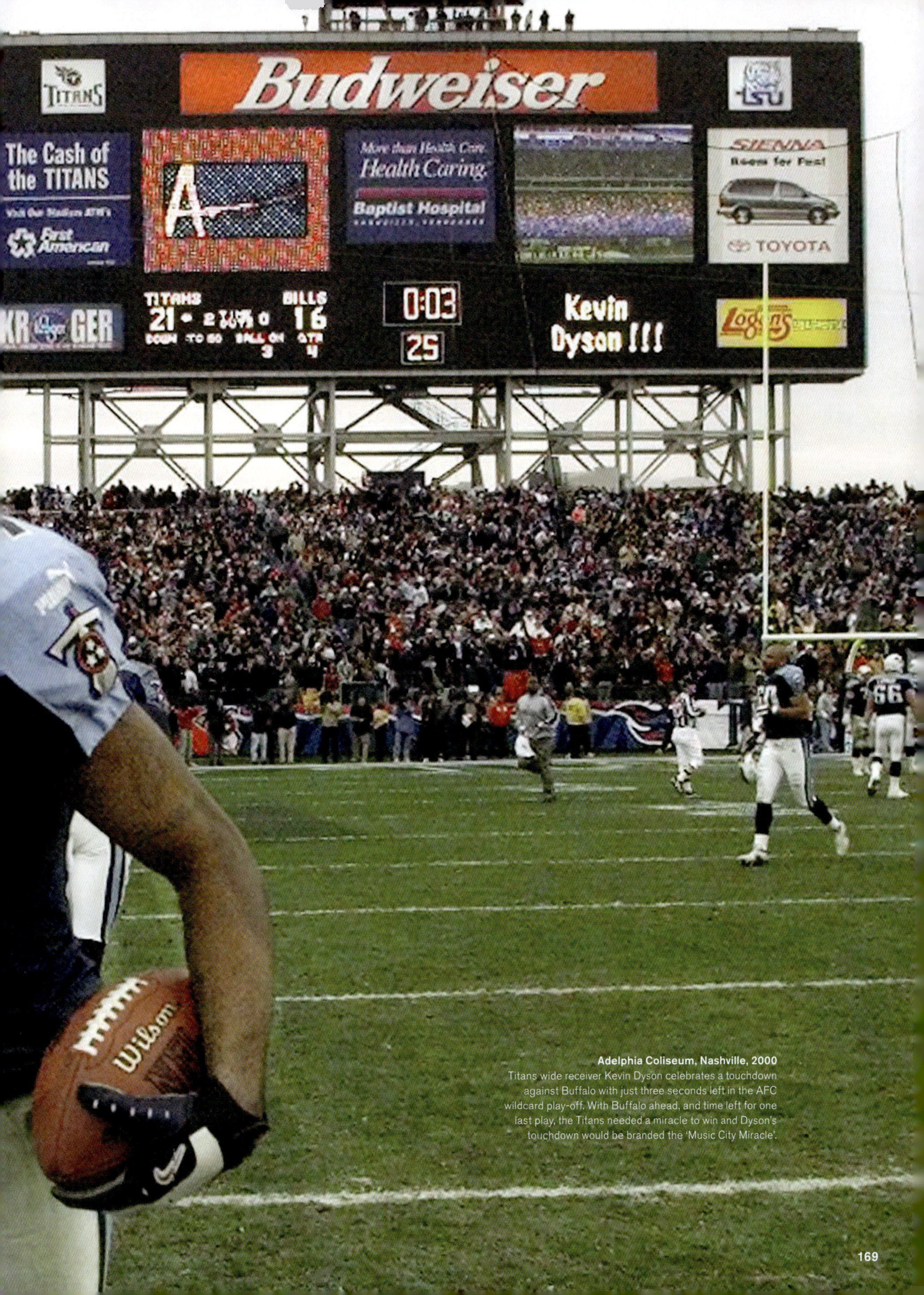

Adelphia Coliseum, Nashville, 2000

Titans wide receiver Kevin Dyson celebrates a touchdown against Buffalo with just three seconds left in the AFC wildcard play-off. With Buffalo ahead, and time left for one last play, the Titans needed a miracle to win and Dyson's touchdown would be branded the 'Music City Miracle'.

Atlanta Falcons: Est. 1965

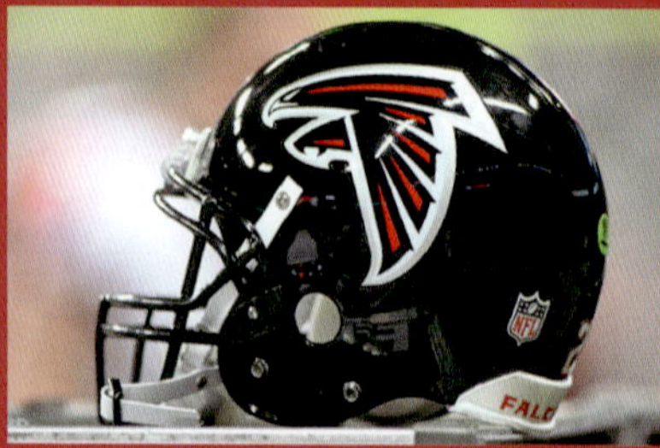

NFC West Champions: (2) 1980, 1988

NFC South Champions: (4) 2004, 2010, 2012, 2016

NFC Conference Champions: (2) 1998, 2016

Super Bowl record: 0-2

Jpon foundation Atlanta were ready to join the AFL, which vas the catalyst for the NFL to offer them a place and get one over their competition. Their inclusion would create an uneven number of 15 clubs in the league, so a year later the NFL brought in New Orleans Saints to even things up. The new Atlanta team needed a second name and members of the public were asked to send in uggestions. The winner was school teacher Julia Elliot who wrote, 'The falcon is proud and dignified, with great courage and fight. It never drops its prey. It is deadly and has a great sporting tradition.'

Atlanta Falcons didn't drop their prey for their first 12 seasons, because they were the prey. It would take them 12 campaigns before making it to the play-offs, where in the 1978 season they beat the Eagles in an all-bird derby but lost to the Cowboys in the divisional play-off. By the 1998 season they had made it to their first NFC Championship game where they beat the Vikings 30-27 in overtime (a game famous for kicker Gary Anderson missing a field goal that would have won it for Minnesota) to book a place in the Super Bowl where they would end up losing 34-19 to John Elway's Broncos.

There is no easy way to lose a Super Bowl; however the manners of some defeats will hit harder than others. Atlanta will forever look back on their second Super Bowl, in the 2016 season, and be traumatised. After a scoreless first quarter, the Falcons came out firing in the second and scored two touchdowns; and at 14-0 it was already at the point where if New England won then it would be the greatest Super Bowl comeback of all time. Near the end of the quarter Tom Brady then threw an interception which was returned for a 'pick six' by Falcons cornerback Robert Alford, making it 21-0. Two seconds before half-time, the Patriots scored a field goal, which would end up being crucial. The Falcons got another touchdown in the third quarter to make it 28-3, and the game was over. With two minutes to go in the third it was still 28-3 and the sports writers who covered the game told of how they had already written most of their articles by this point. Ben Volin of the *Boston Globe* said, 'I probably had a good 600 words written already about how the Patriots were outclassed and they couldn't handle the speed on either side of the ball.' Doug Kyed of the New England Sports Network said, 'The story I did was going to be "Three Reasons why the Patriots Lost".' In the BBC's Super Bowl coverage the talk among the pundits turned to, 'Is this now the end for Tom Brady?'

But Brady still had three Super Bowl wins left in him starting with this game against Atlanta. Three touchdowns and a field goal for New England had tied the game up and a nightmare was unravelling for the Falcons; and to make matters worse the equalising touchdown required a two-point conversion. The biggest regret for Atlanta is that the win should have been sealed with the score at 28-20. With four minutes and six seconds on the clock they were on the Patriots' 23-yard line, well within field goal range to make it a two-score game. However, Matt Ryan was sacked on the 35-yard line, which then got followed by a ten-yard penalty in the next play, meaning they were well out of range for the three points. When the game went into overtime everyone knew that the Patriots had so much momentum they would win, which they did 34-28, in what could just be the greatest ever Super Bowl

Carolina Panthers: Est. 1993

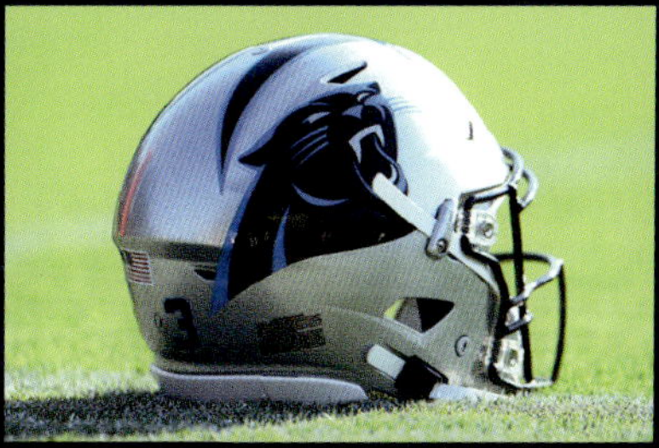

NFC West Champions: (1) 1996

NFC South Champions: (5) 2003, 2008, 2013, 2014, 2015

NFC Conference Champions: (2) 2003, 2015

Super Bowl record: 0-2

In a league that already had Lions, Bengals, and a whole host of other scary animals, the NFL added two more big cat teams in 1995 with the inclusion of the Jaguars and the Panthers as the league expanded to 30 teams. Despite being located in the east, Carolina were originally placed in the NFC West before the NFC South was created in 2002. The team are based in the city of Charlotte in the state of North Carolina; however, the state of South Carolina also considers the Panthers their team, and the governor in the South declared 30th July as 'Carolina Panthers Day'.

In only their second season, the Panthers were just one game away from being in the Super Bowl. No expansion team had ever got that far after just two years in the league. It was good to see someone new, as up to that point in the late 1990s there had not been one NFC Championship game that didn't feature the Giants, Cowboys, 49ers, Rams, or the Redskins. The Panthers would lose to the Green Bay Packers, but in the 2003 season they played the Eagles for a place in the Super Bowl and beat them 14-3. In their ninth season Carolina had made it to the showpiece game and were facing Tom Brady's New England Patriots who were looking to add a second Super Bowl to their list of honours. Despite no scoring in the first and third quarters of Super Bowl 38, the game was considered one of the best to have been played, and was only decided in the final seconds. The Patriots were favoured to win, and were 29-22 ahead before Jack Delhomme threw a touchdown pass to Ricky Proehi and Carolina were level; and it looked like being the first Super Bowl that would go into overtime. However, the Panthers' punter returned the ball with a kick that went out of bounds at the Patriots' 40-yard line, giving Brady and co. a great field position for one more drive to win the game – which was exactly what happened.

Carolina would be back in the NFC Championship game in the 2005 season but would lose to Seattle, then ten years later they would make it all the way to Super Bowl 50 to face Denver. The 2015 Carolina Panthers had been a formidable outfit, and were favourites to beat the Broncos; they had finished the regular season 15-1, and at one point were 14-0 before losing to the Falcons in the penultimate game. Charismatic quarterback Cam Newton was as devastating running with the ball into the endzone as he was throwing it there, and was named the regular-season MVP. In the divisional play-off they blew away Seattle by taking a 31-0 lead at half-time, then destroyed the Cardinals 49-15 to book a place in the Super Bowl.

Coach Ron Rivera had been to the Super Bowl in the 1985 season with Chicago; however for his Panthers team this was a new experience, and that would be evident against the Broncos, who had been to a Super Bowl two years earlier and their defence would dominate this game. Before his first snap, Newton, as he always does, said a prayer, but in a manner that hinted of being slightly overwhelmed by the occasion. He would end up being sacked seven times overall, and Denver would turn the ball over a total of four times. Defensively the Panthers did perform well, and only allowed one touchdown which came about because their offence had lost the ball near their own endzone (the other Denver touchdown came from their defence after a sack on Newton). They too had created multiple turnovers, but it wasn't enough to bring a first world title to the Carolinas.

New Orleans Saints: Est. 1966

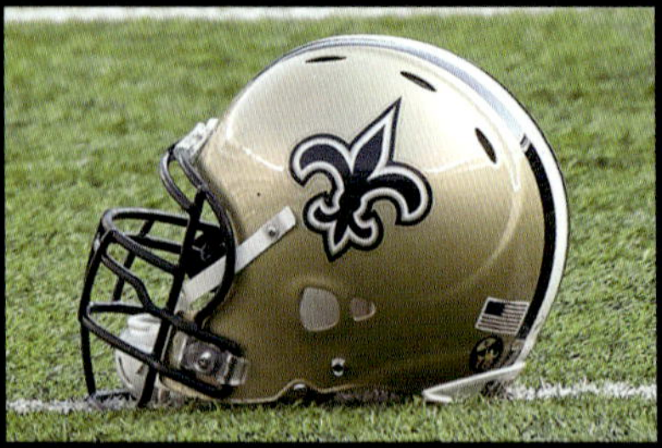

NFC West Champions: (2) 1991, 2000

NFC South Champions: (7) 2006, 2009, 2011, 2017, 2018, 2019, 2020

NFC Conference Championships: (1) 2009

Super Bowl titles: (1) 2009

Super Bowl record: 1-0

'When the Saints Go Marching In' is a famous jazz song associated with New Orleans and when the city got a team as part of the NFL's 1960s expansion, it's fair to say that the first 21 years were rather difficult. Not only did they not make the play-offs in that period, but they didn't produce one winning season; their best record in that time being 8-8 in 1979 and 1983. By the 2000 season, the Saints finally won their first ever post-season game beating the Rams, but would lose to Minnesota in the divisional play-off.

By the 2006 season the Saints made it to the NFC Championship game but would lose 39-14 to the Chicago Bears. A win would have been the ultimate Cinderella story, as a year earlier, Hurricane Katrina had devastated New Orleans, and the Saints' arena, the Superdome, was used as a shelter and a holding area for the people of the city. The hurricane had occurred just before the regular season, and so for the entire 2005 campaign the Saints played many of their home games in other cities including San Antonio (540 miles from New Orleans) where the headquarters would be located until they could return to Louisiana. While in Texas there were rumours that the team could relocate there permanently, and the idea was supported by political figures in the state as well as Dallas Cowboys owner Jerry Jones. The folk of Louisiana were furious at such suggestions; how dare anyone try and take financial advantage of New Orleans's tragedy.

The Saints returned to their hometown in 2006 and by the 2009 season, they finally made it to a Super Bowl, to face the Colts, who were favourites to win by five points and were led by quarterback Peyton Manning. The Saints had a star quarterback of their own in Drew Brees but by the first quarter it was 10-0 to the Colts. The beginning of the third quarter was a massive turning point. The Colts were supposed to have had the first possession of the half; however, the Saints did an audacious onside kick and recovered the fumble. They took advantage of the unexpected possession with a touchdown and were now leading. The Saints were 24-17 ahead with just three minutes to play when a Manning pass was intercepted by Tracy Porter who ran 74 yards for a touchdown to make it 31-17 and the game was over. New Orleans went wild in celebration, five years after the devastation of Katrina.

The Saints felt cheated out of an appearance in Super Bowl 53, which would have seen them take on the Patriots and a dream quarterback matchup of Brady versus Brees. In the NFC Championship game against the LA Rams at the Superdome, the scores were tied at 20-20 and the Saints had a third down on the Rams' 13-yard line, with one minute and 49 seconds left on the clock. LA had just the one timeout left, and another Saints first down would allow them to run the clock down and then score the field goal with no time left for a Rams comeback. Brees threw a pass to Tommylee Lewis who was smashed into by Nickell Robey-Coleman before he could catch the ball; a clear case of pass interference that would give New Orleans a first down, yet no flag came in. Coach Sean Payton was livid that not one of the officials saw fit to call a foul. As a result, the Saints scored the field goal and LA had time on their next possession to level the game, and they would go on to win in overtime. Calls would be made after the game for pass interference situations to warrant a red flag challenge.

Tampa Bay Buccaneers: Est. 1976

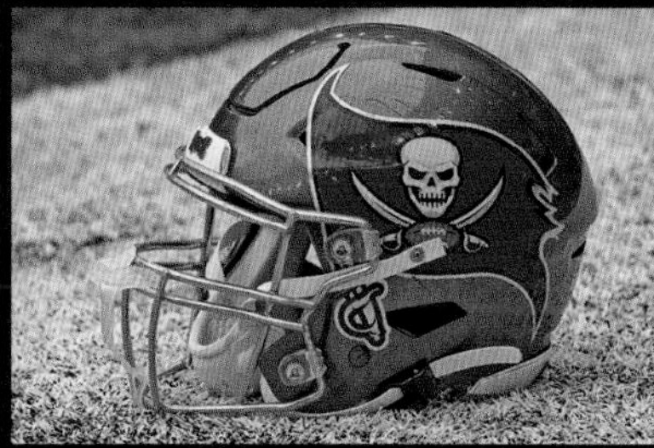

NFC Central Champions: (3) 1979, 1981, 1999

NFC South Champions: (4) 2002, 2005, 2007, 2021

NFC Conference Championships: (2) 2002, 2020

Super Bowl titles: (2) 2002, 2020

Super Bowl record: 2-0

The Buccaneers are a paradox. They have won two Super Bowls, which is more than 17 of the 32 teams in the NFL have achieved; not to mention that they were only founded in 1976, when ten Super Bowls had already happened. Yet despite those two successes, Tampa Bay have the lowest winning percentage of any team in the NFL. Before going into Super Bowl 55 they had won 293 games and lost 439. That one victory against Kansas City in the 2020 season Super Bowl would make little difference to their record, but the overall perception of the Bucs would change massively. Playing Tampa Bay meant playing an elite team, because they now had the most elite quarterback of all time.

When Tom Brady joined Tampa in 2020 there was excitement as well as trepidation. At the age of 42 Brady's last action in the NFL was throwing an interception for the Patriots that got returned for a touchdown in a loss to Tennessee in the play-offs. Despite an opening-day defeat to New Orleans where Brady threw another 'pick six', he would take his new team to the Super Bowl to face defending champs Kansas City.

Aside from Brady, the team were strong all round and the defence would destroy the Kansas offensive line and make Super Bowl 55 a nightmare for quarterback Patrick Mahomes. The attendance was just 24,835 due to Covid restrictions, and no other Super Bowl had felt quite like this one, as well as this being the first time that the game was won by a team playing in their home stadium. With this win, Brady achieved a unique stat of having more Super Bowl wins – seven – than any team had, with Pittsburgh and New England on six.

Tampa made it to the NFC Championship game in the 1979 campaign, in only their fourth NFL season. They lost 9-0 to the Rams but just having got that far was a wholesale improvement to a horrific start to life in the NFL. No one expected things to be easy for the new boys in the 1976 season. Seattle also had their first season in 1976, and had a record of 2-12. Not good, but Tampa lost every single game in a 0-14 nightmare start to their NFL existence. The nightmare continued into the 1977 season as Tampa lost their first 12 games, going to 0-26 since joining the NFL. Then finally on the 13th week of the season the Bucs won a game, beating New Orleans, resulting in the Saints sacking their head coach. Then they won again in week 14 against St Louis, causing the Cardinals to fire their head coach too.

In the 1999 season Tampa nearly made a Super Bowl, narrowly losing to the Rams 11-6 in the NFC Championship game. Three years later in the 2002 season they were back in the NFC Championship game, and beat the Eagles to book a place in the Super Bowl against the Oakland Raiders – in an all-pirate derby. The Raiders' logo is a pirate wearing a football helmet, while the Buccaneers' first logo was a pirate holding a sword between his teeth, though that got changed to a flag with a skull on top of two crossed sabres. As well as 'Pirate-Bowl' the game was known as 'Gruden Bowl' as the Tampa coach Jon Gruden had coached the Raiders between 1998 and 2001. The Raiders were four-point favourites going into the game, but the Bucs would win each quarter and come out on top 48-21. The main narrative for Tampa had been that of a team with the longest losing streak in football; now a new narrative had been set as the Bucs became the youngest team in the NFC to be a Super Bowl champion.

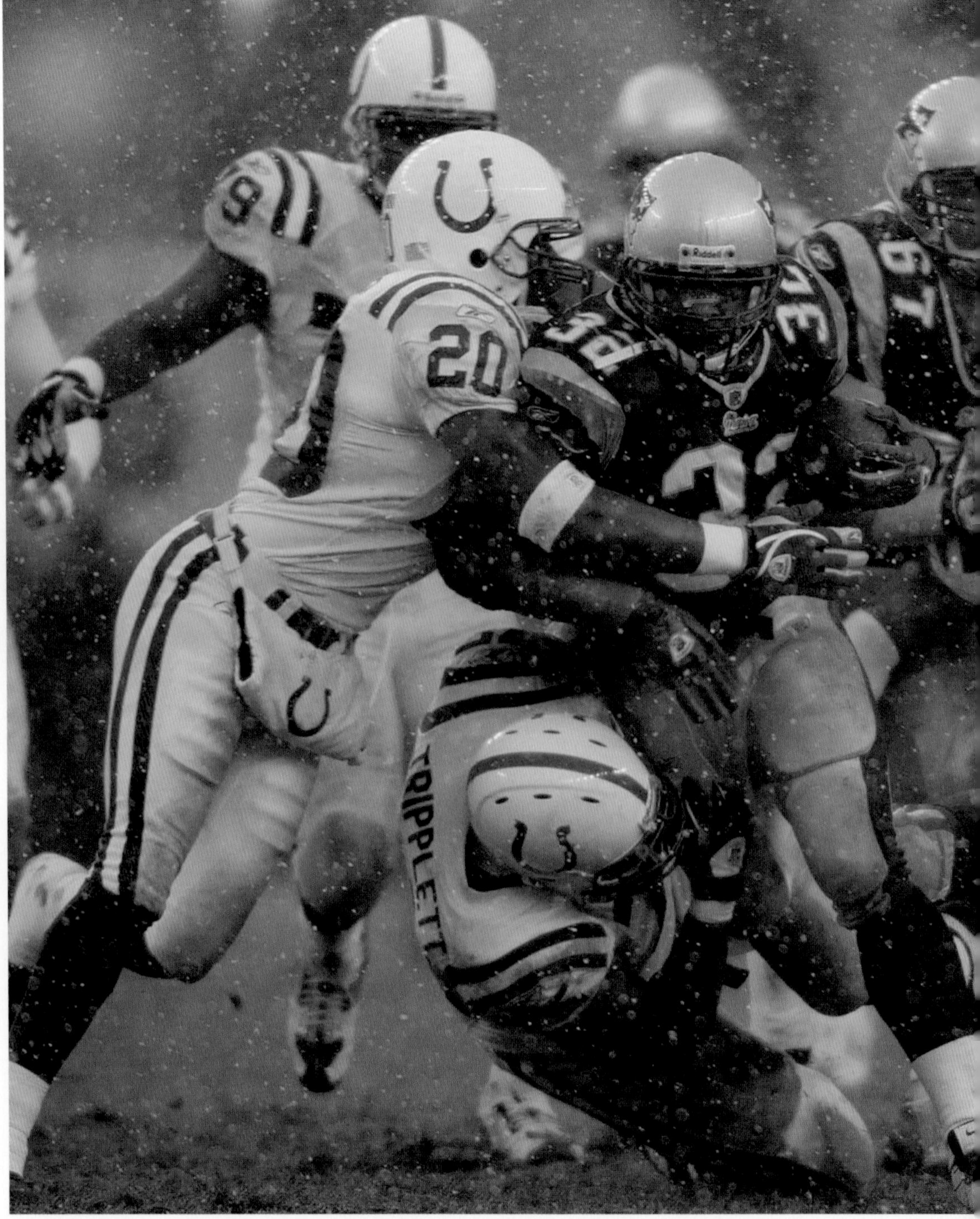
TRIPPLETT

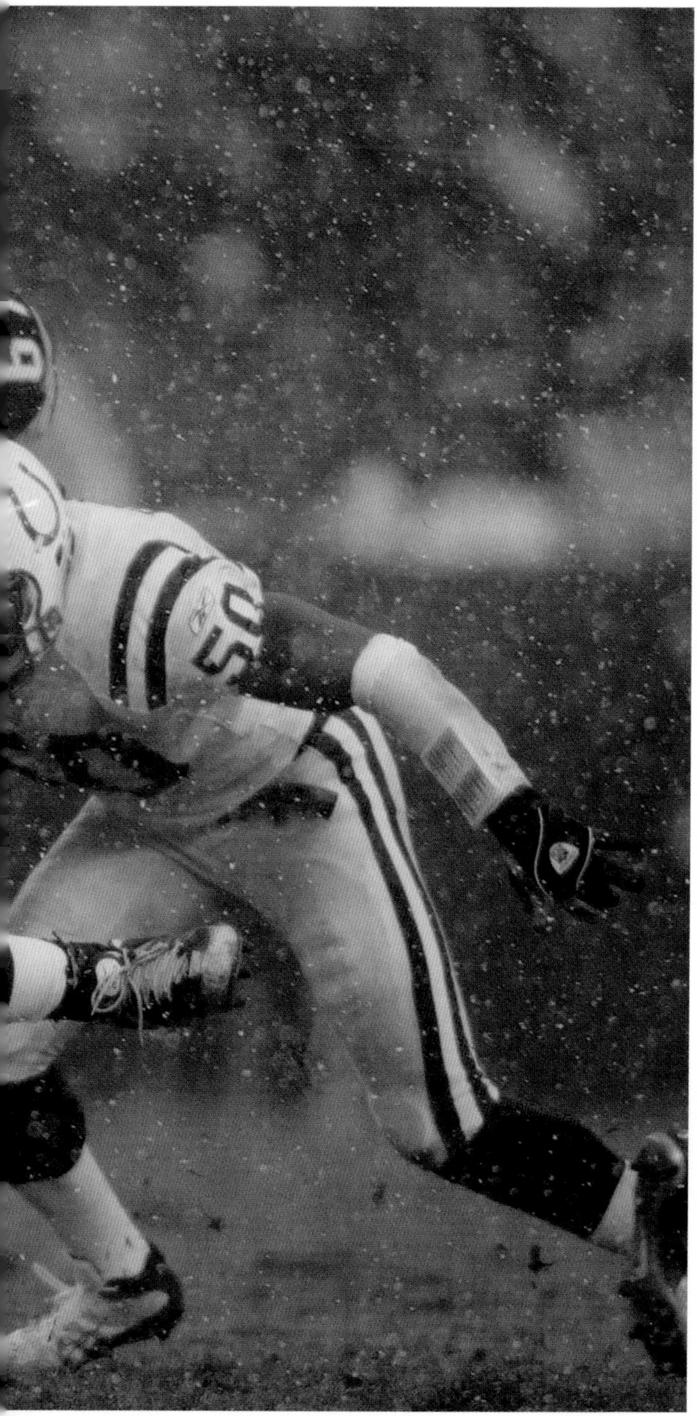

Gillette Stadium, Foxboro, 2004
Patriots running back Antowain Smith charges for a first down against the Colts in the AFC Championship. New England won the game 24-14.

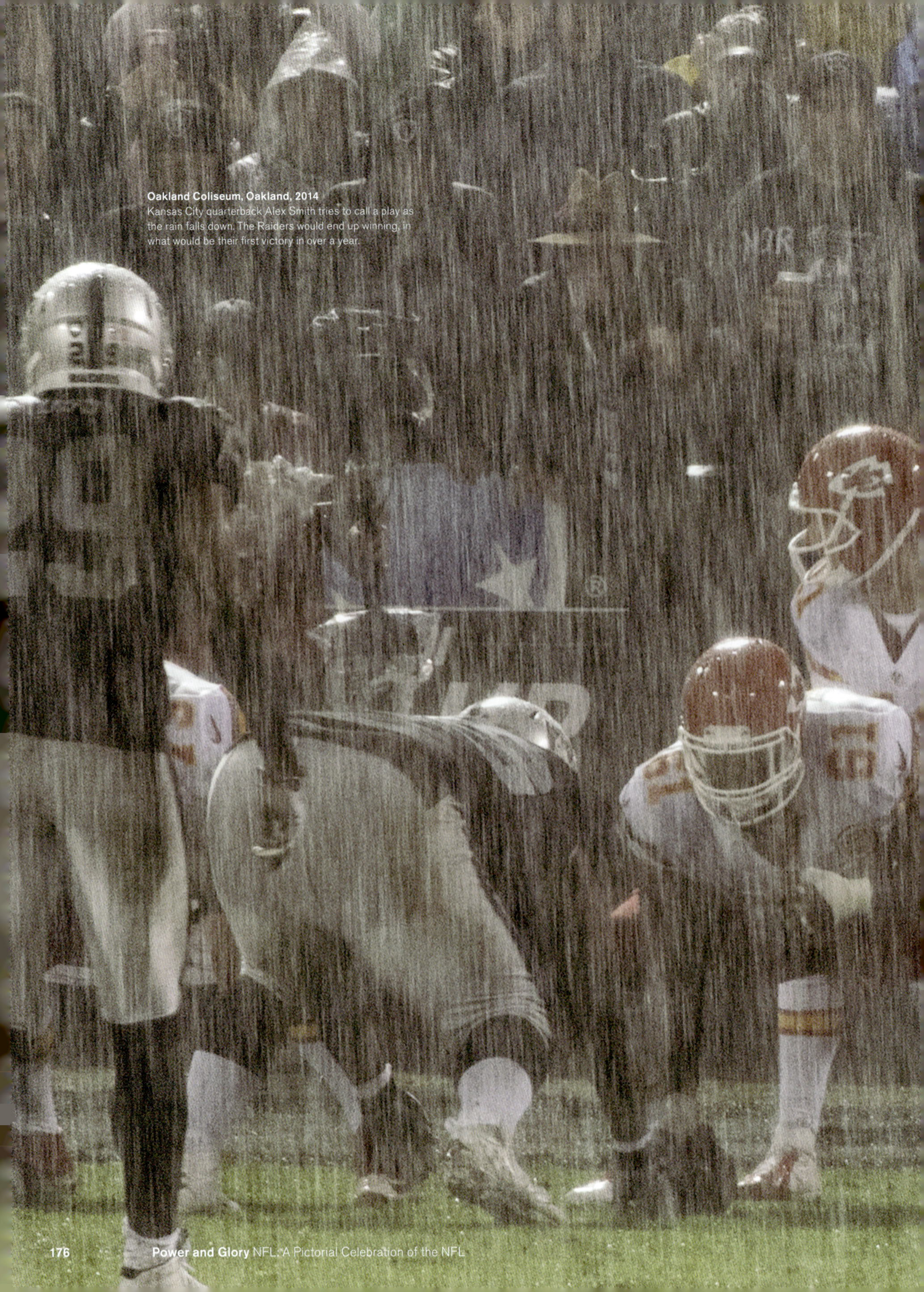

Oakland Coliseum, Oakland, 2014
Kansas City quarterback Alex Smith tries to call a play as the rain falls down. The Raiders would end up winning, in what would be their first victory in over a year.

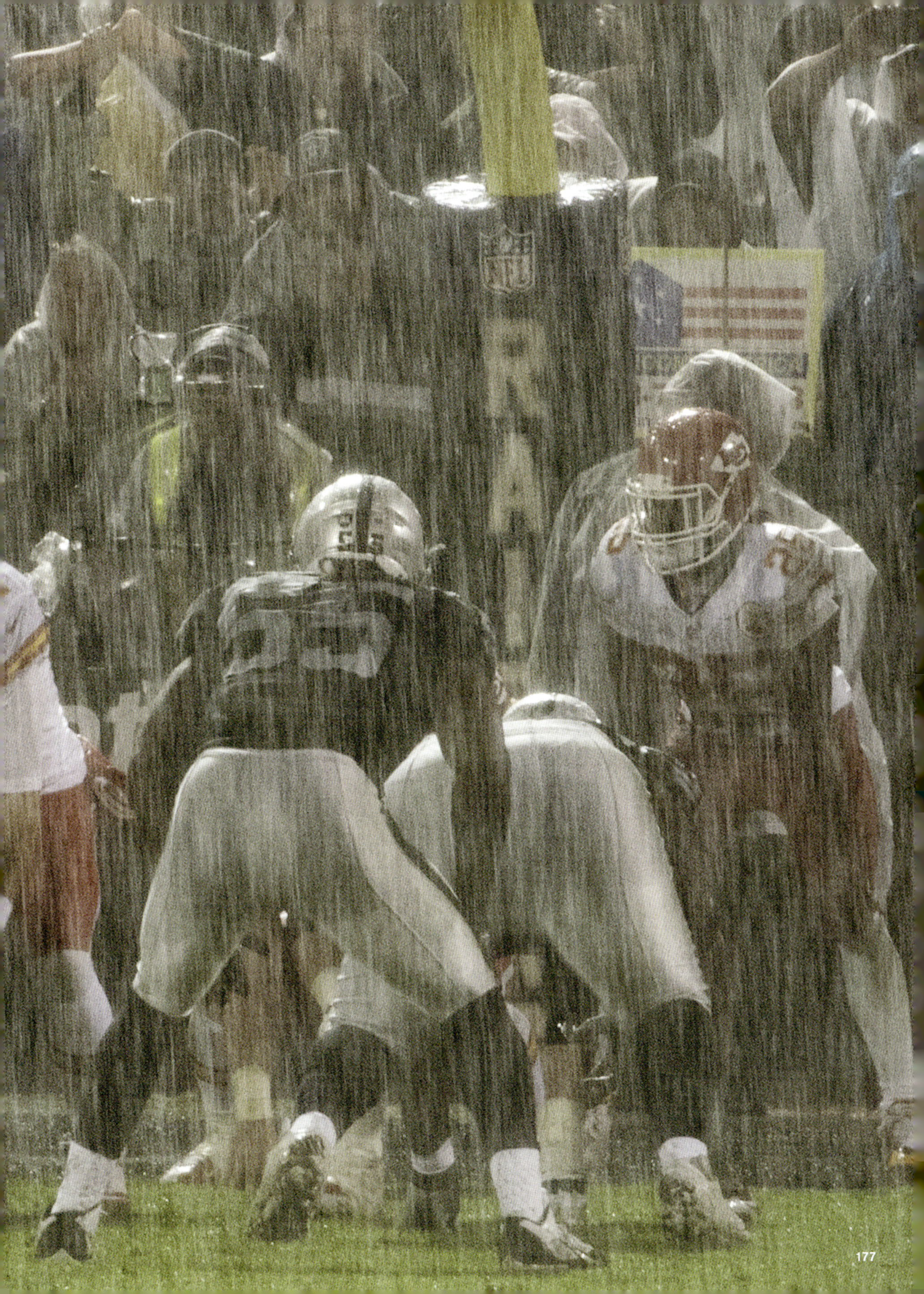

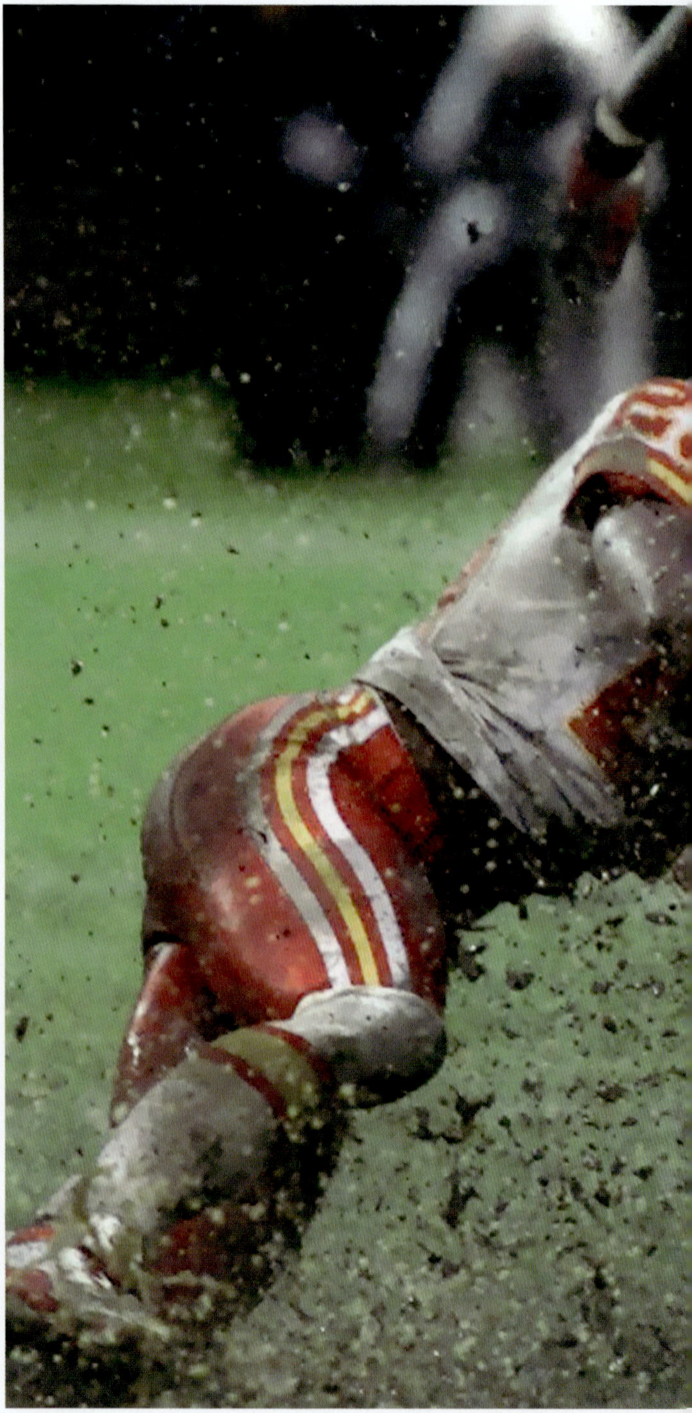

Oakland Coliseum, Oakland, 2002
Kansas City's Jason Belser (29) and John Browning (93) take down Oakland running back Charlie Garner.

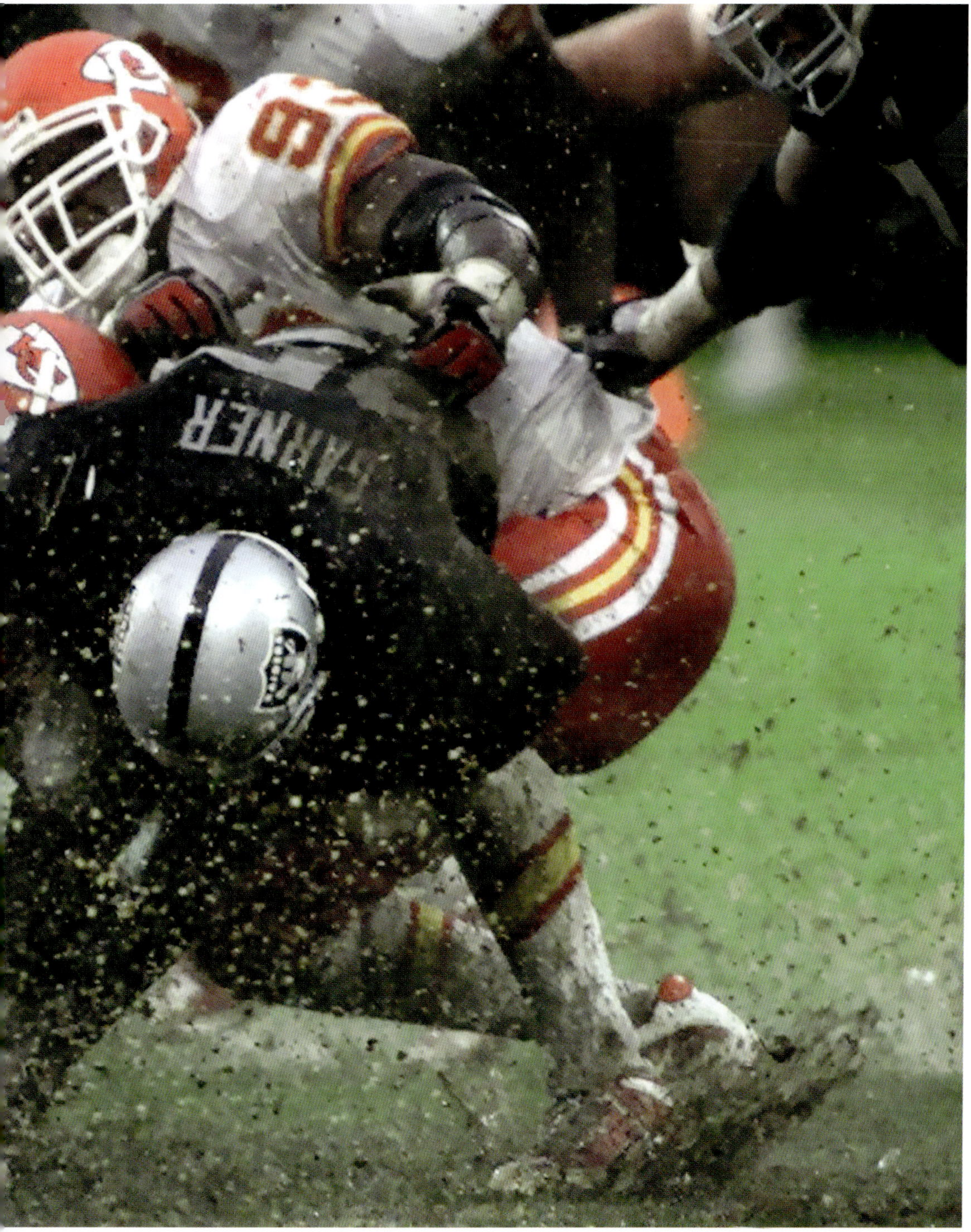

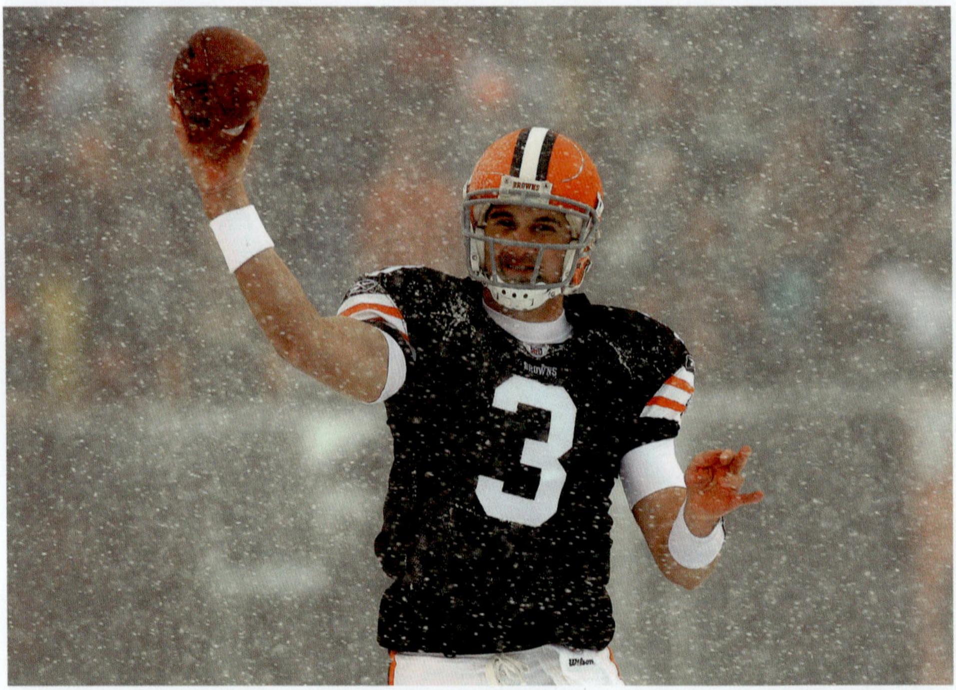

Cleveland Browns Stadium, Cleveland, 2007
Browns quarterback Derek Anderson throws during a snow game against Buffalo.

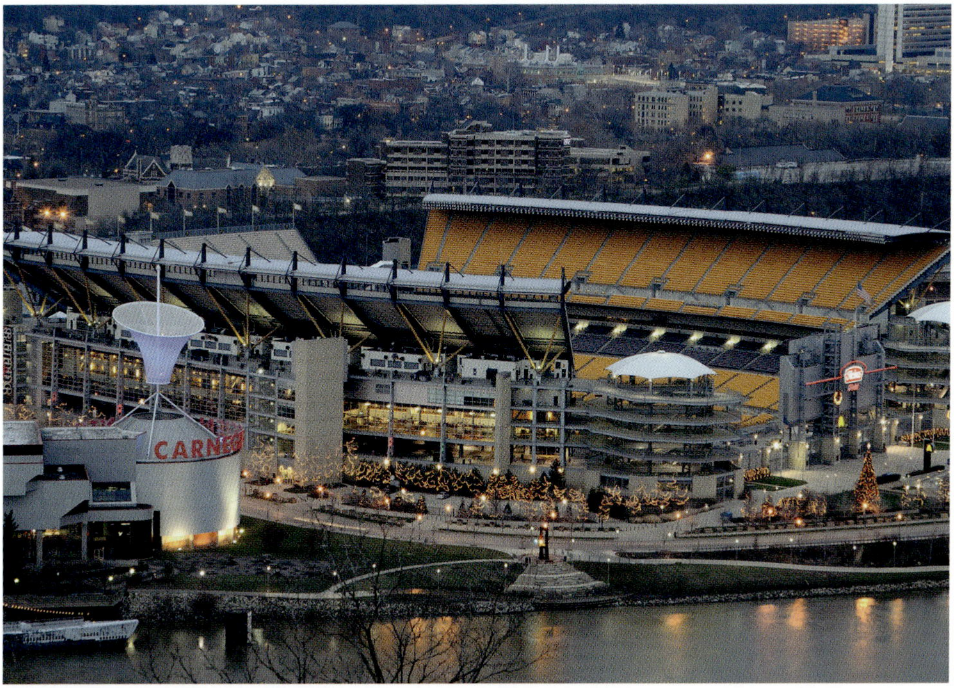

Heinz Field, Pittsburgh, 2010
The waterside home of the Pittsburgh Steelers,
the six-time Super Bowl winners.

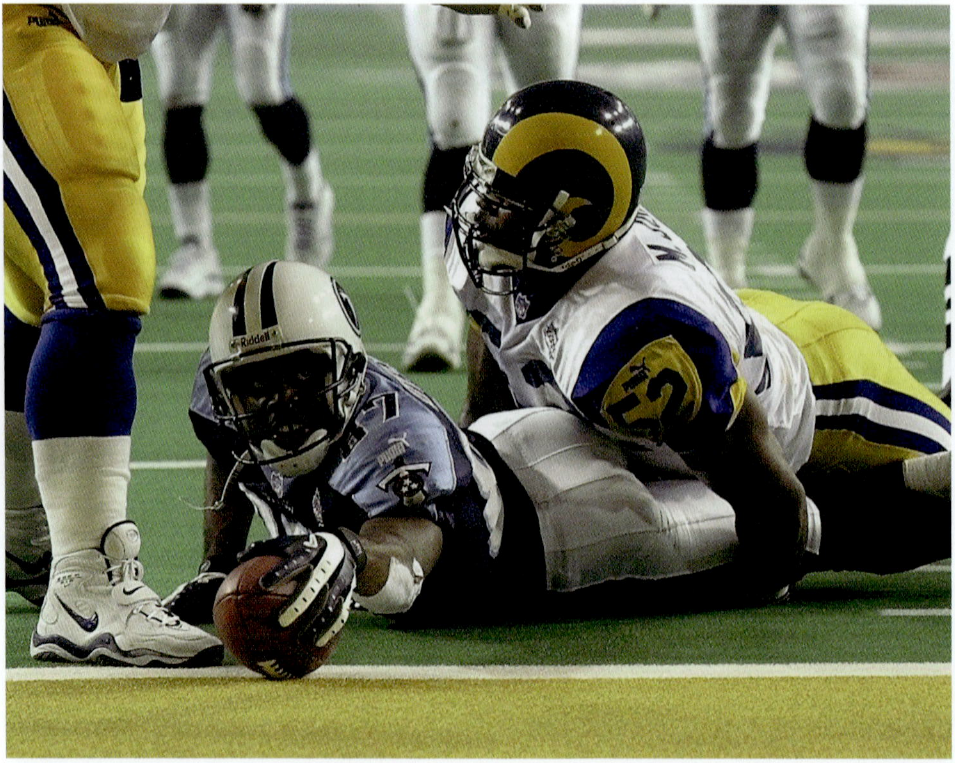

Georgia Dome, Atlanta, 2000
Super Bowl 34 comes to a conclusion in the last play of the game. Tennessee's Kevin Dyson is a yard short of scoring a touchdown and taking the game to overtime, thanks to a last-gasp tackle from St. Louis's Mike Jones (52).

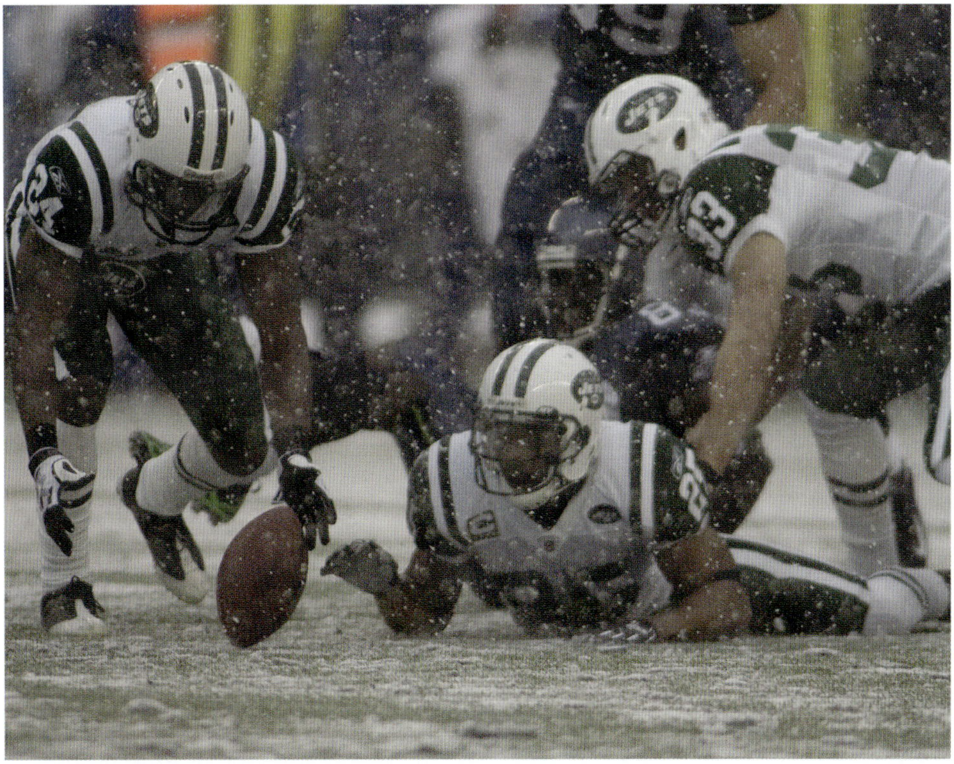

Quest Field, Seattle, 2008
The Jets defence jump upon a fumble by the Seahawks and gain a turnover.

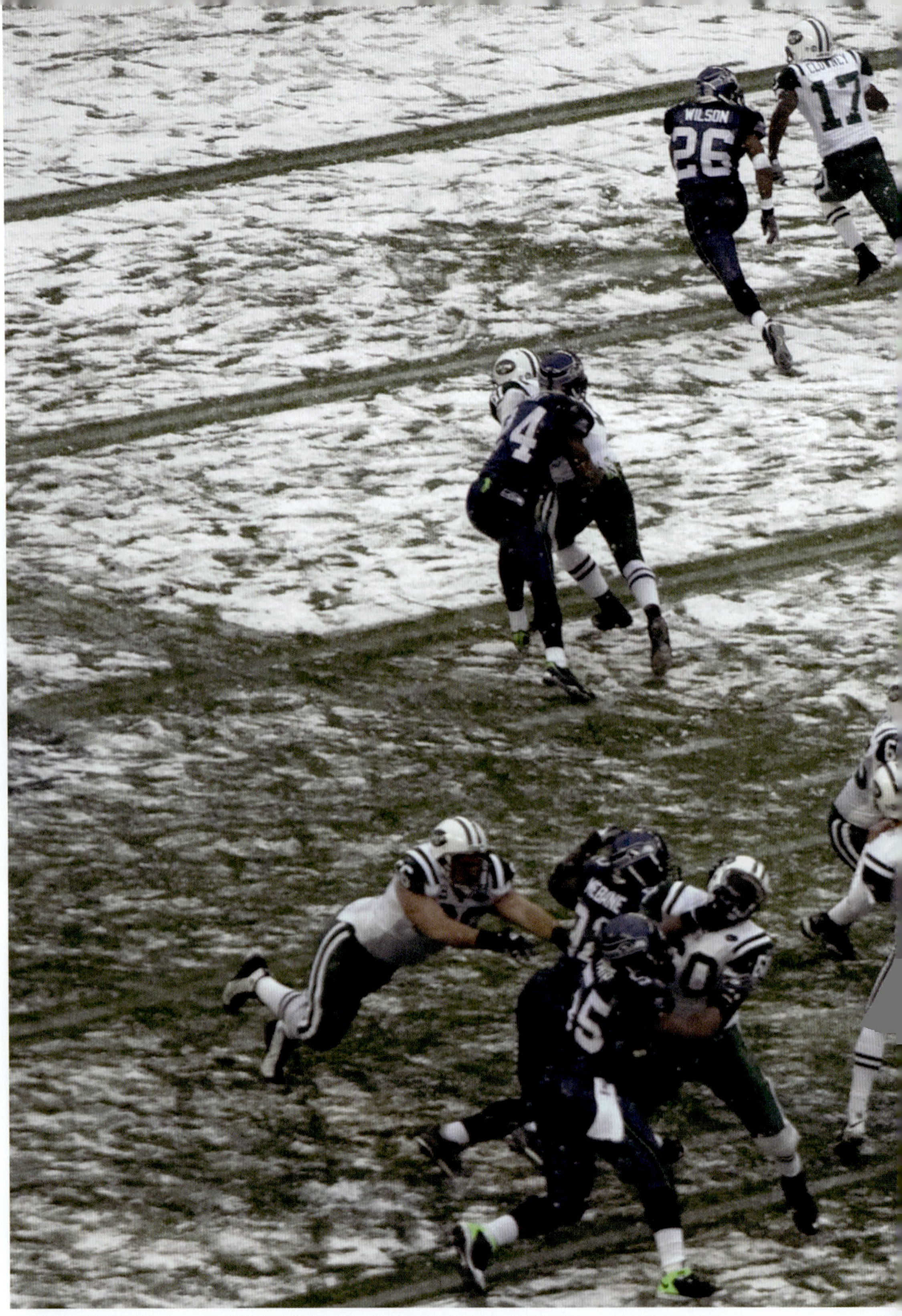

Quest Field, Seattle, 2008
Jets quarterback Brett Favre throws a pass in snow and icy conditions in Seattle. In their last home game of the season the Seahawks would win 13-3.

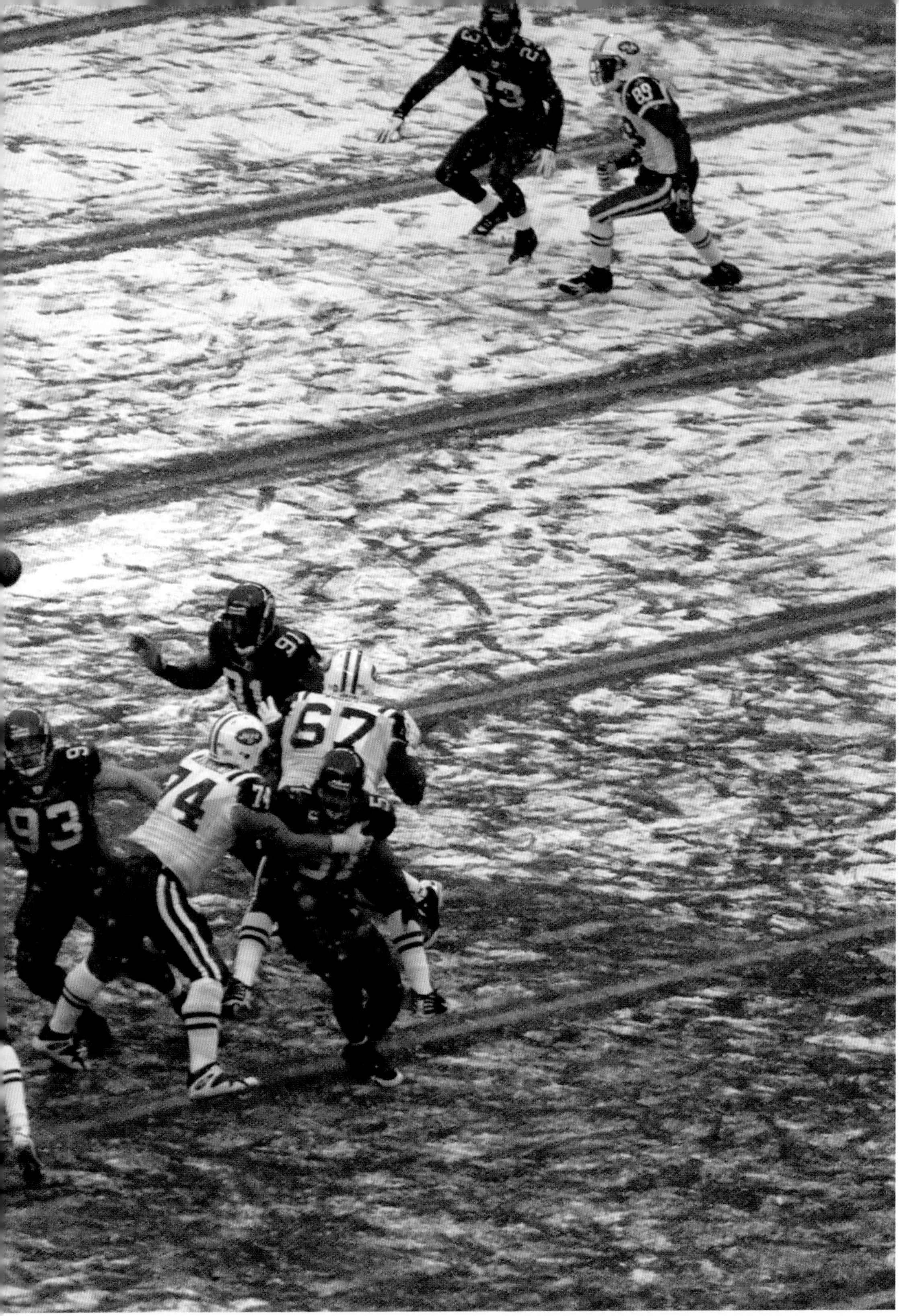

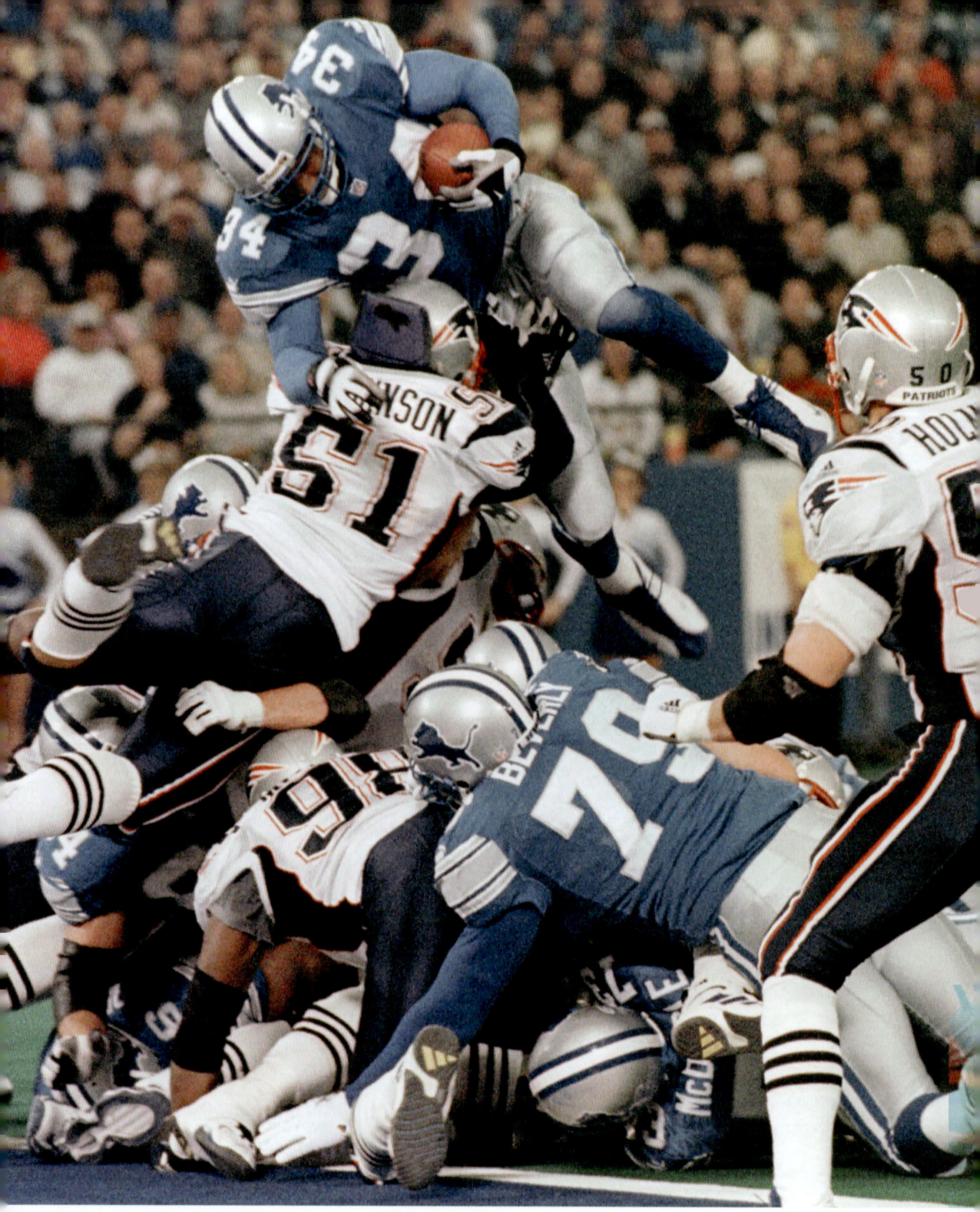

34
NSON
51
50
PATRIOTS
HOL
BEVERLY
79

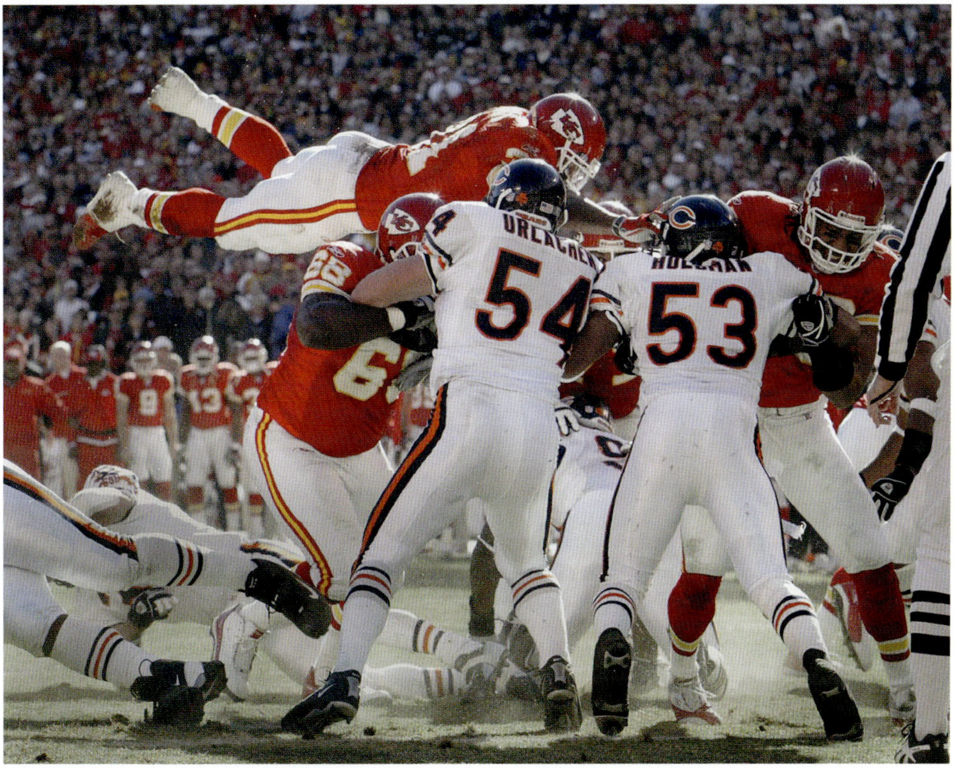

Pontiac Silverdome, Pontiac/Detroit, 2000
It's Thanksgiving Day, therefore in keeping with tradition the Lions will be playing a home game. Here, Detroit's James Stewart (24) jumps over the New England defence to score a touchdown in a 34-9 victory for the home team.

Arrowhead Stadium, Kansas City, 2003
Kansas running back Priest Holmes does an impression of Superman, however is held short of the goal line by the Bears defence. Holmes scored on the very next play and set a record for the most touchdowns in a single season (27).

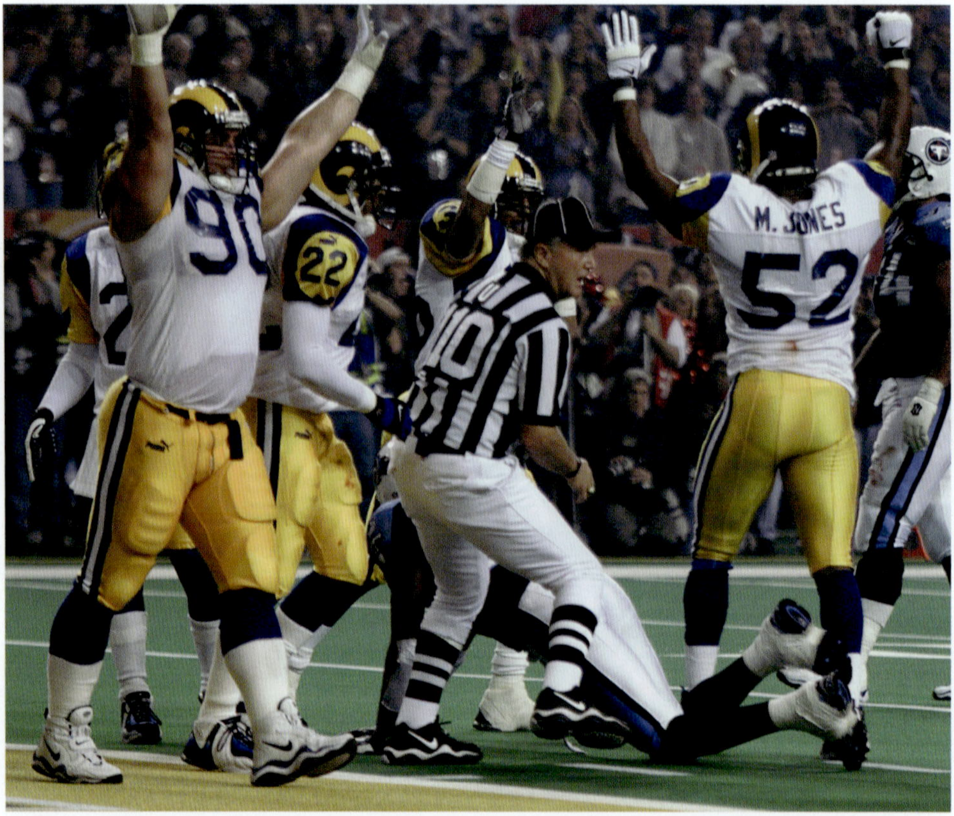

Georgia Dome, Atlanta, 2000
St. Louis players celebrate the end of Super Bowl 34, and a win against the Titans, after they stopped Kevin Dyson in the final play in the 'one yard' Super Bowl.

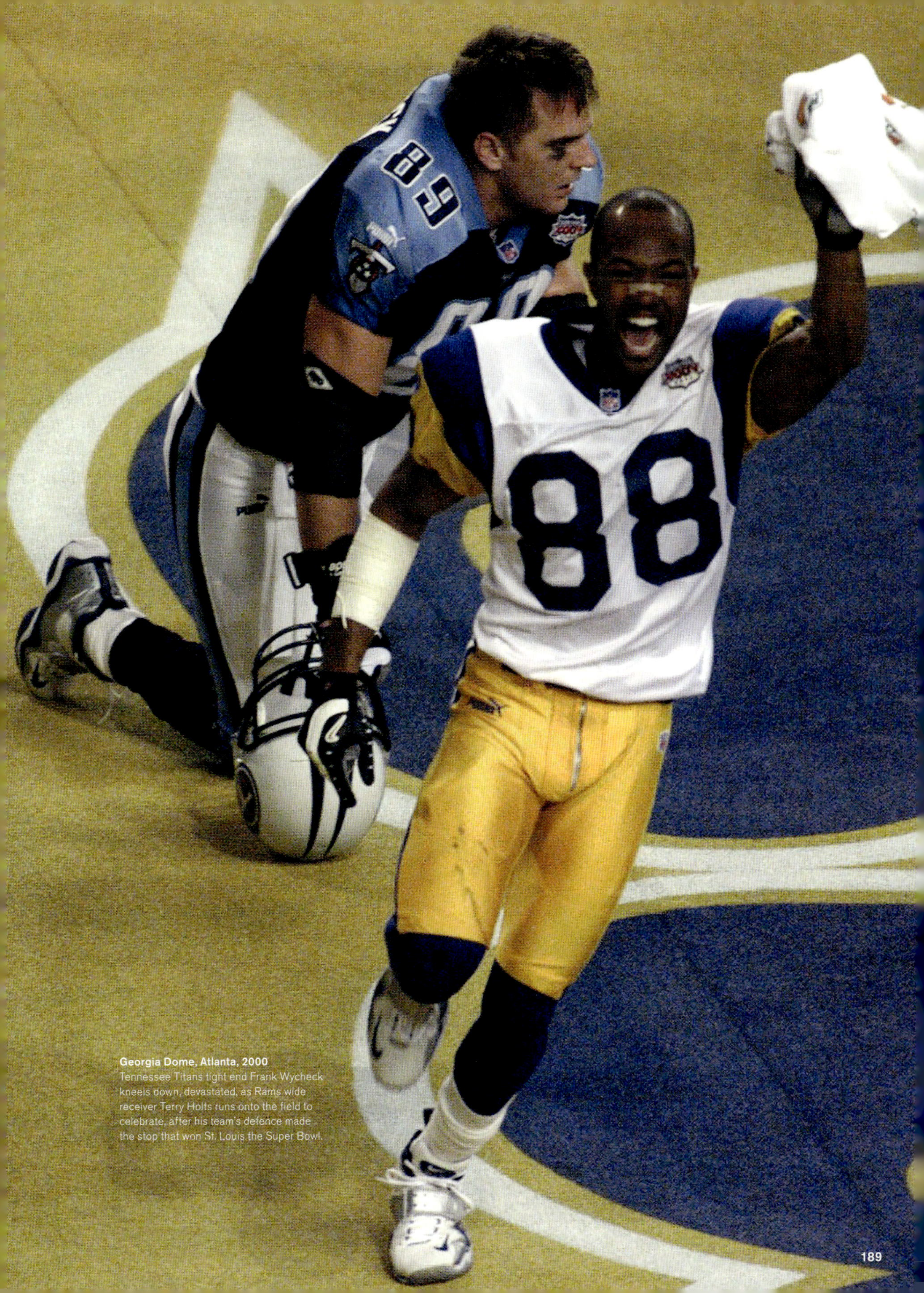

Georgia Dome, Atlanta, 2000
Tennessee Titans tight end Frank Wycheck kneels down, devastated, as Rams wide receiver Terry Holts runs onto the field to celebrate, after his team's defence made the stop that won St. Louis the Super Bowl.

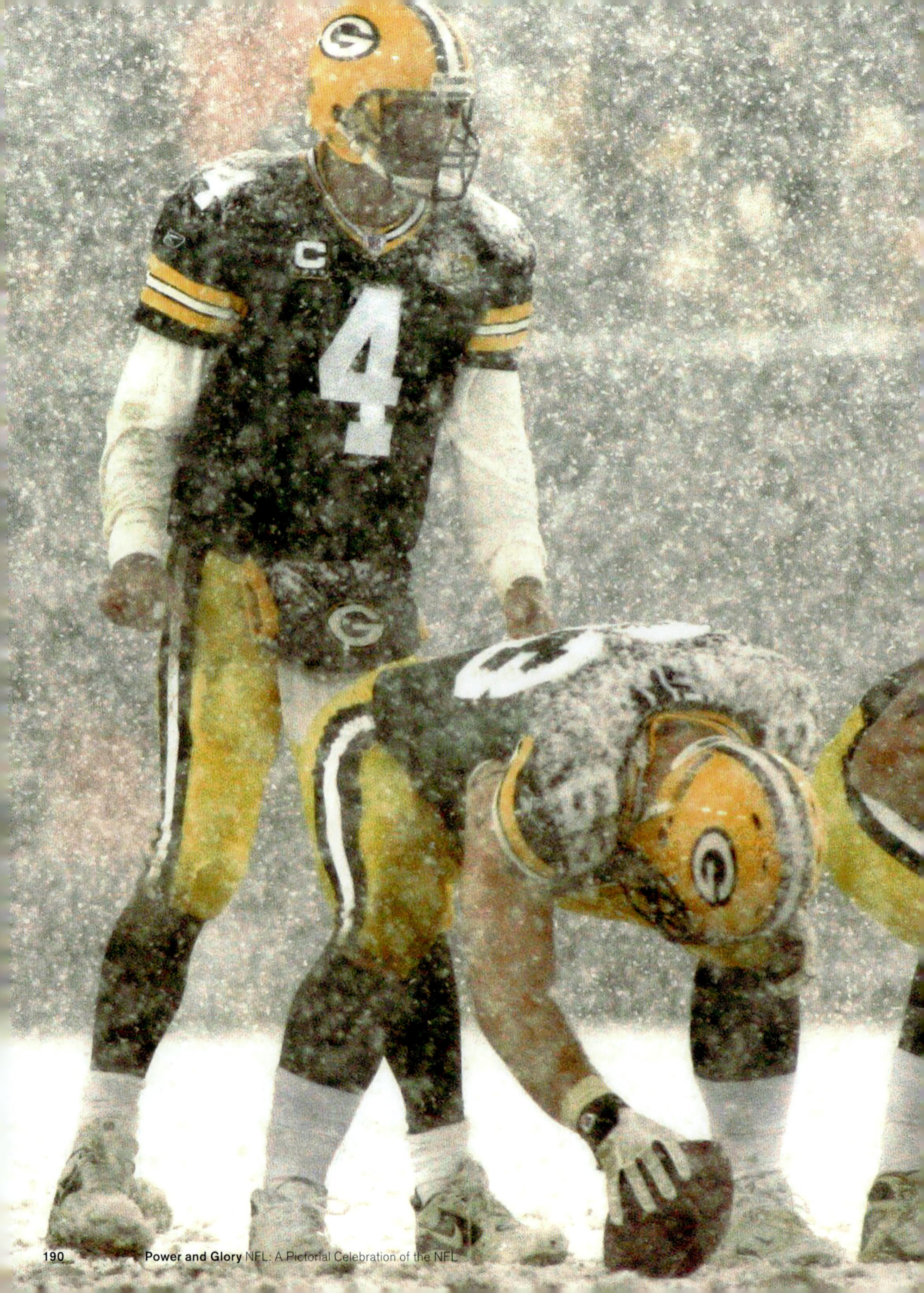

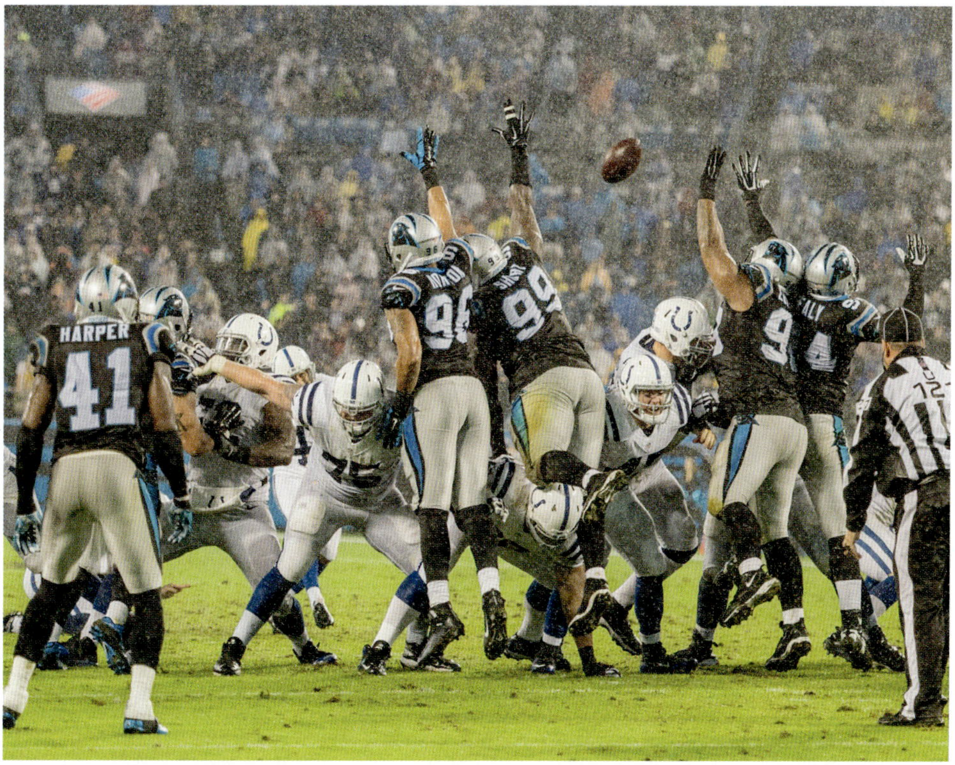

Lambeau Field, Green Bay, 2007
A typical January in Green Bay. Packers quarterback Brett Favre battles the conditions in a divisional play-off win against Seattle.

Bank of America Stadium, Charlotte, 2015
The Carolina Panthers attempt to stop a field goal against Indianapolis.

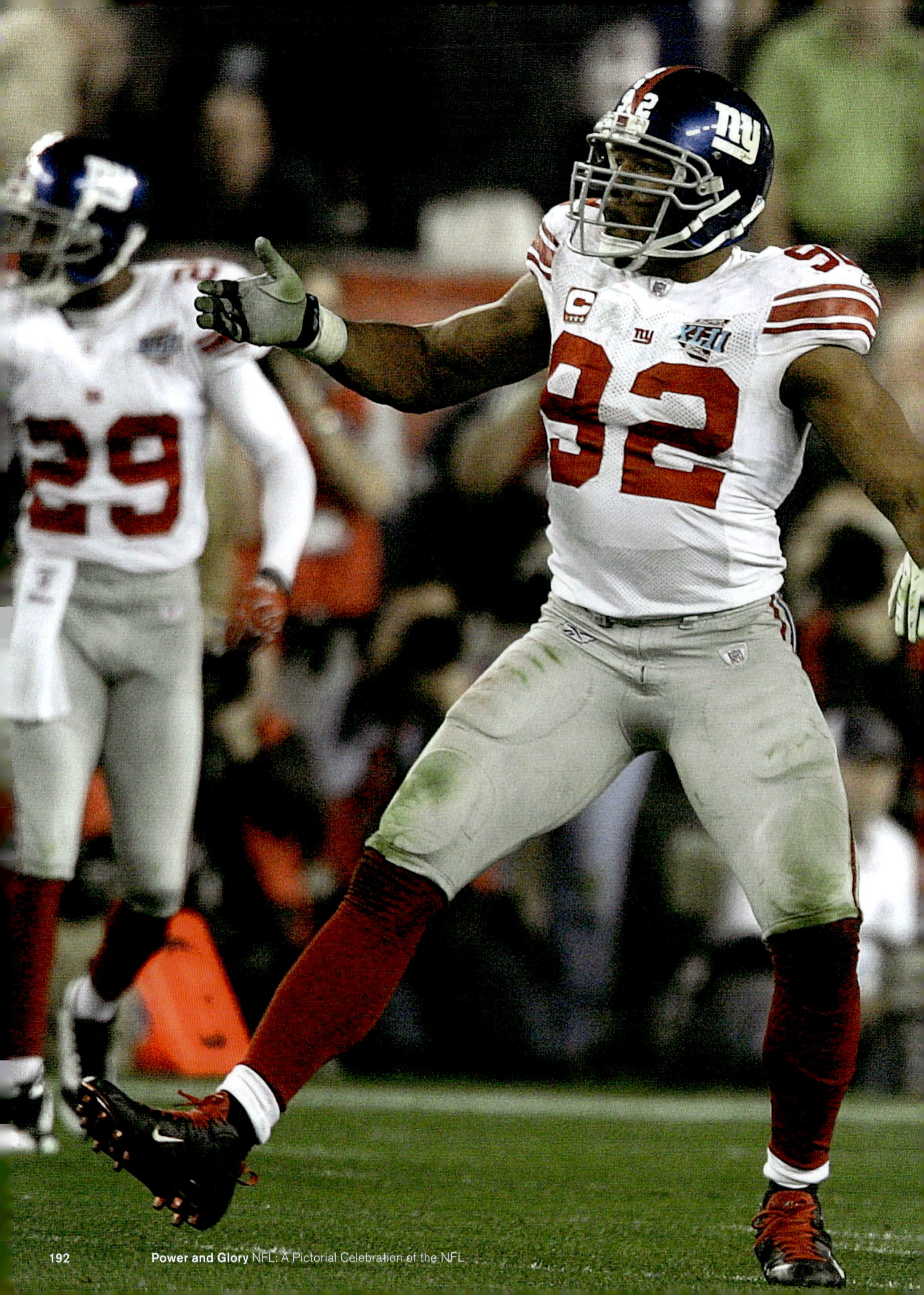

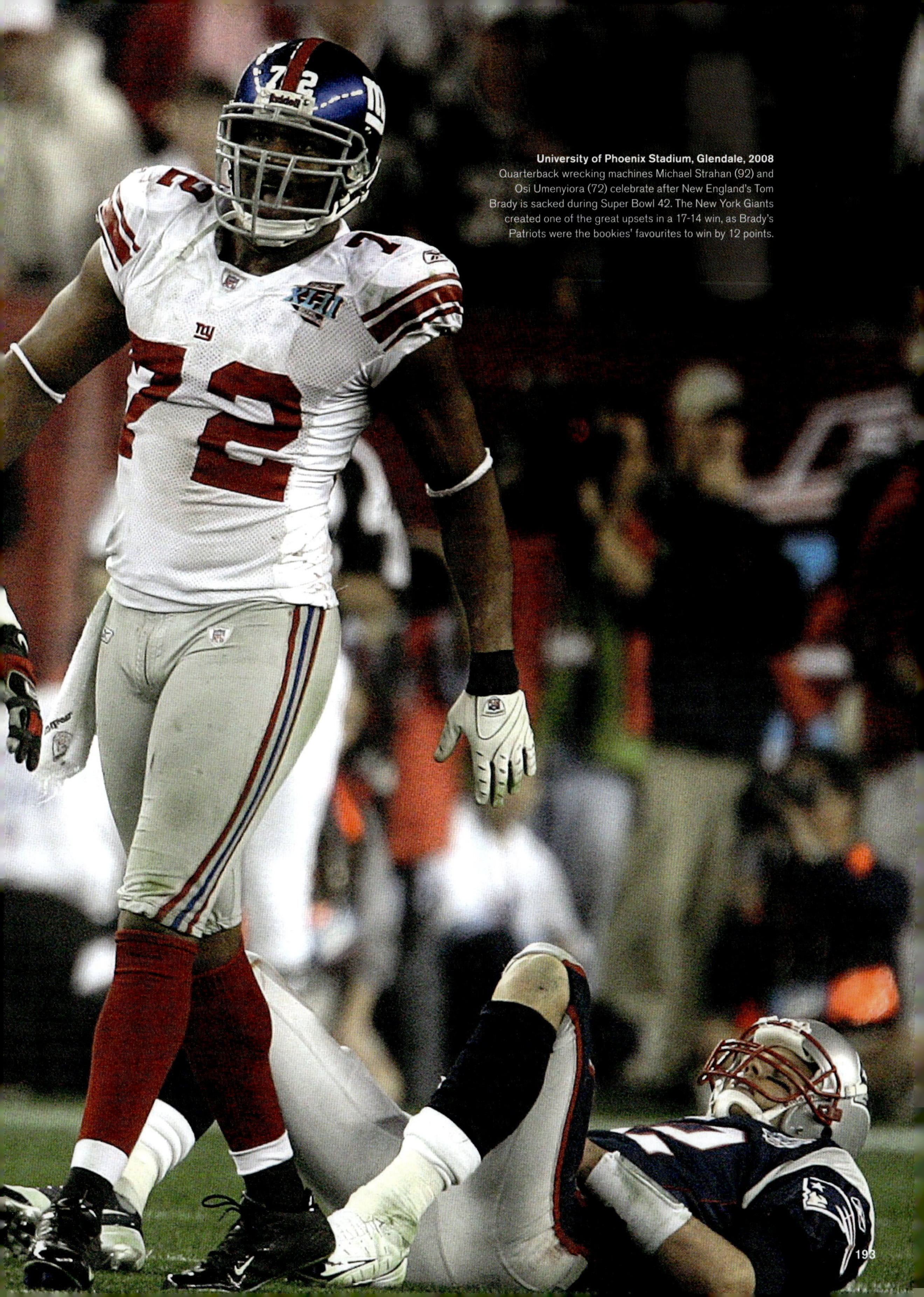

University of Phoenix Stadium, Glendale, 2008
Quarterback wrecking machines Michael Strahan (92) and Osi Umenyiora (72) celebrate after New England's Tom Brady is sacked during Super Bowl 42. The New York Giants created one of the great upsets in a 17-14 win, as Brady's Patriots were the bookies' favourites to win by 12 points.

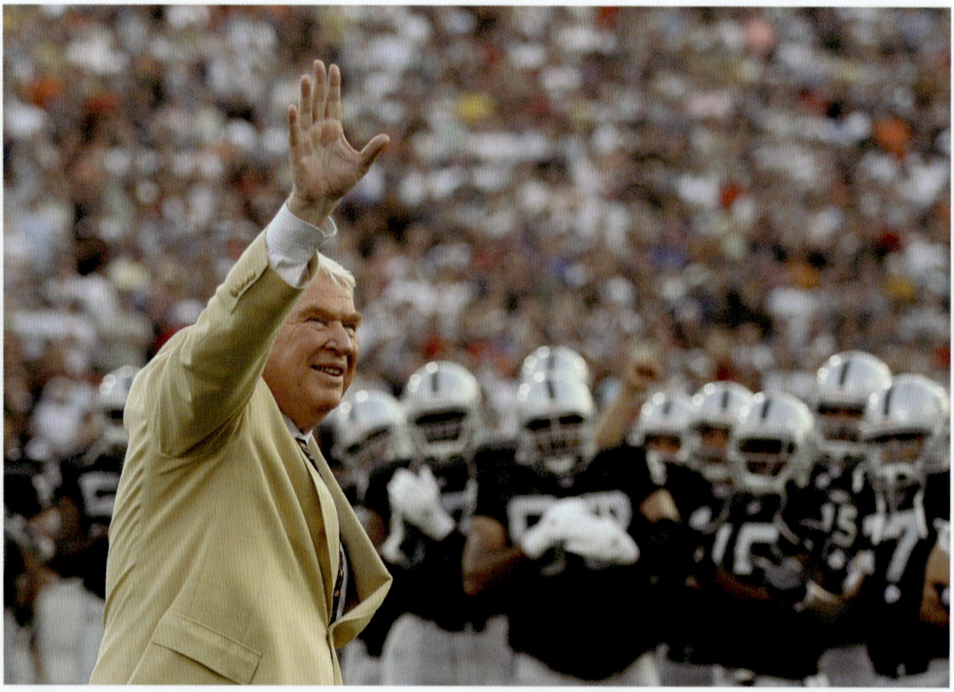

Fawcett Stadium, Canton, 2006
During a Hall of Fame presentation game between the Raiders and the Eagles, the legendary Raiders coach John Madden waves to the crowd. Madden was as famous for being a broadcaster as he was for being a coach, and he died in December 2021 at the age of 85.

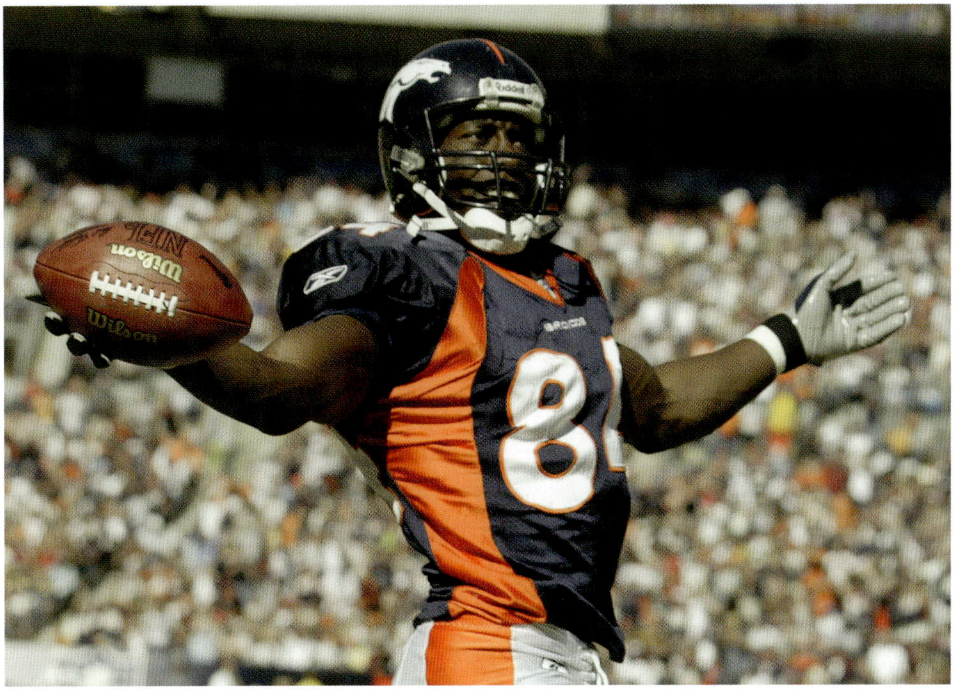

Mile High Stadium, Denver, 2003
Broncos tight end Shannon Sharpe celebrates scoring a touchdown against Detroit. Sharpe won three Super Bowl rings (two with Denver, one with Baltimore) and today has a successful career as a sports pundit.

Dallas Cowboys: Est. 1960

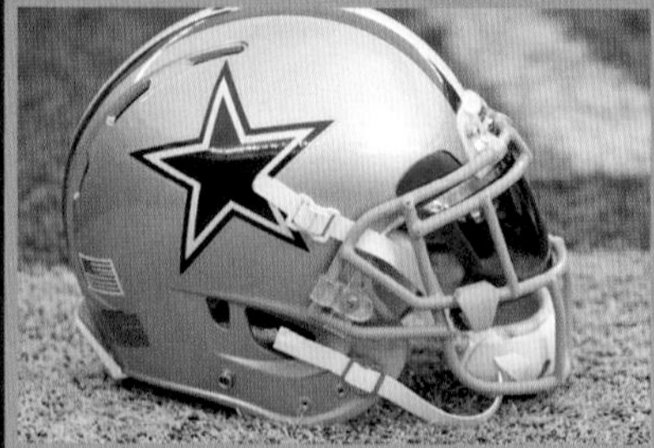

NFC East Champions: (21) 1970, 1971, 1973, 1976, 1977, 1978, 1979, 1981, 1985, 1992, 1993, 1994, 1995, 1996, 1998, 2007, 2009, 2014, 2016, 2018, 2021

NFC Conference Championships: (8) 1970, 1971, 1975, 1977, 1978, 1992, 1993, 1995

Super Bowl titles: (5) 1971, 1977, 1992, 1993, 1995

Super Bowl record: 5-3

The NFC East is probably the division with the most intense rivalry. None of the four teams get along, although New York, Washington and Philadelphia can agree on one thing – they all hate Dallas the most; with that feeling of animosity compounded by the Cowboys' claim to being 'America's Team'. Dallas are a lot younger than their divisional rivals and do not even pre-date the AFL. When they were formed in 1960, the NFL was a northern league, played in states that get freezing cold in the winter. The introduction of the Cowboys changed that, but the team struggled badly in their early years, not registering a winning record in their first six seasons. They started winning in 1966, the season when the NFL and AFL experimented with the idea of the Super Bowl. Dallas came close to getting to the first two Super Bowls but lost the NFC Championship on both occasions to the Packers, including the famous 'ice bowl' game in 1967 at Lambeau Field – the coldest game in the history of the league.

Under the guidance of coach Tom Landry, the Cowboys registered an incredible 20 straight winning seasons between 1966 and 1985, the NFL's longest winning streak. During that period, they made it to the post-season 18 times, and competed in ten NFC Championship games, along with five Super Bowl appearances. When Dallas registered a record of 7-9 in the 1986 season it was the first losing campaign they had suffered since season 1964. The 'Big D' made it to Super Bowl 5 but would lose to the Colts. The following season, in 1971, they were back and this time beat the Dolphins to win their first Super Bowl. In the 1975 season they lost Super Bowl 10 to the Steelers, then two seasons later they beat the Broncos 27-10 to win Super Bowl 12. The season after that, they got to Super Bowl 13 but once again would lose to the Steelers.

In the first three seasons of the 1980s Dallas made it to the NFC Championship game, but would lose on all three occasions, then success would dry up until the 1990s. In the 1992 season they beat the San Francisco 49ers in the NFC Championship game and Buffalo to win the Super Bowl, amazingly repeating the feat against the same two teams the following season to win back-to-back titles. The rivalry with the 49ers was becoming legendary and the win against Buffalo in the 1993 season Super Bowl put Dallas equal with Pittsburgh and the 49ers as the overall record holders with four Super Bowl wins each.

San Francisco then won the 1994 season Super Bowl, giving them the record of five. It was then fitting that the following season's showpiece game was Dallas vs Pittsburgh, to see who would level up with the 49ers on five overall wins. Dallas were heavy favourites to win, which they did 27-17, to equal the record as well as become the first team to win three Super Bowls in four seasons. By the mid-1990s the Cowboys and 49ers had acquired ten Super Bowl victories between them and were the kings of the NFL, although by the time of writing neither has added to that total. Dallas have not even made it to an NFC Championship game since the 1995 season, and have only won four post-season games in that time. As success on the field dried up the price tag didn't and Dallas are considered the world's most valuable sports club at an eye watering $6bn, with owner Jerry Jones saying his price tag is $10bn.

New York Giants: Est. 1925

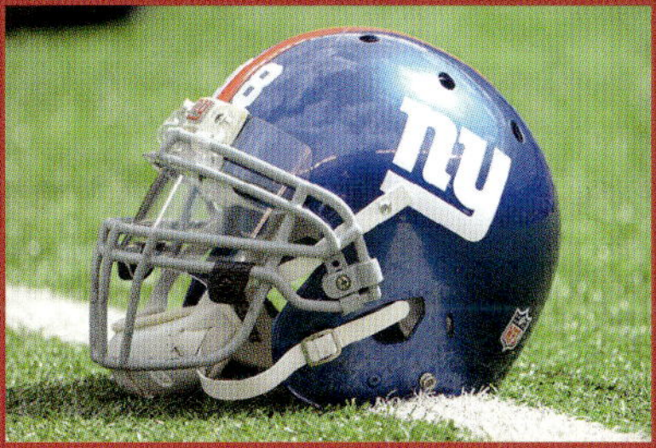

NFL Championships pre-1970 merger (4): 1927, 1934, 1938, 1956

NFC East Champions: (8) 1986, 1989, 1990, 1997, 2000, 2005, 2008, 2011

NFC Conference Champions: (5) 1986, 1990, 2000, 2007, 2011

Super Bowl titles (4): 1986, 1990, 2007, 2011

Super Bowl record: 4-1

The 'Big Blue' are the fourth oldest team in the league and were NFL champions for the first time in 1927, just two years after being founded. Three more championships followed in seasons 1934, 1938 and 1956; with the 1956 team having Vince Lombardi as the offence coach, while Tom Landry coached the defence. Both those legendary names would go on win Super Bowls as head coaches with other teams in the 1960s and 1970s, the very same period of time as the Giants were in decline. Between 1964 and 1980 they didn't appear in one play-off game, and would only register two winning seasons.

The Giants' first home, the Polo Grounds, was located in Manhattan, before they moved to the Yankee Stadium in the Bronx between 1956 and 1973. After spending a couple of years in the state of Connecticut, the team returned to New York City in 1975 to play a season in the borough of Queens. Since that time they have played home games in the state of New Jersey, along with their city neighbours the Jets. By the 1981 season, the Giants had drafted outside linebacker Lawrence Taylor who would end up in the conversation as being the best ever defensive player. The team started to make trips to the post-season and by the 1986 campaign they made it to their first Super Bowl, to face Denver. The Giants won 39-20 and for the first time in 30 years were champions of the NFL. A second championship would follow in the 1990 season when they beat Buffalo in Super Bowl 25, in a game that highlighted just how thin the margins are between triumph and tribulation, as Buffalo's last-second field goal attempt went just wide of the post as the Giants celebrated in relief.

Upon entering the 2007 season Super Bowl, not many people put up a case for the Giants to beat New England who up to this point had a season record of played 18, won 18. New York, in contrast, had a 10-6 regular-season record, but in the play-offs they had battled past Tampa, Dallas and Green Bay to get to the big game. In the NFC Championship game against the Packers, the Giants were also up against the freezing Wisconsin conditions in which defensive end Osi Umenyiora recalled that he couldn't feel his arms, his legs, his face, and other more delicate parts of his anatomy! The Patriots were 12-point favourites to which Umenyiora said, 'It's almost as if we shouldn't have turned up. We went in with an extreme sense of anger. We went in with an extreme sense of disrespect. And because we felt we were better on the defensive line where the game, back then, was won and lost we knew we had a chance. We're like "we're going to destroy Tom Brady!" and that is exactly what we did.'

With one minute and 15 seconds left on the clock the Giants were trailing 14-10, and had a third down in their own half. As quarterback Eli Manning took possession of the ball on third down, he was grabbed hold of, and it looked like he would be sacked. Instead, he managed to wriggle out of trouble and launched a high and hopeful pass downfield. David Tyree leapt up, made the catch of his life, and as he came down managed to hold on to the ball with one hand which he wedged against his helmet. The Giants would go on to score the winning touchdown in what was considered one of the NFL's biggest upsets. To prove the result wasn't a fluke, the Giants beat New England once again four seasons later in Super Bowl 46.

Philadelphia Eagles: Est. 1933

Former names: Phil-Pitt 'Steagles' (1943)

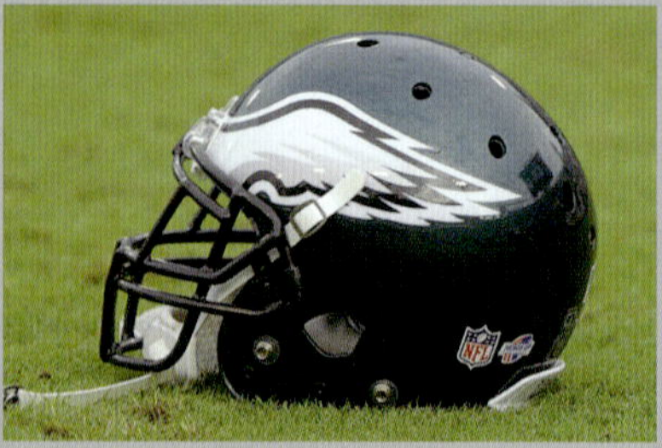

NFL Championships pre-1970 merger: (3) 1948, 1949, 1960

NFC East Champions: (11) 1980, 1988, 2001, 2002, 2003, 2004, 2006, 2010, 2013, 2017, 2019

NFC Conference Championships (3): 1980, 2004, 2017

Super Bowl titles: (1) 2017

Super Bowl record: 1-2

Philadelphia lost their first ten seasons in the NFL, before merging with Pittsburgh for one season in 1943 to become the Steagles. By the end of the decade the Eagles were two-time NFL champions, after winning the championship game in consecutive seasons without conceding a point in either (7-0 versus the Cardinals in 1948, and 14-0 against the Rams in 1949). A third NFL championship came in the 1960 season with a victory over the Green Bay Packers, but it would be a long time before the Eagles would be champions again.

Being in the NFC East over the decades, along with Washington, New York and Dallas, has been tough, as no other team in the NFL got lumbered with three other divisional rivals so strong (apart from the Cardinals who spent some years in the NFC East before moving divisions). Before the millennium, the Eagles had won the NFC East only twice, although this century they have accumulated the most divisional wins putting them above both New York and Washington for overall NFC East titles. The division has recently been nicknamed the 'NFC Least' due to the poor record of all four teams in the last few seasons, but overall, no division comes close to the glory of the NFC East, which boasts the most Super Bowl wins with 13 (AFC East comes in second with nine). Super Bowl victory number 13 for the NFC East in the 2017 season was the one that meant Philly had finally added to the overall tally, and could now look their bitter division rivals in the eye.

The team's name was inspired from the symbol of an eagle that was on a President Roosevelt document designed to help the country get through the Great Depression. The depression for the Eagles would include the early years of the Super Bowl era, and between seasons 1961 and 1977 they would not make one post-season. Coach Dick Vermeil took over in 1976, form improved, and by the 1980 season they finally made it to a Super Bowl. Despite being favourites, they would lose to Oakland, and would have to wait another 24 years before getting back. Three NFC Championship games were lost in a row between seasons 2001 and 2003, then in 2004 they beat the Falcons in the NFC Championship game to book a place in Super Bowl 39 against New England. The Patriots were favourites but the game would only be settled in the last drive from which the Eagles failed to score the touchdown they needed, with some reports suggesting that quarterback Donovan McNabb was vomiting and couldn't communicate during the final plays.

There would be an Eagles-Patriots Super Bowl rematch in the 2017 season. Philadelphia had made it to the Super Bowl despite quarterback Carson Wentz getting injured and being replaced by backup Nick Foles. When Wentz hobbled off towards the end of the regular season not many people backed the Eagles to go all the way, but the team were a strong all-round unit, and beat Atlanta in the divisional play-off, to be followed by a thrashing of the Vikings in the NFC Championship game. The Patriots were five-point favourites to win Super Bowl 52, but in a back-and-forth game the Eagles scored a crucial fourth-quarter touchdown from Zach Ertz, to win 41-33, and finally the great stigma of not having won a Super Bowl was lifted off the city of Philadelphia, which went wild in celebration. Foles had gone from a journeyman, to a Super Bowl MVP, and the Eagles were no longer the one club in the NFC East with no Super Bowl win, which in turn made the division the first, and to date the only, where all four teams have won at least one Super Bowl.

Washington Commanders: Est. 1932

Former names: Boston Braves (1932); Boston Redskins (1933–1936); Washington Redskins (1937–2019); Washington Football Team (2020–2021)

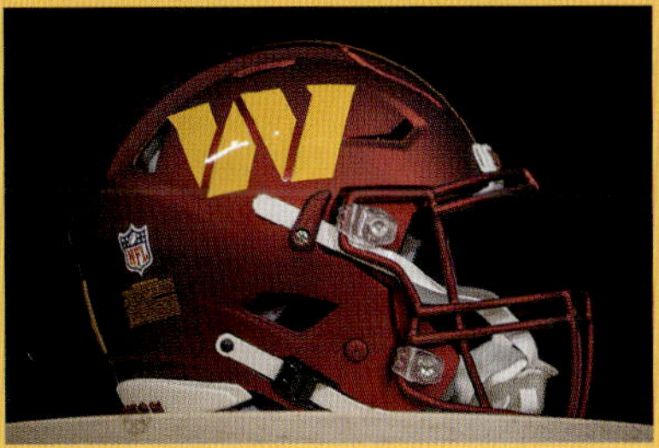

NFL Championships pre-1970 merger: (2) 1937, 1942

NFC East Champions: (9) 1972, 1983, 1984, 1987, 1991, 1999, 2012, 2015, 2020

NFC Conference Championships (5): 1972, 1982, 1983, 1987, 1991

Super Bowl titles: (3) 1982, 1987, 1991

Super Bowl record: 3-2

Like other NFL powerhouses of years gone by such as the Cowboys, Dolphins, Raiders and 49ers, Washington are another superclub who have spent too long without glory – their profile and status not in sync with their lack of success on the field in recent years. Off the field, there has also been wider news issues, with the biggest talking point being the branding itself after the name 'Redskins' was labelled as racist. For years, pressure groups demanded change and so in 2020 they simply became the Washington Football Team, to be followed by an announcement in early 2022 that the new permanent name was the Washington Commanders, in relation to the president of the United States being known as the commander-in-chief. The new logo was simply a 'W' and the announcement of the name was met with a general lack of enthusiasm.

The team started out in Boston before moving to the capital city in 1937, and they became NFL champions in their debut season in Washington, beating Chicago Bears in the championship game. The Redskins would win another NFL title in the 1942 season, once again beating Chicago; however, the following year, the Bears beat them for the NFL championship, and from the mid-1940s Washington would enter into a long period of decline. From 1946 to 1970 they never made the post-season once, and only registered four seasons that carried a winning record. Things would change in the 1970s; although Washington never won a Super Bowl they would register winning campaigns and were NFC champions in 1972 after beating their hated rival Dallas 26-3. They would lose the Super Bowl that year to Miami, and the Super Bowl rematch between these two clubs would happen ten years later in the 1982 season, and this time Washington beat the Dolphins to be champions of the NFL for the first time in 40 years. The following season, the Redskins were back in the Super Bowl to play the Raiders, and were favourites to defend their title, but would get beat heavily 38-9.

Perhaps the most iconic Washington 'team' came in the 1987 season, as it was more than one team. 1987 was the 'Year of the Scab' when the players across the league went on a strike over contract issues, and were replaced by players who had day jobs or – in the case of replacement 'scab' quarterback Tony Robinson – allowed out of prison to be in the squad. He would play in one game, a victory over Dallas in which the Cowboys had started players who had crossed the picket line. The striking Washington players were the most united on the picket line, and would confront the 'scabs' on their way to training. Eventually the crowd got behind the 'scabs' and their overall record was 3-0 which played a major part in the team winning the NFC East with an 11-4 record. The strikers left the picket line and returned to action to book a place in the showpiece game where they would destroy the Broncos 42-10, with Doug Williams becoming the first black quarterback to win a Super Bowl.

A few of the 'scab' players had been kept in the squad, but most went back to their day jobs, and unfortunately for Robinson, he was sent back to prison. They did not receive gold rings for the Super Bowl victory, and many argued that they played a vital role in Washington's regular season. In 2018, Tony Robinson and the other replacement players received rings, over 30 years since the 'Year of the Scab'.

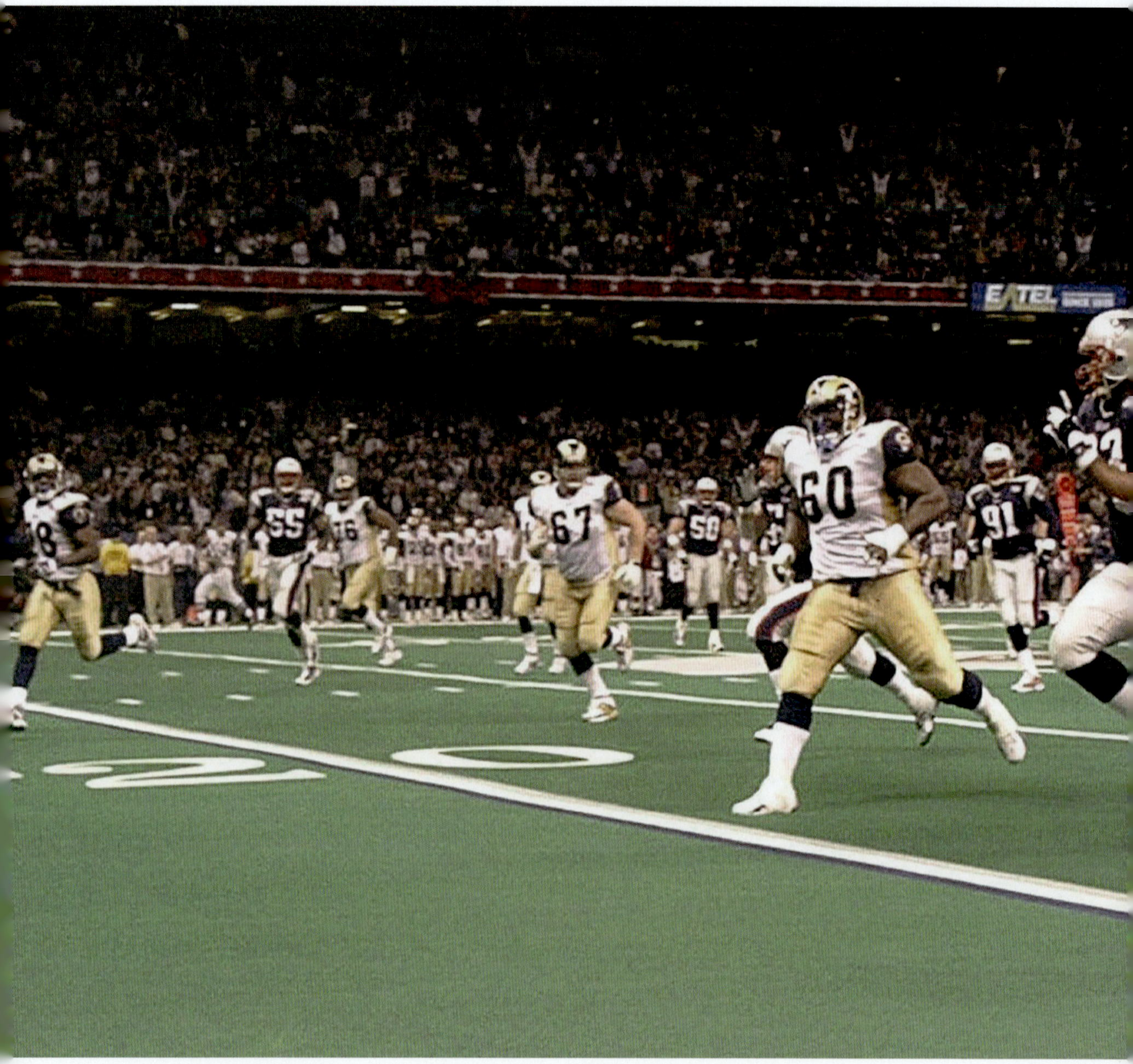

Louisiana Superdome, New Orleans, 2002
At Super Bowl 36, New England corner back Ty Law, runs for a touchdown after intercepting a pass from Rams quarterback Kurt Warner. This was Tom Brady and Bill Belichick's first of six Super Bowl triumphs.

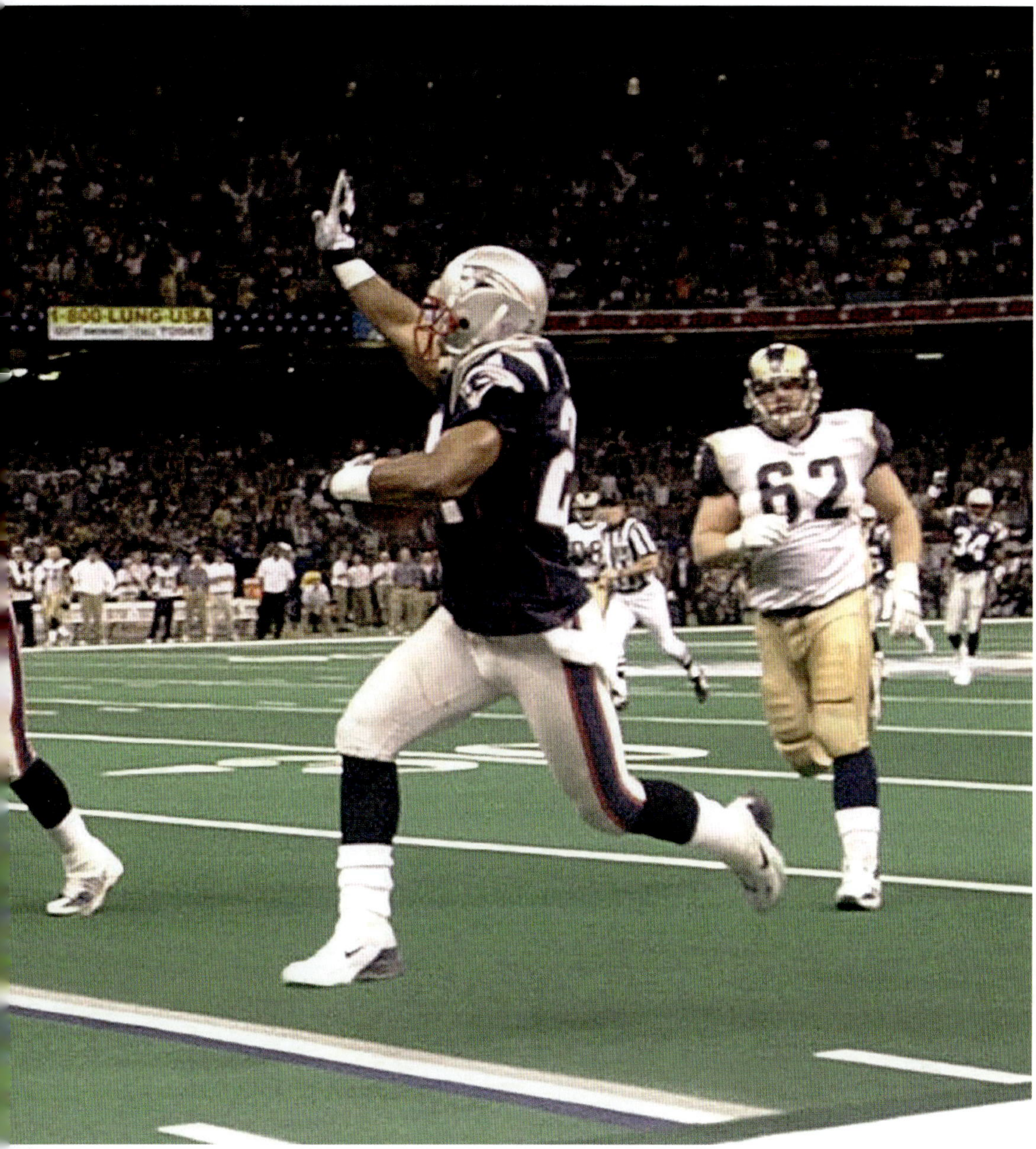
1-800-LUNG-USA
62

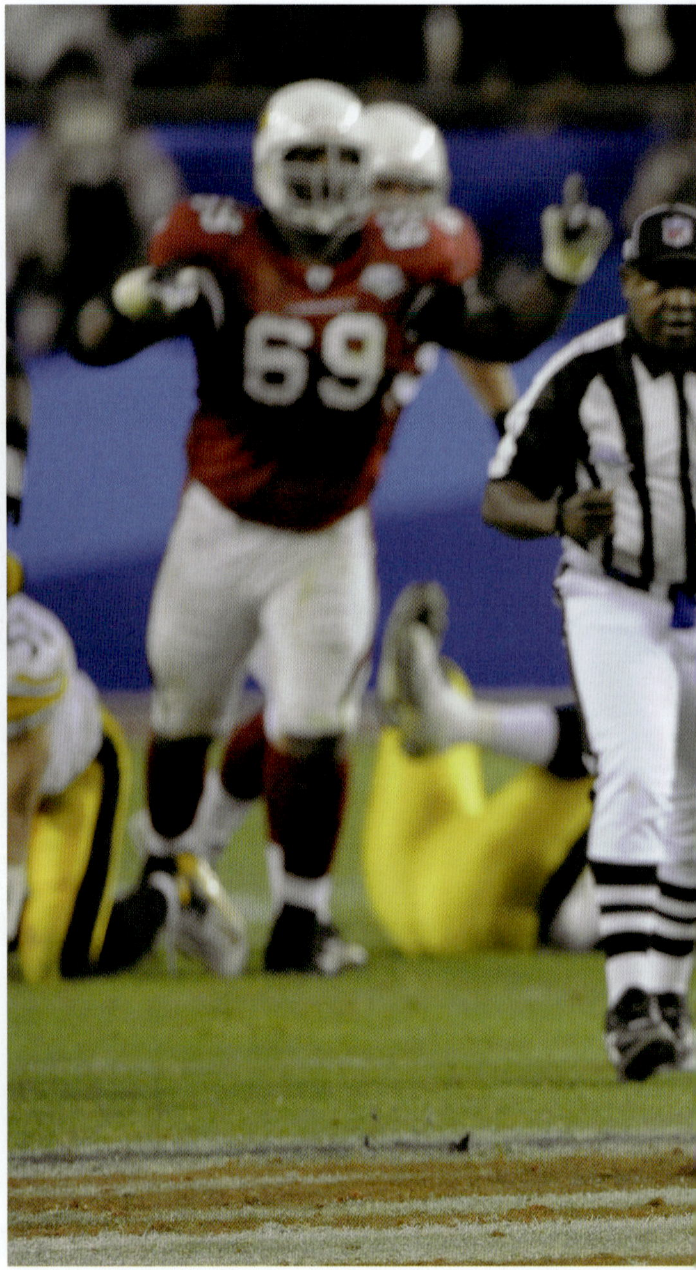

Raymond James Stadium, Tampa, 2009
Late in the game, Arizona's Larry Fitzgerald finds a gap in the middle of the field to score a touchdown and put the Cardinals on the brink of winning the Super Bowl. The lead lasted until there were 35 seconds left on the clock, as Pittsburgh scored a touchdown to break the Cardinals' hearts.

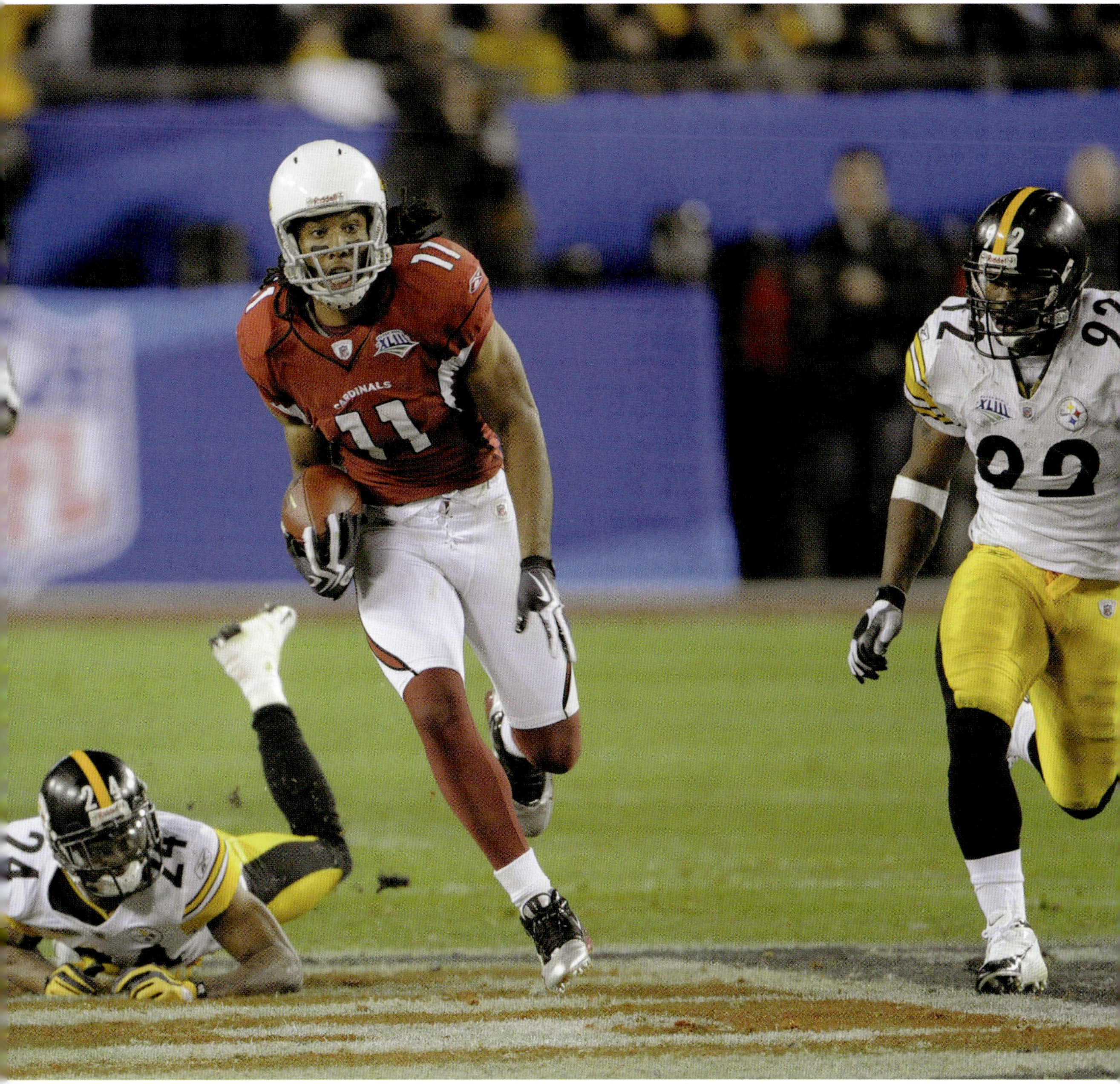
CARDINALS

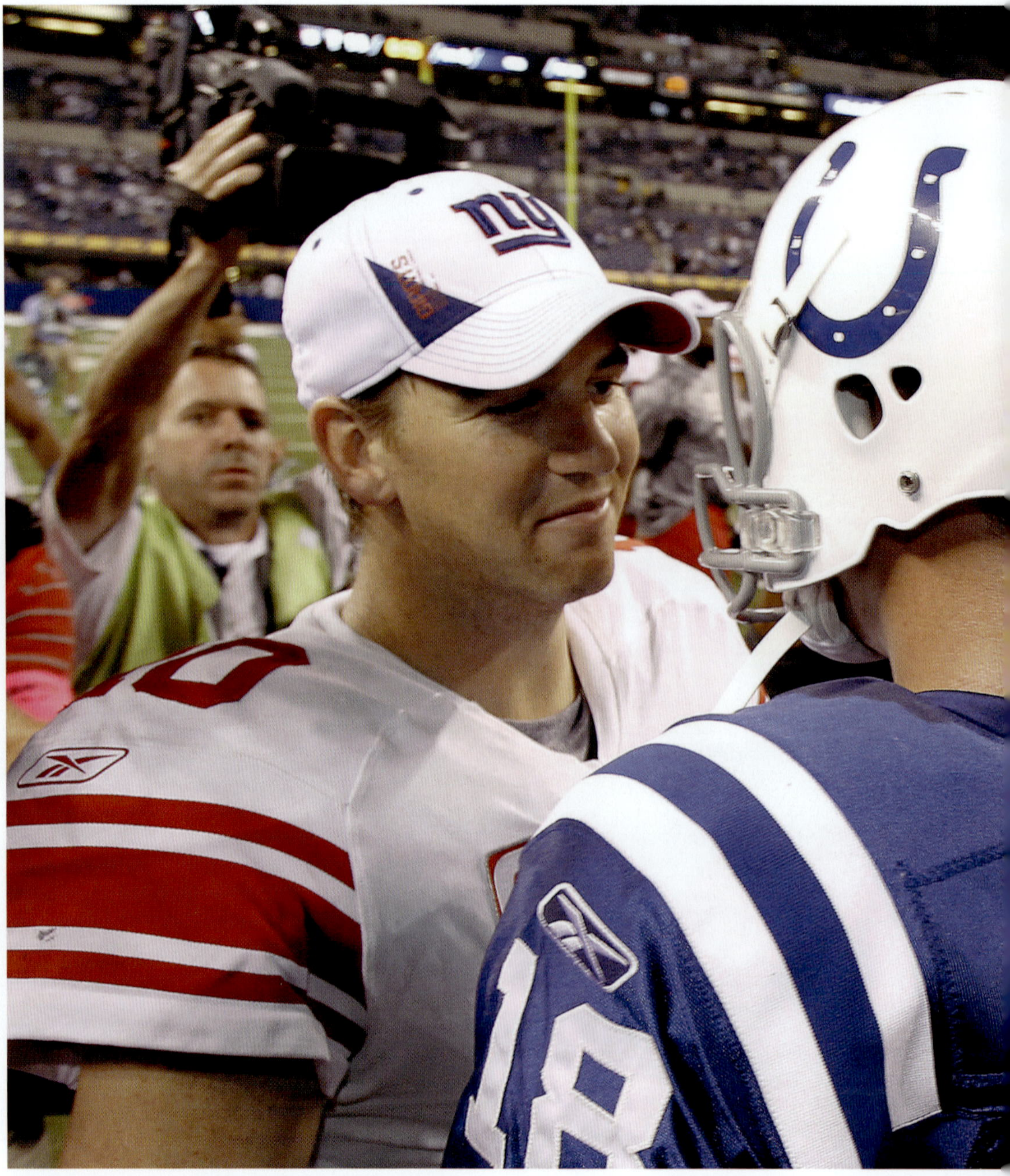

Lucas Oil Stadium, Indianapolis, 2010
Giants quarterback Eli Manning greets his brother Peyton Manning after Peyton's Colts defeated New York 38-14. Both brothers would end their careers having won two Super Bowl rings each.

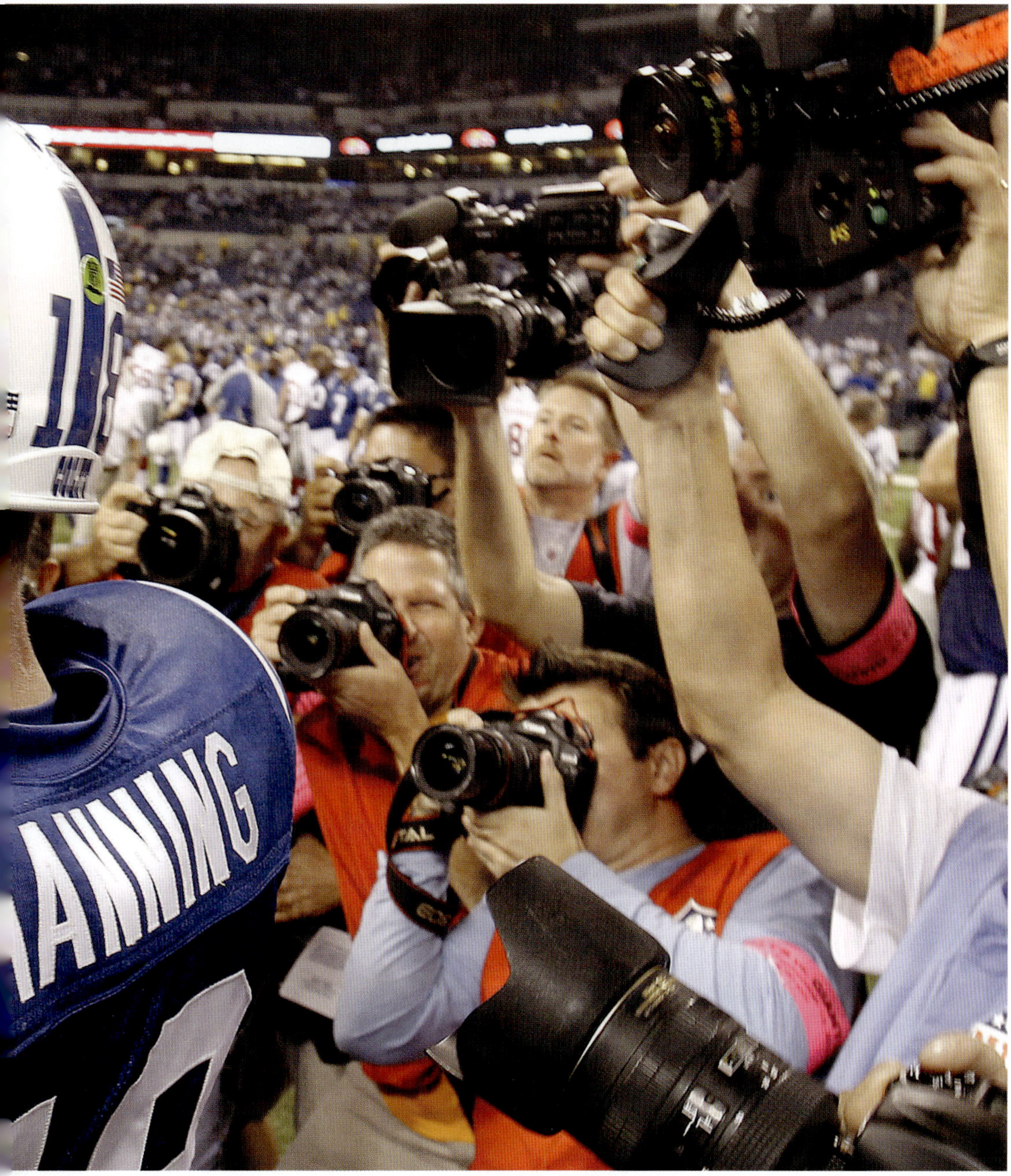
MANNING

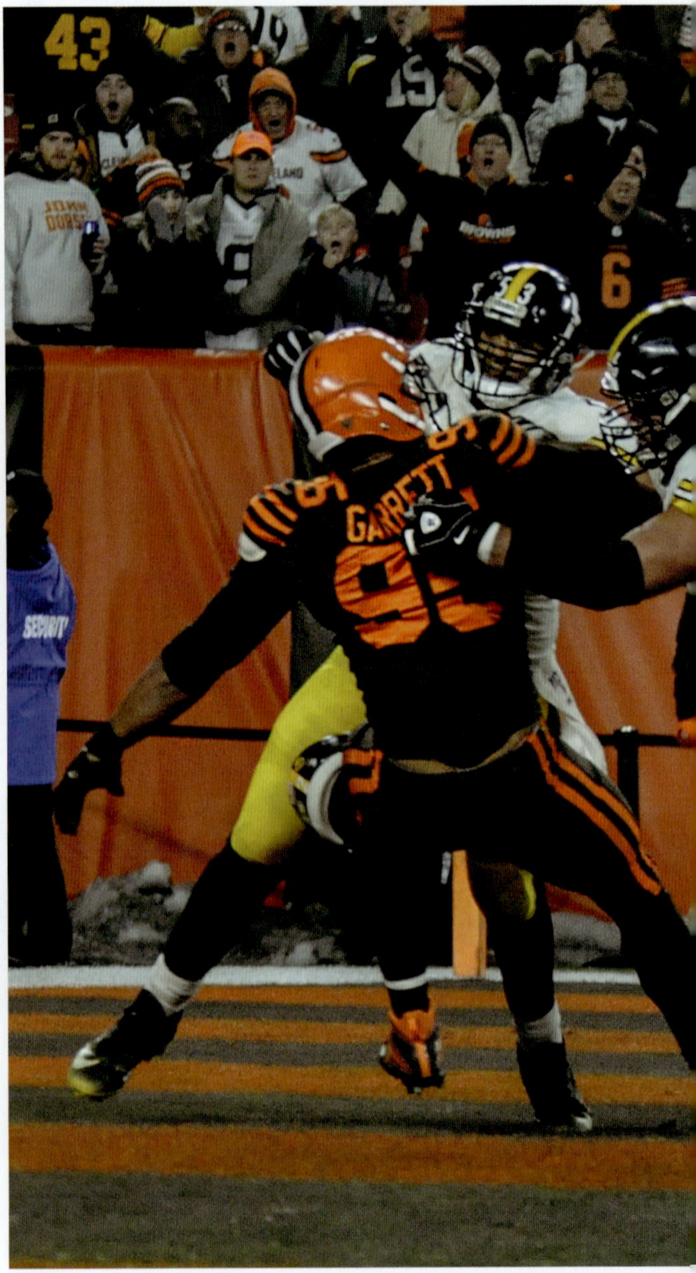

First Energy Stadium, Cleveland, 2019
Cleveland's Miles Garrett (95) is dragged away from Pittsburgh Steelers quarterback Mason Rudolph (2) by Rudolph's team-mates. In a moment of madness Garrett had struck Rudolph over the head with the quarterback's own helmet, and the Cleveland man would receive a fine and suspension for the incident.

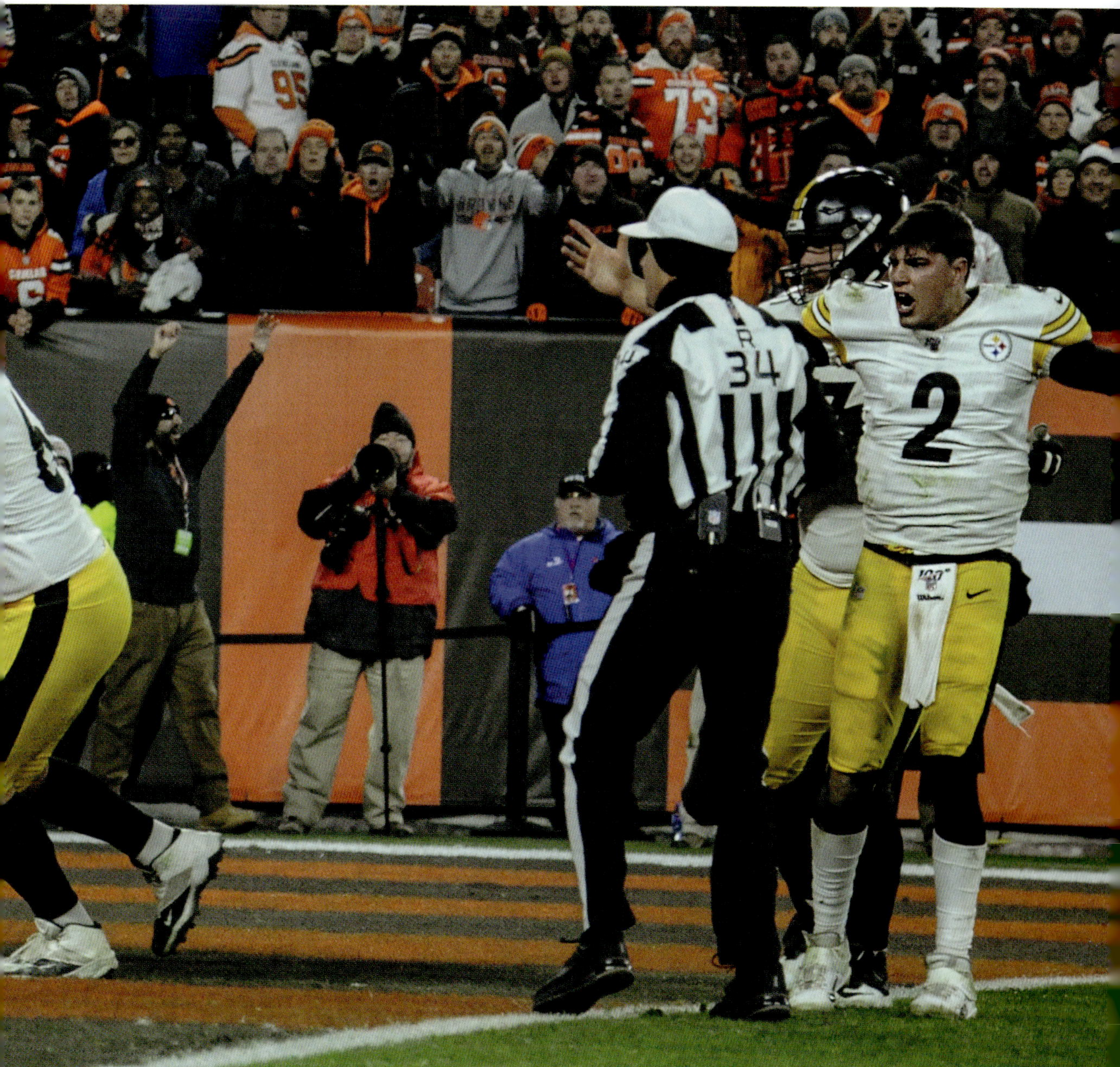
R
34
2

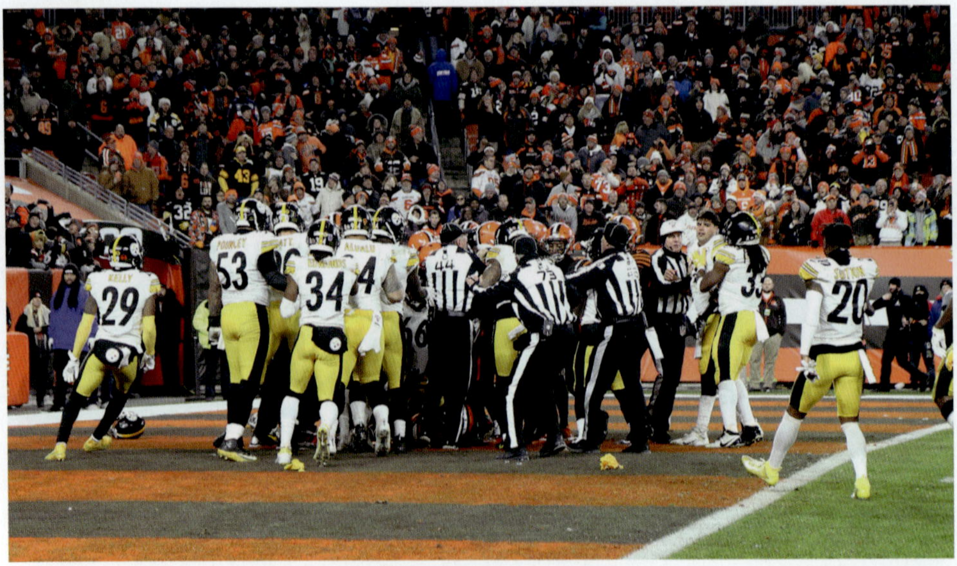

First Energy Stadium, Cleveland, 2019
The resulting brawl from the Miles Garrett/Mason Rudolph incident from the previous pages.

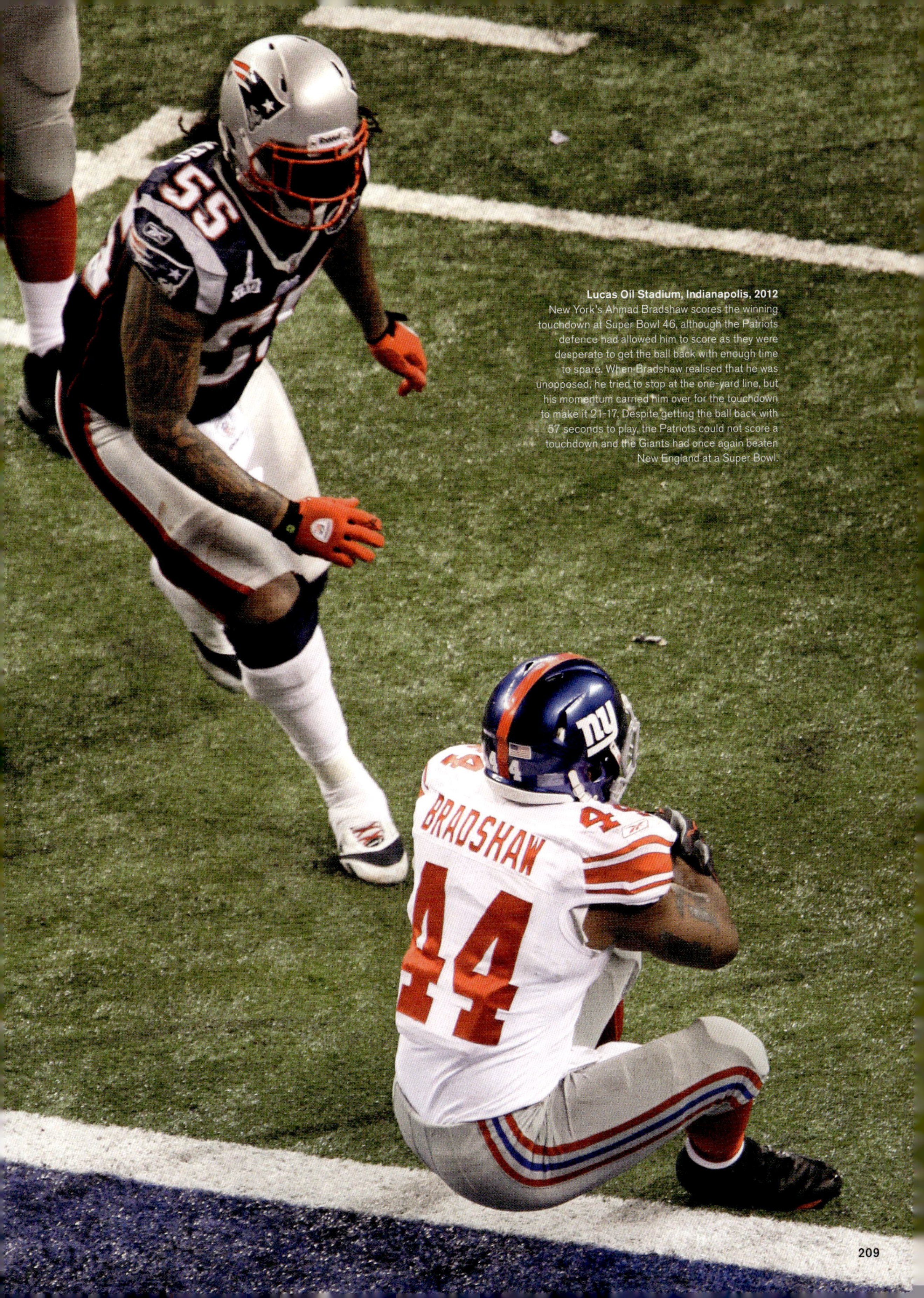

Lucas Oil Stadium, Indianapolis, 2012
New York's Ahmad Bradshaw scores the winning touchdown at Super Bowl 46, although the Patriots defence had allowed him to score as they were desperate to get the ball back with enough time to spare. When Bradshaw realised that he was unopposed, he tried to stop at the one-yard line, but his momentum carried him over for the touchdown to make it 21-17. Despite getting the ball back with 57 seconds to play, the Patriots could not score a touchdown and the Giants had once again beaten New England at a Super Bowl.

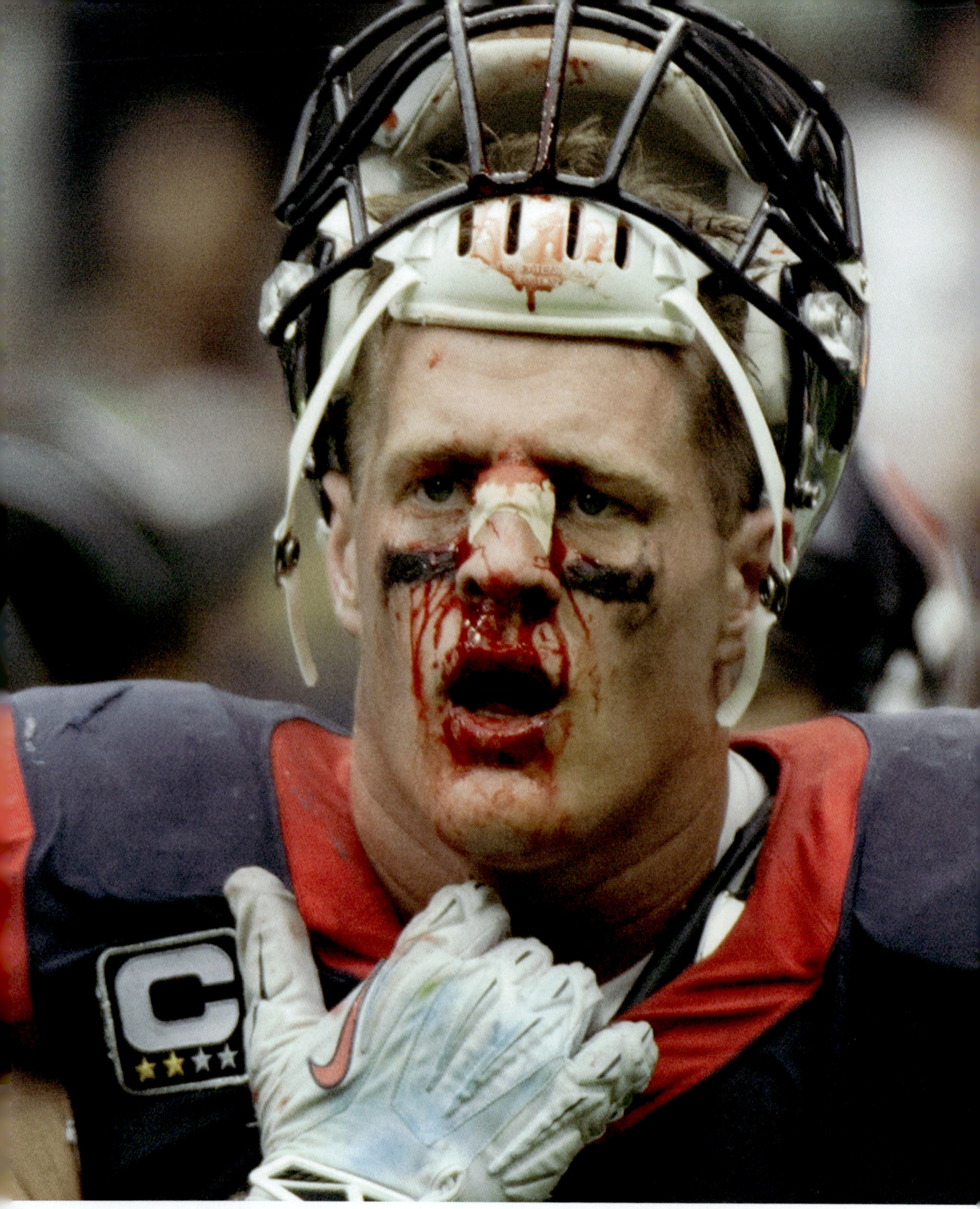
C

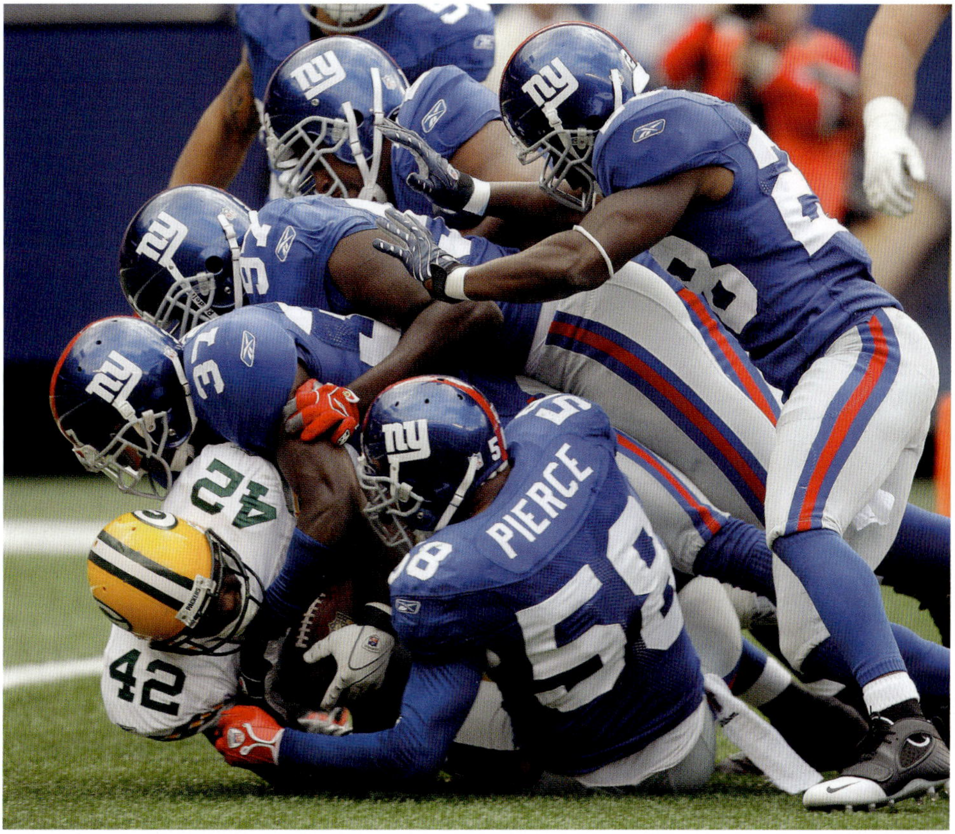

NRG Stadium, Houston, 2013
Dominant and powerful Texans defensive end J.J. Watt is bloodied during a game against Seattle.

MetLife Stadium, East Rutherford, 2007
The New York Giants defence do a 'gang tackle' to stop Green Bay Packers running back DeShawn Wynn.

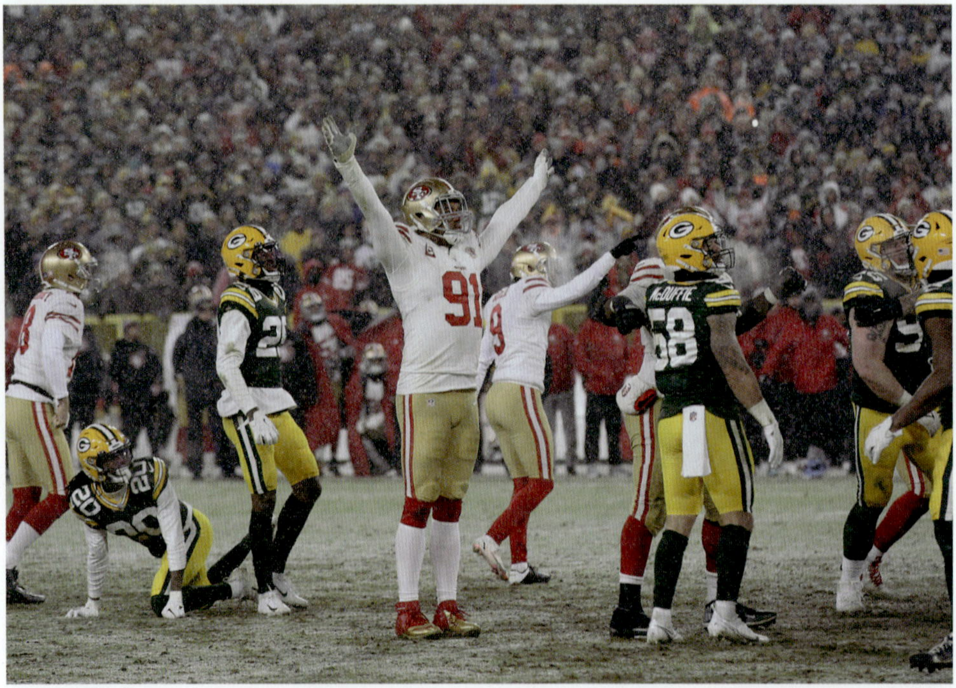

Lambeau Field, Green Bay, 2022
The San Francisco 49ers celebrate a last-second field goal against the Green Bay Packers, to advance to the NFC Championship game.

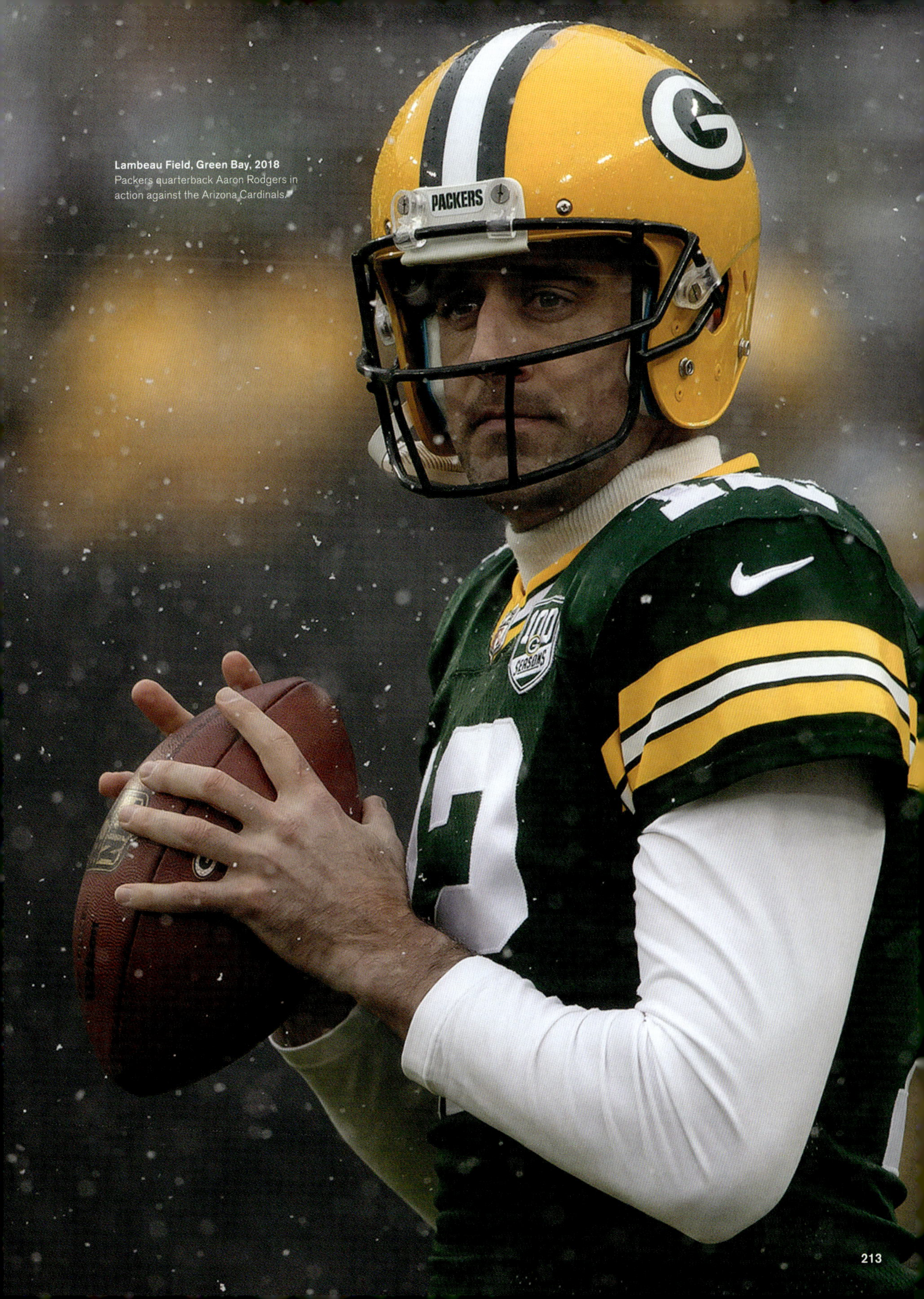

Lambeau Field, Green Bay, 2018
Packers quarterback Aaron Rodgers in action against the Arizona Cardinals.

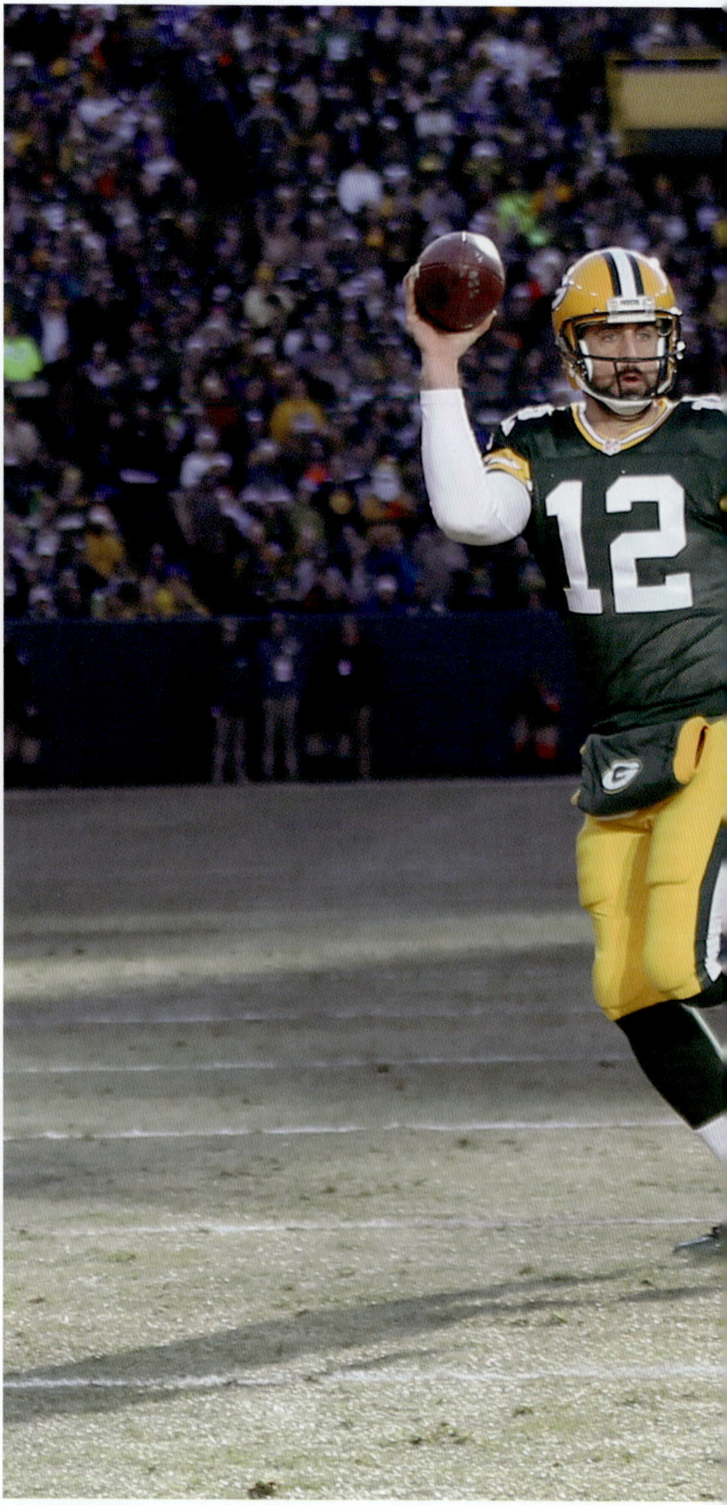

Lambeau Field, Green Bay, 2016
Living legend Aaron Rodgers looks for an opening in a home game versus the Minnesota Vikings. Rodgers' standard of performance has earned him four MVP awards for the regular season.

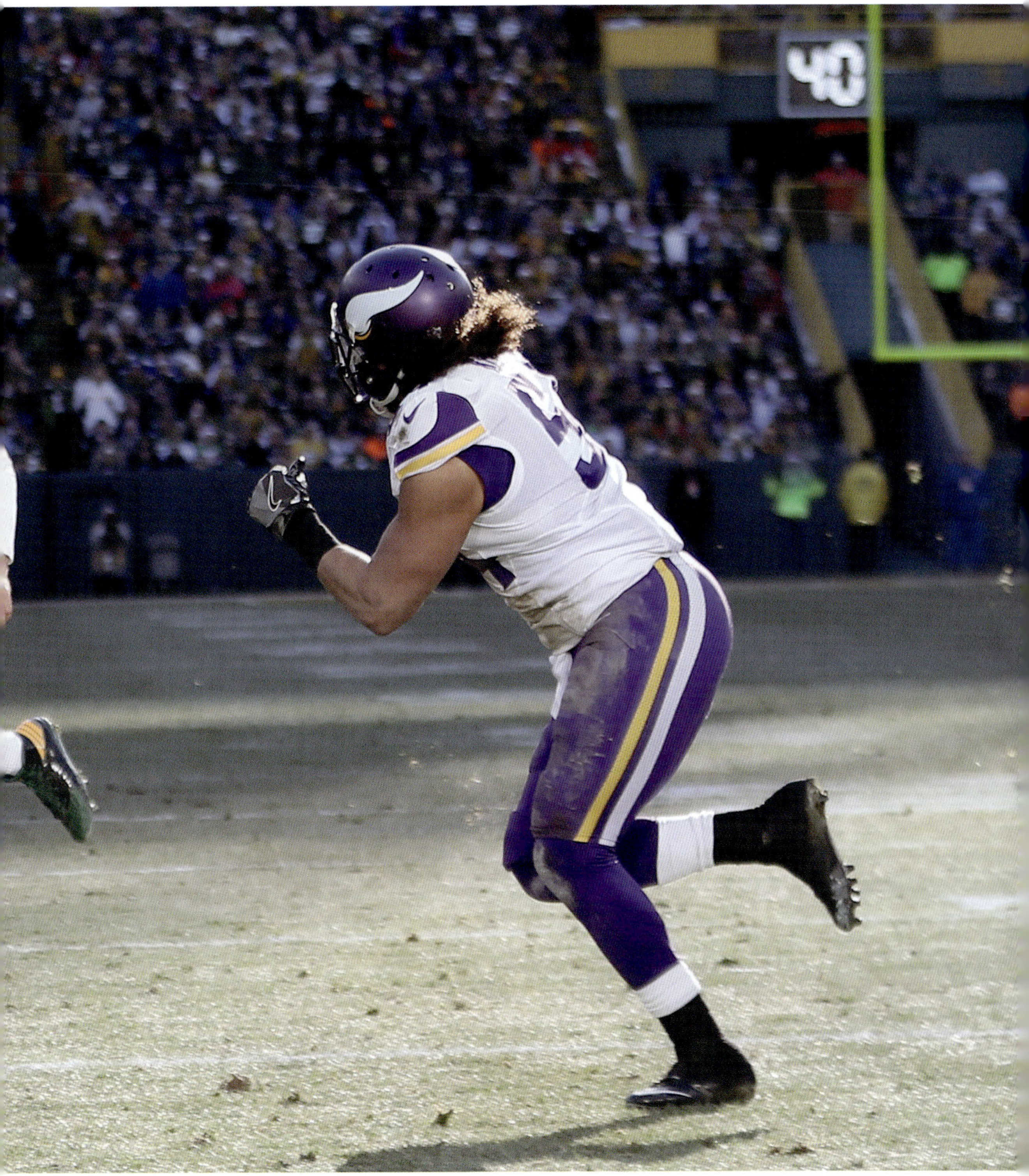
40

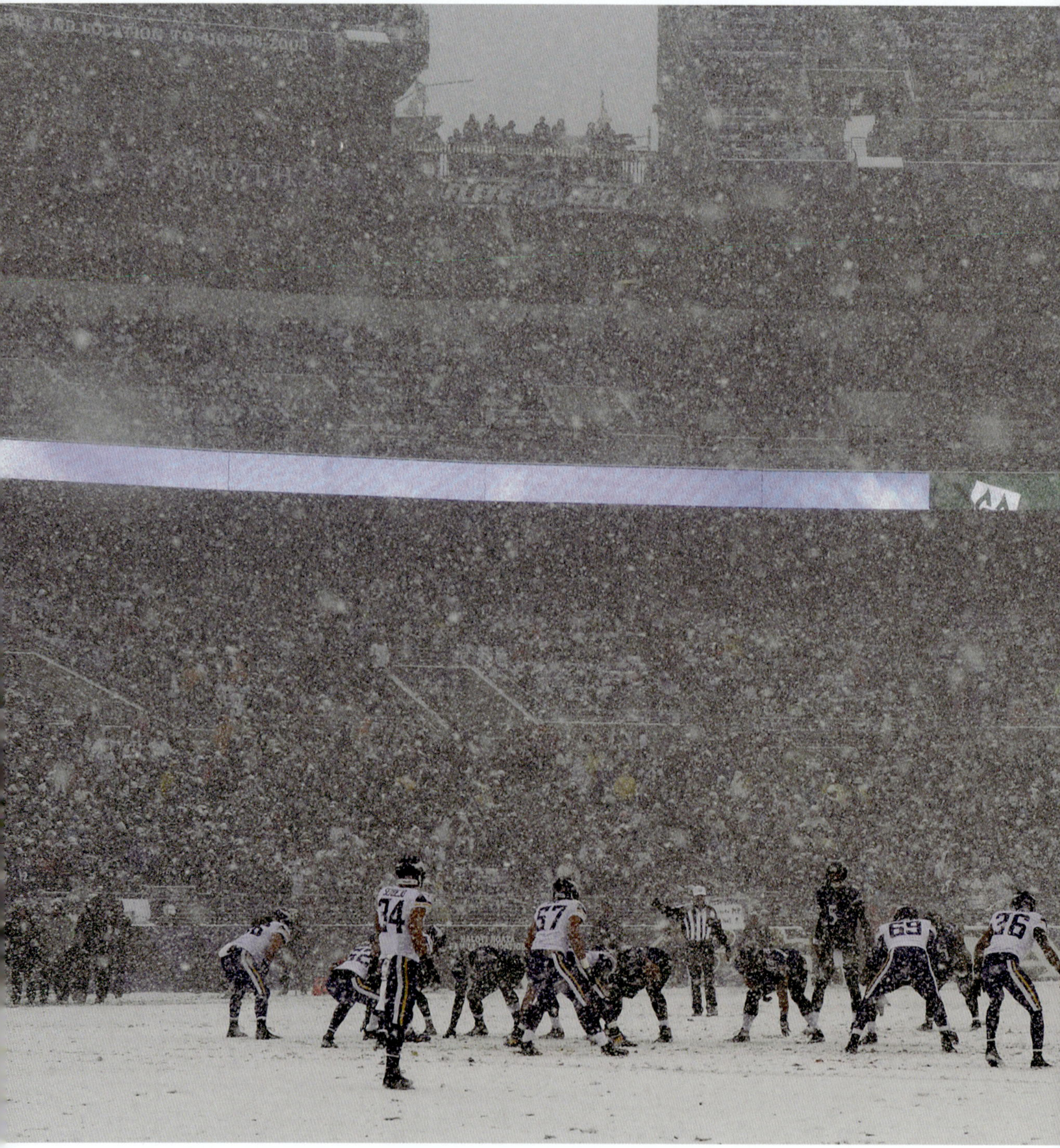

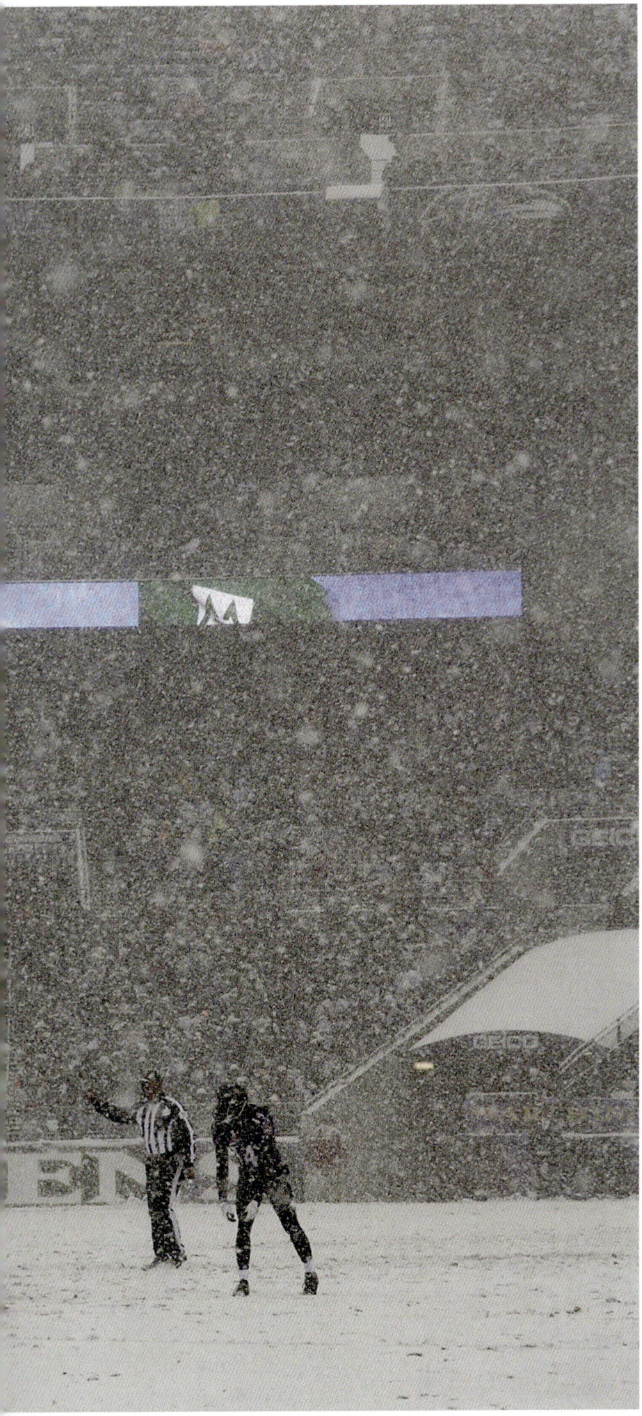

M&T Bank Stadium, Baltimore, 2013
The Baltimore Ravens and Minnesota Vikings play in a snow blizzard. The Ravens would win the game 29-26.

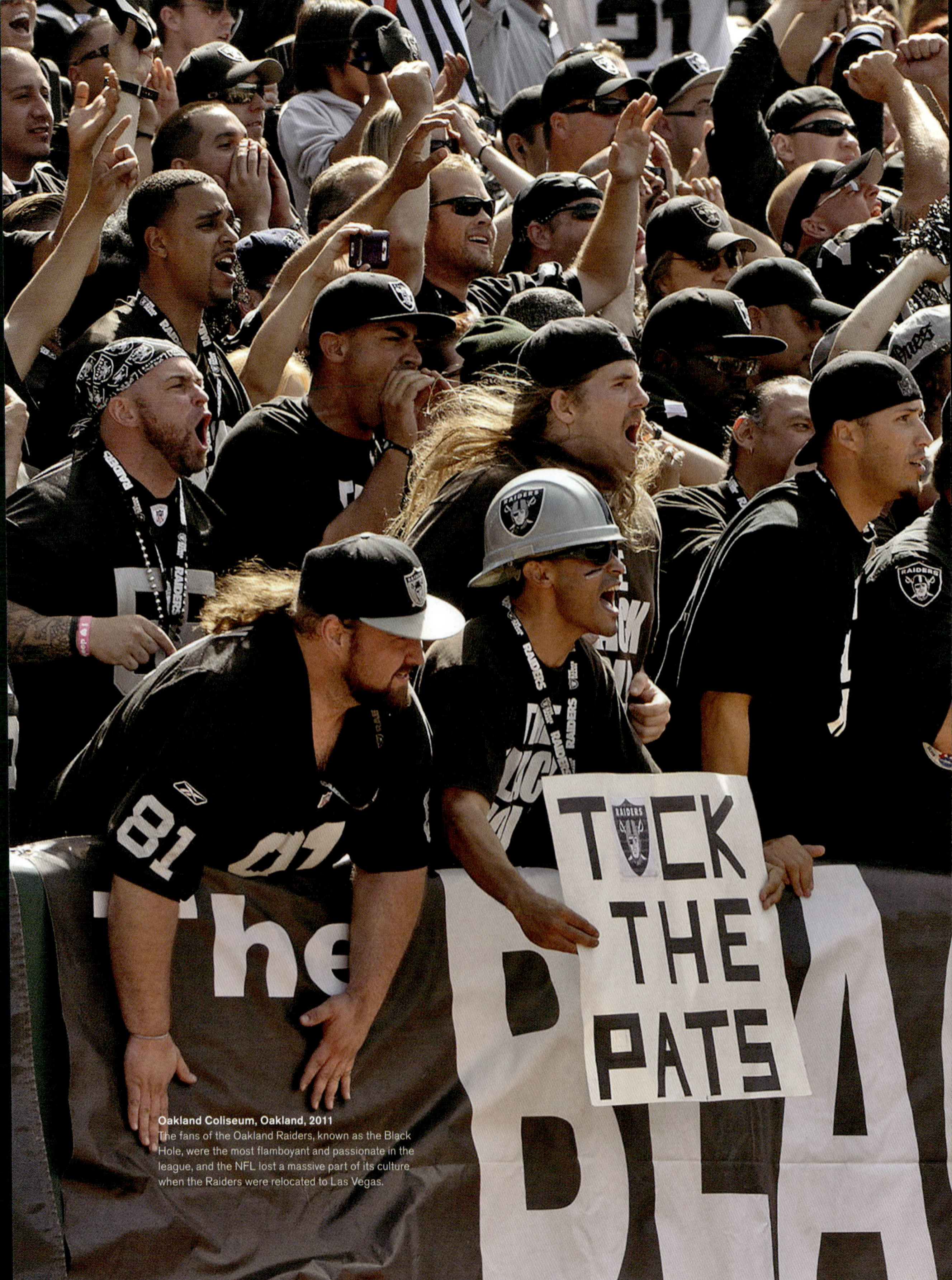

Oakland Coliseum, Oakland, 2011
The fans of the Oakland Raiders, known as the Black Hole, were the most flamboyant and passionate in the league, and the NFL lost a massive part of its culture when the Raiders were relocated to Las Vegas.

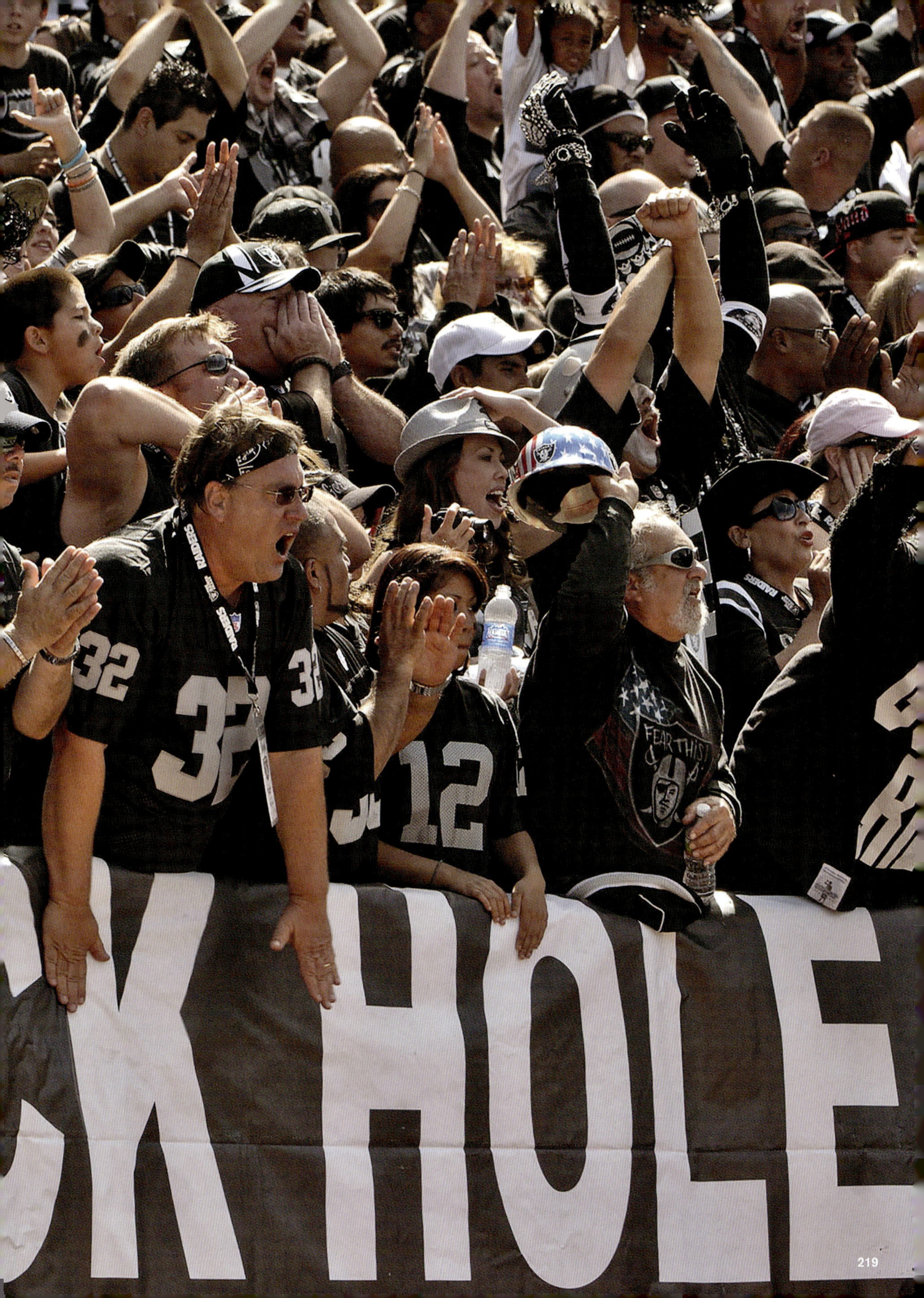
CK HOLE
FEAR THIS!

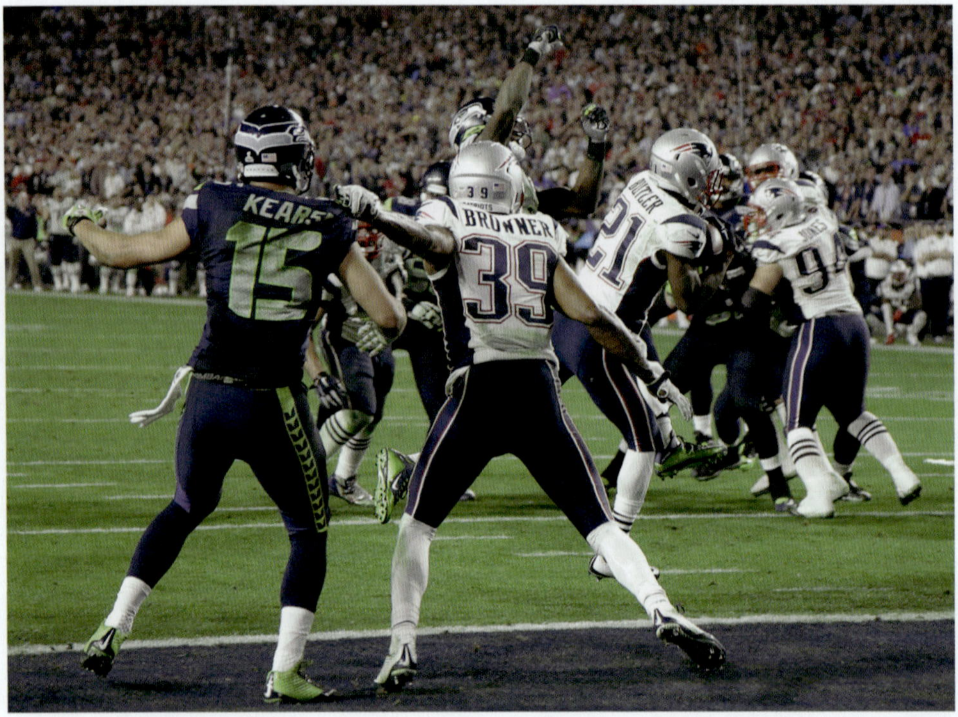

University of Phoenix Stadium, Glendale, 2015
A stunning moment in Super Bowl 49, between New England and defending champions Seattle. With the score 28-24 to the Patriots, with 26 seconds to go, Seattle have the ball on the New England one-yard line, and are in a great position to win the game. However, Malcolm Butler (21) intercepts the pass from Russell Wilson, to seal the win for the Patriots.

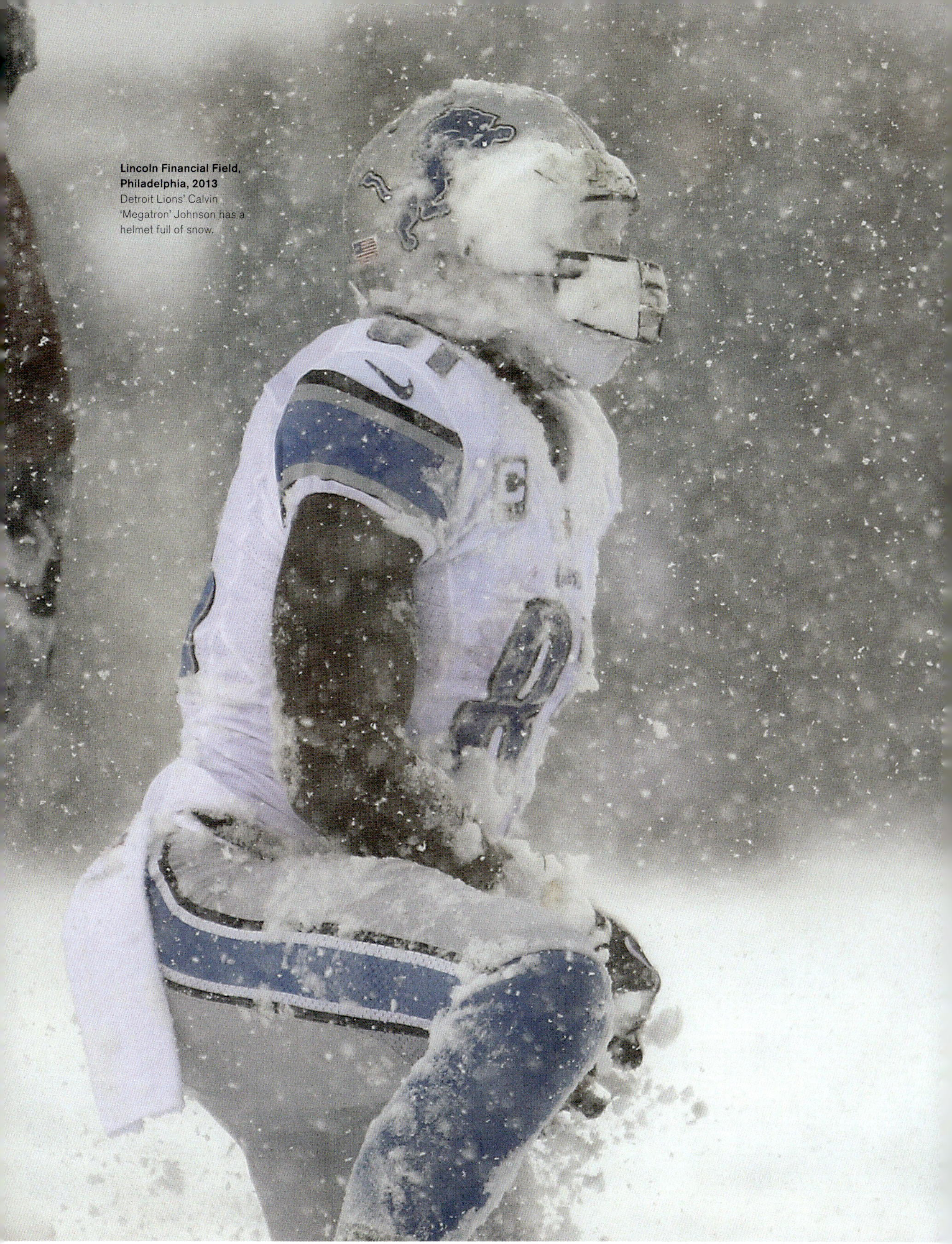

Lincoln Financial Field, Philadelphia, 2013
Detroit Lions' Calvin 'Megatron' Johnson has a helmet full of snow.

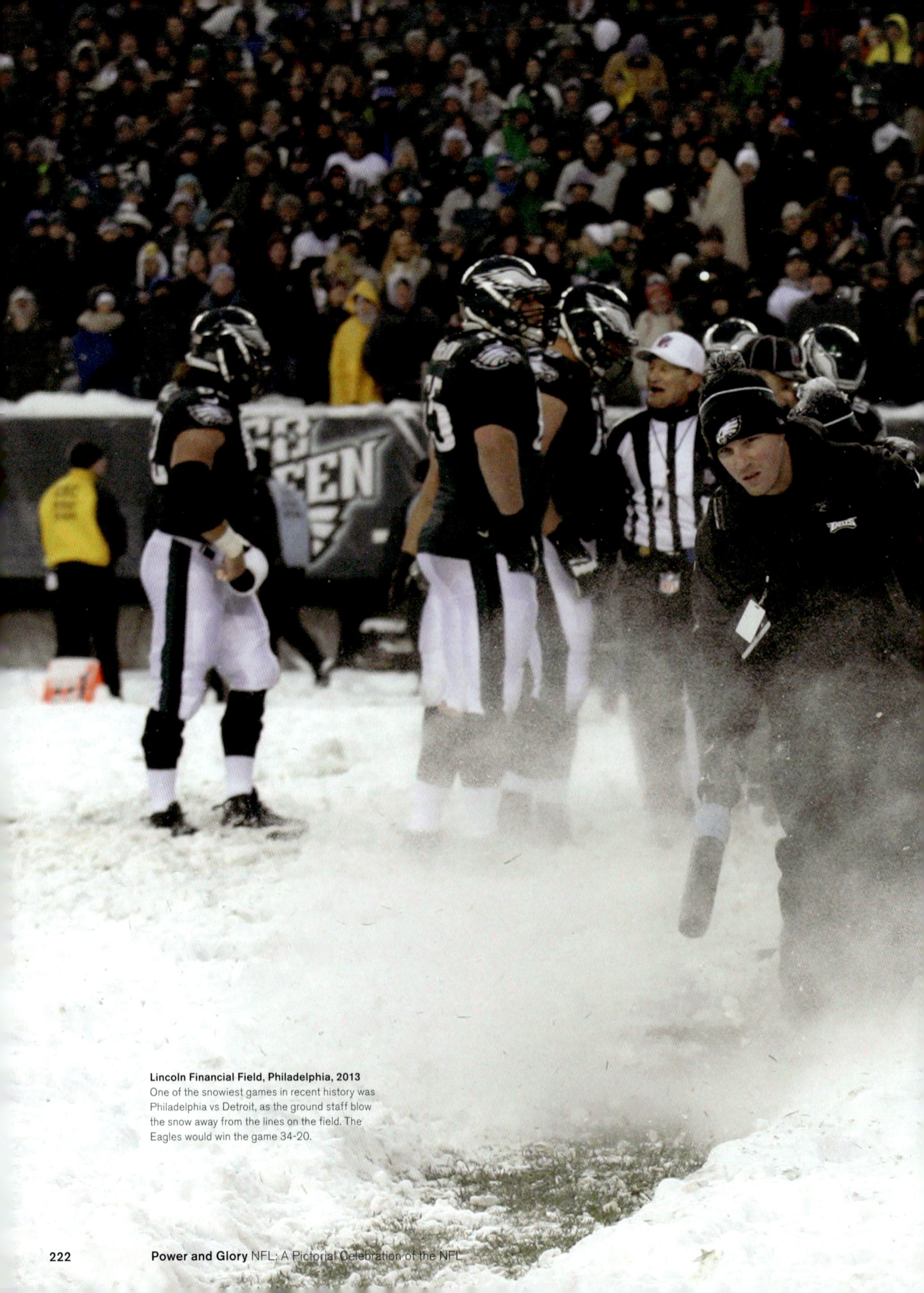

Lincoln Financial Field, Philadelphia, 2013
One of the snowiest games in recent history was Philadelphia vs Detroit, as the ground staff blow the snow away from the lines on the field. The Eagles would win the game 34-20.

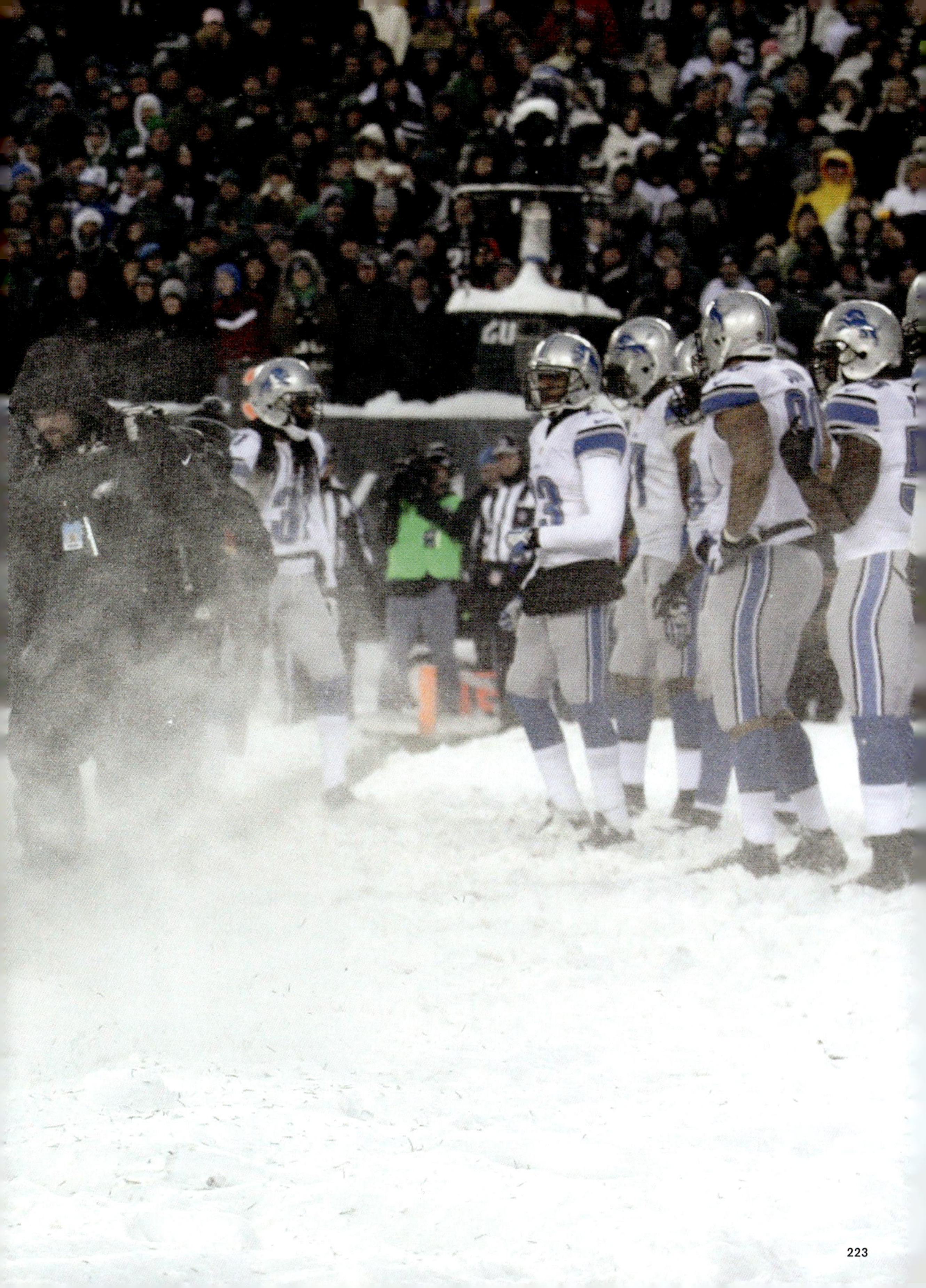

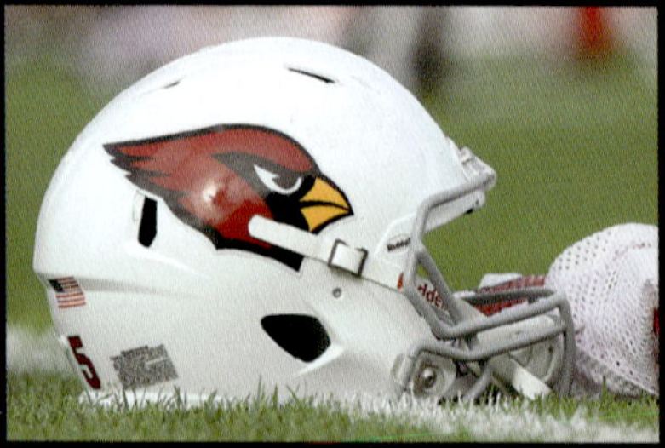

NFL Championships pre-1970 merger: (2) 1925, 1947

NFC East Champions: (2) 1974, 1975

NFC West Champions: (3) 2008, 2009, 2015

NFC Conference Champions: (1) 2008

Super Bowl record: 0-1

Arizona Cardinals: Est. 1898

Former names: Racine Cardinals (1920–1921); Chicago Cardinals (1922–1943, 1945–1959), Card-Pitt (1944), St Louis Cardinals (1960–1987), Phoenix Cardinals (1988–1993)

In English football, Notts County are recognised as the oldest professional club. They play in the same city they were founded in and there is no lack of credibility regarding their longevity. The Arizona Cardinals are the oldest team in the NFL, despite there being 1,754 miles that separate Phoenix and Chicago. The fans who watch the Arizona Cardinals are not the grandchildren of the fans who watched the Chicago Cardinals win two NFL Championships in 1925 and 1947, and who had a fierce rivalry with the Chicago Bears. Or the relatives of the fans who watched the St Louis Cardinals for the 27 years the team was in Missouri. However, the Cardinals are officially recognised as being founded in 1898 and along with the Bears they have been ever present since the first NFL season in 1920.

The last time the 'Cards' were the NFL champions was when they beat Philadelphia 28-21 in the 1947 season Championship game. The following year they had a chance to reclaim their title and once again were playing the Eagles in the decider, however they lost 7-0, in one of the worst weather games ever played. The field had four inches of snow and the match only went ahead because the players insisted that they wanted to play. With no post-season in 11 years and being overshadowed by city rivals the Bears, in 1959 the team moved 300 miles south to St Louis; and of all the places to relocate, they moved to a city that already had a team called the St Louis Cardinals. The baseball team had been established since 1900, played in red and white and had the little red bird as the team logo. To avoid confusion, the folk of St Louis referred to the football team as the 'Gridbirds' or 'Big Red'. While in St Louis the team only made the post-season on four occasions.

After the 1970 NFL/AFL merger the Cardinals had been placed in the NFC East along with Dallas, New York, Washington and Philadelphia. It was a tough division and the Cardinals would only register two NFC East titles before being moved to the NFC West in 2002. It had been a while since they were located in the east of the country and they had left St Louis to relocate to Arizona in 1988. Owner Bill Bidwill blamed poor attendances for wanting to move away from St Louis, the low numbers being brought on by the fact that the team had been mediocre for so many years. Jacksonville and Baltimore were considered for relocation, but the team moved way out west and became the Phoenix Cardinals.

In the 1998 season they made the play-offs and won their first post-season game since 1964 by beating Dallas in the wildcard. After the 1998 season the now-named Arizona Cardinals went nine years in a row without a post-season, but then in the 2008 campaign, they won three play-off games and made it to the Super Bowl to face Pittsburgh, in one of the all-time classics. The Cardinals were trailing 20-7 going into the fourth quarter, but would make a fightback and with 2:45 left on the clock, Larry Fitzgerald caught a pass on his own 40-yard line, saw a gap in the middle of the field, and ran 60 yards for a touchdown that put Arizona 23-20 ahead. It looked like the oldest team in the league would achieve Super Bowl glory, but with 35 seconds left Pittsburgh scored a touchdown to win 27-23.

Los Angeles Rams: Est. 1936

Former names: Cleveland Rams (1936–1942, 1944–1945); Los Angeles Rams (1946–1994); St Louis Rams (1995–2015)

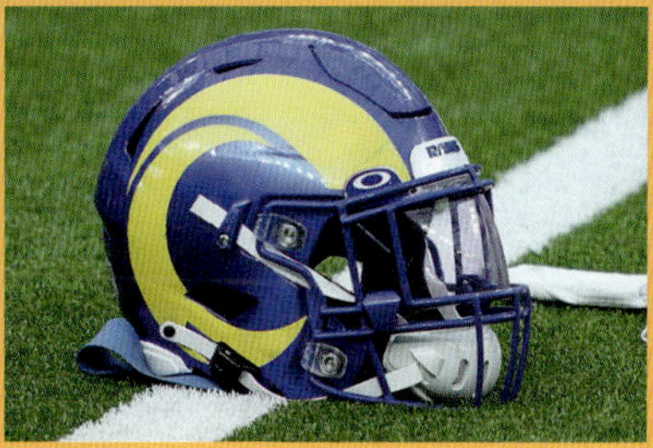

NFL Championships pre-1970 merger: (2) 1945, 1951

NFC West Champions: (14) 1973, 1974, 1975, 1976, 1977, 1978, 1979, 1985, 1999, 2001, 2003, 2017, 2018, 2021

NFC Conference Champions: (5) 1979, 1999, 2001, 2018, 2021

Super Bowl titles: (2) 1999, 2021

Super Bowl record: 2-3

The Rams played nine seasons in Cleveland before moving 2,344 miles to Los Angeles in 1946. In their last season in Ohio they won their first ever title by beating Washington 15-14 in the NFL Championship game. The LA Rams averaged huge home attendances, so at the start of the 1960s the newly formed LA Chargers moved to San Diego rather than compete with a more popular neighbour – the opposite scenario to what would happen years later in 2016/17 when both teams moved back to LA at the same time.

After the 1970 NFL/AFL merger, the Rams were placed in the NFC West division and the 1970s would see them be contenders but struggle to make it over the line. They won the NFC West seven years in a row during the decade, but would lose four NFC Championship games in a row before finally winning one in the 1979 season and reaching the Super Bowl. They faced Pittsburgh who were favoured to win by ten points, but going into the fourth quarter the Rams were ahead 19-17. They would lose 31-19, and the next time they would be back in a Super Bowl the team would go by the name of the St Louis Rams.

By the 1990s the crowd attendances in LA were on the decline and the ownership applied for a move 1,824 miles away to St Louis, who had just lost the Cardinals to Arizona. Refreshingly, the NFL voted it down – with the reasoning being that the Rams had 50 years of history in LA and loyalty should be shown to the people of the city (what happened to that principle!). A lawsuit later, and the NFL voted in favour of the move – and the Rams were off to Missouri.

The era in St Louis saw the most celebrated Rams team, known as 'The greatest show on turf'. Between 1999 and 2001 the Rams' offence was explosive and set records. They lost the 2001 season Super Bowl to the Patriots by a field goal in the last second, although two years earlier they had been champions for the first time with a 23-16 win over the Tennessee Titans, in one of the most dramatic finishes to a Super Bowl game. With 1:54 left on the clock, Isaac Bruce caught a 73-yard touchdown reception from MVP quarterback Kurt Warner (who had a film, *American Underdog*, made about his life) and the Rams were ahead. Tennessee had a chance to level the game at the end, as Kevin Dyson caught a pass on the ten-yard line and ran towards the endzone, but linebacker Mike Jones would make the stop and win the game for the Rams in the 'one yard Super Bowl'. A period of decline followed, and from 2005, St Louis would go 11 straight seasons without making one post-season appearance and not registering one winning season. Owner Stan Kroenke, who is from Missouri, then moved the Rams back to LA, and is now as popular in the city of St Louis as dry rot.

At the time of writing, the LA Rams are the Super Bowl champions after beating Cincinnati in a thrilling encounter. LA were trailing 20-16 late into the fourth quarter, before Matthew Stafford threw a game-winning touchdown to Cooper Kupp. There was still time left on the clock for the Bengals to win the game, but the Rams' defence, led by the formidable Aaron Donald, held firm, and for the second year in a row the Super Bowl was won by a team playing in their home stadium.

San Francisco 49ers: **Est. 1944**

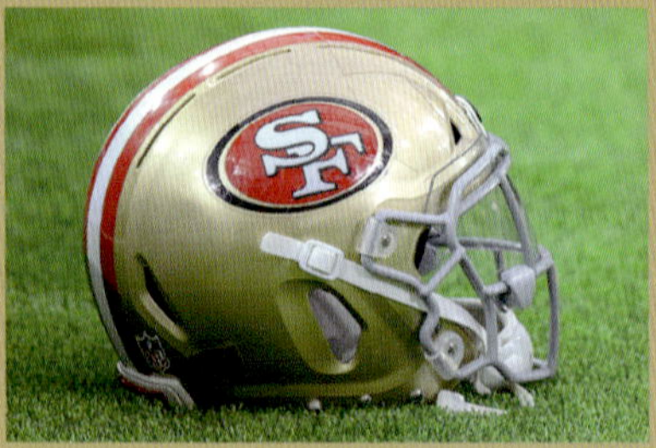

NFC West Champions: (20) 1970, 1971, 1972, 1981, 1983, 1984, 1986, 1987, 1988, 1989, 1990, 1992, 1993, 1994, 1995, 1997, 2002, 2011, 2012, 2019

NFC Conference Championships: (7) 1981, 1984, 1988, 1989, 1994, 2012, 2019

Super Bowl titles: (5) 1981, 1984, 1988, 1989, 1994

Super Bowl record: 5-2

With a name inspired by the 1849 Californian gold rush, the 49ers started out in the AAFC before the league merged with the NFL in 1950. Their early years would be mediocre and only produced four post-season appearances until the season of 1981. The drafting of 89th pick Joe Montana in 1979 would be the most significant acquisition for San Francisco, and a move that would take a club with an unremarkable history to owning a record number of Super Bowl wins. The first came in the 1981 season with a 26-21 win over Cincinnati. Three years later in the 1984 season they were back in the Super Bowl to face a Miami team with Dan Marino, a young quarterback who had set records that season; however, it would be 'Golden Joe' Montana who was victorious in a 38-16 victory and he was now a two-time winner, while Marino would not play in another Super Bowl.

By the 1985 season wide receiver Jerry Rice was on the roster, and his relationship with Montana would be one of the most celebrated quarterback/receiver partnerships in the league's history. Montana and Rice's 49ers won Super Bowl 23 in the 1988 season with a late touchdown against Cincinnati with just 34 seconds left on the clock. Montana led the team to so many fourth-quarter comebacks that he gained the nickname 'Comeback Kid'. The following season they went into Super Bowl 24 as 12-point favourites against Denver and beat them 55-10; which was the most points ever scored at a Super Bowl and today still stands as the biggest winning margin.

With four Super Bowl wins in one decade San Francisco were the undisputed kings of the 1980s – and they had one more Super Bowl to add in the 1990s, however Montana had moved on to Kansas and was replaced by quarterback Steve Young who had been a backup for the 49ers' conquests of the previous decade. Against San Diego, in Super Bowl 29, less than 90 seconds had passed when Young threw a 44-yard touchdown pass to Jerry Rice to open the scoring; the 49ers would go on to win 49-26 and surpass Dallas and Pittsburgh to be the first team to win five Super Bowl titles.

Despite being separated by 1,732 miles, the 49ers' most significant rivals over the years were the Dallas Cowboys. It was a rivalry based purely on the fact that both teams were top contenders in the NFC and the feud started when the two teams played one another three times in play-off games between seasons 1970 and 1972. Before the glory days of the 1980s, the early 1970s was the one time in the 49ers' history where they had been top contenders. They made it to two NFC Championship games, yet Dallas beat them on both occasions, along with beating them in the divisional play-off in 1972. In the 1981 Super Bowl-winning season the 49ers finally beat Dallas in the NFC Championship game. The Cowboys got their revenge in the 1992 and 1993 NFC Championship games, beating San Francisco on both occasions, but then the following year the 49ers beat Dallas to get to Super Bowl 29. The two dominant teams of the NFC would not meet again in the play-offs until the 2021 season, when San Francisco won the wildcard 23-17.

Both Dallas and San Francisco would see their joint record of five Super Bowl wins overtaken by Pittsburgh and New England; however the 49ers hold a record of most appearances in an NFC Championship game with 17, compared to the 14 of the Cowboys.

Seattle Seahawks: Est. 1974

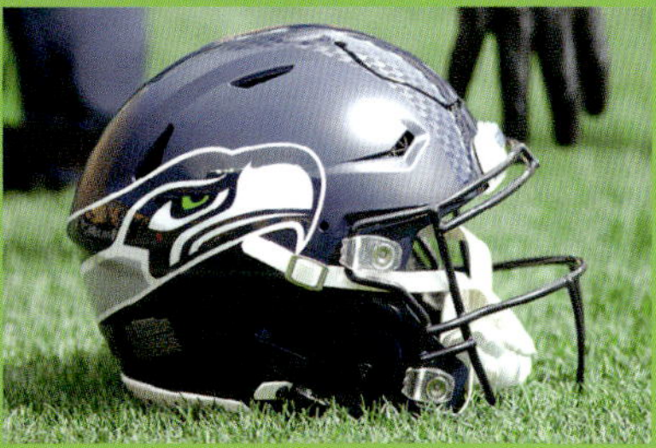

AFC West Champions: (2) 1988, 1999

NFC West Champions: (9) 2004, 2005, 2006, 2007, 2010, 2013, 2014, 2016, 2020

NFC Conference Championships: (3) 2005, 2013, 2014

Super Bowl titles: (1) 2013

Super Bowl record: 1-2

The Seahawks first entered the league in 1976 along with Tampa Bay as part of an NFL expansion, and they were placed in the AFC West. It hadn't just been a city without an NFL team, it was an entire region of north-western America. The nearest other NFL team to Seattle is San Francisco, who are over 800 miles away, so the Seahawks' core fanbase incorporates neighbouring states such as Oregon, Idaho, Montana and areas of western Canada including Vancouver. The team from Washington state has in recent years built up a reputation as a perennial contender, and also has a formidable support. On two occasions the Seahawks' crowd, known as the '12th man' have set decibel records that got them into the *Guinness Book of World Records*.

Seattle are the only team to have played in both the AFC and NFC Championship games. The team was moved to the NFC West in 2002 and in the past two decades the Seahawks have been the most consistent team in that division, reaching three Super Bowls in that time. The first, in the 2005 season, saw Seattle lose 21-10 to the Pittsburgh Steelers. The 2013 season saw an all-round strong Seahawks team; Russell Wilson was gaining a reputation as a dynamic quarterback, running back Marson Lynch was known as 'Beast Mode' and the dominant defence got nicknamed the 'Legion of Boom'. In an era of tight Super Bowls won by small margins, Seattle's win against Denver in Super Bowl 48 bucked the modern trend. Denver were the bookies' favourites to win by a two-point margin but were blown away 43-8 in what was the third biggest winning margin in Super Bowl history, and the biggest ever win by a team who were underdogs.

This Super Bowl was unusual for two reasons; firstly, this was the first one played where two teams used to be in the same division, as Seattle used to be in the AFC West before being moved to the NFC. Being hosted in New York it was also the only Super Bowl to be played in the cold, as normally the game is played in warmer climate states, or indoor arenas. Seattle went ahead in the first possession as the Denver offence fumbled a snap in their own endzone and it was 2-0 with just 12 seconds gone. By half-time it was 22-0, and there was never a phase in the game when Denver were not being dominated.

The following season, the Seahawks were back in the Super Bowl after a thrilling fourth-quarter comeback against Green Bay in the NFC Championship game, when they were losing 19-7 with just three minutes to go. The Super Bowl against New England was also a classic, and the biggest 'what if?' in Seahawks history. In a tight contest, the Patriots were four points ahead late on in the fourth quarter. The Seahawks needed a touchdown to win and Wilson led a drive that got them a first down on the Patriots' one-yard line. There was enough time left on the clock to complete four plays as Seattle still had a timeout, but Wilson threw the ball on the first down and it was intercepted by New England's Malcolm Butler. The 'Legion of Boom' defence stood on the touchline distraught, their emotions summed up by the shocked and disgusted expression of cornerback Richard Sherman. No one could understand why Seattle didn't run the ball with Marshawn Lynch, and questions were asked over whose call it was to throw the ball. Offensive coordinator Darrell Bevell said that it was his call, while coach Pete Carroll said it was 'all my fault'.

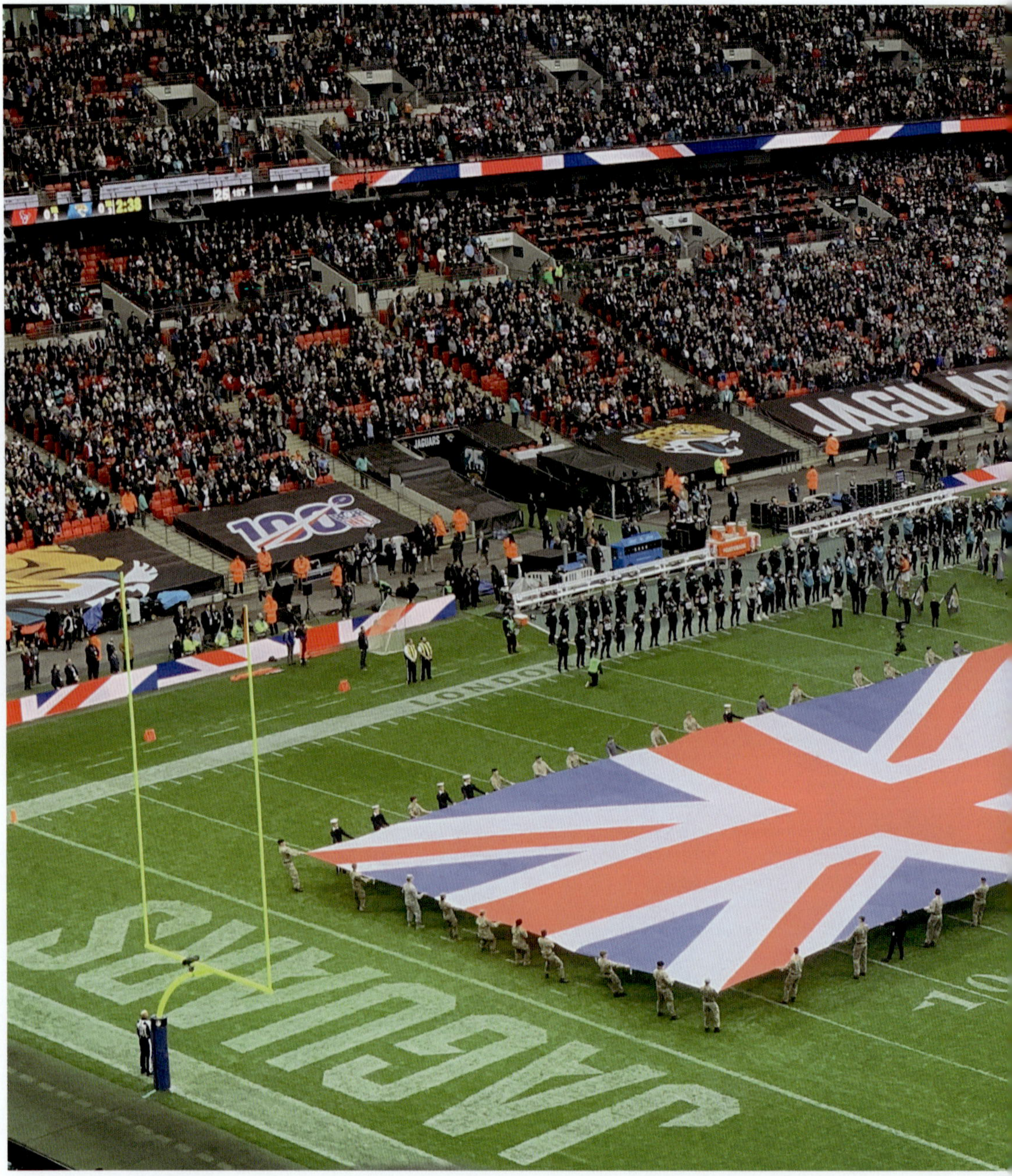

Wembley Stadium, London, England, 2019
Pageantry before the Jaguars take on the Texans in the International Series at Wembley. Regular season games in the UK started in 2007, and Jacksonville have played the most times with eight appearances, winning four and losing four. Houston won this game 26-3.

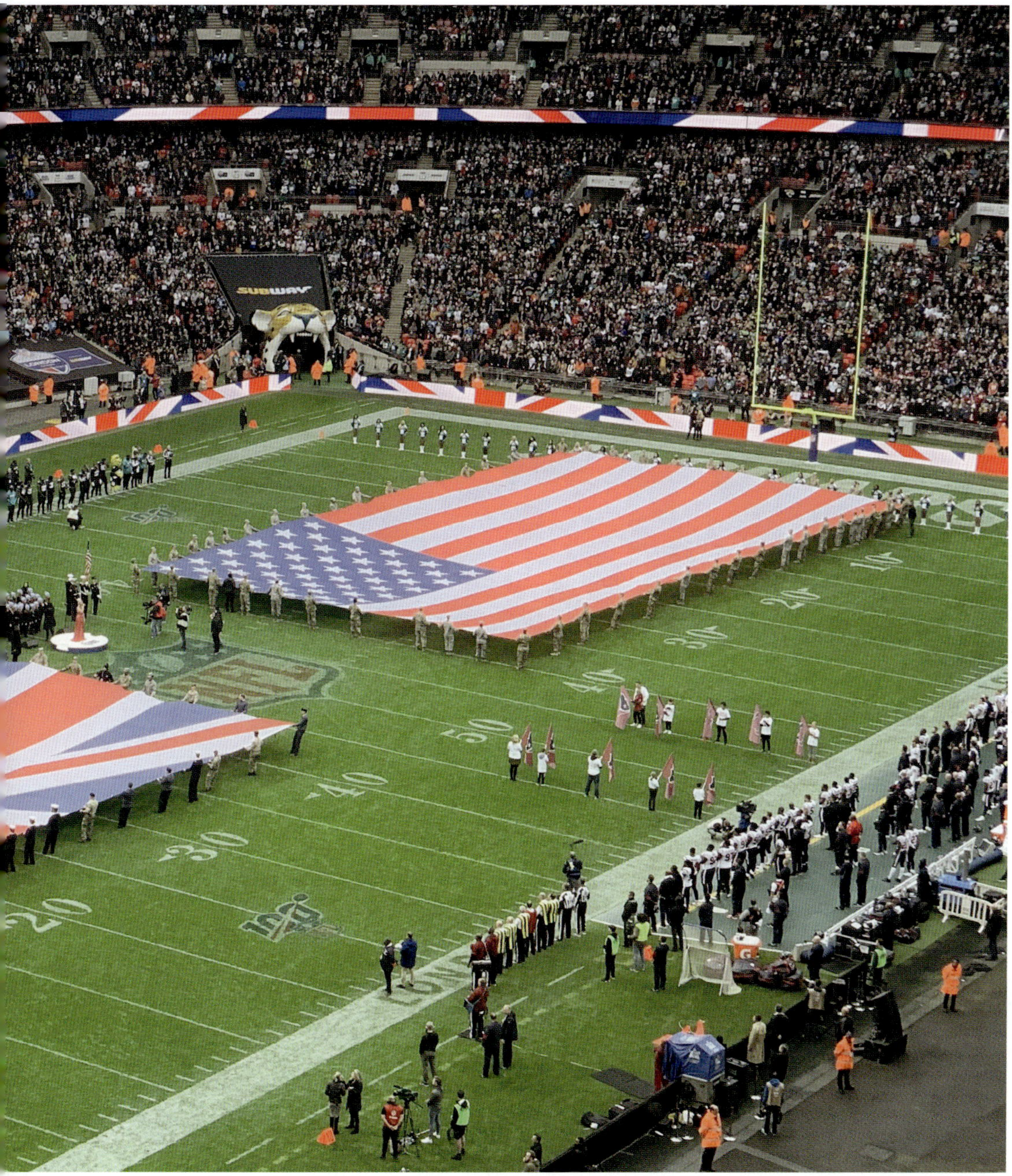
SUBWAY

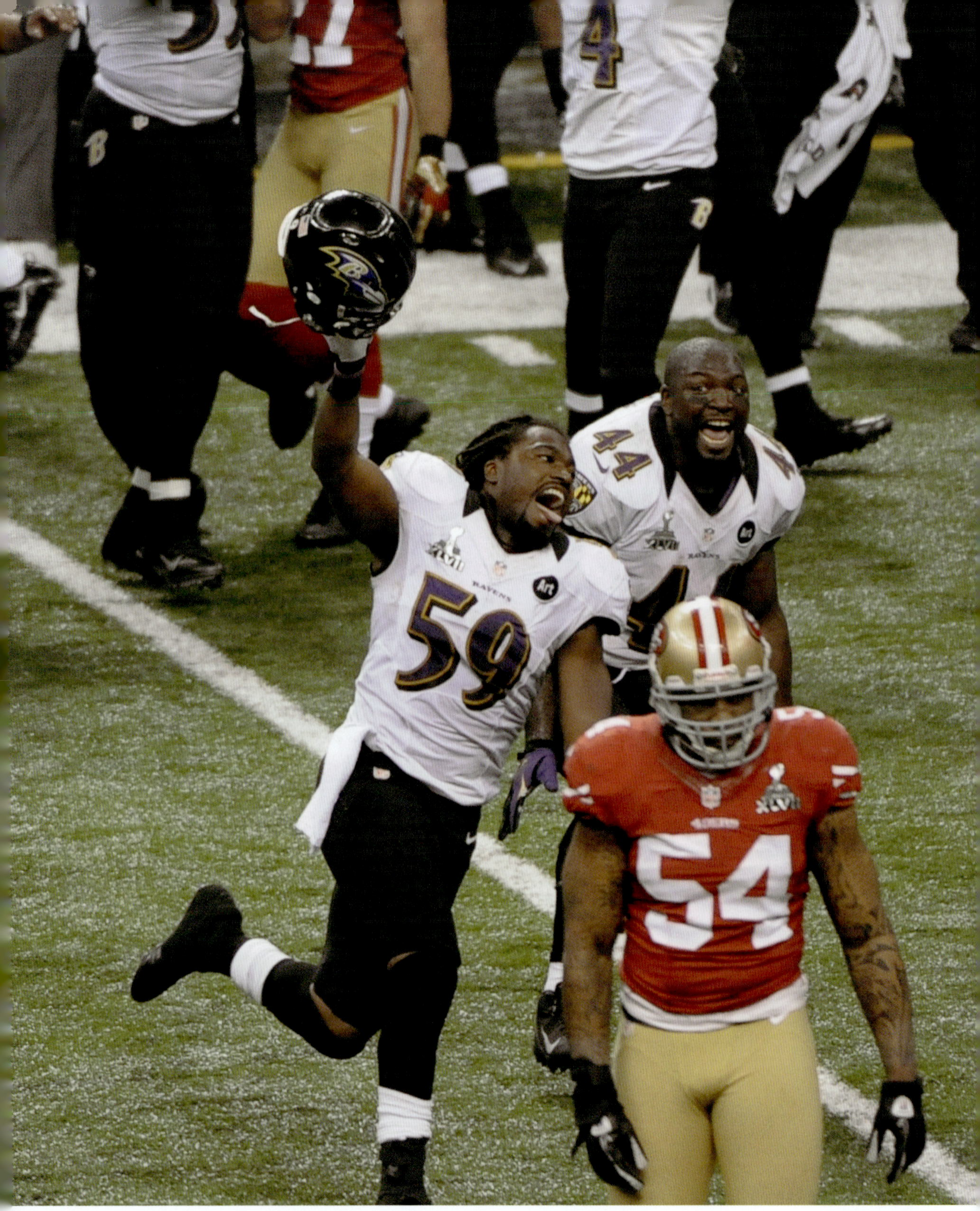

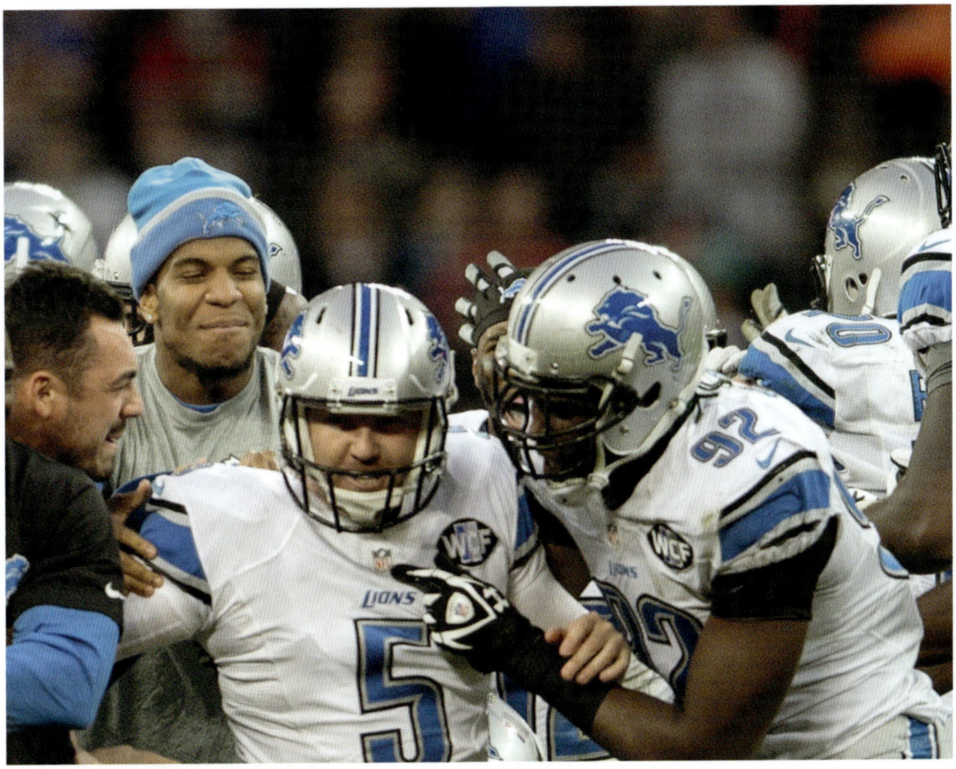

Mercedes-Benz Superdome, New Orleans, 2013
The Baltimore Ravens have just beaten San Francisco 34-31 in Super Bowl 47, as Dannell Ellerbe (59) and Vonta Leech (44) run onto the field in celebration.

Wembley Stadium, London, England, 2014
The Detroit Lions players mob their kicker Matt Prater (5) after he converts the field goal that beats the Atlanta Falcons at Wembley, 'the home of legends'.

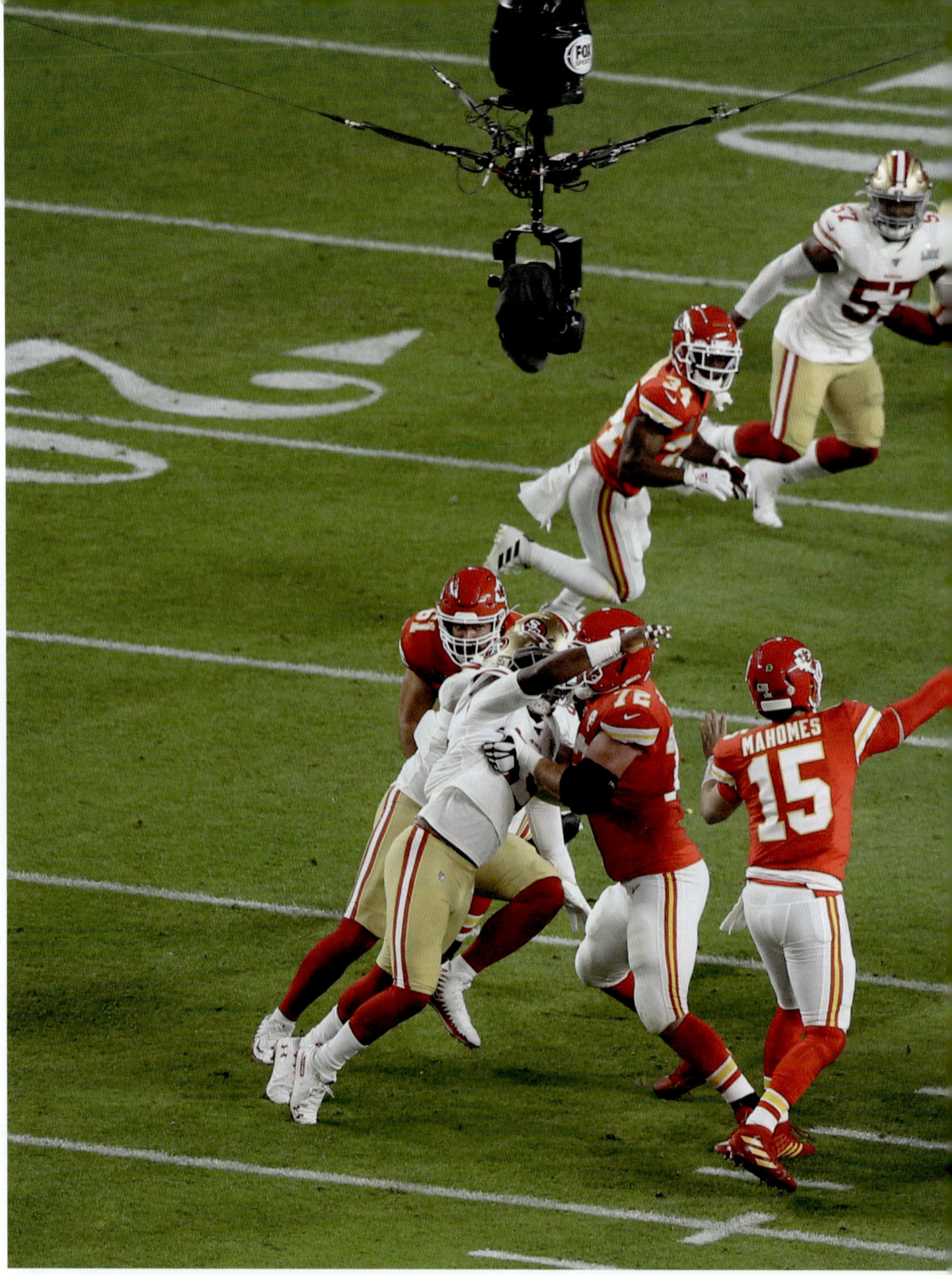

Hard Rock Stadium, Miami, 2020
Patrick Mahomes throws a pass as Kansas City beat the 49ers at Super Bowl 55. The game was a coming of age for the superstar quarterback as he led his team to a fourth-quarter comeback after the Chiefs were trailing by 10 points. Not long after this game, the world was sent into confusion and chaos because of the Covid 19 pandemic, and due to restrictions, this would be the last fully attended NFL game until the start of the 2021 season.

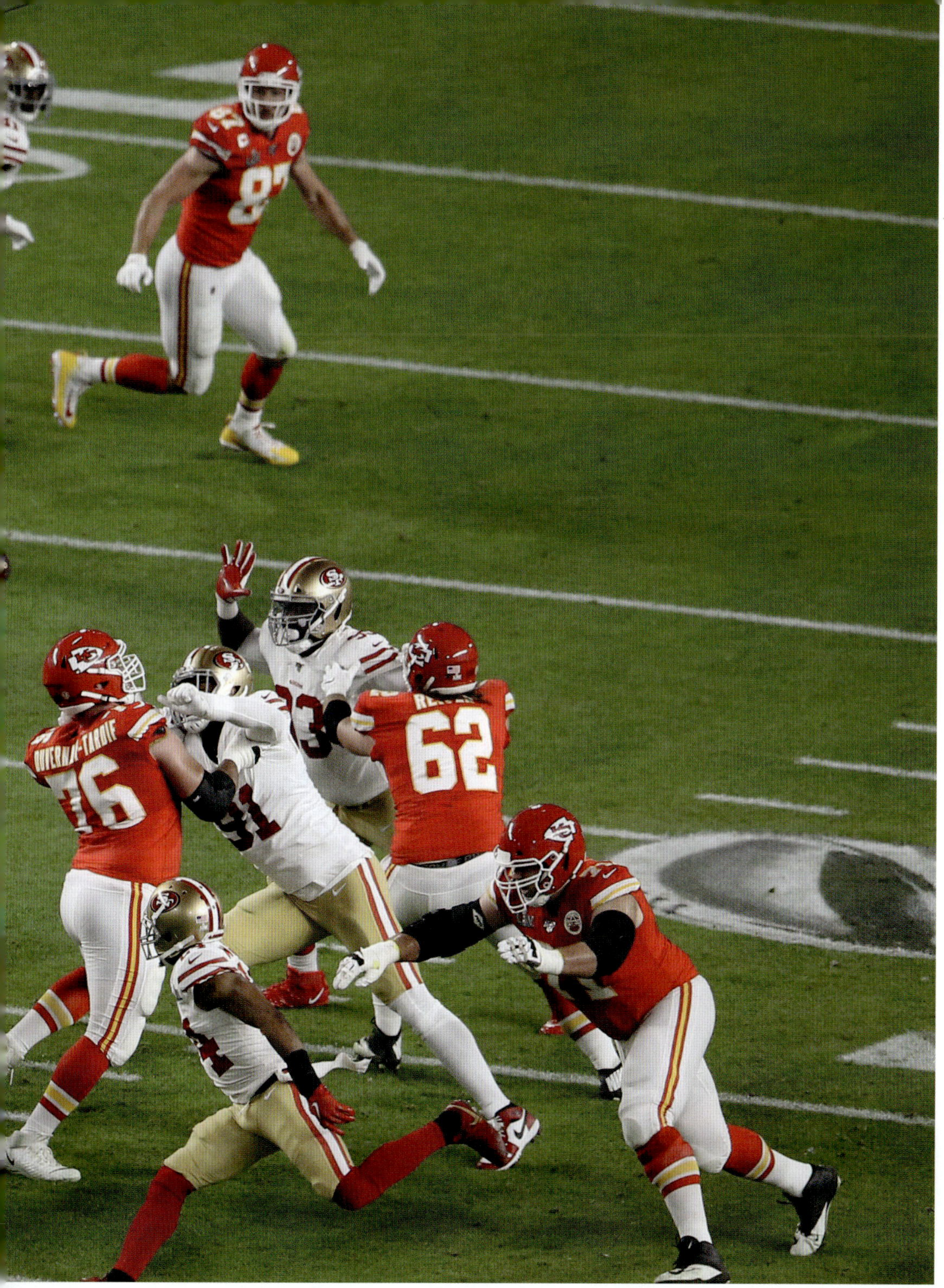

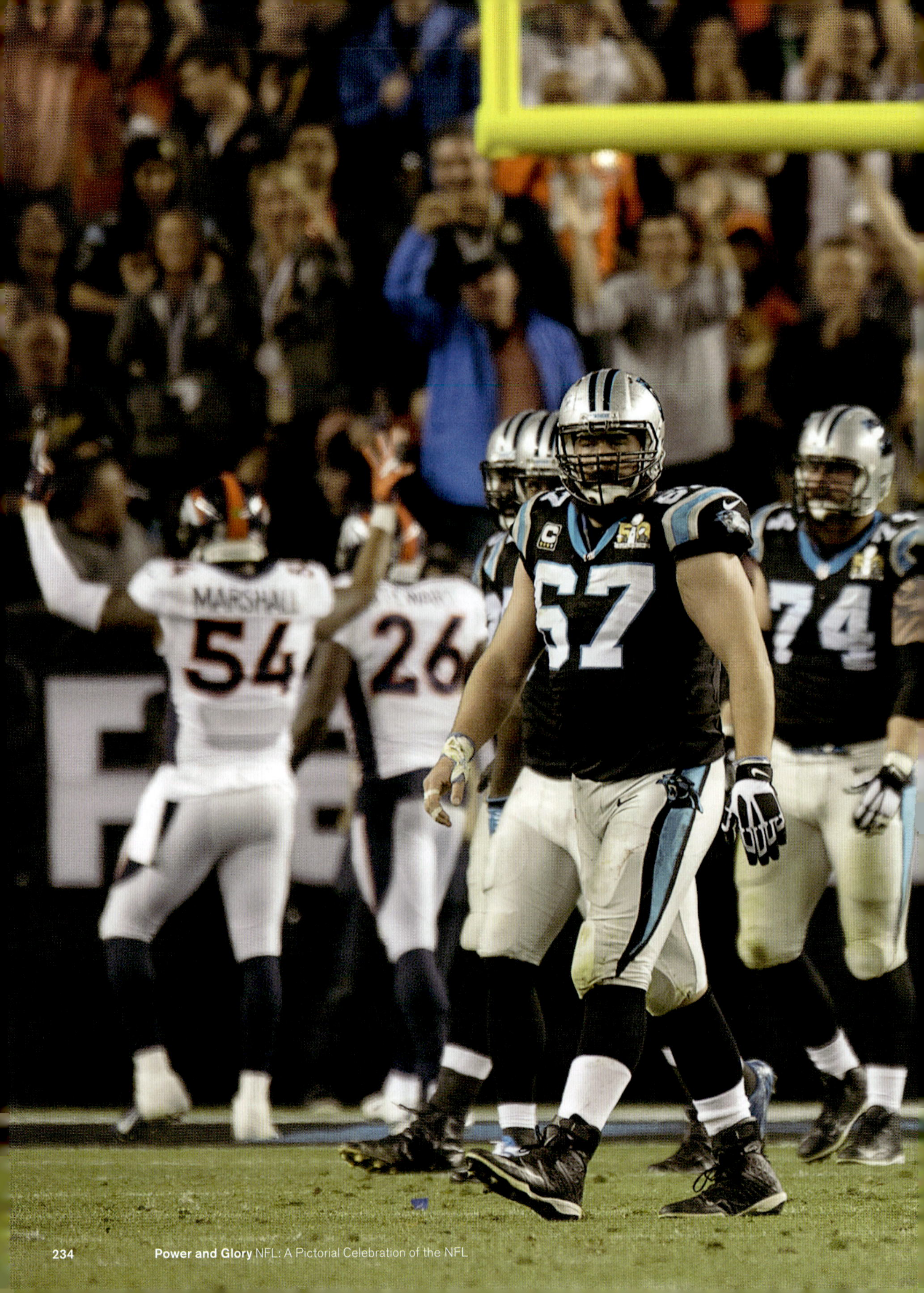
MARSHALL
54
26
67
74

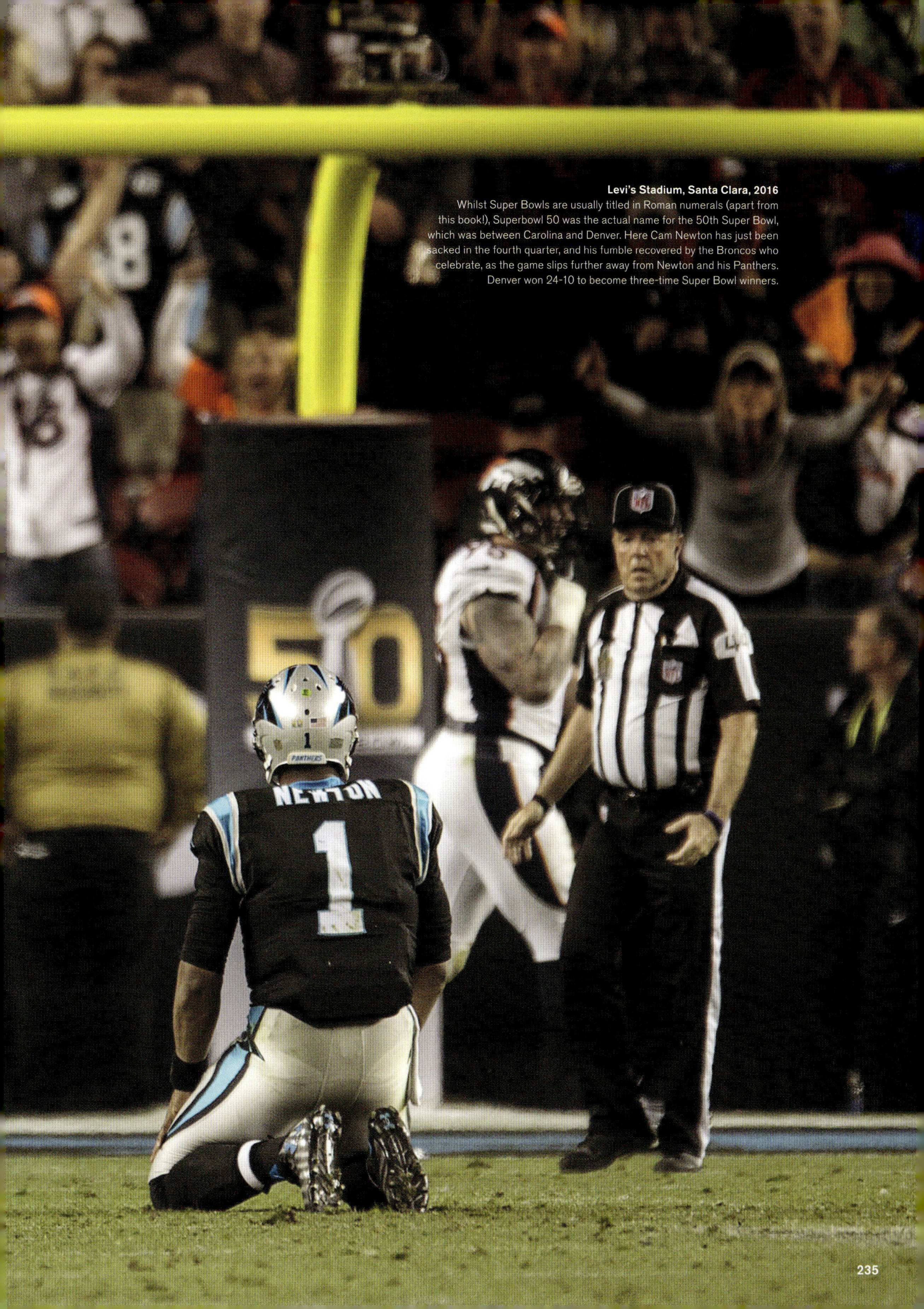

Levi's Stadium, Santa Clara, 2016

Whilst Super Bowls are usually titled in Roman numerals (apart from this book!), Superbowl 50 was the actual name for the 50th Super Bowl, which was between Carolina and Denver. Here Cam Newton has just been sacked in the fourth quarter, and his fumble recovered by the Broncos who celebrate, as the game slips further away from Newton and his Panthers. Denver won 24-10 to become three-time Super Bowl winners.

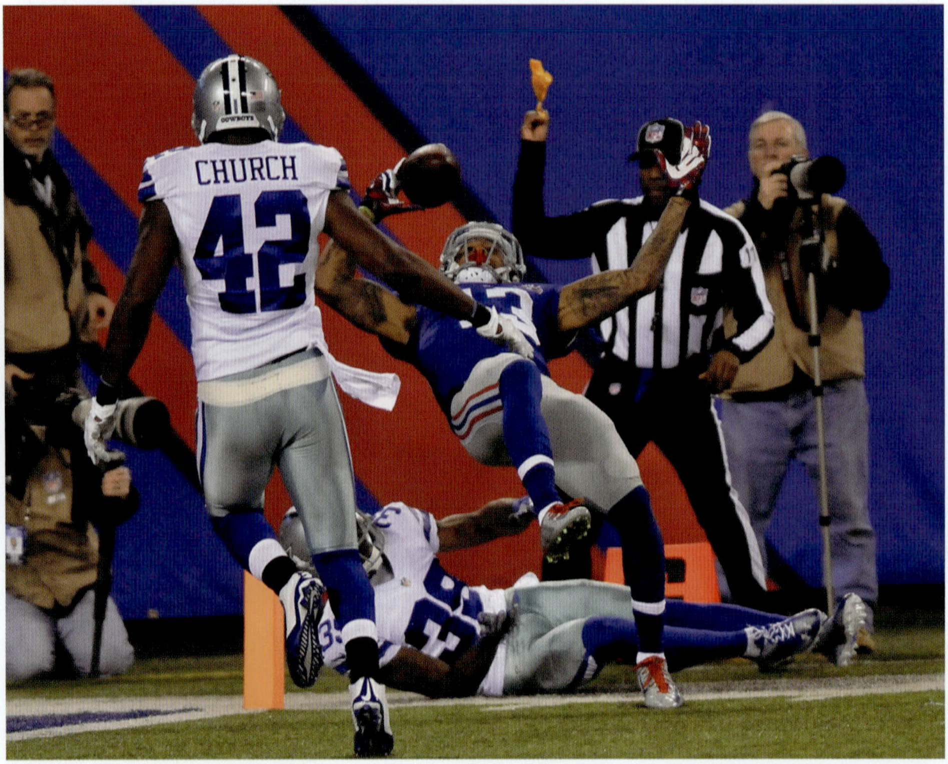

MetLife Stadium, East Rutherford, 2014
New York Giants wide receiver Odell Beckham catches with one hand for a touchdown against Dallas. In the commentary box, NBC's Chris Collinsworth described it as the best catch he'd ever seen.

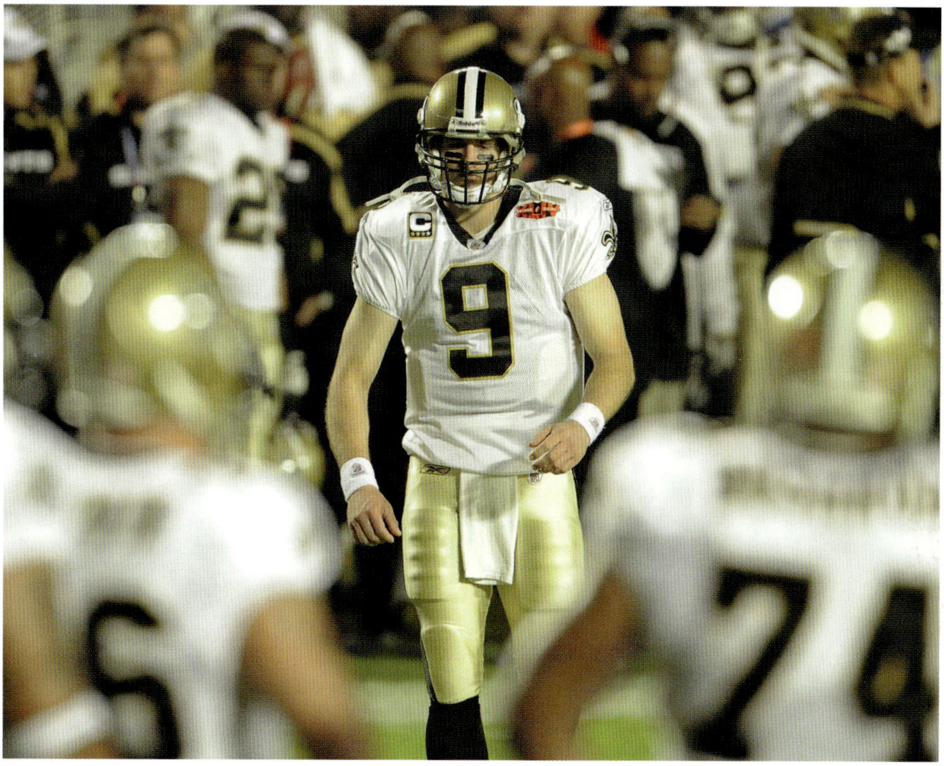

Sun Life Stadium, Miami, 2010
New Orleans quarterback Dree Brees during Super Bowl 44, as the Saints beat the Colts 34-17.

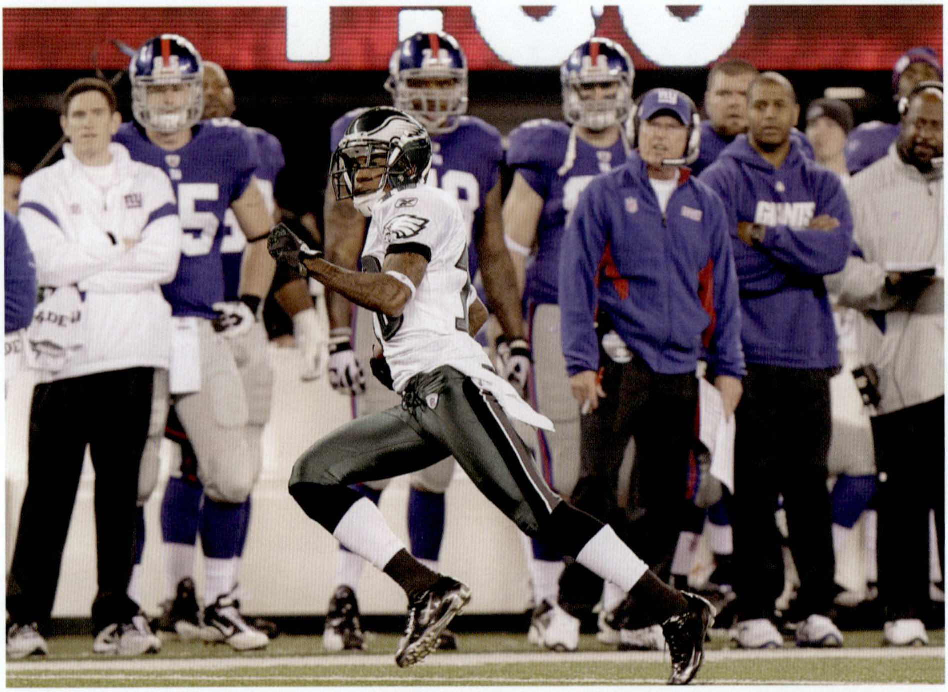

New Meadowlands Stadium, East Rutherford, 2010
A sweet moment for Philadelphia against bitter rivals New York, in what was branded 'The Miracle at the New Meadowlands'. With just over seven minutes to go in the game, the Giants were ahead 31-10. A comeback seemed impossible, yet the Eagles scored three quick touchdowns to level the score. Then in the final play, with 10 seconds to go, DeSean Jackson catches a badly directed punt from the Giants kicker, and runs 70 yards for the winning touchdown. In the background is Giants head coach Tom Coughlin watching on in utter disgust at what is transpiring.

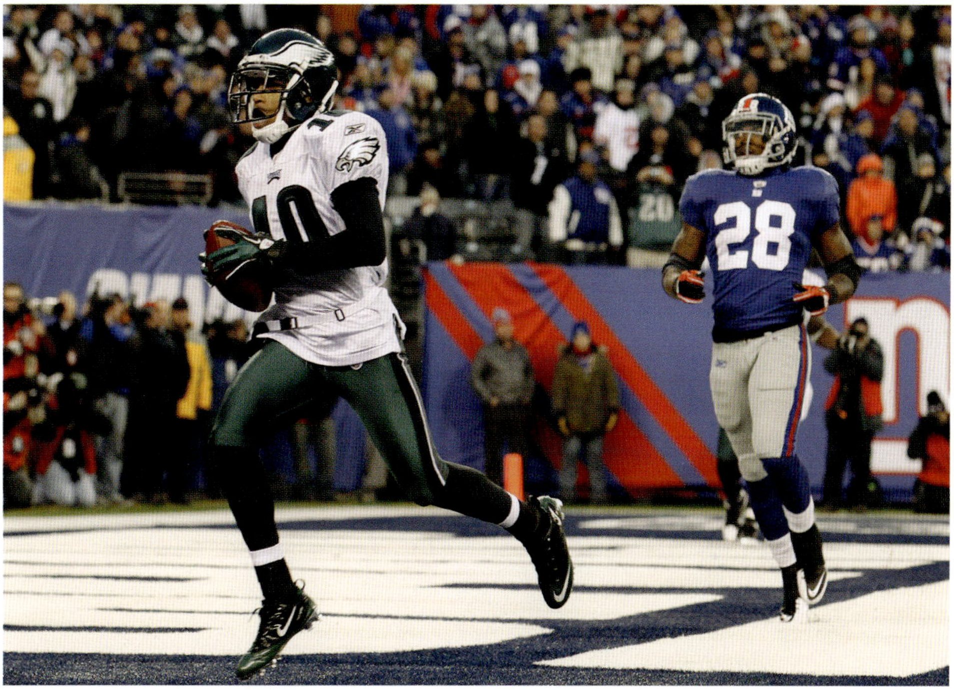
28

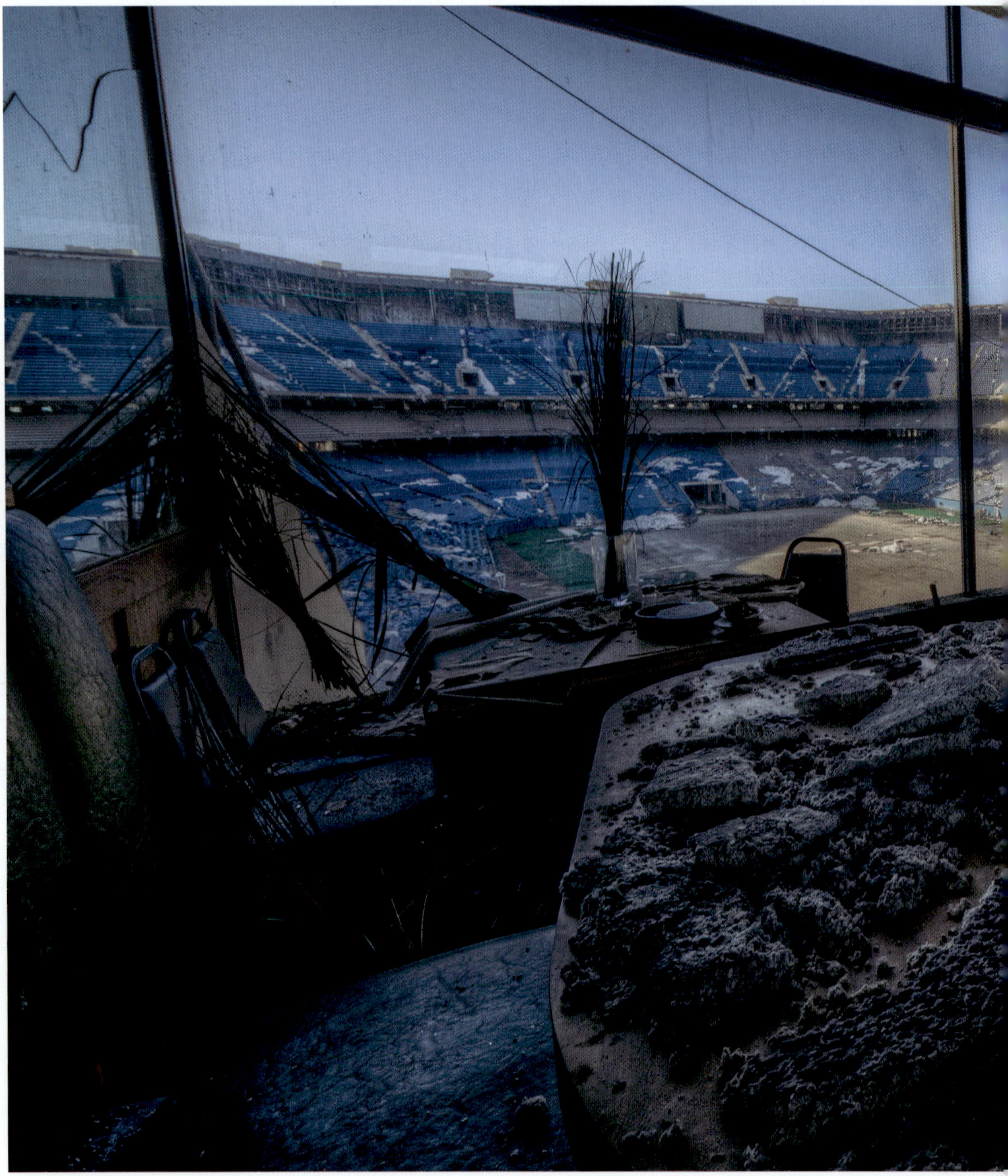

Pontiac Silverdome, Pontiac/Detroit, 2015
The rotting, and now roofless, remains of what once was a state-of-the-art modern stadium. The Silverdome was home to the Detroit Lions between 1975 and 2001 and was demolished in 2017.

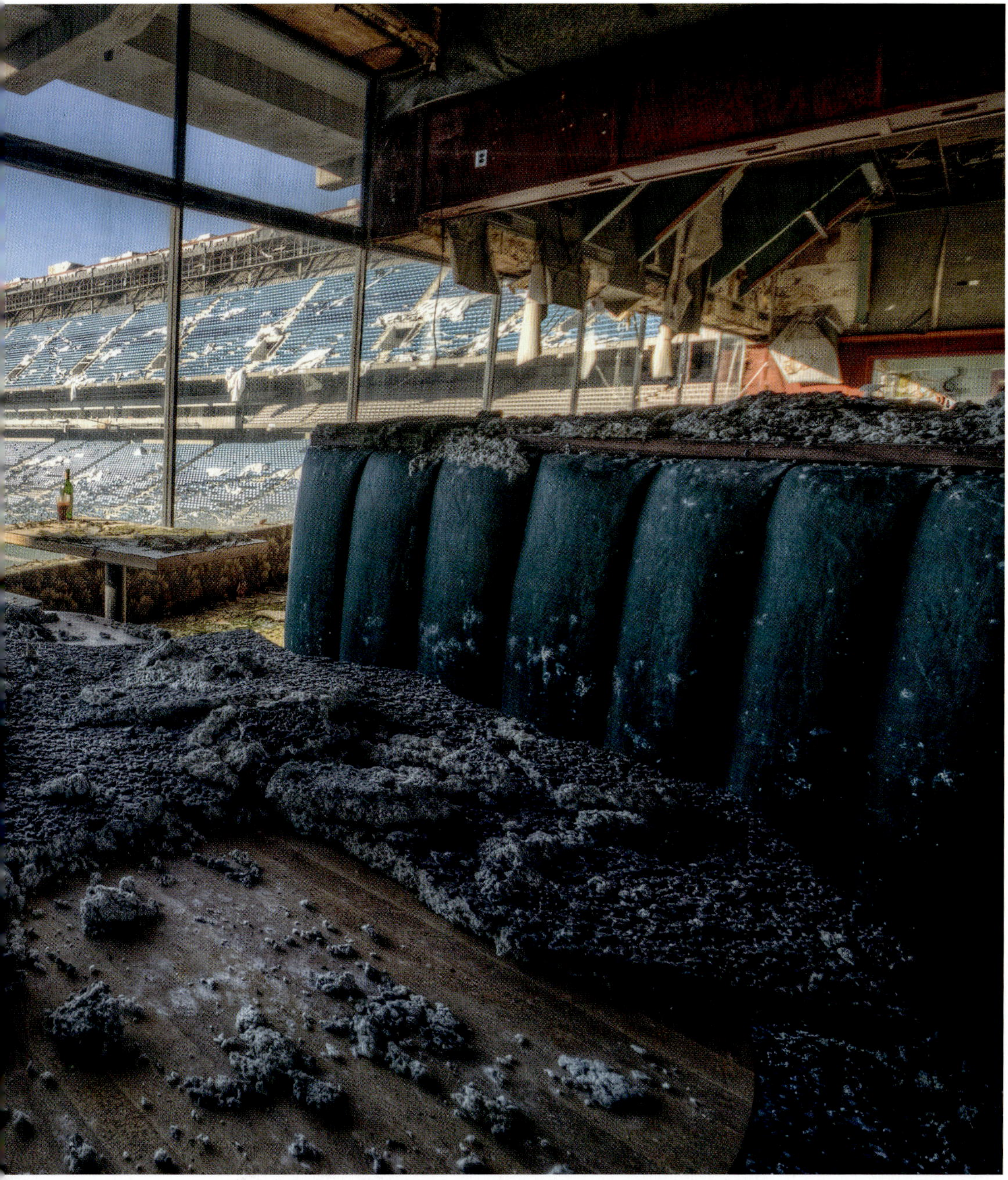

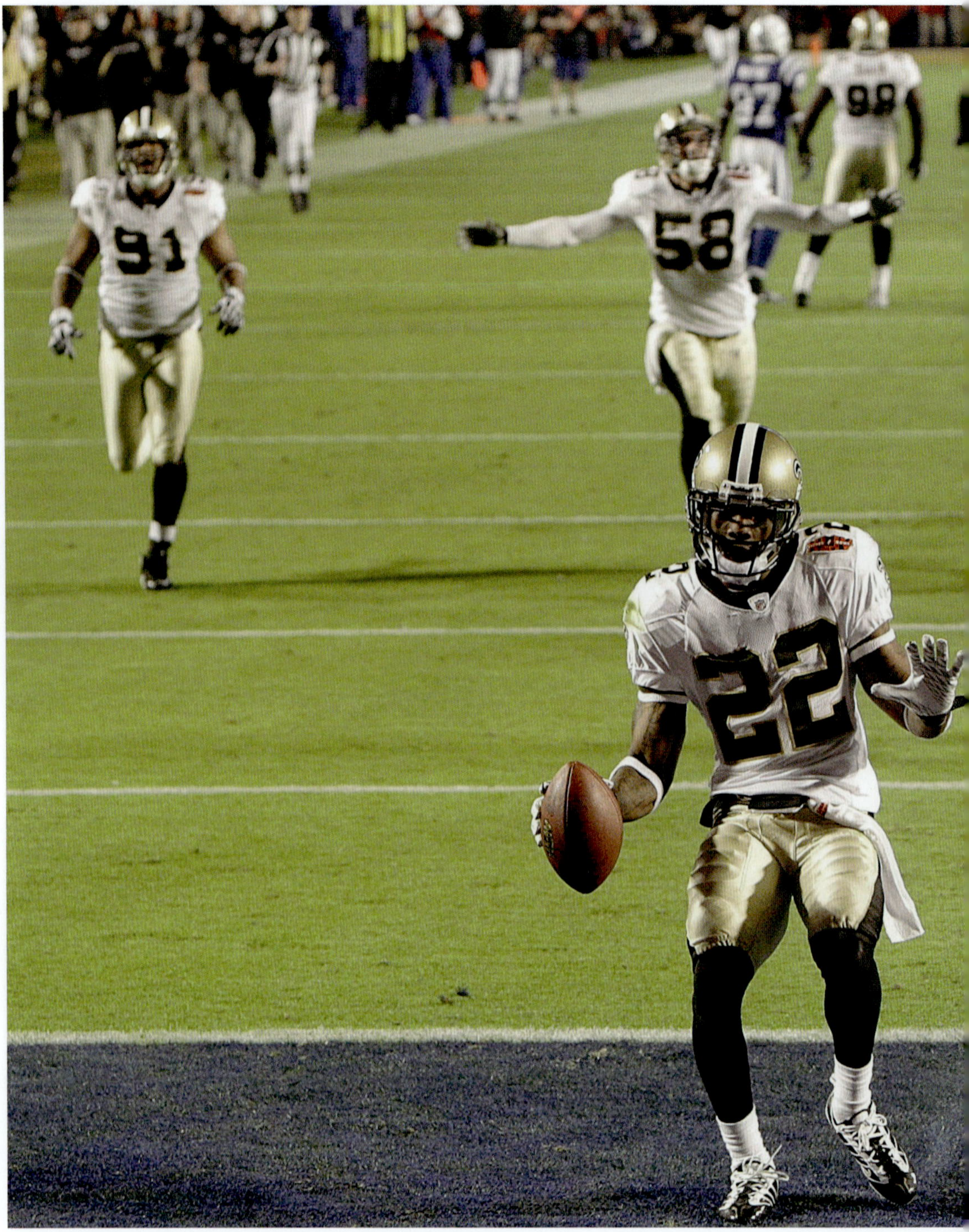

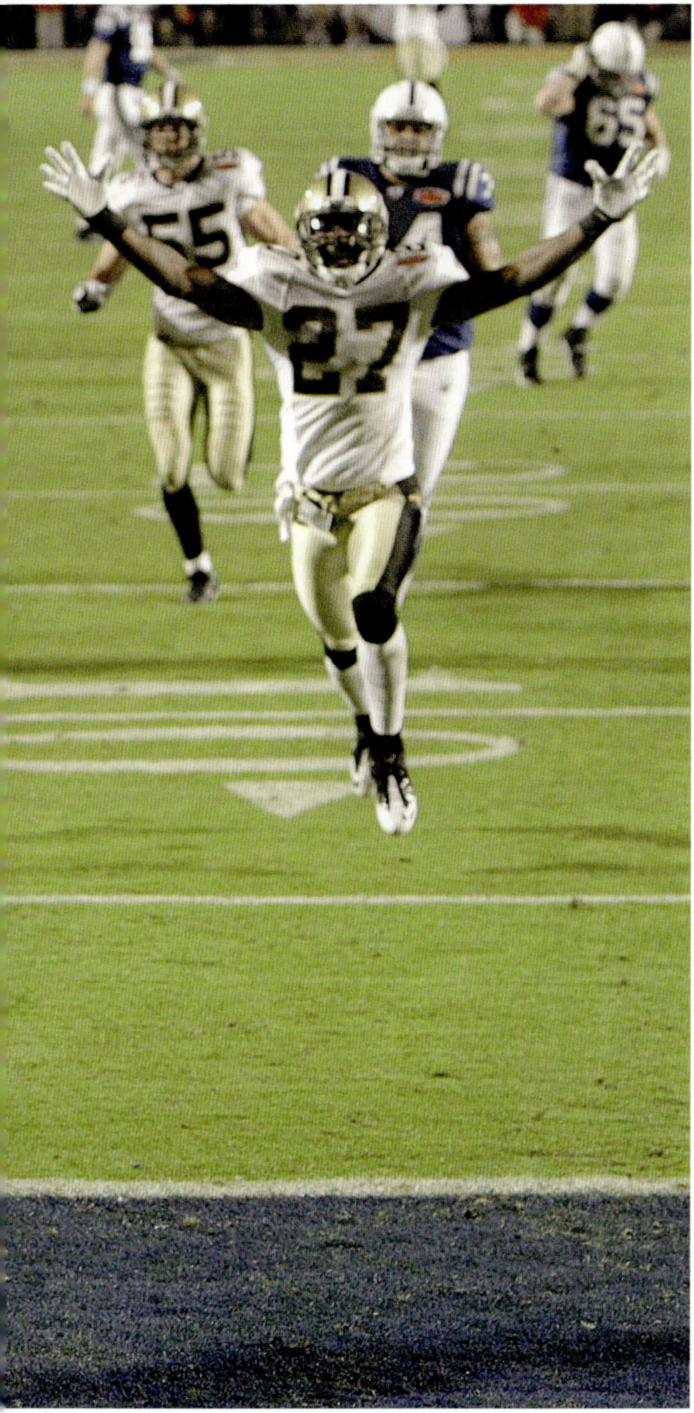

Sun Life Stadium, Miami, 2010
Late on in Super Bowl 44, New Orleans cornerback Tracy Porter has just intercepted a pass from Peyton Manning and scored a touchdown that confirms New Orleans as world champions for the first time ever.

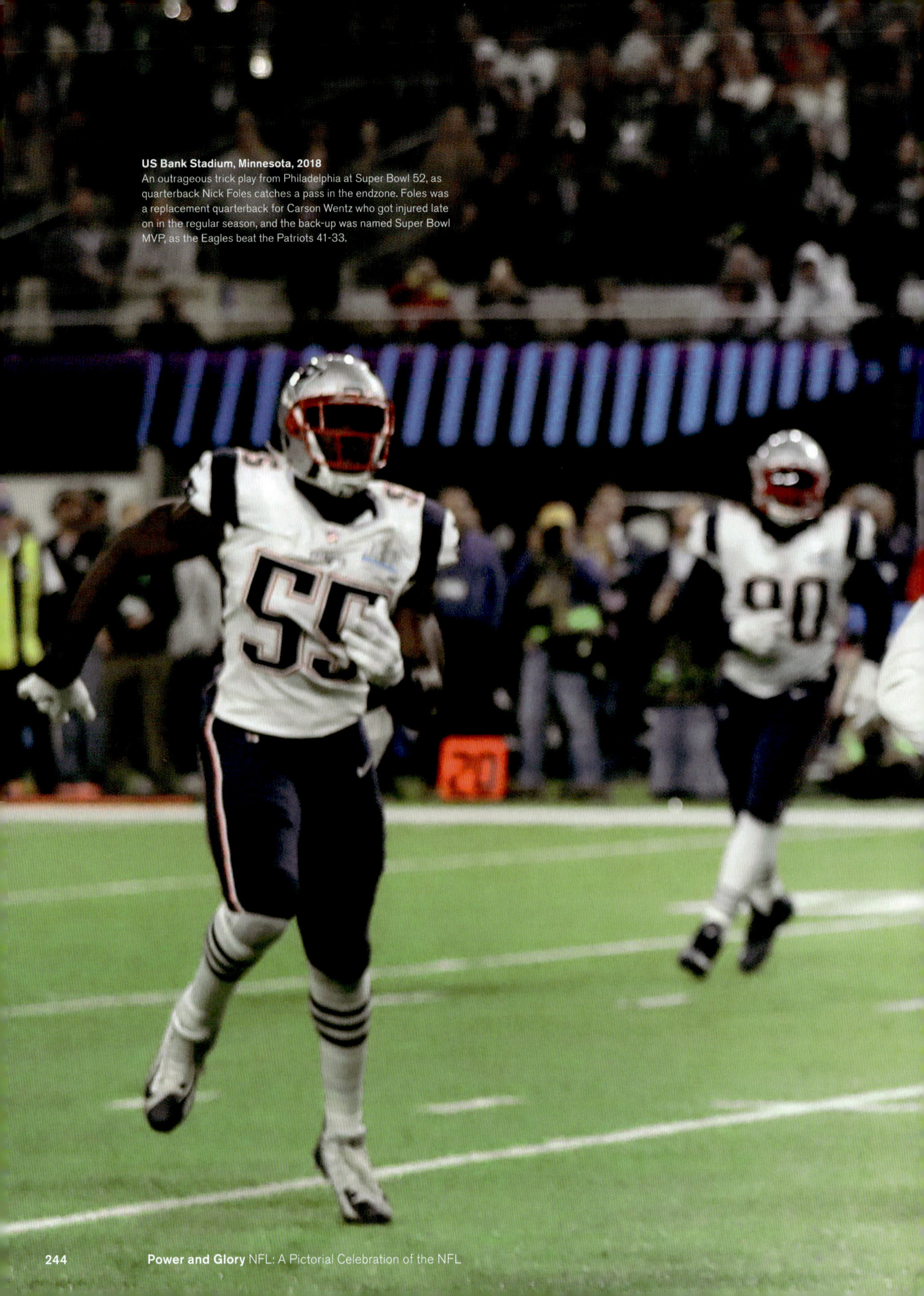

US Bank Stadium, Minnesota, 2018
An outrageous trick play from Philadelphia at Super Bowl 52, as quarterback Nick Foles catches a pass in the endzone. Foles was a replacement quarterback for Carson Wentz who got injured late on in the regular season, and the back-up was named Super Bowl MVP, as the Eagles beat the Patriots 41-33.

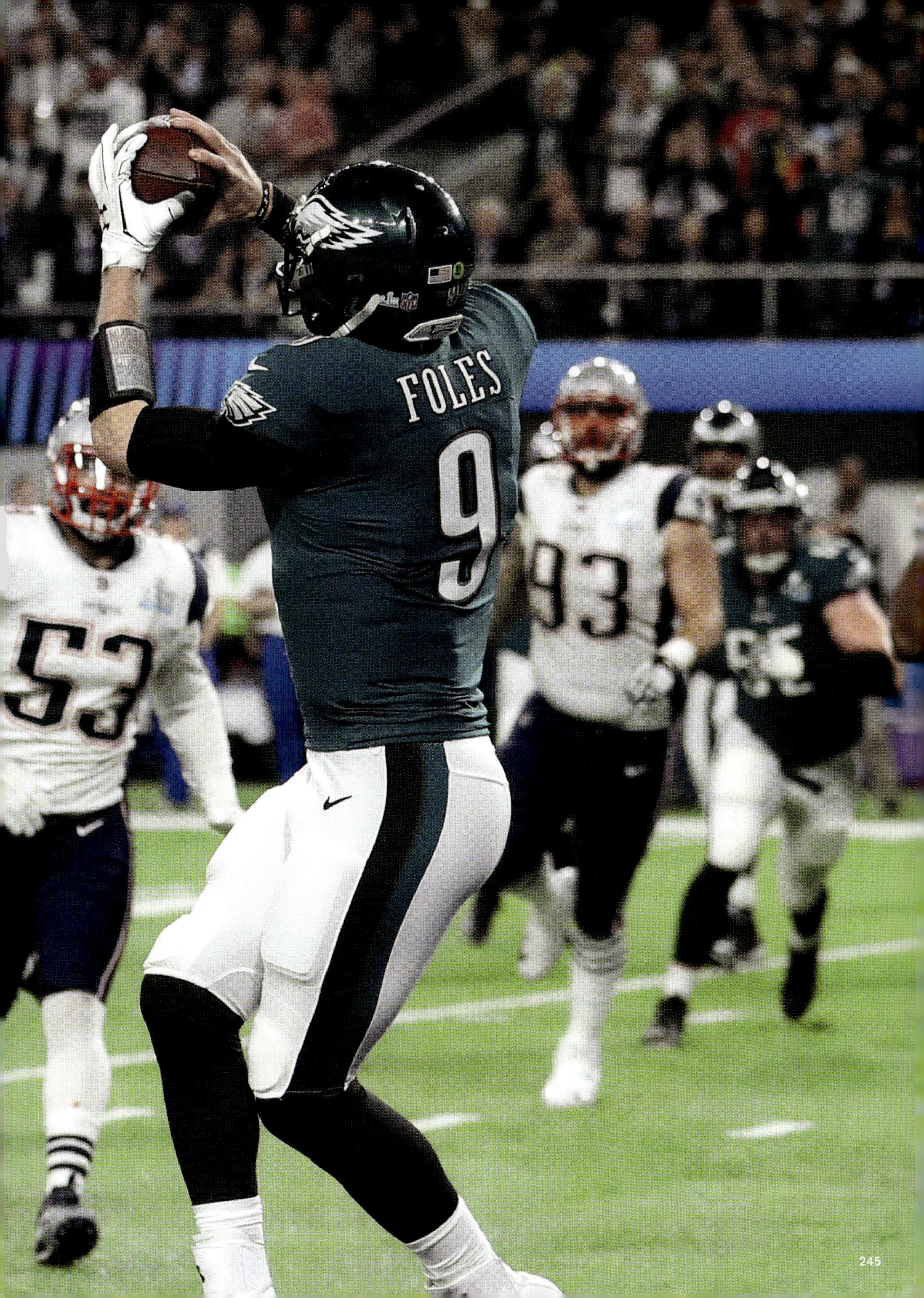
FOLES
9
93
53

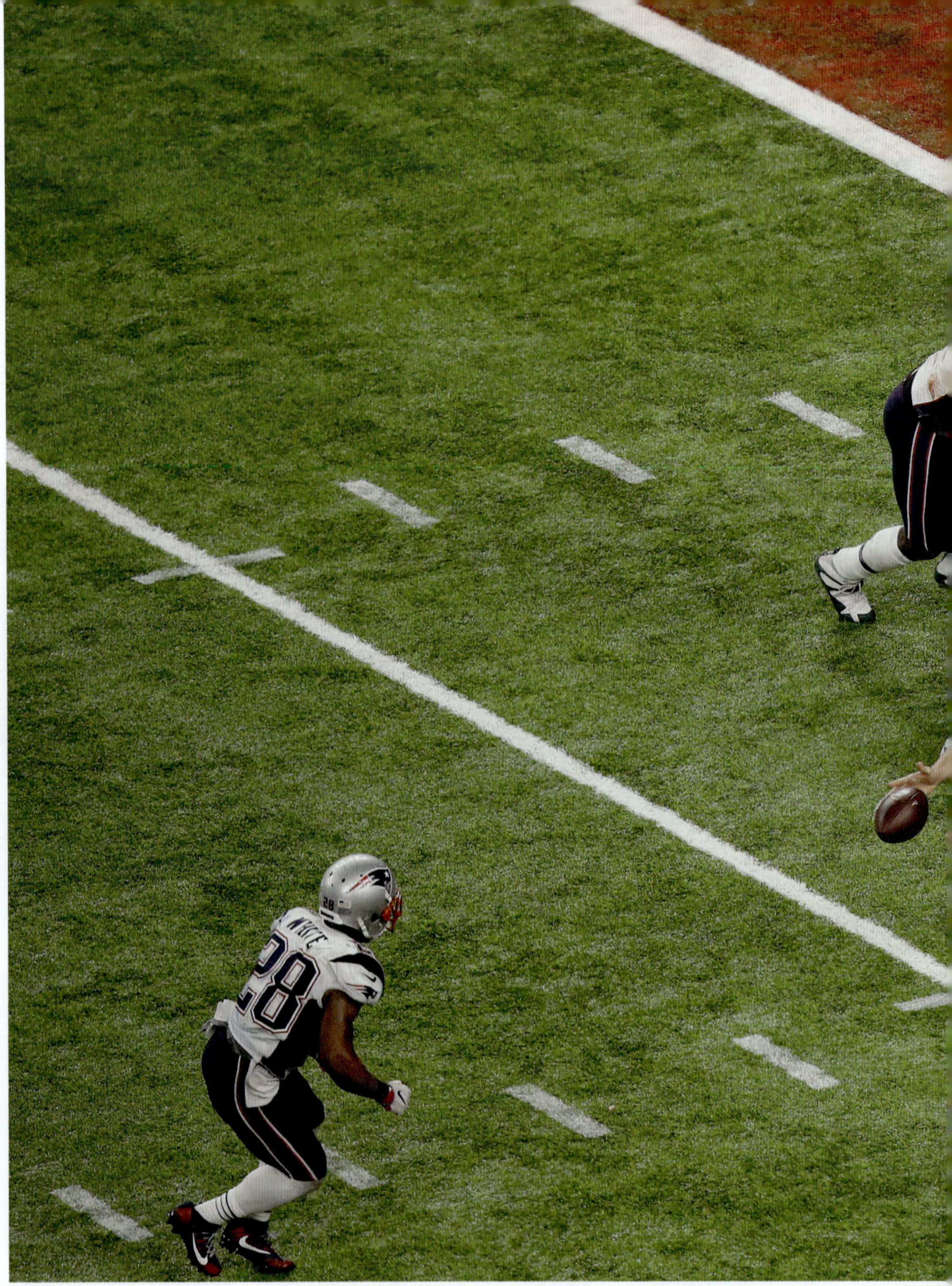

NRG Stadium, Houston, 2017
One of the most incredible Super Bowls is coming to a climax as New England's Tom Brady hands the ball to James White (28) to run for the winning touchdown in overtime. The Atlanta Falcons had led 28-3, yet a remarkable late comeback saw the Patriots overcome the biggest points margin in Super Bowl history.

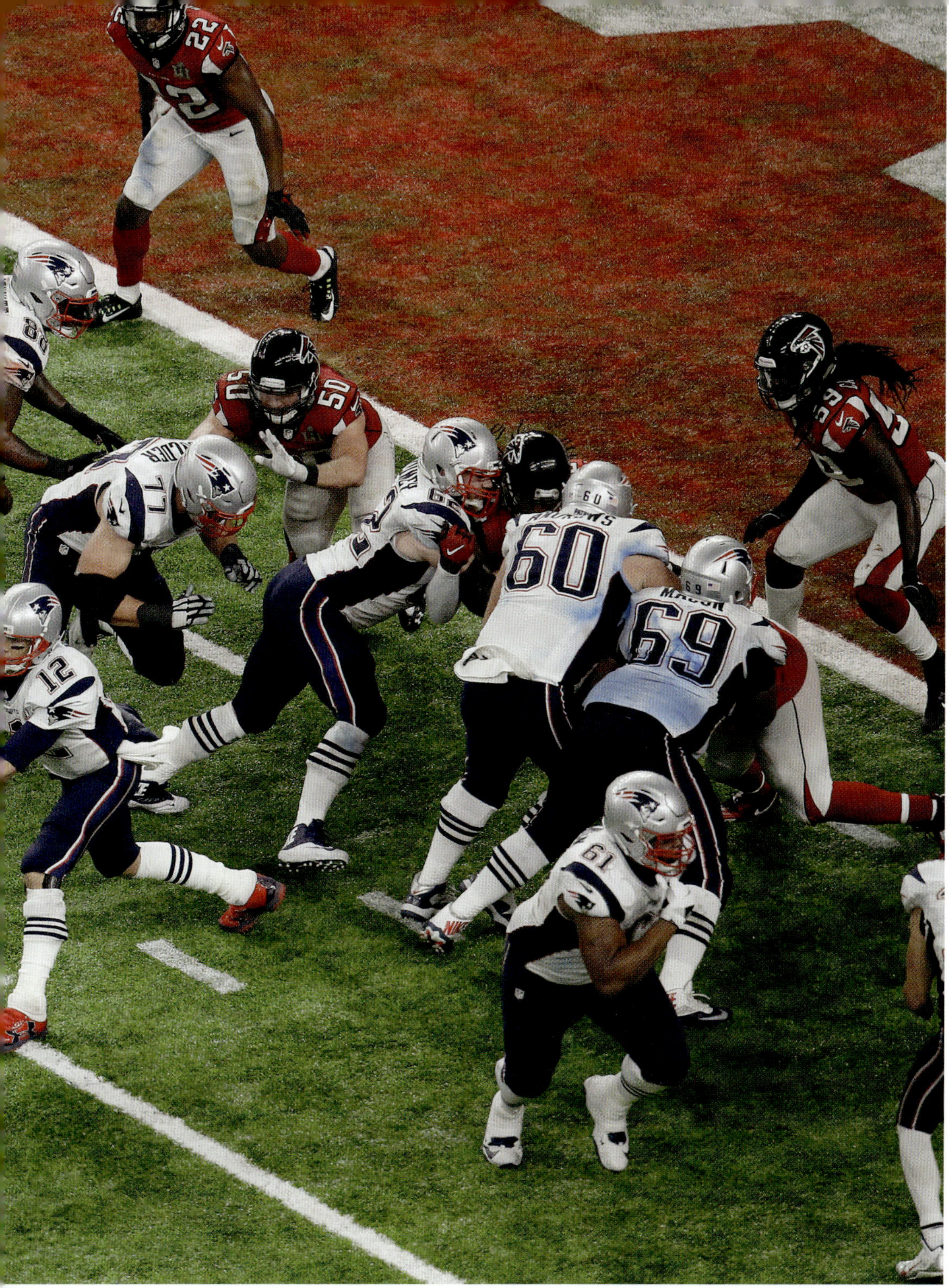

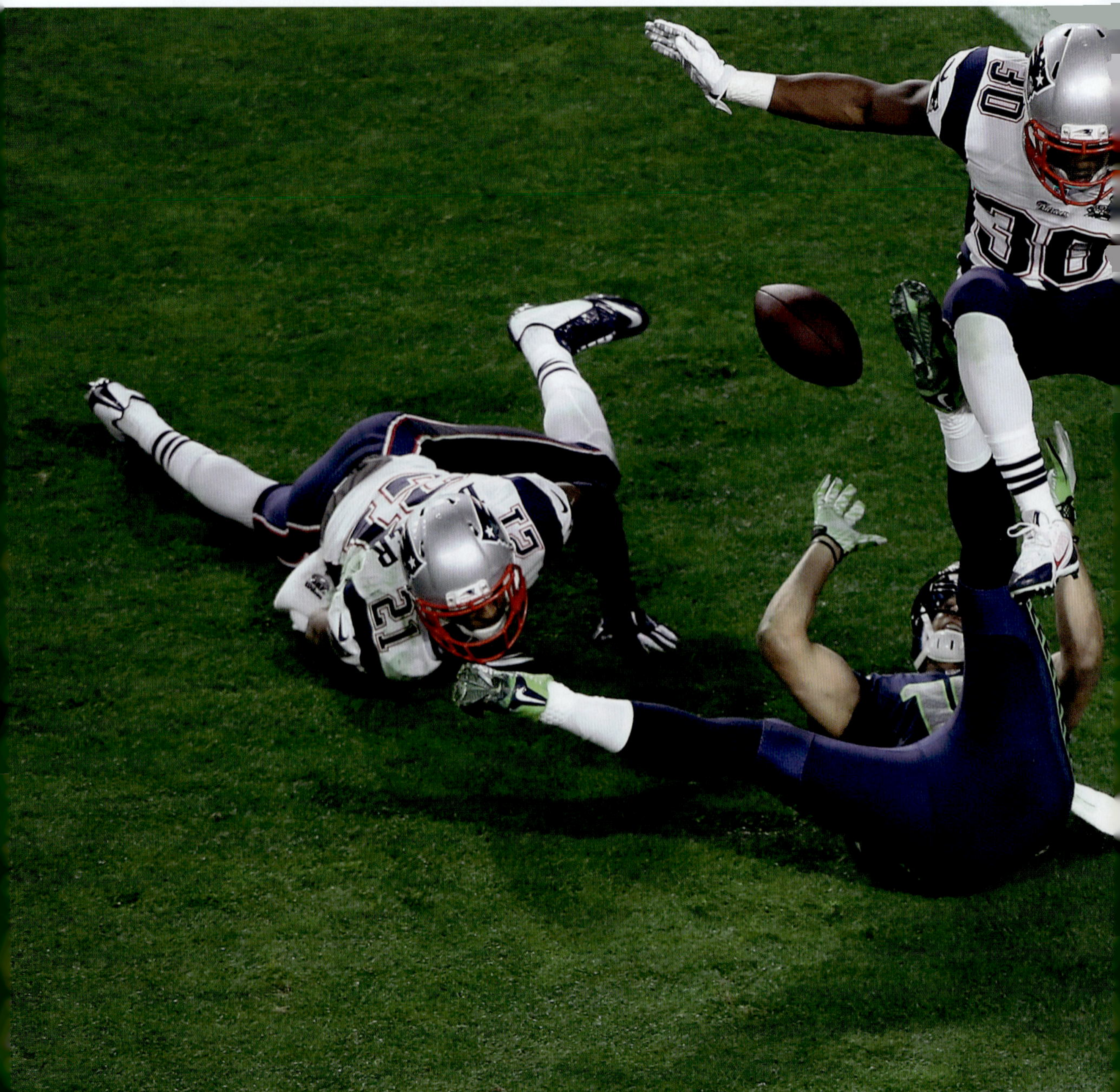

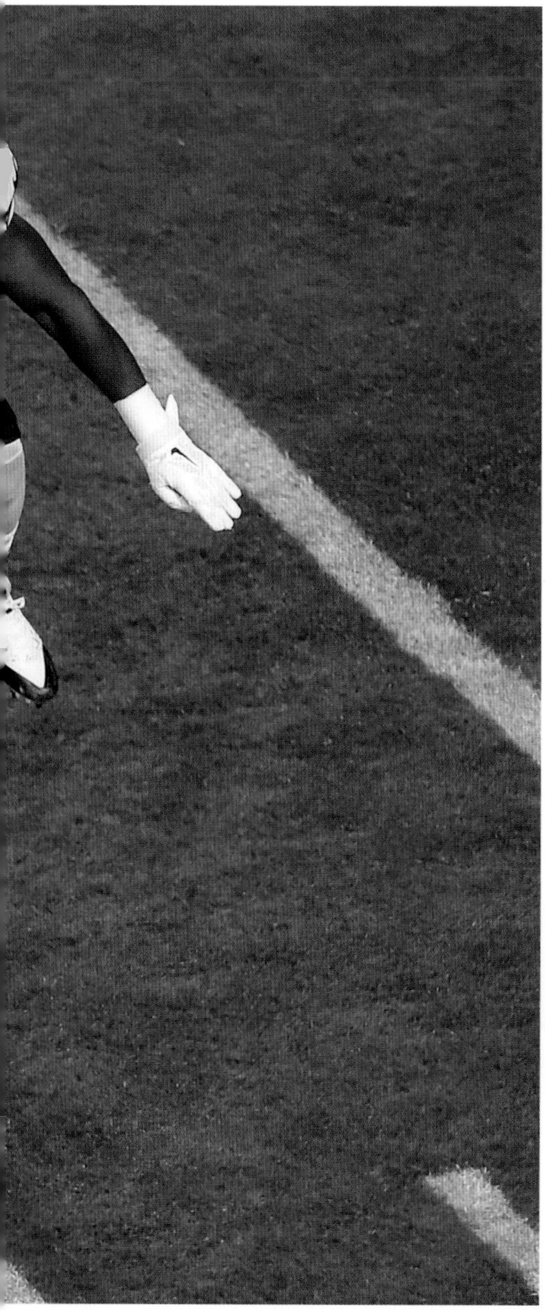

University of Phoenix Stadium, Glendale, 2015
One of the most bizarre catches in Super Bowl history. Late on in the game, Seattle's wide receiver Jermaine Kearse gets a second chance to catch the ball, as it bounces off his body and into his arms. With the clock ticking down it was a crucial moment, however Malcolm Butler (21) who here lies on the turf, would make a crucial catch himself that would prevent Seattle from a game-winning touchdown.

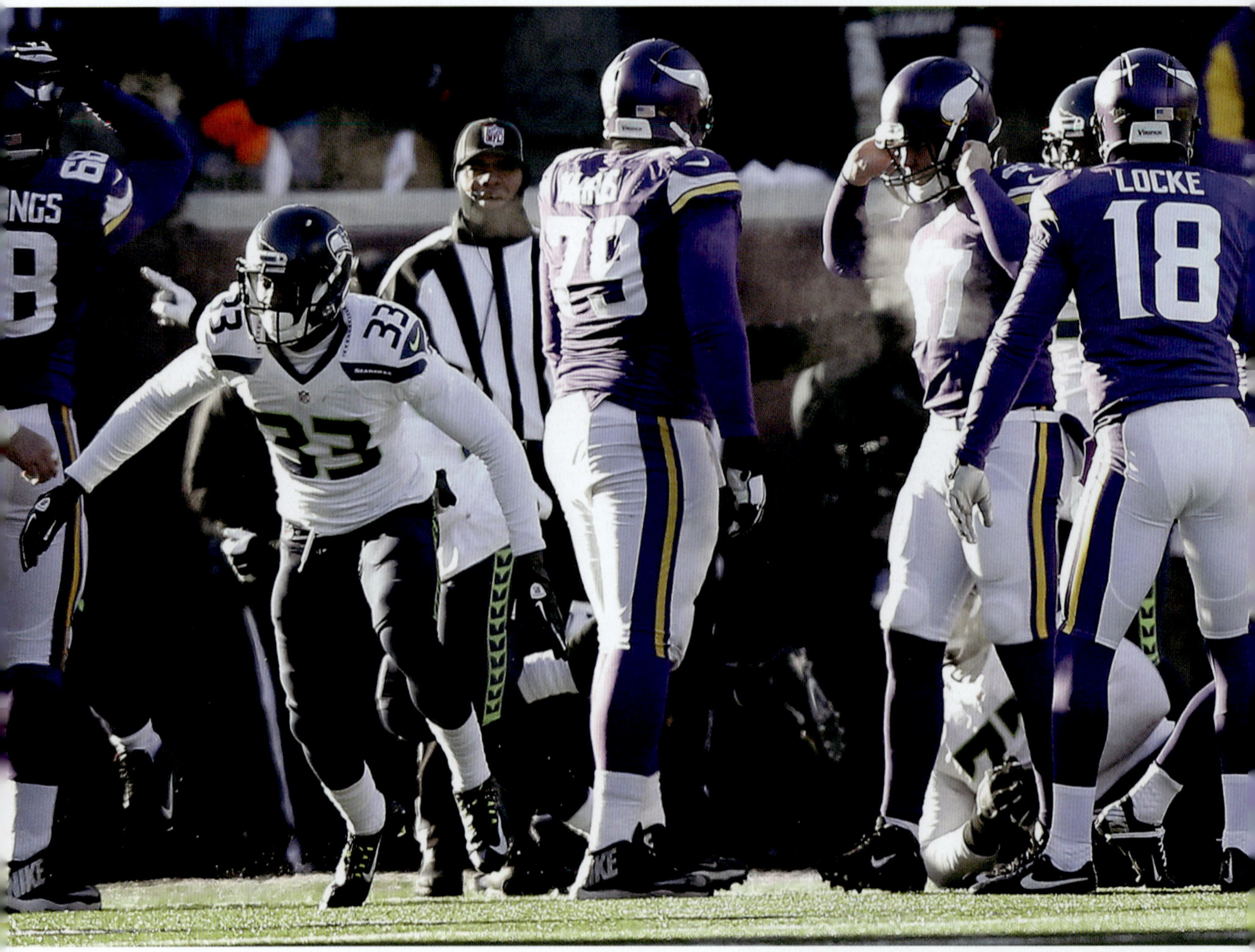

TFC Bank Stadium, Minneapolis, 2016
A terrible moment for Vikings kicker Blair Walsh (3). He has just missed a last-second field goal against Seattle that would have taken Minnesota to the divisional play-off. Seattle cannot believe their luck, as they come through victorious in one of the coldest weather games in recent NFL history.

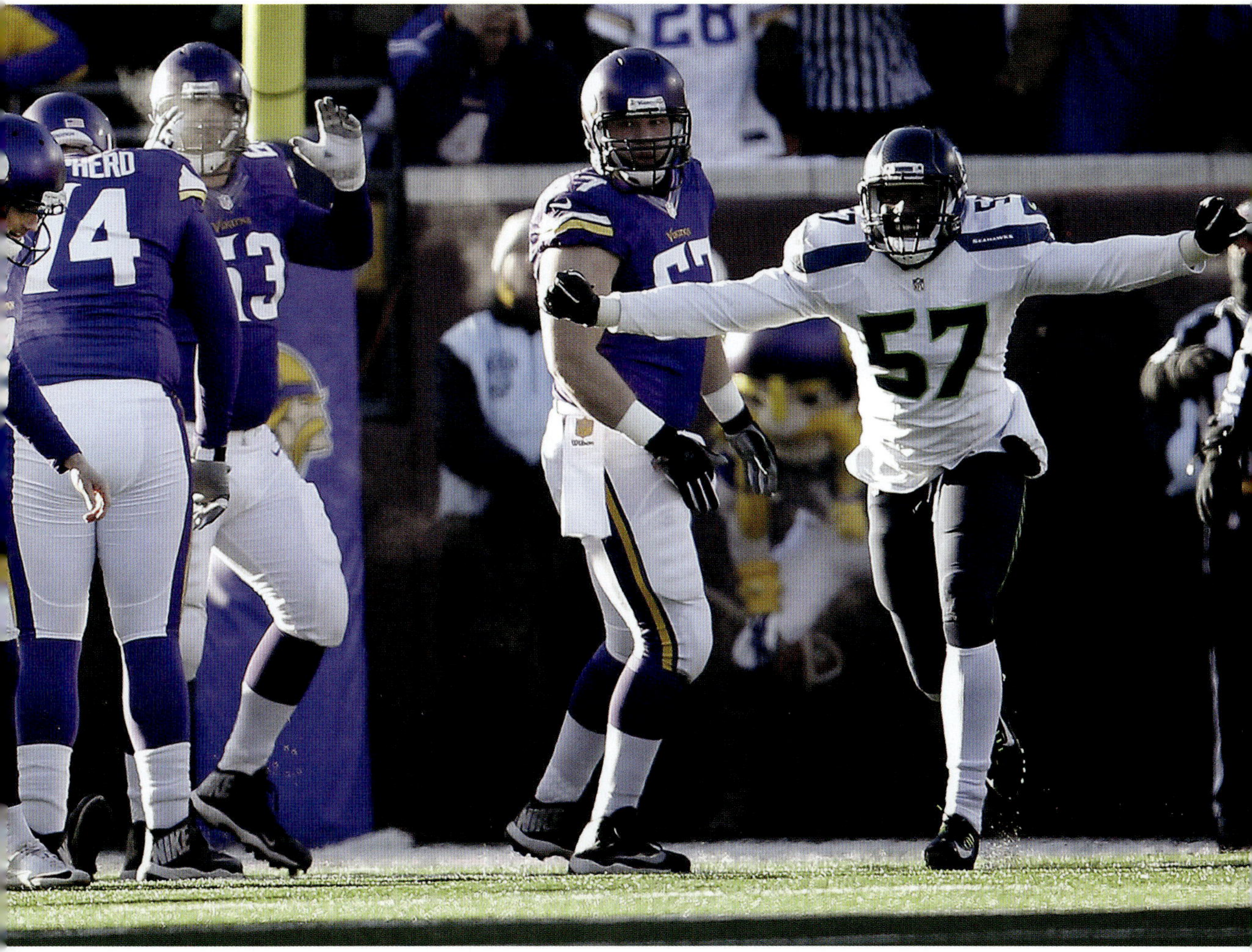

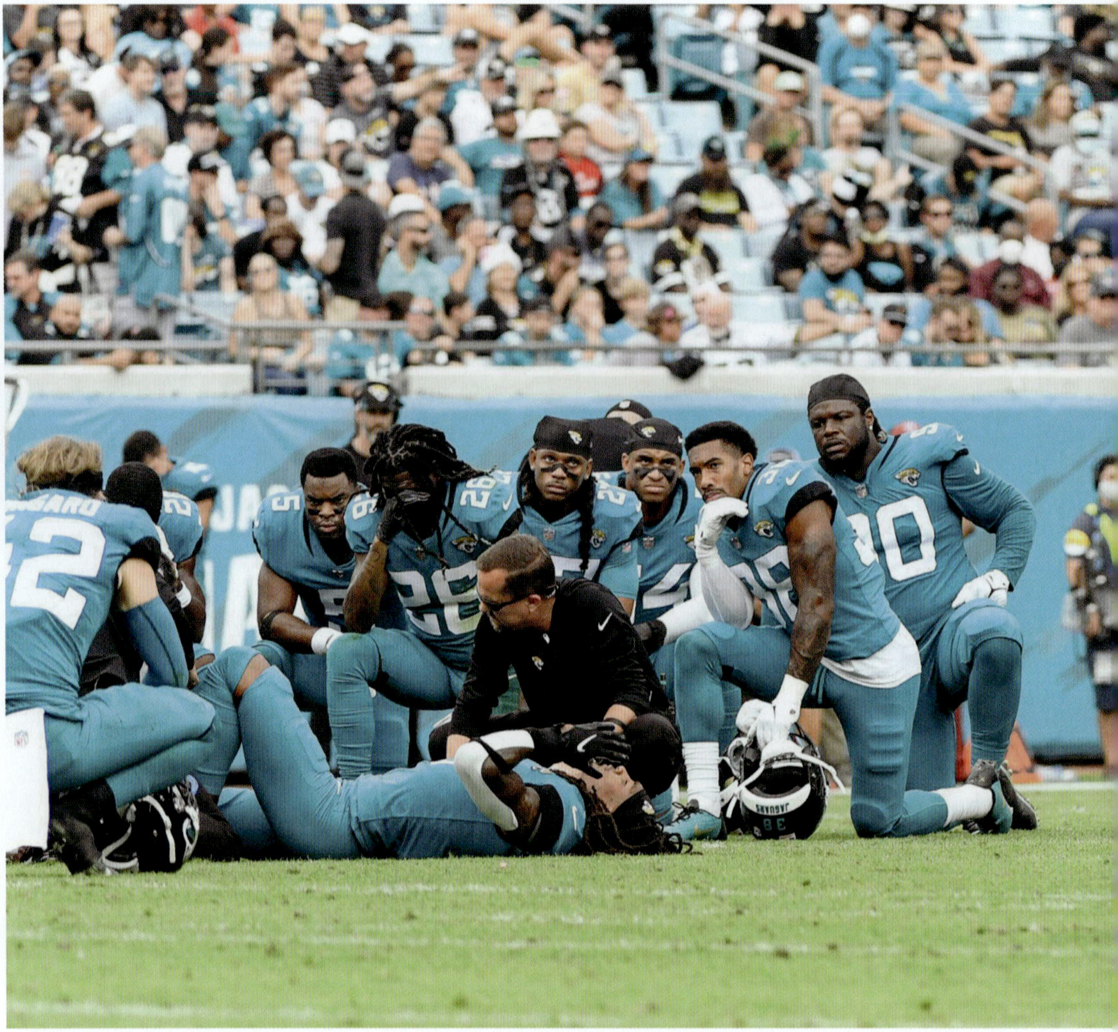

TIAA Bank Field, Jacksonville, 2021
Houston and Jacksonville players kneel down in concern for injured Jacksonville free safety Rayshawn Jenkins who lies on the floor with a leg injury.

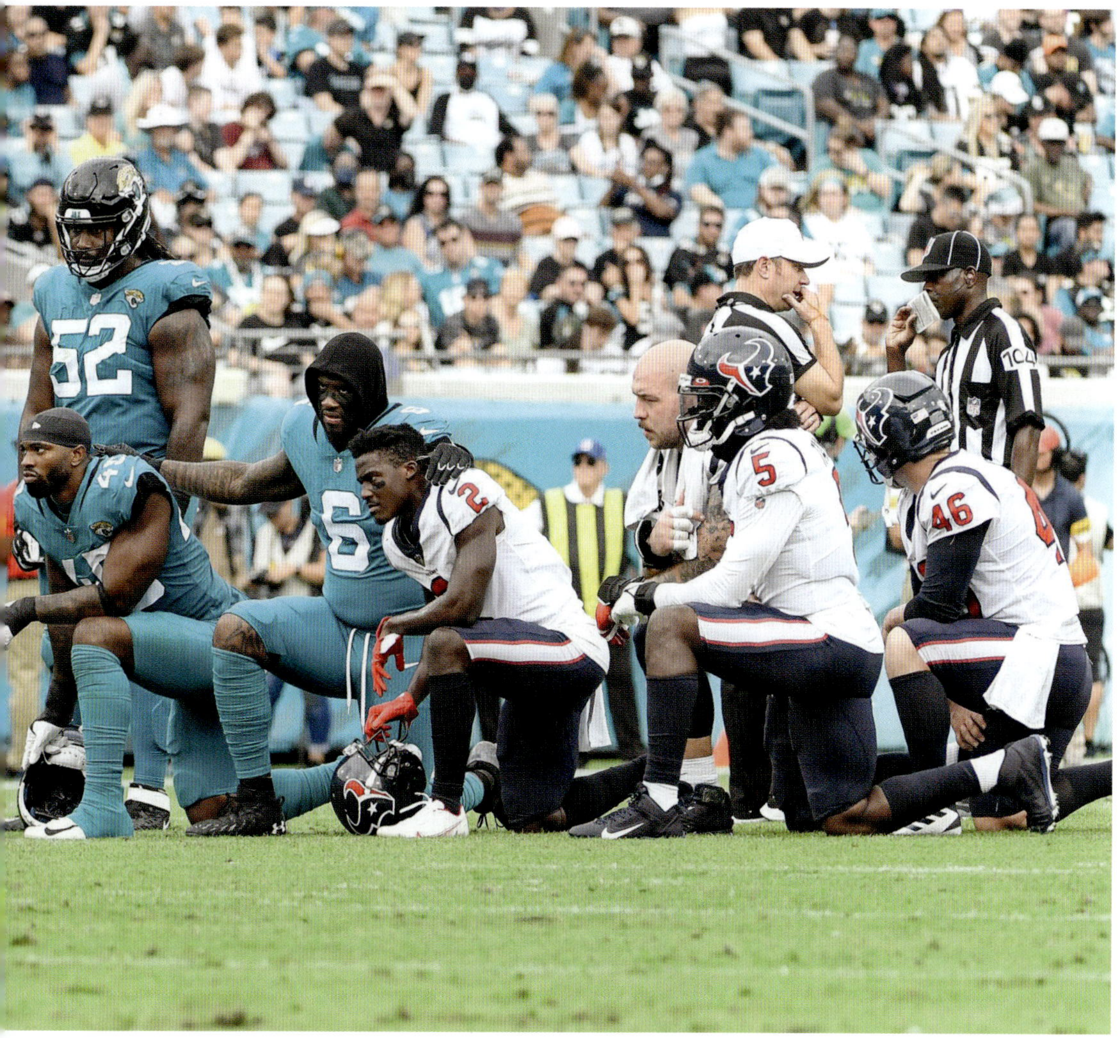

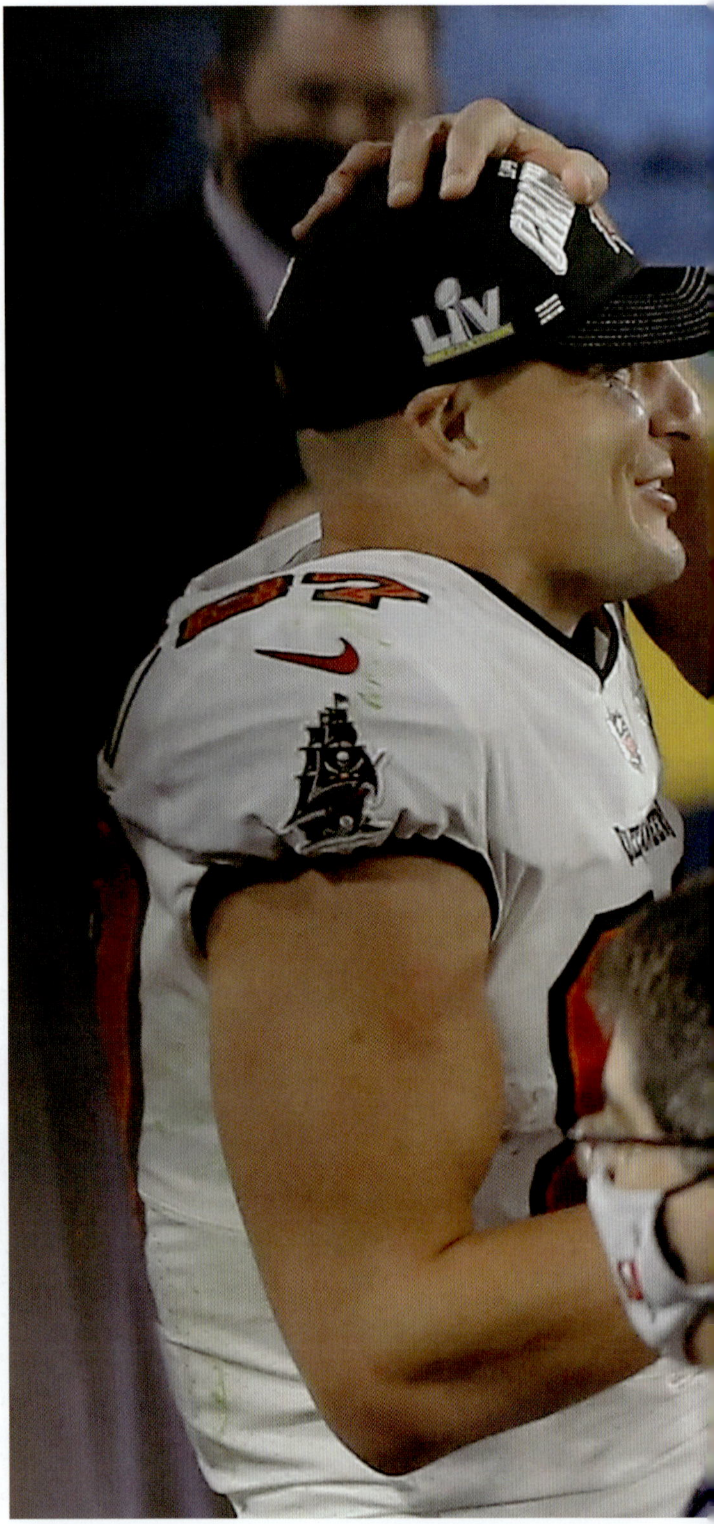

Raymond James Stadium, Tampa, 2021
Tom Brady (right) and Rob Gronkowski (left) celebrate another Super Bowl victory, this time for Tampa Bay who have beaten defending champions Kansas City 31-9. Gronkowski won three Super Bowls with New England, and one with Tampa Bay. Brady won six Super Bowls with New England and one with Tampa Bay. His seven overall Super Bowl wins makes Brady, not a team, the overall record holder for the most ever Super Bowl titles.

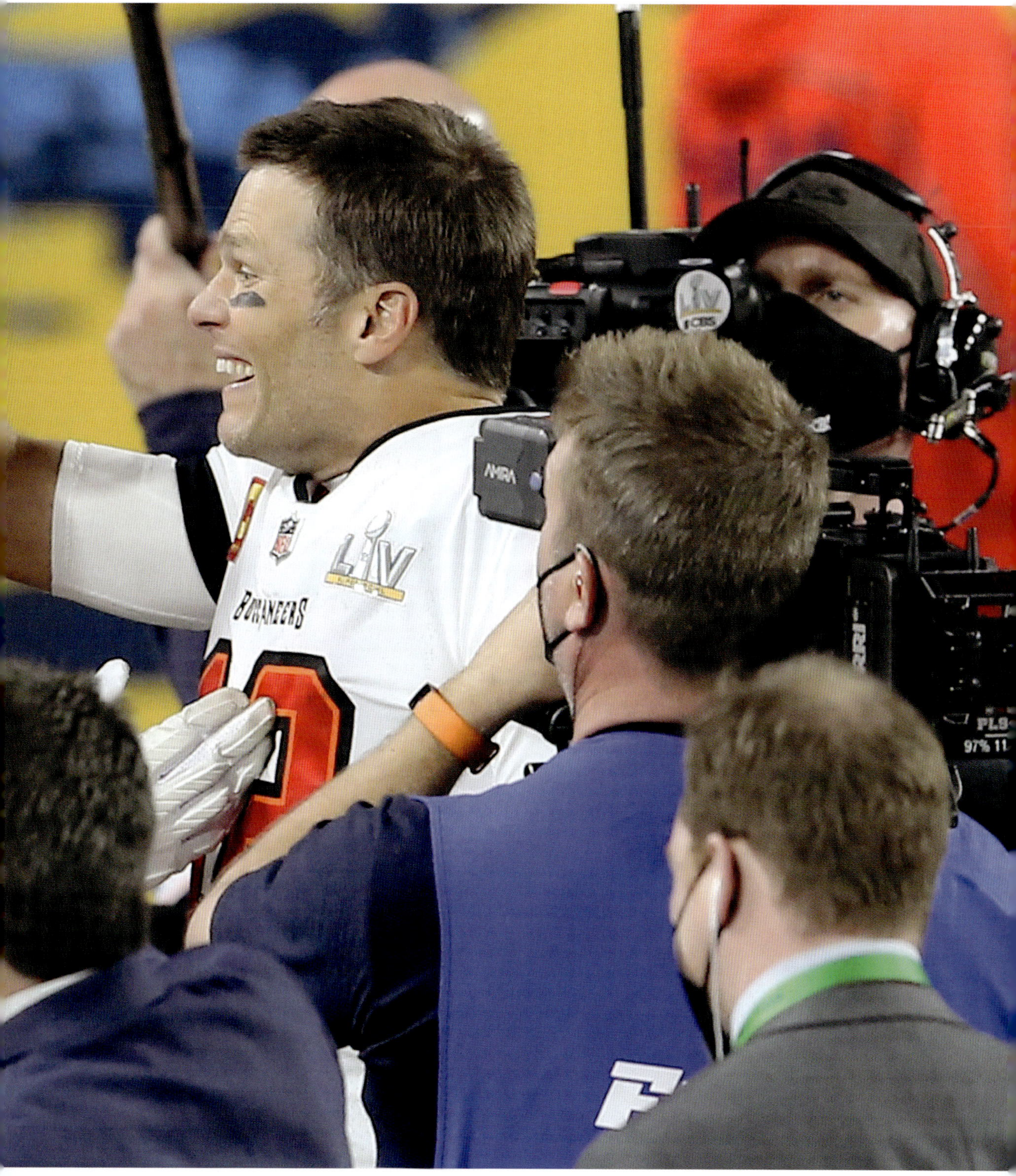

More from Matt Bazell

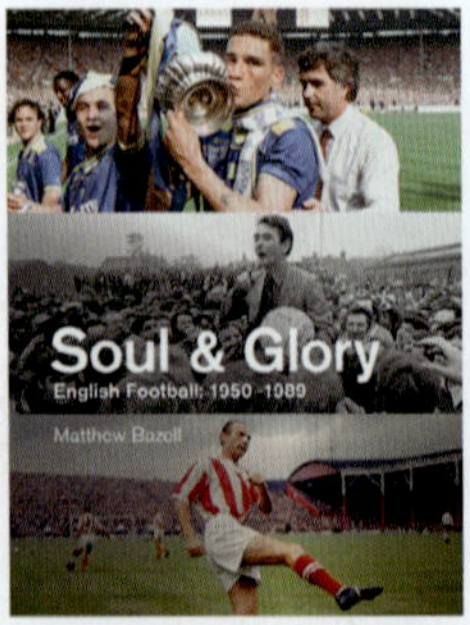

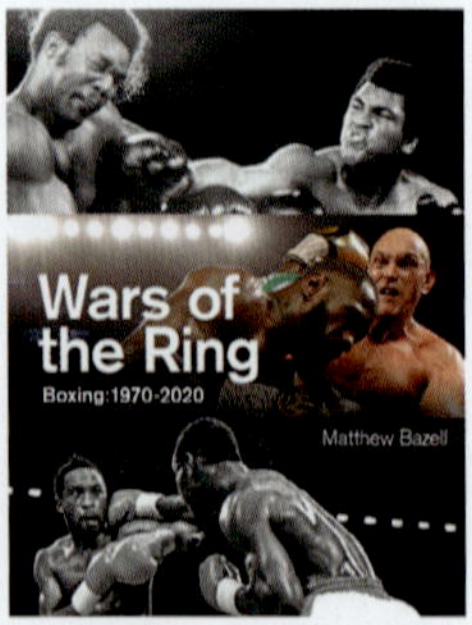

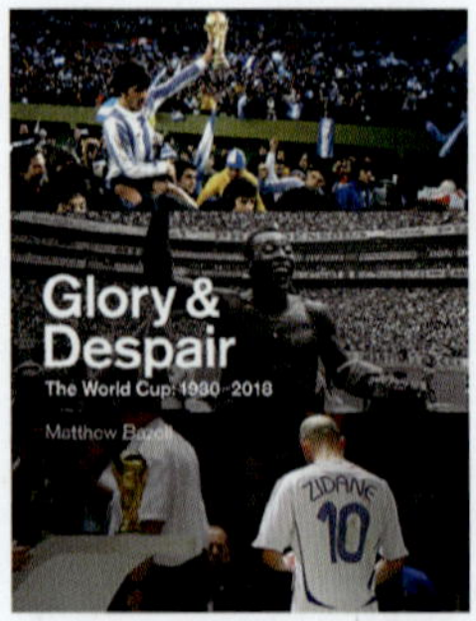

Authors notes and dedication

A small number of photos in this book feature AFL games, which was a separate league to the NFL. However, the league would merge into the NFL in 1970, and as the photos feature current NFL teams, I felt these images could be used. With the exception of Super Bowl 50, a Super Bowl is officially titled by using Roman numerals. However, for this book, I have used the numbers that most of us are used to and automatically understand upon first glance.

I would like to thank everyone who has bought a copy of this book for supporting authors and print media. Thanks to my parents Catherine Bazell and Ben Bazell for proofreading duties. I would like to say thanks to Pitch Publishing for sharing the same vision of the book as I did, and for being easy to work with. I'd like to dedicate the book to my nieces the double V's ... Veronica Bazell and Vivienne Delaney.

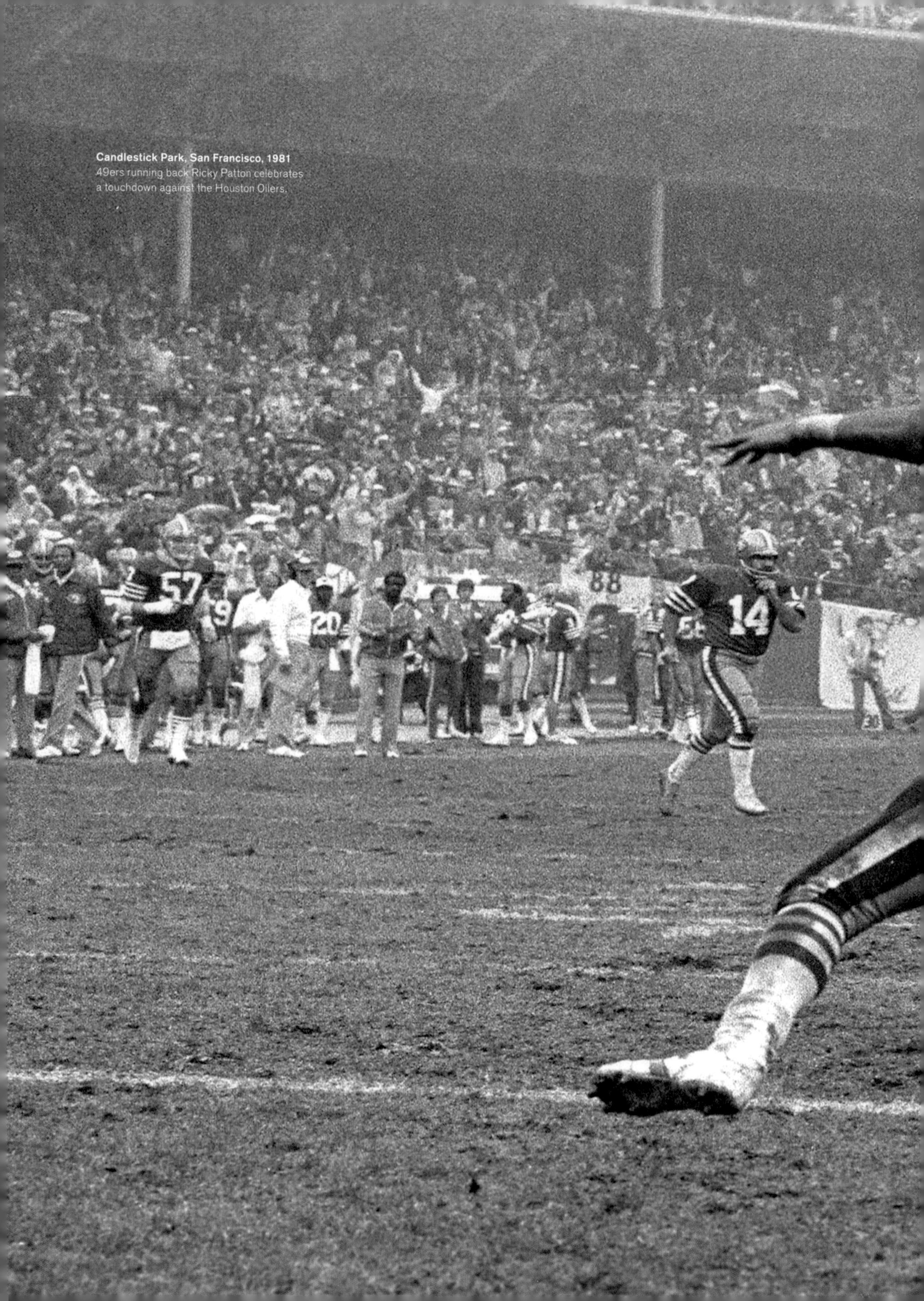

Candlestick Park, San Francisco, 1981
49ers running back Ricky Patton celebrates a touchdown against the Houston Oilers.